CW00429519

The Perfect Matrimony

The Perfect Matrimony

Samael Aun Weor

GLORIAN

Glorian Publishing
PO Box 209
Clinton, CT 06413 USA
glorian.org

© 2024 Glorian Publishing
All rights reserved.

A translation of *El Matrimonio Perfecto,* 1950.

No part of this book may be reproduced in any form or by any means, electronic or mechanical, including photography, recording, or by any information storage and retrieval system or technologies now known or later developed, without permission in writing from the publisher.

Library of Congress Cataloging-in-Publication Data

Names: סמאל און ואור, Samael Aun Weor, 1917-1977, author.

Title: The Perfect Matrimony / Conceived and written by Samael Aun Weor; translated and edited by Glorian Publishing.

Identifiers: LCCN 2024934850 (print)

Subjects: LCSH: Sex--Religious aspects

Classification: LCC HQ12-449

LC record available at: https://lccn.loc.gov/2024934850

ISBN 978-1-943358-21-2

Glorian Publishing books are printed on acid-free paper and meet the guidelines for permanence and durability of the Production Guidelines for Book Longevity of the Council on Library Resources.

Printed in the United States of America.

Glorian Publishing is a non-profit organization. All proceeds go to further the distribution of these books. For more information, visit glorian.org

Contents

Illustrations

Introduction

I have written this book for the few. I state "for the few" because many people do not accept it, comprehend it, or want it.

When the first edition of *The Perfect Matrimony* appeared
[in 1950], it produced great enthusiasm among students of
all schools, lodges, religions, orders, sects, and esoteric societ-
ies. The outcome of that enthusiasm was the formation of the
Gnostic movement.[1] This movement began with a few understanding people. Afterwards, it became broadly international.

Many students of esotericism studied this book; however,
only a few understood it. Many of them, enthusiastic with the
enchanting theme of *The Perfect Matrimony,* joined the ranks of
the Gnostic movement. Nonetheless, those who did not leave
the Gnostic movement can be counted on the fingers of one
hand. Many swore loyalty in front of the altar of Gnosis; however, in reality, they unquestionably violated their sworn oaths.
Some seemed to be true apostles, which even made it seem a
sacrilege to doubt them. Nevertheless, in the long run we had
to realize with infinite pain that they were also traitors. Often it
was enough for some of these false brothers and sisters to read
a book or to listen to a new lecturer who had just arrived in the
city in order to withdraw from the Gnostic movement.

Therefore, in this battle for the new Age of Aquarius[2]—which
began on the 4th of February, 1962, between 2 and 3 o'clock
in the afternoon—we had to learn that the abyss is filled with
sincerely mistaken people who have very good intentions.

The perfect matrimony and the Cosmic Christ[3] are the synthesis of all religions, schools, orders, sects, lodges, yogas, etc.

---

1   "The universal Christian Gnostic movement is non-sectarian. The
     Gnostic movement is made up of the army of world salvation, of all
     spiritual schools, lodges, religions, and sects... The Gnostic movement is
     made up of people from all religions, schools..." —Ch.9 and 19
2   Approximately every 2,160 years, our planet passes from the influence of
     one constellation to another.
3   "The Cosmic Christ is a force, as electricity is a force, or as gravity is a
     force, etc. The Cosmic Christ is beyond the personality, individuality, and
     the 'I.'"

Indeed, it is unfortunate that so many who discovered the practical synthesis have left it in order to fall into an intricate labyrinth of theories.

Tradition states that in the center of the labyrinth there is the synthesis, that is to say the labrys[4] of the temple. Etymologically, the word labyrinth originates from the word labrys, a double-edged ax, a symbol of the masculine and feminine sexual forces.

LABRYS

Indeed, whosoever finds the synthesis and afterwards leaves the center and returns to the complicated corridors of theories (which form the labyrinth of the mind) commits the greatest foolishness.

Christ and Sexual Magic[5] represent religious synthesis.

If we make a comparative study of religions, we shall then discover phallicism at the foundation of all schools, religions and esoteric sects. Let us remember Peristera,[6] the nymph of Venus' entourage, who was transformed by love [Eros] into a dove. Let us remember the virtuous Venus. Let us remember the processions of the god Priapus of the august ancient Rome of the Caesars, when the priestesses of the temple, filled with ecstasy, majestically carried an enormous phallus made out of sacred wood. Hence, Freud (the founder of psychoanalysis) correctly stated that religions have a sexual origin.

---

4   Greek λάβρυς. "...double-headed axe; a familiar emblem of Cretan sovereignty shaped like a waxing and a waning moon joined together back to back, and symbolizing the creative as well as the destructive power of the goddess." —Robert Graves, *The Greek Myths*

5   The word magic comes from magh- "to be able, to have power." From Persian magu "priest, one of the members of the learned and priestly class," from O.Pers. magush; Sanskrit mahas, "power"; Latin magis and German mebr, that mean "more." The word magic is derived from the ancient word "mag" that means priest. Genuine magic is the power of a priest or holy person to help others. Real magic is the work of a priest. A real magician is a priest. Sexual magic is how priests and priestesses direct their sexual power. See Sexual Magic in the glossary.

6   Ancient Greek Περιστερά, literally "dove."

PRIESTESSES OF VESTA TENDING THE SACRED FIRE.

The mysteries of fire are contained within the perfect matrimony. All the religions of the fire are totally sexual. The vestals[7] were true priestesses of love. With them, the celibate priests reached adepthood.[8] It is unfortunate that the modern vestals (nuns) do not know the key of Sexual Magic. It is unfortunate that the priests of this day and age have forgotten the secret key of sex. We feel profound pain when we see so many yogis ignoring the supreme key of yoga, which is Sexual Magic, the supreme synthesis of all systems of yoga.

People are filled with horror when they hear about Sexual Magic; however, they are not filled with horror when they give in to all kinds of sexual perversion and carnal passion.

---

7   A term derived from Roman religion, referring to a priestess of Vesta. The term refers to a sacred duty performed by virginal (sexually pure) women in many esoteric traditions. In Roman times, while still little girls, they were chosen from prominent Roman families. Their duties included the preparation of sacrifices and the tending of the sacred fire. If any vestal broke her vow of chastity, it is said that she was entombed alive. The vestals had great influence in the Roman state.

8   (Latin) adeptus, "One who has obtained." In esotericism, one who has reached the stage of initiation and become a master in the science of esotericism.

In this book, dear reader, you have the synthesis of all religions, schools and sects. Our doctrine is the doctrine of the synthesis.

There were powerful civilizations and grandiose mysteries within the profound night of the centuries. Back then, the priestesses of love were never missing from the temples. Those who became masters[9] of the White Lodge[10] practiced Sexual Magic with them. The master must be born within us by means of Sexual Magic.

In the sunny land of Khem, there in the ancient Egypt of the Pharaohs, whosoever dared to reveal the Great Arcanum[11] (Sexual Magic) was condemned to death. His head was cut off, his heart was torn out, and his ashes were tossed to the four winds.

In the land of the Aztecs, the men and women who aspired to become adepts, caressed each other, loved each other and practiced Sexual Magic for long periods of time within the courtyards of the temple. Whosoever spilled the Cup of Hermes[12] during these practices in the temple was beheaded for having profaned the temple.

All systems of intimate self-education have Sexual Magic as their ultimate practical synthesis. Every religion, every esoteric cult,[13] has as its synthesis Sexual Magic (the Arcanum A.Z.F.).[14]

---

9   See glossary.

10 The ancient collection of pure human beings who uphold and propagate the highest and most sacred of sciences. It is called "white" due to its purity and cleanliness (ie. the absence of pride, lust, anger, etc.). This "brotherhood" or "lodge" includes men and women of the highest order from every race, culture, creed and religion.

11 (Latin. plural: arcana). A secret, a mystery. The Great Arcanum is the secret of secrets, the core of the teachings.

12 A Hermetic symbol of the sexual power. See glossary.

13 Latin CVLTVS, cultus, "care, labor; cultivation, culture; worship, reverence," from colere, "to cultivate." In modern times the word cult has a decidedly negative implication, but originally the word simply meant "worship." When studying older writings, you will encounter the word used in its positive sense: worship.

14 The practice of sexual transmutation as couple (male-female), a technique known in Tantra and Alchemy. Arcanum refers to a hidden truth or law. A.Z.F. stands for A (agua, water), Z (azufre, sulfur), F (fuego, fire), and is thus: water + fire = consciousness. . Also, A (azoth = chemical

In the mysteries of Eleusis,[15] there was naked dancing and ineffable things. Sexual Magic was the fundamental basis of those mysteries. At that time, no one thought of perversities, because sex was profoundly venerated. Initiates know that the Third Logos[16] works within sex.

We have written this book with broad clarity; we have unveiled what was veiled. Now, whoever wants to self-realize in depth can rightly do so. Behold, here is the guide, here is the complete teaching.

I have already been harassed, humiliated, slandered, persecuted, etc., for teaching the path of the perfect matrimony. This does not matter to me anymore. At first, treason and slander hurt me a great deal; however, I have now become like steel. Hence, treason and slander no longer hurt me. I know all too well that humanity hates the truth and mortally hates the prophets; therefore, it is normal that they hate me for having written this book.

We aspire towards only one thing, only one goal, only one objective: Christification.

It is necessary for each human being to Christify themselves. It is necessary to incarnate the Christ.

In this book we have lifted the veil of the Christic mysteries. We have explained what the Christ-principle is. We have invited all human beings to follow the path of the perfect matrimony in order to attain Christification. We have explained that Christ is not an individual but a universal, cosmic and impersonal principle, which must be assimilated by each human being through Sexual Magic. Yes, indeed, fanatics are scandalized by all of this; yet, the truth is the truth, and we have to say it, even if it may cost us our lives.

The teachings of the Zend *Avesta*[17] contain the Christ-principle and are in accordance with the doctrinal principles contained in the Egyptian *Book of the Dead*. *The Iliad* of Homer,

---

element that refers to fire). A & Z are the first and last letters of the alphabet thus referring to the Alpha & Omega (beginning & end).

15 See glossary.

16 The creative aspect of the holy trinity. See Logos in the glossary.

17 Religious texts of Zoroastrianism.

the Hebrew Bible, the Germanic *Edda* and the Sibylline Books of the Romans contain the same Christ-principle. All these are sufficient in order to demonstrate that Christ precedes Jesus of Nazareth. Christ is not one individual alone. Christ is a cosmic principle that we must assimilate within our own physical, psychic, somatic, and spiritual nature through Sexual Magic.

Among the Persians, Christ is Ormuz, Ahura Mazda, the terrible enemy of Ahriman (Satan), which we carry within us. Amongst the Hindus, Krishna is Christ; thus, the gospel of Krishna is very similar to that of Jesus of Nazareth. Among the Egyptians, Christ is Osiris and whosoever incarnated him was in fact an Osirified one. Among the Chinese, the Cosmic Christ is 伏羲 Fuxi, who composed the *I-Ching* (The Book of Laws) and who dubbed the Dragon Ministers. Among the Greeks, Christ is called Zeus, Jupiter, the father of the gods. Among the Aztecs, Christ is Quetzalcoatl, the Mexican Christ. In the Germanic *Edda*, Baldur is the Christ who was assassinated by Hodur, god of war, with an arrow made from a twig of mistletoe, etc. We can cite the Cosmic Christ within thousands of ancient texts and old traditions which hail millions of years before Jesus. This invites us to embrace that Christ is a cosmic principle contained within the essential principles of all religions.

Indeed, there is truly only one single cosmic religion. This religion assumes different forms according to the times and the needs of humanity. Therefore, religious conflicts are an absurdity, because at their base all religions are only modifications of the universal cosmic religion. Thus, from this point of view, we affirm that this book is not against any religion, school or system of thought. The only objective of this book is to give humanity a key, a sexual secret, a key with which every living being may assimilate the Christ-principle contained within the foundation of all the great religions of the world.

We recognize Jesus-Iesus-Zeus-Jupiter as the new superhuman[18] who totally assimilated the Christ-principle, and be-

---

18   Translated from the German word Übermensch, "highly evolved human being that transcends good and evil," from "Thus Spake Zarathustra" (1883-91), by Friedrich Nietzsche (1844-1900).

MARY AND JESUS   ISIS AND HORUS

came for that reason, a god-human. We consider that we must imitate him. Jesus was a complete human, a true human in the full sense of the word.[19] He attained the absolute assimilation of the universal Cosmic Christ-principle through Sexual Magic.

Those few devotees who understand must rightly study the Gospel of John 3:1-21. In that chapter, the devotee of the perfect matrimony will find pure and legitimate Sexual Magic as taught by Jesus. Obviously, the teaching is written in code; however, the one who has understanding will intuitively understand it.

Modern humanity has committed the mistake of separating the great Master Jesus from all his predecessors who, like him, Christified themselves. This is what has damaged this present humanity. We need to progressively comprehend that all religions are only one religion.

Mary, the mother of Jesus, as well as Isis, Juno, Demeter, Ceres, Maia, etc., correspondingly represent the Cosmic Mother

---

19   Derived from Latin humanus "of man, human," also "humane, philanthropic, kind, gentle, polite; learned, refined, civilized." In classical philosophy, we are not yet human beings, but have the potential to become so. A famous illustration of this is the story of Diogenes wandering around crowded Athens during this day with an illuminated lantern, searching for "anthropos" (a real human being), yet failing to find one. See Human in the glossary.

or Kundalini[20] (sexual fire) from whom the Cosmic Christ is always born.

Mary Magdalene, as well as Salammbô, Matres, Ishtar, Astarte, Aphrodite, and Venus all represent the priestess-wife with whom we must practice Sexual Magic in order to awaken the fire.

The Martyrs, Saints, Virgins, Angels, and Cherubim are the same gods, Demigods, Titans, Goddesses, Sylphs, Cyclops, and Messengers of the gods from Pagan mythology.

All the religious principles of Christianity are Pagan.

Therefore, when the present religious forms disappear, their principles will be assimilated by the new religious forms of the future.

It is necessary to comprehend what the immaculate conceptions are. It is necessary to know that only with the perfect matrimony can Christ be born within the heart of the human being. It is urgent to awaken the fire of Kundalini (the fire of the Holy Spirit) in order to incarnate the Christ. Whosoever awakens the Kundalini transforms oneself (like Ganymede) into the eagle of the Spirit in order to soar to Olympus, to become a cup-bearer for the ineffable gods.

It is lamentable that the Catholic priests have destroyed so many documents and so many valuable treasures of antiquity. Fortunately, they could not destroy them all. During the Renaissance, some marvelous books were discovered by brave priests. Thus, despite the persecutions of the clergy, Dante Alighieri, Boccacio, Petrarch, Erasmus, etc., were able to translate famous books like *The Iliad* and *The Odyssey* of Homer, true books of esoteric science and Sexual Magic. They also translated *The Aeneid* of Virgil, *The Theogony, The Works and Days* of Hesiod, *The Metamorphoses* of Ovid, and other writings of Lucretius, Horace, Tibullus, Titus Livius, Tacitus, Apulius, Cicero, etc. All of this is pure Gnosticism. It is really unfortunate how some ignorant people abandon Gnosis in order to follow systems and methods that ignore Sexual Magic and the perfect matrimony.

---

20   See glossary.

We have investigated all the great Gnostic treasures, and we have delved into the basis of all the archaic religions; thus, we have found the supreme key of Sexual Magic at the base of all cults. Now we deliver this treasure, this key, to this suffering humanity. Many will read this book; however, few will comprehend it.

The topic of this book is exclusively Sexual Magic. Indeed, those who are accustomed to read thousands of books out of pure intellectual curiosity will assuredly miss the opportunity to study this book in depth.

It is worthless to read this book in a hurry. Those who proceed thus are mistaken.

It is necessary to profoundly study this book and to totally comprehend it, not only with the intellect but in all the levels of the mind. The intellect is only a small fraction of the mind. The intellect is not the whole mind. Therefore, whosoever understands this book only with the intellect has not understood it.

Only with internal meditation is it possible to understand this book in all the levels of the mind.

It is urgent to practice Sexual Magic in order to attain Christification. The reader will discover the supreme key of intimate Realization of the Self within this book.

We are not against any religion, school, sect, order, or lodge because we know that all religious forms are manifestations of the great cosmic universal infinite religion latent in every atom of the cosmos.

We teach the synthesis of all religions, schools, orders, lodges, and beliefs. Our doctrine is the doctrine of the synthesis.

Sexual Magic is practiced in esoteric Christianity. Sexual Magic is practiced in Zen Buddhism. Sexual Magic is practiced amongst the initiated yogis. Sexual Magic is practiced amongst the Mohammedan Sufis. Sexual Magic was practiced in the initiatic colleges of Troy, Egypt, Rome, Carthage, Eleusis. Sexual Magic was practiced by the mysterious Maya, Aztec, Inca, Druids, etc.

Therefore, Sexual Magic and the Cosmic Christ are the synthesis of all religions, schools, and sects. We teach the doctrine of the synthesis. This doctrine could never be contrary to the diverse religious forms. Our teachings are found within all religions, schools, and beliefs. If the reader makes a serious study of all the religions of the world, one will discover the phallus and uterus as the synthesis of all mysteries.

There has never been any authentic religion or school of mysteries where the Cosmic Christ and the mysteries of sex were absent.

The doctrine of the synthesis cannot harm anyone, because it is the synthesis of all.

We invite the devotees of all cults, schools, and beliefs to make a comparative study of religions.

We invite the students of all the diverse systems of intimate self-education to study the sexual esotericism from all the secret schools of mysteries.

We invite all yogis to study sexual yoga and white tantra from India, without which no yogi is able to attain absolute liberation.

Whatever be the name, Sexual Magic and Christ are the synthesis of all esoteric studies, religious forms, or educational systems.

The attacks of which we have been victims, the persecutions, anathemas, and excommunications etc., are because of ignorance and lack of study.

Any religious form or esoteric system enriches itself with the synthesis. The synthesis cannot harm anyone. This is the doctrine of the synthesis. We intensely love all religious forms. We know that all religious forms are the loving manifestation of the great cosmic universal religion.

The supreme religious synthesis is found within the perfect matrimony. God[21] is love and wisdom.

The ultimate synthesis of all lodges, orders, schools, sects, systems and methods of intimate realization of the Self, from the East and the West, the North and the South, is found within Christ and within sex.

Inverential peace.

---

21 What is referred to as "God" in this book is not a bearded old man in the clouds. See God in the glossary.

Chapter 1
Love

God as Father is wisdom. God as Mother is love. As Father, God resides within the eye of wisdom. The eye of wisdom is located between the eyebrows. As love, God is found within the heart temple. Wisdom and love are the two basal pillars of the great White Lodge. To love, how beautiful it is to love. Only the great souls can and know how to love. Love is infinite tenderness... Love is the life that beats in every atom as it beats in every sun.

Love cannot be defined because it is the Divine Mother of the world; it is that which comes to us when we really fall in love.

Love is felt within the depths of the heart; it is a delectable experience; it is a consuming fire; it is divine wine, a delight to those who drink it. A simple perfumed handkerchief, a letter, a flower, give rise to great inner uneasiness, exotic ecstasy, and ineffable voluptuousness within the depths of the soul.

No one has been able to define love; it has to be lived, it has to be felt. Only great lovers really know that which is called love. The perfect matrimony is the union of two beings who truly know how to love.

In order that there truly be love, it is necessary for man and woman to adore each other in all the seven great cosmic planes.[22]

In order for there to be love, it is necessary for there to be a true communion of souls in the three spheres of thought, feeling, and will.

When the two beings vibrate in affinity in their thoughts, feelings, and volition, then the perfect matrimony is consummated in the seven planes of cosmic consciousness.

There are people who are married in the physical and ethereal planes, but not in the astral plane. Others are married in the physical, ethereal and astral planes, but not in the mental

---

22   The seven lower sephiroth on the Tree of Life, which correspond to our physical body, vitality, emotion, intellect, willpower, intuition, and spirit.

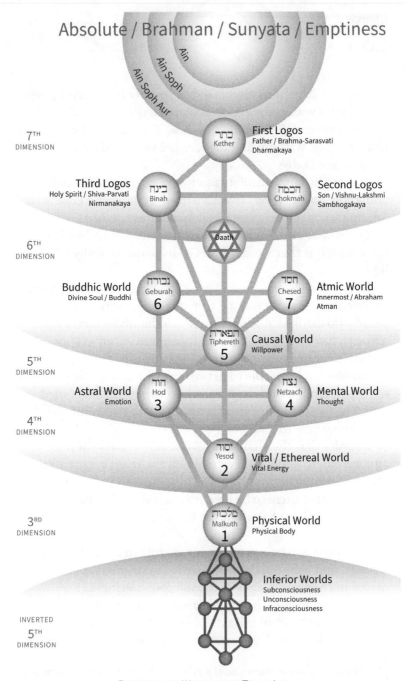

Absolute / Brahman / Sunyata / Emptiness

Ain
Ain Soph
Ain Soph Aur

7TH DIMENSION

First Logos
Father / Brahma-Sarasvati
Dharmakaya

כתר
Kether

Third Logos
Holy Spirit / Shiva-Parvati
Nirmanakaya

בינה
Binah

Second Logos
Son / Vishnu-Lakshmi
Sambhogakaya

חכמה
Chokmah

Daath

6TH DIMENSION

Buddhic World
Divine Soul / Buddhi

גבורה
Geburah
6

Atmic World
Innermost / Abraham
Atman

חסד
Chesed
7

Causal World
Willpower

תפארת
Tiphereth
5

5TH DIMENSION

Astral World
Emotion

הוד
Hod
3

Mental World
Thought

נצח
Netzach
4

4TH DIMENSION

Vital / Ethereal World
Vital Energy

יסוד
Yesod
2

3RD DIMENSION

Physical World
Physical Body

מלכות
Malkuth
1

Inferior Worlds
Subconsciousness
Unconsciousness
Infraconsciousness

INVERTED
5TH DIMENSION

DIMENSIONS AND WORLDS ON THE TREE OF LIFE

plane. Each one thinks in his or her own way; the woman has her religion and the man another; they do not agree in their thoughts, etc.

There are marriages with affinity in the worlds of thought and feeling, but that are absolutely opposed in the world of will. These marriages crash constantly; they are not happy. The perfect matrimony should be performed in the seven planes of cosmic consciousness. There are marriages that do not even reach the astral plane, hence there is not even sexual attraction; these are true failures. Such a marriage is founded exclusively on matrimonial formality.

Some people live a matrimonial existence in the physical plane with a given mate; however, in the mental plane they lead a married life with a different spouse. Rarely in life do we meet a perfect matrimony. For there to be love, it is necessary that there be affinity of thought, feeling, and will.

Where there is arithmetical calculus, there is no love. Unfortunately, in modern life, love implies the bank account, commerce, and celluloid material. In those homes where there are only additions and subtractions, there is no love.

When love leaves the heart, it rarely returns. Love is an elusive child. The marriage that is consummated without love and is based solely on economic and social interest is really a sin against the Holy Spirit.[23] This type of marriage inevitably fails.

Lovers often confuse desire with love, and the worst of all is that they get married believing they are in love. Therefore, when the sex act is consummated and carnal passion is satisfied, then disenchantment arrives and the terrifying reality remains.

Lovers should analyze themselves before getting married to see if they are really in love. Passion is mistaken easily for love. Love and desire are absolute opposites.

Whosoever is truly in love is willing to shed even their last drop of blood for their beloved.

---

23   The Christian name for the third aspect of the Holy Trinity, or "God." On the Kabbalistic Tree of Life, this is the third sephirah, called Binah, "intelligence." This force has many names in other religions. It is the creative aspect of divinity. See Logos in the glossary.

KRISHNA, AN INCARNATION OF CHRIST, WITH HIS WIFE RADHA

Examine yourself before you get married. Do you feel capable of shedding even your last drop of blood for the being you adore? Would you be capable of giving your life so that your beloved could live? Reflect and meditate. Is there a true affinity of thought, feeling, and will with the being whom you adore? Remember that if complete affinity does not exist, then your marriage, instead of being a heaven, will be a true hell.

Do not let yourself get carried away by desire. Kill not only desire, but moreover, the shadow itself of the tempting tree of desire.

Love begins with a flash of delectable affinity. It is substantiated with infinite tenderness and it is synthesized with supreme adoration.

A perfect matrimony is the union of two beings who absolutely adore each other. In love, there are neither plans nor bank accounts. If you are making plans and calculations, it is because you are not in love. Reflect on it before you take the great step. Are you really in love? Beware of the illusion of desire. Remember that the flame of desire consumes life and then the dreadful reality of death remains.

Contemplate the eyes of the being you love; lose yourself in the joy of their eyes, but if you want to be happy, don't let yourself get carried away by desire.

You who are in love, do not confuse love with passion.

Analyze yourself in depth. It is urgent to know if your beloved belongs to you in spirit. It is necessary to know if you are
in complete affinity with your loved one in the three worlds of
thought, feeling, and will.

Adultery[24] is the cruel result of the lack of love. The woman
who is truly in love would prefer death to adultery. The man
who commits adultery is not truly in love.

Love is terribly divine. The blessed Goddess Mother of the
world is what we call love.

With the terrifying fire of love, we can transform ourselves
into gods in order to enter into the amphitheater of cosmic
science with full majesty.

---

24   In the scriptures of Judaism and Christianity, the word adultery is
     usually placed as the translation for נאף na'aph, "to perform voluntary
     violation of the marriage bed." Adultery is sexual infidelity. See glossary
     for a full explanation.

The creation of the Philosophical Stone (Christ, the Son of Man)

18TH CENTURY ALCHEMICAL PAINTING

Chapter 2

The Son of Man

"God is love, and his love creates
and creates anew."

The delectable words of love lead to the ardent kiss of adoration.

The sexual act is the real consubstantiation of love in the tremendous psycho-physical reality of our nature.

Something is created when a man and a woman unite sexually. In those moments of supreme adoration, he and she are really only one androgynous being with powers to create like the gods.

The Elohim[25] are male and female. Man and woman united sexually during the supreme ecstasy of love are really one terrifically divine Elohim.

In those moments of sexual union, we are really in the laboratorium-oratorium[26] of holy Alchemy.[27]

In those moments, the great clairvoyants[28] can see the sexual pair enveloped in terribly divine splendors. We have then entered into the sanctum regnum[29] of high magic. With these dreadfully divine forces, we can disintegrate the devil we carry within and transform ourselves into great hierophants.[30]

As the sexual act is prolonged, as the delightful caresses of beloved ecstasy increase, one feels an enchanting spiritual voluptuousness. We are then charging ourselves with universal electricity and magnetism; terrifying cosmic forces accumulate

---

25 Usually mistranslated as "God," אלהים Elohim is actually a plural Hebrew word with deep meanings. See glossary.
26 (Latin, indicating a place of work and prayer) A reference to the practice of Alchemy, originating from an illustration by Heinrich Kunrath.
27 Al-Kimia: "to fuse with the highest" or "to fuse with God." See glossary.
28 Those who can see other dimensions. See glossary.
29 Latin, "holy kingdom."
30 From Greek (Hierophantes) High priest, judge or interpreter of sacred mysteries or arcane knowledge.

in the depths of the soul; the chakras[31] of the astral body[32] sparkle; the mysterious forces of the great cosmic mother[33] flow through all the channels of our organism.

The ardent kisses, the intimate caresses, are transformed into miraculous notes which movingly resound within the aura of the universe.

We have no way of explaining those moments of supreme pleasure. The serpent of fire[34] is agitated; the fires of the heart are enlivened, and there upon the forehead of the sexually united beings shine the terrifying rays of the Father, full of majesty.

If man and woman know how to withdraw without the spasm,[35] if in those moments of delightful enjoyment they have the willpower to control the animal ego,[36] and if at that point they retire from the sexual act without ejaculating the semen[37] (neither inside the womb, nor outside of it or to the side of

---

31 See glossary.
32 What is commonly called the astral body is not the true astral body, it is rather the lunar protoplasmatic body, also known as the kama rupa (Sanskrit, "body of desires") or "dream body" (Tibetan rmi-lam-gyi lus). The true astral body is solar (being superior to lunar nature) and must be created, as the Master Jesus indicated in the Gospel of John 3:5-6. The solar astral body is created as a result of the third initiation of major mysteries (serpents of fire), and is perfected in the third serpent of light. "One knows that one has an astral body when one can use it, as one knows that one has feet, because one can walk with them, or hands because one can use them; likewise, one knows that one has an astral body when one can travel with it." —Samael Aun Weor, Gnostic Cult to Agnostos Theos
33 The Divine Mother. See glossary.
34 Kundalini. See glossary.
35 Orgasm in both men and women.
36 From the Latin for "I" and similar to the Greek Εγώ. In esotericism, the term ego is very different from the Freudian definition. In practical spirituality, the term ego refers to psychological constructs in the mind that trap the consciousness. See glossary.
37 Latin, literally "seed of plants, animals, or people; race, inborn characteristic; posterity, progeny, offspring," figuratively "origin, essence, principle, cause." In other words, semen is not just a fluid in masculine bodies. Semen refers to the sexual energy of any creature or entity. In esotericism, "semen" is a term used for the sexual energy of both masculine and feminine bodies. To "ejaculate the semen" is to orgasm, whether male or female.

it, nor in any other place) they will have performed an act of Sexual Magic. This is what is called in esotericism the Arcanum A. Z. F.[38]

With the Arcanum A. Z. F., we can retain all that marvelous light, all those cosmic currents, all those divine powers. Then, Kundalini, the sacred fire of the Holy Ghost, awakens in us and we become terribly divine gods.

However, when we ejaculate the semen, the cosmic currents merge with the universal currents and then penetrate the souls of the two beings with a bloody light, the luciferic[39] forces of evil, fatal magnetism. Then, Cupid[40] leaves, weeping. The gates of Eden[41] are locked; love becomes disillusionment. Disenchantment arrives and the black reality of this valley of tears is all that remains.

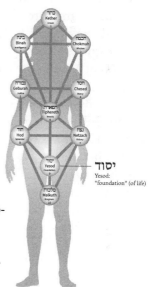

When we know how to withdraw before the sexual spasm, the igneous serpent of our magical powers awakens.

The Kabbalists speak of the Ninth Sphere.[42] The Ninth Sphere of the Kabbalah is sex.

The descent into the Ninth Sphere was, in the ancient mysteries, the highest trial to prove the supreme dignity

---

38   The practice of sexual transmutation as couple (male-female), a technique known in Tantra and Alchemy. Arcanum refers to a hidden truth or law. A.Z.F. stands for A (agua, water), Z (azufre, sulfur), F (fuego, fire), and is thus: water + fire = consciousness. Also, A (azoth = chemical element that refers to fire). A & Z are the first and last letters of the alphabet thus referring to the Alpha & Omega (beginning & end).

39   See glossary.

40   The Roman name of the Greek Ερως, Eros, "love." See Eros in the glossary.

41   Judeo-Christian symbol of primordial purity and happiness. Hebrew עדן Eden means "bliss, pleasure, delight." See glossary.

42   In Kabbalah, a reference to the sephirah Yesod of the Tree of Life (Kabbalah). When you place the Tree of Life over your body, you see that Yesod is related to your sexual organs.

of the hierophant. Hermes, Buddha, Dante, Zoroaster, etc. had to descend to the Ninth Sphere in order to work with the fire and water, the origin of worlds, beasts, humans and gods. Every authentic and legitimate White Initiation[43] begins there. The Son of Man[44] is born in the Ninth Sphere. The Son of Man is born of water and fire. When the alchemist has completed their work in the mastery of fire, they receive the Venustic Initiation.[45] The betrothal of the soul[46] to the Lamb[47] is the greatest festival of the soul. That great Lord of Light enters her. He becomes human; She becomes divine. From this divine and human mixture, that which with so much certainty the beloved one called "the Son of Man" is born.

The greatest triumph of supreme adoration is the birth of the Son of Man in the manger of the world.

The man and woman who love each other are truly two miraculous, harmonious harps, an ecstasy of glory, that which cannot be defined, because if it is defined, it is disfigured. That is love. The kiss is the profound mystic consecration of two souls who adore each other, and the sexual act is the key with which we become gods. Gods, is God. All of you who truly love, know that God is love. To love, how beautiful it is to love. Love is nourished with love; only with love are the alchemical weddings possible.

---

43   See Initiation in the glossary.

44   "When the Beloved One [Christ] becomes transformed into the soul, and when the soul becomes transformed into the Beloved One, that which we call the Son of Man is born from this ineffable, divine, and human mixture. The great Lord of Light, being the Son of the living God, becomes the Son of Man when he transform himself into the Human Soul. The Sun-Man is the result of all our purifications and bitterness. The Sun-Man is divine and human. The Son of Man is the final outcome of the human being. He is the child of our sufferings, the solemn mystery of the transubstantiation." —Samael Aun Weor, *The Aquarian Message* (1960)

45   See glossary.

46   Here, soul refers to the sephirah Geburah, the divine soul, which is feminine. See Soul in the glossary.

47   "The Lamb is our interior angel, that is to say, our Innermost." A reference to the sephirah Chesed, the Innermost Spirit.

Jesus, the Beloved One, reached the Venustic Initiation in the Jordan. At the moment of baptism, Christ entered within the beloved Jesus through the pineal gland. The Word[48] was made flesh and lived amongst us, and we beheld his glory as the Father's only son, full of grace and truth.

> "Whosoever knows, the Word gives power to. No one has uttered it; no one will utter it, except the one who has the Word incarnated." —Huiracocha

In the Apocalypse [of St. John], the saint of Revelation describes to us the Son of Man, the Son of our kisses, with the following verses:

"I was in the spirit on the Lord's day, and heard behind me a great voice (the Word), as of a trumpet.

"Saying, I am Alpha and Omega, the first and the last: and, what thou seest, write in a book, and send it unto the seven churches which are in Asia; unto Ephesus (the coccygeal magnetic center), and unto Smyrna (the prostatic magnetic center), and unto Pergamos (the solar plexus located in the region of the navel), and unto Thyatira (the magnetic center of the heart), and unto Sardis (the magnetic center of the creative larynx), and unto Philadelphia (the eye of wisdom, the clairvoyant center located between the eyebrows), and unto Laodicea (the crown of the saints, the magnetic center of the pineal gland).

"And I turned to see the voice that spake with me. And being turned, I saw seven golden candlesticks; And in the midst of the seven candlesticks one like unto the Son of Man, clothed with a garment down to the foot (the white linen tunic of every master; the tunic of glory. The seven candlesticks which the saint of Revelation saw are the seven churches of the spinal medulla), and girt about the paps with a golden girdle.

---

48   Greek λόγος, from λέγω lego "I say," means Verb or Word. The unifying principle. The Logos is the manifested deity of every nation and people; the outward expression or the effect of the cause which is ever concealed. (Speech is the "logos" of thought). The Logos has three aspects, known universally as the Trinity, Trikaya, or Trimurti. See glossary for more.

"His head and his hairs were white like wool, as white as snow; and his eyes were as a flaming fire (always immaculate and pure);

"And his feet like unto fine brass, as if they burned in a furnace; and his voice as the sound of many waters (the human waters, the semen).

"And he had in his right hand seven stars (the seven angels who govern the seven churches of the spinal medulla); and out of his mouth went a sharp two-edged sword (the word); and his countenance was as the sun shineth in his strength.

"And when I saw him, I fell at his feet as dead. And he laid his right hand upon me, saying unto me, fear not; I am the first and the last, I am he that liveth, and was dead; and, behold, I am alive for ever more, Amen, and have the keys of hell and of death." —Christian Bible, Revelation 1:10-18

When the inner Christ enters the soul, he is transformed into her. He is transformed into her and she into him; he becomes humanized and she becomes divine. From this human and divine alchemical mixture, that which with so much certainty our beloved savior called the Son of Man is born.

The alchemists say that we should transform the moon into the sun. The moon is the soul. The sun is Christ. The transformation of the moon into the sun is only possible with the help of fire, and this can only be lit with the amorous connubium of the perfect marriage.

A perfect marriage is the union of two beings: one who loves more, and the other who loves better.

The Son of Man is born of water and fire. Water is the semen. Fire is the Spirit. God shines upon the perfect couple. The Son of Man has power over the flaming fire, over the impetuous air, over the boisterous waves of the ocean, and over the perfumed earth.

The sexual act is mightily terrific with just reason. The Apocalypse states:

"Him that overcometh will I make a pillar in the temple of my God, and he shall go no more out..." —Christian Bible, Revelation 3:12

Chapter 3
The Great Battle

In Jeremiah 21:8, it is written,

"Behold, I set before you the way of life, and the way of death."
Man and woman can use sexual intercourse and the delights
of love and kisses in order to become gods or demons.
From the dawn of life, a great battle has raged between the
powers of light and the powers of darkness. The secret root of
that battle lies in sex.

There is a correct interpretation of the mysteries of sex. The
white magicians never ejaculate the semen. The black magicians always ejaculate the semen. The white magicians make
the igneous serpent of our magical powers ascend through the
medullar canal. The black magicians make the snake descend
towards the atomic infernos of the human being.

Gods and demons live in eternal struggle. The gods defend
the doctrine of chastity.[49] The demons hate chastity. The root
of the conflict between gods and demons is found in sex..

The great battle takes place in the Astral Light.[50] The Astral
Light is the deposit of all of great Nature's past, present and
future forms. The Astral Light is the Azoth and Magnesia[51] of
the ancient alchemists, Medea's flying dragons, the Christians'
INRI, the Tarot of the Bohemians. The Astral Light is a terrific
sexual fire springing forth from the Sun's nimbus and is fixed
to the Earth by the force of gravity and the weight of the atmosphere. The Sun is the one that attracts and repels that enchanting and delightful light. The Astral Light is Archimedes'
lever. The old sage said, "Give me a fulcrum and I will move the
universe."

---

49 Sexual purity, not abstinence. See glossary.
50 The vital substance in Nature upon which all things subsist. See
    glossary.
51 Menabadus says: "He who joins quicksilver to the body of magnesia, and
    the woman to the man, extracts the secret essence..."

The semen is the human being's astral liquid. The semen is the Astral Light. The semen is the key to all powers and the key to all empires.

The Astral Light has two poles, one positive and the other negative. The ascending serpent is positive. The descending serpent is negative. When it ascends, it is the brazen serpent that healed the Israelites in the wilderness. When it descends, it is the tempting serpent of Eden.

When we know how to adore and kiss with infinite tenderness and supreme chastity, the serpent ascends. When we enjoy lust ardently and spill the cup, the serpent precipitates itself inebriated with madness towards the atomic infernos of the human being.

In the region of light live the beings who adore each other. In the region of darkness live the souls who become inebriated with the chalice of lust, and who after getting drunk spill the cup. Those souls are consumed in the fire of their own lust.

The Earth is ruled by Christ and Javhe[52] who live in eternal struggle. Christ is the leader of gods. Javhe is the chief of demons.

Javhe is that terribly perverse demon who tempted Christ when he took him atop a high mountain and showed him all the kingdoms of the world and the glory of them. Thus, when tempting Christ, Javhe said, "ITABABO. All these things will I give thee, If thou wilt fall down and worship me." Christ answered and said unto him, "Get thee behind me, Satan: for it is written, Thou shalt not tempt the Lord thy God, but thou shalt worship the Lord thy God, and him only shalt thou serve."[53]

Javhe is a terribly perverse fallen angel. Javhe is the genius of evil. Christ is the leader of the great White Lodge, and Javhe, his antithesis, is the chief of the great Black Lodge.[54] The powers of

---

52   Often spelled Yahweh or Yahwe, and intentionally confused with Jehovah since they are both spelled the same way in Hebrew: יהוה. While Jehovah is a very positive and potent name of God, Yahve (Jahve) is the name of a demon who has been misleading humanity for ages. You can read his story in *The Revolution of Beelzebub*.

53   Read Matthew 4 and Luke 4 in the Christian Bible.

54   A term that describes the multitude of creatures who seek power, glory, fear, envy, lust, vengeance, domination, etc. and use whatever means

light and darkness live in eternal struggle and that struggle is
rooted in sex. The semen is the battlefield. In the semen, angels and demons fight to the death. The medullar bone of the
great conflict between angels and demons is sex. There is the
problem. There is the root of all the white and black doctrines.
Christ has his program of action, Javhe has his. The chosen
follow the Christ. The great majority of human beings fanati-
cally follow Javhe. Nevertheless, they all hide behind the cross.

In the astral cross, there is a mutual struggle between the
columns of angels and demons. Facing each angel, there is a
demon.

Every human being has his double. Behold the mystery of
the twin souls. The Lamas say that Devadatta was the brother
and the rival of Buddha. He is the king of Hell.

The double is similar in everything to his own double. The
doubles are analogous; they have the same tendencies, with
the differences of the analogies of opposites. Facing a white
astrologer, there is a black astrologer. If a master teaches white
Sexual Magic, his double will teach black Sexual Magic. The
doubles are similar in everything but antithetical.

The physiognomy and the body of the doubles are similar
because they are twins. This is one of the great mysteries of
esotericism. Every white soul has a black double, a contrary
soul that antagonizes and combats him.

Love and anti-love mutually fight each other. Anael is the
angel of love. Lilith is his tenebrous double. Lilith represents
anti-love. In ancient times, Iamblicus, the great theurgist, invoked these two genii and then out of a river two children appeared: love and anti-love, Eros and Anteros, Anael and Lilith.
The multitudes who witnessed Iamblicus's miracle prostrated
themselves before the great theurgist.

The disciple of the rocky path that leads to Nirvana[55] is
filled with ecstasy when he has the joy of contemplating Anael,
the angel of love.

---

necessary to get what they want; in other words, they are ruled by desire,
and use desire to manipulate others. It is called "black" because it is
corrupted by the ego, desire, attachment, etc.
55 Sanskrit निर्वाण, "extinction" or "cessation"; Tibetan: nyangde, literally

Anael presents himself before those who invoke him, who know how to call him. Anael is a beautiful child of the dawn. In the presence of the angel of love, we feel ourselves returning to the lost innocence of Eden. Anael's hair is like a golden waterfall falling onto his alabaster shoulders. The face of the angel of love has the rosy color of dawn. Anael wears a white tunic and he is indescribably beautiful. Anael is the angel of music and love, the angel of beauty and tenderness, the delightful cupid of all lovers, the ecstasy of all adoration.

Lilith[56] is Anael's rival sibling, his evil antithesis, a terribly evil child, the infernal angel of all great amorous deceptions, a monarch of the atomic hells of the human being.

Lilith cannot resist the look of the angel of love, but is the shadow of that angel. Lilith has the presence of a terribly evil child. Lilith's hair is in disarray and discolored. The evil face and the black and blue tunic tells us clearly of a world of cruelty and bitterness.

Anael represents the positive ray of Venus. Lilith represents the negative ray of Venus.

The traditions of the great Kabbalists state that Adam had two wives: Lilith and Nahemah.[57] Lilith is the mother of abor-

---

"the state beyond sorrow." In general use, the word nirvana refers to the permanent cessation of suffering and its causes, and therefore is a state of consciousness rather than a place. Yet, the term can also apply to heavenly realms, whose vibration is related to the cessation of suffering. In other words, if your mind-stream has liberated itself from the causes of suffering, it will naturally vibrate at the level of Nirvana (heaven). "Samsara, 'circling,' is to spin from one place to another. Nirvana is to have cut through this circling."—Padmasambhava, *The Cycle of Vital Points*

56   (also Lilit; Hebrew לילית, "the night visitor") An ancient symbol appearing in Sumerian mythology (4000 BC). In the Zohar she is described as the feminine half or the first "wife" of Adam (the first man), and is the origin of many demonic spirits (elementaries) who plague mankind, including the sucubi and incubi generated by masturbation and sexual fantasy. "...Lilith, the great mother of the demons..." —Zohar

57   "Rabbi Chiya quotes, "And the sister of Tuval Kayin was Naamah" (Beresheet 4:22). Why do the scriptures mention her name, Naamah (tender)? It is because people were seduced by her, and spirits and demons. Rabbi Yitzchak said that the sons of Elohim, Aza, and Azael were seduced by her. [...] Adam had intercourse with the female spirits for 130 years until Naamah came. Because of her beauty, she led the

LILITH TEMPTING ADAM AND EVE

tions, pederasty, sexual degeneration, homosexuality, infanticides, etc...

Nahemah is the mother of adultery. Nahemah seduces with the enchantment of her beauty and her virginity.

When a man is unfaithful to his wife (who was given to him by the lords of the law) he receives a luciferic mark between the eyebrows. When a man marries a woman who does not belong to him, when he performs a marriage which is in violation of the law, it is easy to recognize the error because on the day of the wedding, the bride appears to be bald. She covers so much of her head with a veil that the hair does not show.[58] The woman does this instinctively. Hair is the symbol of modesty in the woman, and in the weddings of Nahemah it is prohibited to display the hair. This is the law.

---

sons of Elohim, Aza and Azael astray. She bore them. Evil spirits and demons spread out from her into the world. They wander around the world during the night, deriding human beings and causing nocturnal pollution. Wherever they find people sleeping alone in their own homes, they hover over them and cling to them, arousing lustful desires and having offspring by them." —Zohar

58 Traditionally, long hair symbolizes sexual purity (ie. Samson). When someone becomes sexually defiled through fornication or adultery, they must shave their heads. These symbols appears in the internal worlds and in dreams.

The angels of light and the angels of darkness live in eternal struggle. The root of the great battle between the powers of light and darkness is in sex.

According to the great law, every planet has two polarities.

The positive ray of Mars is represented by Elohim Gibor. The negative ray of Mars is represented by the double of this Elohim. This double is called Andrameleck. The perverse demon Andrameleck is now reincarnated in China.

The supreme leader of the positive ray of the Moon is Jehovah. Chavajoth is exactly his antithesis, his rival brother. Jehovah directs the positive ray of the Moon. Chavajoth directs the negative ray of the Moon. Jehovah teaches white Sexual Magic. Chavajoth teaches black Sexual Magic.

There are two moons: the white moon and the black moon. The universal, feminine forces of sexuality are represented in the two moons.

Creation is the outcome of the evolving processes of sound.

Sound is the expression of sexuality. The angels create with the sexual power of the creative larynx.

The primordial, unmanifested sound (through its incessant, evolving processes) is converted into energetic forms of stabilized, dense matter. The unmanifested, primordial sound is the still, small voice. The primordial sound contains in itself the masculine-feminine sexual forces. As we descend into the difficult abyss of matter, these forces multiply and become more complicated. The positive pole of sound is the miraculous force which attracts us towards the unmanifested Absolute[59] where only happiness reigns. The negative pole of sound is the

---

59   Abstract space; that which is without attributes or limitations. Also known as sunyata, void, emptiness, Parabrahman, Adi-buddha, and many other names. "In the Absolute we go beyond karma and the gods, beyond the law. The mind and the individual consciousness are only good for mortifying our lives. In the Absolute we do not have an individual mind or individual consciousness; there, we are the unconditioned, free and absolutely happy Being. The Absolute is life free in its movement, without conditions, limitless, without the mortifying fear of the law, life beyond spirit and matter, beyond karma and suffering, beyond thought, word and action, beyond silence and sound, beyond forms." —Samael Aun Weor, *The Major Mysteries*

tenebrous force which attracts us to this valley of bitterness. The positive pole is solar, Christic, divine. The negative pole is lunar and is represented by the Moon. The shadow of the white moon is Lilith. The origin of fornication[60] is in Lilith. The origin of separate individuality is in Lilith.

The origin of the "I" is the black moon. The black moon is Lilith.

Jehovah works with the white moon. Chavajoth works with the black moon. The creation of the phenomenal universe is impossible without the intervention of the lunar forces. Unfortunately, the dark forces of the black moon intervene and harm creation.

The Sun and the Moon represent the positive and negative poles of sound. The Sun and the Moon originate creation.

The Sun is positive and the Moon negative. The Sun is the husband and the Moon is the wife; the devil Lilith gets in between and harms the great work; as above so below. The man is the Sun and the woman is the Moon. Lilith is the Satan[61] that seduces them both and leads them to fornication and to the Abyss. Lilith is the black moon, the dark aspect of the white moon, the origin of the "I" and of separate individuality.

Jehovah does not have a physical body. Chavajoth has a physical body. Chavajoth is now reincarnated in Germany; he poses as a war veteran and works for the great Black Lodge.

In the inner worlds, the black magician Chavajoth dresses in a red tunic and wears a red turban. This demon cultivates the mysteries of black Sexual Magic in a tenebrous cavern. He has many European disciples.

Jehovah lives normally in Eden. Eden is the ethereal world. Everyone who returns to Eden is received by Lord Jehovah. The door of Eden is sex.

In the astral, there are temples of light and temples of darkness, and where the light shines more clearly, the darkness becomes more dense.

---

60 Orgasm, or any misuse of sexual energy. See glossary.
61 Hebrew שטן, opposer, or adversary.

In Cataluña, Spain, there is a marvelous temple in the Jinn state.[62] This is the Temple of Montserrat. The Holy Grail is guarded in that temple. It is the silver chalice from which Jesus, the Christ, drank the wine during the Last Supper. The coagulated blood of the redeemer of the world is contained in the Holy Grail. Tradition tells us that at the foot of the Savior's cross the Roman senator Joseph of Arimathea filled that chalice with royal blood. The blood flowed from the wounds of the Beloved One and the chalice was filled.

A group of masters of the great White Lodge live in the Temple of Montserrat. They are the Knights of the Holy Grail.

In other times, the Temple of Montserrat and the Holy Grail were visible to the whole world. Later, that temple with its Holy Grail was made invisible. The temple exists in the Jinn state. The temple with its Holy Grail was submerged into hyperspace. Now we can only visit that temple with the astral body or with the physical body in the Jinn state.

A physical body can be taken out of the tridimensional world and placed in the fourth dimension. All this can be performed through the wise use of hyperspace. Soon, astrophysics will demonstrate the existence of hyperspace. The indigenous tribes of America had a profound knowledge of the Jinn science. In Mexico, the Tiger Knights knew how to place the physical body in hyperspace. In America, there are lakes, mountains and temples in the Jinn state. In Mexico, the Temple of Chapultepec is found in Jinn state (it is located in hyperspace). The Master Huiracocha[63] received the initiation in this temple.

---

62 Arabic; literally "hidden from sight," from the root جُنّ / جَنّ j-n-n which means 'to hide, conceal'. The Jinn state is the condition that results from moving physical matter into the fourth dimension. It remains in the fourth dimension and retains its physical characteristics, but disappears from the physical world.

63 Huiracocha is a master in the internal worlds, who had an incarnation that was known as Dr. Arnold Krumm-Heller. He established "Fraternatis Rosicruciana Antiqua" (The Ancient Rosecrucian Fraternity) in Mexico City. He was the Dean of Linguistics at the University of Mexico City, was of high rank in the Mexican Army, and was a Doctor of Medicine at the University of Berlin.

Next to every temple of light, there is a temple of darkness. Where the light shines brighter, there the darkness by contrast turns denser.

The Knights of the White Grail should inevitably fight against the Knights of the Black Grail.

The witchcraft salon located in Salamanca, Spain, is the fatal antithesis of the Temple of Montserrat.

Let us study this curious analogy of opposites. The Temple of the White Grail is a splendid monastery of the great light. The Temple of Salamanca is a splendid monastery of darkness.

The monastery of Montserrat has two floors. The witchcraft salon also has two floors. The Temple of Montserrat is surrounded by beautiful and sweet gardens. The witchcraft salon also is surrounded by romantic gardens where each flower exhales a breath of death.

Both are splendid edifices. In both buildings, truth and justice are well spoken of. In both temples, order and culture reign. In both temples, sanctity and love are spoken of. This will astound the reader, and one might question oneself, "How is it possible that in the temples of evil, sanctity and love are well spoken of?" Please, dear reader, don't be disconcerted.

Remember, dear sibling, that the Knights of the Black Grail are wolves dressed in sheep's clothing. The adepts of the left-hand[64] love to ejaculate the Christonic semen; that is why they are black magicians. Their philosophy is the philosophy of fatality.[65] For them, all good is evil. For them, all evil is good. The doctrine of Javhe is divine for them. The doctrine of Christ is diabolical for them; the lords of darkness hate the Christ. The children of the Abyss hate the Divine Mother. In their regions, they violently attack all those who invoke the Divine Mother or her beloved son.

If the esoteric investigator goes into the witchcraft salon with the astral body, one will inevitably find a beautiful, spiral staircase which leads to the most secret place of the precinct. This is an elegant salon furnished with the splendid luxury of

---

64 See glossary.
65 "destined for disaster, quality or state of causing death or destruction, something leading to a fatal outcome"

the lordly mansions of the seventeenth century. There shine
The One Thousand and One Night mirrors, the enchanted rugs,
and all of Nahemah's evil beauty. The governor of that man-
sion of fatality is Don Ramón Rubifero, distinguished Knight
of the Black Grail, horrible demon of darkness.

How unfortunate are those disciples who visit the witchcraft salon! Nahemah's fatal beauty will seduce them with all
the delightful magic of her enchantments. Then they will roll
down into the bottomless pit where we hear only the crying
and the gnashing of teeth. For them it would have been better
not to have been born at all or "to have had a millstone tied
around their necks and been thrown into the depths of the
sea."[66]

In the Temple of Montserrat shines the glory of the silver
chalice with the blood of the redeemer of the world. In the
Temple of Salamanca shines the darkness of the Black Grail.
In the Temple of Montserrat, cosmic festivals are celebrated.
In the Temple of Salamanca, profane dances and disgusting
witches' Sabbaths are celebrated. The Knights of the Holy Grail
worship the Christ and the Divine Mother. The Knights of
the Black Grail worship Javhe and great Nature's fatal shadow.
That shadow is called Santa Maria.[67] The kingdom of Santa
Maria is the Abyss. The great battle between the powers of light
and darkness is as ancient as eternity.

The medullar bone of that great battle is sex. The white
magicians want the serpent to ascend. The black magicians
want the serpent to descend. The white magicians follow the
way of the perfect marriage. The black magicians love adultery
and fornication.

There are masters of the great White Lodge. There are masters of the great Black Lodge. There are disciples of the great
White Lodge. There are disciples of the great Black Lodge.

The disciples of the great White Lodge know how to move
consciously and positively in the astral body. The disciples of
the great Black Lodge also know how to travel in the astral
body.

---

66   A reference to a saying of Jesus in Matthew 18:6, Mark 9:42, Luke 17:12.
67   This is not Mary the mother of Jesus, but her mirror opposite.

As children all of us heard many stories of witches and fairies. Our grandmothers used to always tell us stories of witches
that at midnight rode on their brooms and traveled through
the clouds. Although it will seem incredible to many students
of esotericism, Theosophy, Rosicrucianism, etc., those witches
really do exist. They do not ride brooms as grandmothers
believe, but they do know how to travel through the air. The
so-called "witches" travel with their body of flesh and bone
through space. They know how to make use of hyperspace and
travel from one place to another with the physical body. Soon
astrophysics will discover the existence of hyperspace. It can be
demonstrated with hypergeometry. When a body submerges
into hyperspace, it is then said that it has entered the Jinn
state. The body in the Jinn state escapes the law of gravity.
Then it floats in hyperspace.

There is volume and hypervolume. The so-called "witches"
move in the hypervolume of curved space in which we live.

Curved space does not belong exclusively to the planet
Earth. Curved space corresponds to the infinity of the starry
heavens.

If cyclones constitute proof of terrestrial spiral motion,
it is then very certain that the spiral rotation of all the suns,
constellations and worlds is concrete evidence of the curvature
of space.

The white magicians also know how to place the physical
body in the Jinn state. Jesus walked on the waters of the Sea of
Galilee by making intelligent use of hyperspace. Buddha's disciples, by making use of hyperspace, could traverse through a
rock from side to side. In India there are yogis who, by making
use of hyperspace, can pass through fire without being burned.

Peter, by using hyperspace, escaped from prison and saved
himself from the death penalty. The great yogi Patanjali states
in his aphorisms[68] that by practicing a samyama[69] on the physical body, it becomes as light as cotton and can float on air.

---

68 The Yoga Sutras
69 (Sanskrit संयम, "holding together, control, self-control") Perfect control
    of the mind. "The three [dharana, dhyana, and samadhi] together
    constitute samyama." —Patanjali, Yoga Sutras 3:4

A samyama consists of three tempos: concentration, meditation, and ecstasy. First, the yogi concentrates on the physical
body. Second, one meditates on the physical body inducing
sleep. Third, full of ecstasy, one gets up from the bed with the
body in the Jinn state. Then, one enters into hyperspace and
escaping from the law of gravity, floats in the air.

The devotees of Santa Maria (witches and warlocks) do the
same thing with the formulas of black magic.

With their bodies in Jinn state, the white magicians enter
into a higher dimension. The black magicians enter into a
lower dimension with their body in the Jinn state.

In Nature, there is always the subtraction and addition of
infinite dimensions. We leave a dimension to enter another
one, either higher or lower. This is the law.

The kingdom of Santa Maria is the abyss of failures. The
kingdom of light is the region of the gods.

In the kingdom of light only those who have attained the
state of supreme chastity can live. In the abyss, chastity is a
crime and fornication is law.

Whosoever sees the elegant salon of Javhe-Tzimus will be
dazzled by the luxury and happiness. There, one will meet
thousands of black magicians with gifts of terribly evil beauty.
The innocent soul who enters those evil regions could very easily go astray, to the wrong way, and fall forever into the abyss of
perdition. Nahemah's evil beauty is dangerous.

In the temples of light, we only witness love and wisdom.
There, the tenebrous ones cannot enter because they live in a
lower dimension.

Nahemah's beauty is fatal. Those beings who loved so
much, those beings who swore to love each other forever could
have been happy. Unfortunately, enchanted by Nahemah's
beauty, they adored someone else's spouse and fell into the
abyss of desperation.

In the salon of Javhe-Tzimus, the beauty of Nahemah fatally
shines.

The black magicians have a sacred symbol. This symbol is
the copper cauldron. The white magicians have the holy cross
as their sacred symbol. The latter is phallic. The insertion of

the vertical phallus into the horizontal uterus forms the cross.
The cross has the power to create. There can be no creation
without the sign of the holy cross. Animal species are crossed;
atoms and molecules are crossed to perpetuate life.

The blessed roses of spirituality
bloom on the cross of the perfect marriage. The perfect marriage is the union
of two beings: one who loves more and
the other who loves better. Love is the
best religion available to the human
species.

The black magicians hate the perfect
marriage. Nahemah's fatal beauty and
Lilith's sexual crimes are the antithesis
of the perfect marriage.

THE ORIGINAL SYMBOL OF THE
ROSICRUCIAN BROTHERHOOD.

The white magician worships the
inner Christ. The black magician worships Satan. This is the
"I," the me, myself, the reincarnating ego. In fact, the "I" is the
specter of the threshold[70] itself. It continually reincarnates
to satisfy desires. The "I" is memory. In the "I" are all of the
memories of our ancient personalities. The "I" is Ahriman,
Lucifer, Satan.

Our real Being is the inner Christ. Our real Being is of a universal nature. Our real Being is not a superior or inferior "I."
Our real Being is impersonal, universal, divine. He transcends
every concept of "I," me, myself, ego, etc.

The black magician strengthens his Satan and upon this
he bases his fatal power. Satan's form and size result from the
degree of human evil. When we enter the path of the perfect
marriage, Satan loses his volume and ugliness. We need to dissolve Satan. This is only possible with the perfect marriage.

We need to elevate ourselves to the angelic state. This is only
possible by practicing Sexual Magic with a priestly spouse.
Angels are perfect human beings.

There are two kinds of Sexual Magic: black and white.
Those who practice white Sexual Magic never ejaculate the se-

---

70 A variation on the name "guardian of the threshold," explained in
chapter 19.

men. Those who practice black Sexual Magic always ejaculate the semen.

The Bons[71] and Drukpas[72] of the "Red Cap" ejaculate the semen which they later collect from within the vagina. This semen mixed with the feminine sexual fluid is reabsorbed once again through the urethra, utilizing a tenebrous procedure. The fatal result of that Black Tantra is the awakening of the serpent in an absolutely negative form. Then, instead of ascending through the medullar canal, it descends towards the atomic hells of the human being. This is Satan's horrifying tail. Through this procedure, the Bons and Drukpas forever separate themselves from the inner Christ and forever sink into the terrifying Abyss.

No white magician ejaculates the semen; the white magician treads the path of the perfect marriage.

Bons and Drukpas of the "Red Cap" want (by means of their fatal procedure) to unite the solar and lunar atoms in order to awaken the Kundalini. The result of their ignorance is separation from the inner God forever.

The white magicians blend the solar and lunar atoms in their own sexual laboratory. This is what the perfect marriage is for. Blessed be woman. Blessed be love.

The great battle between the black and the white magicians has its root in sex. The tempting serpent of Eden and the brazen serpent which healed the Israelites in the wilderness fight against each other. When the serpent ascends we become angels; when it descends we become demons.

---

71   (or Bhons) The oldest religion in Tibet. It was largely overshadowed (some say persecuted) by the arrival of Buddhism. Early on, Samael Aun Weor had accepted the statements of earlier investigators which described the Bon religion as essentially black, but upon further investigation he discovered that they are not necessarily black, just extreme in some practices.

72   See glossary.

During Sexual Magic, the three breaths of pure Akasha[73] that descend through Brahman's thread are reinforced.[74] When a magician ejaculates the semen, they lose billions of solar atoms that are replaced by billions of diabolical atoms, which the sexual organs collect with the nervous movement that takes place at the time of the ejaculation of semen.[75] The satanic atoms try to ascend to the brain through Brahman's thread, but the three breaths of Akasha precipitate them to the Abyss. When they crash against the black atomic god[76] residing in the coccyx, the snake awakens and moves downward to form the devil's tail in the astral body.

Angels are perfect human beings. The perfect marriage is necessary in order to rise to the angelic state. Demons are perverse beings.

There are two types of Sexual Magic: white and black.[77] Those who practice white Sexual Magic never in their lives spill the semen. Those who practice black Sexual Magic spill the semen.

The Bons and Drukpas of the Black Lodge of Tibet spill the semen. These tenebrous beings, after spilling their semen retrieve it from within the feminine vulva with a special instrument. Later, they reabsorb it through the urethra using a black power, a variety of Vajroli Mudra,[78] which we do not divulge so as not to propagate the fatal science of darkness.

---

73 Sanskrit आकाश; or akasa "Space, sky, atmosphere, vacuity, ether, free or open space, subtle and ethereal fluid, heaven, god brahma." From akash, "to be visible, appear, shine, be brilliant." The most subtle level of matter. See glossary.

74 Sanskrit ब्राह्मणादि "channel of Brahma" from ब्रह्मन् Brahma, the highest form of divinity, and nadī नदी, "river, conduit, artery." A subtle conduit in the center of the spinal column, through which energy can flow. It is closed unless one is transmuting sexual energy.

75 This occurs in men and women who orgasm. The "ejaculation of semen" is the orgasm in both sexes.

76 To learn what this means, read *The Dayspring of Youth* by M.

77 These symbolic colors indicate their purity: white represents purity, black represents corruption.

78 Sanskrit वज्रोली, from vajra वज्र "thunderbolt, lightning, diamond, adamantine" and mudra मुद्रा "seal, stamp." Vajroli Mudra refers to esoteric practices in Hindu and Tibetan Yogas that traditionally were kept secret and only practiced under the supervision of an experienced

The black magicians believe they can mix the solar and lunar atoms in this way to awaken the Kundalini. The result is that instead of ascending through the medullar canal, the spinal fires descend towards the atomic hells of the human being and turn into the tail of Satan.

The white magicians mix the solar and lunar atoms in their own sexual laboratory without committing the crime of spilling any seminal liquor.

Thus, the Kundalini awakens positively and ascends victoriously through the medullar canal. This is the angelic way.

The white magician aspires to the angelic state. The lords of the dark countenance want to reach the grade of Anagarikas.[79]

The souls who follow the way of the perfect marriage unite with their inner God and rise to the kingdom of the superhuman.

The souls who hate the way of the perfect marriage separate from their inner God and submerge into the Abyss.

The white magician makes the sexual energy ascend through the sympathetic canals of the spinal medulla. These two cords are entwined around the spinal medulla, forming the holy eight. These are the two witnesses of the Apocalypse.[80]

"Fill your chalice, sibling, with
the sacred wine of light."

Remember, the chalice is the brain. You need the eyes of the eagle and the igneous wings.

---

teacher, albeit with variation and opposing uses. Some vajroli techniques (such as the one taught by Samael Aun Weor) are positive and valuable, but most are degenerated, ranging from useless to dangerous, especially today with the proliferation of "experts" who lack any real experience of the truth, or who are actually black magicians.

79   Sanskrit अनगारिका "homeless one." The term is commonly applied to those who have renounced worldly things but are not full fledged monks or nuns. The word Anagarika is also used as a title among black magicians.

80   Two currents along the spine, also called Ida and Pingala, Adam and Eve, Od and Obd, etc. "And I will give power unto my two witnesses, and they shall prophesy a thousand two hundred and threescore days, clothed in sackcloth. These are the two olive trees, and the two candlesticks standing before the God of the earth." —Revelation 11

The tenebrous ones struggle to take you from the real path. Know that the three gravest dangers which await the student are the mediums of spiritualism, the false prophets and prophetesses, and sexual temptations.

This is the path of the razor's edge; this path is full of dangers inside and out.[81]

Live alert and keep a watchful eye as the watchman in wartime. Do not let yourself be caught off guard by those who consider sex a purely animal function without any spiritual transcendence of any kind. As a rule, false prophets hate sex and exhibit novel doctrines to surprise the weak, to fascinate them, and to lead them to the Abyss.

Do not become confused by the false statements of the tenebrous ones. Remember that spiritualist mediums often serve as vehicles for black entities. These entities pose as saints and advise against the perfect marriage. Usually, they declare themselves to be Jesus Christ or Buddha, etc., to cheat the fools.

Beware of the temptations that await you. Be prudent and watchful.

Remember that in sex is found the great battle between the powers of light and darkness.

Everyone who enters the path of the perfect marriage must be very careful of the three very grave dangers. The tenebrous ones struggle tirelessly to take you from the path of the perfect marriage.

Do not be seduced by the sublime doctrines that advise the ejaculation of the semen, because they are of black magic. The king of the diabolical atoms awaits in the coccyx for the opportunity to awaken the serpent negatively, in order to direct it downward. With the ejaculation of semen, the black atomic god receives a formidable electrical impulse, enough to awaken the serpent and direct it toward the atomic hells of the human being. This is how the human being becomes a demon. Thus, this is how one falls into the Abyss.

---

81   "A sharpened razor's edge is hard to cross —The dangers of the path— wise seers proclaim them!" —Katha Upanishad 3:14

Dante and Virgil observe the suffering in the Abyss.

Chapter 4

The Abyss

Kabbalistic traditions state that Adam had two wives: Lilith and Nahemah. Lilith is the mother of abortions, homosexuality, and in general, all kinds of crimes against Nature. Nahemah is the mother of malignant beauty, passion, and adultery. Thus, the Abyss is divided into two large regions: the spheres of Lilith and Nahemah. Infrasexuality[82] reigns sovereign in these two large regions.

The Sphere of Lilith

In the infrasexual sphere of Lilith abide those who hate sex, for example, monks, anchorites, preachers of pseudo-esoteric type sects, pseudo-yogis who abhor sex, nuns, etc. All such infrasexual people (by the mere fact that they are infrasexual) often have an affinity with people of intermediate sexuality. Thus, it is not difficult to find homosexuality within many convents, religions, sects and schools of a pseudo-esoteric type.

Infrasexual people consider themselves to be highly superior to those of normal sexuality. They are disdainful of people of normal sexuality, considering them inferior. All of the taboos, restrictions, and prejudices that currently condition the lives of people of normal sexuality were firmly established by infrasexual people.

We heard about the case of an old anchorite who preached a certain pseudo-occult doctrine. Everyone venerated this man considering him to be a saint. He appeared to be a master and people worshiped him. Finally, one poor woman discovered the truth, when he proposed a sexual union against Nature to her, supposedly in order to initiate her. In reality, this anchorite was an infrasexual. Nevertheless, this man had taken the vows of chastity. This man mortally hated the Arcanum A.Z.F. (Sexual Magic). He considered it to be dangerous. However, he had no

---

82   Inferior sexual behavior. The use of sexual energy that leads to suffering.

problem proposing extra-vaginal unions to his devotees because he was really an infrasexual.

Who would have doubted this man? He appeared to be a saint. This is what the people believed. His followers considered him a master. He hated sex. Yes, he mortally hated sex. This is a characteristic of infrasexual, degenerated people.

The worst of the matter is that they consider themselves superior to people of normal sexuality. They feel they are super-transcendent, and they manage to seduce people of normal sexuality, converting them into their followers. In our mission, which is to divulge Gnostic esotericism, we have had the opportunity to study infrasexual people. We often hear them repeating the following phrases: "You Gnostics are selfish because all you ever think of is your Kundalini and Sexual Magic." "You are sexual fanatics." "Sexual Magic is purely animalistic." "Sex is something very vulgar; I am a spiritualist and I abhor all that is materialistic and vulgar." "Sex is filthy." "There are many paths to God." "I live only for God and am not interested in the rubbish of sexuality." "I follow the doctrine of chastity and abhor sex," etc. This is precisely the language of infrasexual people. They are always self-sufficient, always so proud in their feeling of superiority to people of normal sexuality.

An infrasexual woman who hated her husband said to us, "I would only practice Sexual Magic with my guru." She said this in the presence of her husband. This woman had no sexual relations with her husband because she supposedly hated sex. Nevertheless, she was willing to practice Sexual Magic, but only with her guru. She had an affinity with the guru because he too was an infrasexual. This is the "saint" mentioned earlier in this chapter, the one who enjoyed suggesting to his female devotees to have sexual unions, against Nature, with him.

We heard about the case of the arch-hierophant who hated women and who often uttered phrases such as, "Women! I kick them with my feet." He preached a doctrine, and his followers adored him as if he was a god. He was always surrounded by adolescents. Thus, this is how he spent his time, until the police uncovered everything. He was a homosexual, a corrupter of minors; yet, he had the same pride of all infrasexual people, which is feeling super-transcendent, ineffable, and divine. The sphere of Lilith is the sphere of great heresy. These people no longer have the possibility of redemption because they hate the Holy Spirit.

"All manner of sin shall be forgiven, except the sin against the Holy Ghost." —Christian Bible, Matthew 12:31

Sexual energy is an emanation of the Divine Mother. Whosoever renounces the Cosmic Mother, whosoever hates the Divine Mother, whosoever profanes the energy of the Divine Mother, shall sink into the Abyss forever. There they will have to pass through the Second Death.[83]

The Psychology of the Sphere of Lilith

The sphere of Lilith is characterized by its cruelty. The psychology of this sphere has various aspects: monks and nuns who hate sex, homosexuality in convents, homosexuality outside of monastic life, induced abortions, people who love masturbation, criminals of the brothel, people who enjoy torturing others, etc. In this sphere we find the most horrible crimes reported in police records: horrible cases of bloody crimes of homosexual origin, terrifying acts of sadism, homosexuality in jails, lesbianism, terrifying psychotic criminals, those who enjoy making their loved one suffer, horrible infanticides, patricides, matricides, etc. In this sphere we also find pseudo-occultists who would rather suffer from nocturnal pollution than get married, people who mortally hate the Arcanum A. Z. F. and the perfect matrimony, people who believe that they can reach God while hating sex, anchoritic people who abhor sex and who consider it vulgar and gross.

---

83 A mechanical process in nature experienced by those souls who within the allotted time fail to reach union with their inner divinity (i.e. known as self-realization, liberation, religare, yoga, moksha, etc). The Second Death is the complete dissolution of the ego (karma, defects, sins) in the infernal regions of nature, which after unimaginable quantities of suffering, proportional to the density of the psyche, in the end purifies the Essence (consciousness) so that it may try again to perfect itself and reach the union with the Being.

The Sphere of Nahemah

The sphere of Nahemah seduces with the enchantment of her malignant beauty. In this infrasexual sphere we find the "Don Juans and femme fatales." The world of prostitution unfolds in this sphere. The infrasexual men of Nahemah feel very manly. Men who have many women live in this sphere. They feel happy in adultery. They believe themselves to be very manly; they are unaware that they are infrasexual.

In the sphere of Nahemah we also find millions of prostitutes. These poor women are victims of the fatal charm of Nahemah. In the sphere of Nahemah we find elegant ladies of high social standing. These people are very happy within adultery. That is their world.

In the infrasexual region of Nahemah we find a sweetness that moves the soul: virgins that seduce with the charm of their tenderness, very beautiful seductive women, men who abandon their homes bewitched by the enchantment of these most precious beauties. In this region we also find indescribable beauty, uncontrollable passions, beautiful salons, elegant cabarets, soft beds, delightful dances, orchestras of the abyss, unforgettable romantic words that cannot be forgotten, etc.

The infrasexual people of Nahemah sometimes accept the Arcanum A.Z.F. (Sexual Magic) but fail because they are unable to avoid the ejaculation of semen. They almost always withdraw from the perfect matrimony uttering horrible things against it. We have heard them saying: "I practiced Sexual Magic and sometimes I was able to remain without spilling the semen. I was an animal enjoying the delicious passions of sex." After withdrawing from the path of the razor's edge, represented by the spinal medulla, they seek refuge in some seductive doctrine of Nahemah. If they are lucky enough not to fall into the sphere of Lilith, they continue ejaculating the seminal liquor. Such is their infrasexual world.

The Psychology of the Sphere of Nahemah

The infrasexual inhabitants of the sphere of Nahemah are very touchy. They are the ones who utter phrases such as, "Offense is cleansed with blood." "I killed because I am a man of honor." "My honor was slighted." "I am a wronged husband," etc. The Nahemah type of man is the one who jeopardizes his life for any lady. He is the passionate lover of luxury, a slave to social prejudice, the friend of drunkenness, banquets, parties, very elegant fashions, etc. These people consider the perfect matrimony to be something impossible, and when they accept it, they last for only a short time on the path because they fail. This type of person enjoys sex in a bestial manner. When these people accept the Arcanum A.Z F., they utilize it to enjoy lust. As soon as they find some seductive doctrine that offers them refuge, they then withdraw from the perfect matrimony.

The Mystique of Nahemah

Sometimes we find mystical types in the infrasexual sphere of Nahemah who neither drink, eat meat, nor smoke, or they are very religious, though not vegetarians. The mystical type of Nahemah is only passionate in secret. They intensely enjoy sexual passions, even though later they pass terrible judgements against sexual passion. Sometimes they accept the Arcanum A.Z.F., but they withdraw in a short while when they find some consoling doctrine which provides them with phrases like this, "God said 'grow and multiply." "The sexual act is a purely animal function and spirituality has nothing to do with it," etc. Then the infrasexual one from Nahemah, in finding justification for ejaculating the seminal liquor, leaves the path of the perfect matrimony.

VAJRASATTVA

Vajrasattva represents the power to purify
ourselves of psychological defects.

Chapter 5

Normal Sexuality

We understand people of normal sexuality to be those who
have no sexual conflicts of any kind.
Sexual energy is divided into three distinct types. First: the
energy having to do with the reproduction of the race and the
health of the physical body in general. Second: the energy having to do with the spheres of thought, feeling, and will. Third:
the energy that is related with the divine Spirit of man.

Indeed, sexual energy is without a doubt the most subtle
and powerful energy normally produced and transported
through the human organism. Everything that a human being
is, including the three spheres of thought, feeling and will, is
none other than the exact outcome of distinct modifications
of sexual energy.

The control and storage of sexual energy is certainly difficult due to the tremendously subtle and powerful nature of
this energy. In addition, its presence represents a source of immense power that can result in a true catastrophe if one does
not know how to handle it.

Within the organism, there are certain canals through
which this powerful energy must normally circulate. When this
energy infiltrates the delicate mechanism of other functions,
failure is the violent outcome. In this case, extremely delicate
centers in the human organism are damaged, and in fact, the
individual becomes an infrasexual.

All negative mental attitudes can lead directly or indirectly
to these violent and destructive catastrophes of sexual energy.
Hatred of sex, hatred of the Arcanum A.Z.F., disgust or repugnance towards sex, disdain for sex, an underestimation of sex,
fear of sex, passional jealousy, sexual cynicism, sexual sadism,
obscenity, pornography, sexual brutality, etc., turn the human
being into an infrasexual.

Sex is the creative function through which the human being
is a true god. Normal sexuality results from total harmony and
concordance with all the other functions. Normal sexuality

bestows upon us the power to create healthy children, to create in the world of art or the sciences. Any negative mental attitude towards sex produces infiltration of this powerful energy into other functions, which provokes frightening catastrophes, fatally resulting in infrasexuality.

All negative mental attitudes compel the sexual energy, forcing it to circulate through canals and systems fit for mental, volitive, or any other type of energy less powerful than sexual energy. The result is fatal because that type of canal and system, unable to endure the tremendous voltage of the very powerful sexual energy, gets heated and blows out, as does a wire that is too thin and fine when a high power electrical current passes through it.

When man and woman unite sexually in the perfect matrimony, they are truly ineffable gods in those voluptuous moments. Man and woman united sexually form a divine androgynous being, a male-female Elohim, a terrifically divine divinity. The two halves, separated since the dawn of life, are united for one instant in order to create. This is ineffable, sublime; this is a thing of paradise...

Sexual energy is dangerously volatile and potentially explosive. During the secret act, during sexual ecstasy, the pair is surrounded by a tremendous, terrifically divine energy. In these moments of utmost joy and ardent kisses, which ignite the depths of the soul, we are able to retain that marvelous light to purify and totally transform ourselves. When we spill the glass of Hermes, when the loss occurs, the light of the gods withdraws, leaving an open door for the red and sanguinary light of Lucifer to enter the home. Then the enchantment disappears and disillusion and disenchantment take its place. After a short time, the man and woman start out on the path of adultery because their home has become an inferno.

It is characteristic of Nature to mobilize enormous reserves of creative energy in order to create any cosmos. Yet Nature only employs an infinitesimal quantity of its enormous reserves in order to carry out its creations. Man loses six or seven million spermatozoa in one seminal ejaculation; however, only one infinitesimal spermatozoon is needed to engender a child.

In Lemuria, no human being ejaculated the semen. Then, couples united sexually in the temples to create. During those moments, the lunar hierarchies knew how to utilize one spermatozoon and one egg in order to create without the necessity of the couple reaching the orgasm and seminal ejaculation. No one spilled the semen. The sexual act was a sacrament which was only performed within the temple. Women in those times gave birth to children without any pain, and the serpent was raised victoriously through the medullar canal. In that epoch, human beings had not yet left Eden. All of Nature obeyed them, and they knew neither pain nor sin. The tenebrous Lucifers were the ones who showed humans how to spill the semen. The original sin of our first parents was the crime of spilling the semen. That is fornication. When the paradisiacal human beings fornicated, they then entered the kingdom of the Lucifers. The human being of this day and age is luciferic.

It is absurd to spill six or seven million spermatozoa when only one is needed in order to create. One sole spermatozoon escapes easily from the sexual glands without the necessity of spilling the semen. When human beings return to the starting point, when they re-establish the sexual system of Eden, the sacred serpent Kundalini will again rise victoriously in order to convert us into gods. The sexual system of Eden is normal sexuality; the sexual system of the luciferic human is absolutely abnormal.

Not only does one fornicate physically, but there is fornication also in the mental and astral worlds. Those who engage in lustful conversations, those who read pornographic magazines, those who attend movie houses where passionate, erotic films are shown waste enormous reserves of energy. Those poor people utilize the finest and most delicate substance of sex, wasting it miserably in the satisfaction of their brutal mental passions.

Sexual fantasy produces psycho-sexual impotence. There are sick people whose sexual organs function normally. They appear to be normal people, but the instant the man tries to connect the male member with the vulva, the erection diminishes and the phallus falls, leaving them in the most horrible state of despair [the same reaction happens with women]. They have lived in sexual fantasy, and when they actually find themselves facing the stark reality of sex, which has nothing to do with fantasy, they become confused and are unable to respond to that reality as they should.

The sexual sense is tremendously rapid and formidably subtle, thanks to its very fine and imponderable energy. The molecular level where the sexual sense acts is millions of times faster than thought waves. The logical mind and fantasy are stumbling blocks for the sexual sense. When the logical mind with all of its reasoning, or when sexual fantasy with all of its erotic illusions wants to control the sexual sense or direct it within its illusions, then it is fatally destroyed. The logical mind and sexual fantasy destroy the sexual sense when they try to place it at their service. Psycho-sexual impotence is the most dreadful tragedy that can afflict extravagantly fanciful men and women or purely rational people.

The struggle of many monks, nuns, anchorites, pseudo-yogis, etc., to bottle up sex within their religious fanaticism, to confine it to the prison of their penitence, to muzzle it or sterilize it, to prohibit all creative manifestation, etc., converts the fanatics into slaves of their own passions. They become slaves of sex, incapable of thinking about anything other than sex. These are the ones who are fanatical about sex. These are the degenerated ones of infrasexuality. These people discharge their energy every night with disgusting nocturnal emissions, or acquire homosexual vices, or masturbate miserably. Wanting to confine sex is like wanting to bottle up the Sun. A person like this is the most abject slave of sex without any benefit or true pleasure. A person like this is an unhappy sinner. A woman like this is a sterile mule, a miserable slave of that which she wants to enslave (sex). The enemies of the Holy Spirit are people of the Abyss. It would have been better for these people if they had never been born or "if they tied a millstone around their necks and hurled themselves to the bottom of the sea."

The human being must learn to live sexually. The age of sex, the new Aquarian Age, is at hand. The sexual glands are controlled by the planet Uranus, which is the ruling planet of the constellation of Aquarius. Thus, sexual alchemy is in fact the science of the new Aquarian Age. Sexual Magic will be officially accepted in the universities of the new Aquarian Age. Those who presume to be messengers of the new Aquarian Age, but nevertheless hate the Arcanum A.Z.F., provide more than enough evidence that they are truly impostors, this is because the new Aquarian Age is governed by the regent of sex. This regent is the planet Uranus.

Sexual energy is the finest energy of the infinite cosmos.

Sexual energy can convert us into angels or demons. The image of truth is found deposited in sexual energy. The cosmic design of Adam Christ is found deposited in sexual energy.

The Son of Man, the superhuman, is born from normal sexuality. The superhuman could never be born of infrasexual people. The realm of infrasexual people is the Abyss. The Greek poet Homer said, "It is better to be a beggar on Earth than a king in the empire of shadows." That empire is the tenebrous world of the infrasexuals.

JESUS DEMONSTRATES HIS MASTERY OVER THE SEXUAL WATERS. ENGRAVING BY GUSTAVE DORÉ

Chapter 6

Suprasexuality

Suprasexuality[84] is the result of sexual transmutation. Christ, Buddha, Dante, Zoroaster, Mohammed, Hermes, Quetzalcoatl, and many other great masters were suprasexual. The two great aspects of sexuality are called generation and regeneration. In the preceding chapter we studied conscious generation; now we are going to study regeneration.

By studying the life of animals we discover very interesting things. If we cut a glass snake[85] in half we can be sure that it has the power to regenerate itself. It can totally develop a new half with all of the organs of the lost half. Most worms of the earth and sea also have the power of continuous regeneration. The lizard can regenerate its tail and the human organism its skin. The power of regeneration is absolutely sexual.

The human being has the power to recreate oneself. A human can create the superhuman within oneself. This is possible using sexual power wisely. We can recreate ourselves as authentic superhumans. This is only possible with sexual transmutation. The fundamental key to sexual transmutation is the Arcanum A.Z.F. (Sexual Magic).

The key to all power is found in the union of the phallus and the uterus. What is important is that the couple learns how to withdraw from the sexual act before the spasm, before the seminal discharge. The semen must not be spilled either inside the uterus or outside of it, neither to the sides, nor anywhere else. We speak clearly, so that people will understand, even though some puritanical infrasexual people might consider the former statement to be pornographic.

Human life in itself has no meaning. To be born, to grow, to work hard in order to live, to reproduce oneself as any animal, and then to die is really a chain of martyrdom that the human

---

84   Superior sexuality. Sexual actions that lead to superior results, ie. liberation from the ego, the birth in the superior worlds and creation of the soul, the incarnation of Christ, etc.
85   *Ophisaurus* looks like a snake but is classified as a lizard.

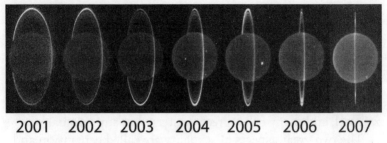

2001   2002   2003   2004   2005   2006   2007

URANUS AS SEEN BY THE NASA/ESA HUBBLE SPACE TELESCOPE.

being carries entangled in his soul. If that is life, it is not worth living. Fortunately, we have in our sexual glands the seed, the grain. From this seed, from the grain, can be born the superhuman, the Adam Christ, the golden child of sexual alchemy. For this, life is certainly worth living.

The path is sexual transmutation. This is the science of Uranus. This is the planet that controls the gonads or sexual glands. This is the planet that governs the constellation of Aquarius.

Uranus has a sexual cycle of eighty-four years. Uranus is the only planet which directs its two poles toward the sun. The two poles of Uranus correspond to the masculine and feminine aspects. These two phases alternate in periods of forty-two years each. The alternating stimuli of the two poles of Uranus govern all the sexual history of human evolution. Epochs in which women undress in order to display their bodies alternate with epochs in which men adorn themselves. Epochs of feminine preponderance alternate with times of intrepid gentlemen. This is the history of the ages.

When the human being reaches a mature age, one is stimulated by the antithetical cycle, opposite to that which governed during infancy and youth. Then we are truly mature. We feel sexually stimulated by the sexual opposite. In reality, maturity is marvelous for the task of sexual regeneration. Sexual sentiments are richer and more mature at forty years of age than at thirty.

The superhuman is not the outcome of evolution. The superhuman is born from the seed. The superhuman is the result of a tremendous revolution of the consciousness. The superhuman is the Son of Man mentioned by Christ. The superhuman is Adam Christ.

Evolution means that nothing is still; everything exists within the concepts of time, space and movement. Nature contains within itself all possibilities. No one reaches perfection with evolution. Some people become better and the vast majority, terribly perverse. This is evolution. The human being of innocence, that paradisiacal human of several million years ago, is now, after much evolution, the human of the atomic bomb, the human of the hydrogen bomb, and the corrupted human of fraud and crime.

Evolution is a process of the complication of energy. We need to return to the point of departure (sex) and regenerate ourselves. The human being is a living seed. The seed, the grain, must make an effort so that the superhuman may germinate. This is not evolution. This is a tremendous revolution of the consciousness. Christ said, and rightly so,

> *"And as Moses lifted up the serpent in the wilderness, even so must the Son of Man be lifted up."* —Christian Bible, John 3:14

The Son of Man is Adam Christ, the superhuman.

With sexual transmutation, we regenerate ourselves absolutely.

The period of sexual ecstasy is always preceded by the period of sexual enjoyment. Thus, the same energy that produces sexual enjoyment, when transmuted, produces ecstasy.

The lamp of the Hermit of the Ninth Arcanum, which is normally found enclosed within the deep caverns of one's sexual organs, must be placed within the tower of the temple. This tower is the brain. Then we become enlightened. This is the

The Hermit

THE NINTH ARCANUM

truly positive path that converts us into masters of samadhi (ecstasy).[86]

Every true technique of internal meditation is intimately related with sexual transmutation. We need to raise the lamp very high in order to illuminate ourselves.

Every novice of Alchemy, after being crowned, begins to move away from the sexual act little by little. The secret connubial becomes increasingly distant in accordance with certain cosmic rhythms marked by the oriental gong. That is how the sexual energies are sublimated until they are absolutely transmuted to produce continuous ecstasy.

The neophyte of Alchemy (who in preceding reincarnations worked on the magisterium of fire) accomplishes the work of the sexual laboratory in a relatively short time. But those who undertake the Magnus Opus (the Great Work) for the first time need at least twenty years of very intense work, and twenty more in order to withdraw very slowly from the work of the laboratory: a total of forty years in order to accomplish all the work. When the alchemist spills the Cup of Hermes, the fire of the laboratory burner is turned off and all the work is lost.

The age of mystical ecstasy begins when the age of sexual pleasure ends.

All those who attain the Venustic Initiation have a very difficult task to accomplish afterwards. This task consists of the transformation of the sexual energies. Just as we can transplant a vegetable, transfer a plant from one flower pot to another, we must also transplant the sexual energy, extract it from the earthly human, and transfer it, transplant it, into the Adam Christ. In Alchemy, it is said that we must liberate the philosophical egg from the filthy putrefaction of matter and deliver it decisively to the Son of Man. The result of this work is astonishing and marvelous. This is precisely the instant when the Adam Christ can swallow his human consciousness. The

---

86   Sanskrit समाधि Literally "union" or "combination," although in context it can have a dizzying number of meanings. Samadhi is a state of consciousness. In general, the word refers to the ultimate stage of yoga, in which the consciousness, freed of the conditioning of the body and mind, experiences its true nature: happiness, insight, joy, freedom, etc. This experience is reached and perfected only through meditation.

consciousness of Adam the sinner must have died before this moment. Only the inner God can devour the soul. Upon reaching this point, the master has Self-realized absolutely. From this moment we have attained continuous ecstasy, the supreme illumination of great hierophants.

The birth of the superhuman is an absolutely sexual problem. We need to be born again in order to enter into the kingdom of the heavens. The superhuman is as different from the human as lightning from a black cloud. Lightning comes from the cloud, but it is not the cloud. Lightning is the superhuman; the cloud is the human. Sexual regeneration activates the powers that we had in Eden. We lost those powers when we fell into animal generation. We re-conquer those powers when we regenerate ourselves. Just as the worm can regenerate its body and the lizard its tail, we can regenerate our lost powers in order to again shine as gods. Sexual energies transplanted in the Adam Christ shine with the immaculate whiteness of divinity. These energies appear then as terrifically divine rays. The grandeur and majesty of the superhuman is tremendous. In reality, the superhuman shines for a moment in the darkness of the ages and then disappears. He becomes invisible to people.

Ordinarily, we can find traces of these kinds of beings in some secret schools of regeneration. Almost nothing is officially known about these schools; however, it is because of them that we know of the existence of those sublime suprasexual beings. The schools of regeneration have periods of public activity and periods of secret work. The planet Neptune cyclically governs the activity of these schools. In the human organism, Neptune has control over the pineal gland. Only with sexual transmutation is this gland of the gods activated. Uranus controls the sexual glands and Neptune controls the pineal gland. Uranus is practical Sexual Alchemy. Neptune is esoteric study. First we must study and then work in the laboratory. Uranus has a sexual cycle of 84 years, and Neptune a cycle of 165 years. The cycle of Uranus is that of an average human life. The cycle of Neptune is that of public activity in certain schools of regeneration. Only through the path of the perfect matrimony do we reach supra-sexuality.

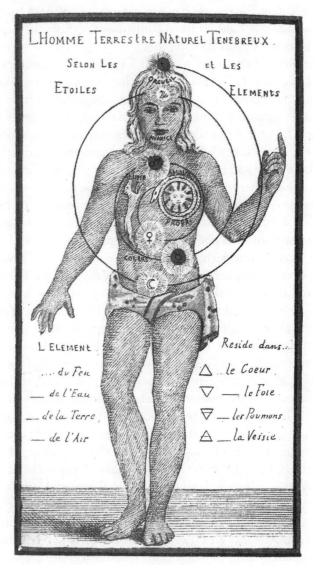

G. GICHTEL, Theosophia practica, 1898

Chapter 7

The Seven Churches

The human being is a triad of body, soul, and Spirit. There is a mediator between the Spirit and the body. This is the soul. We, Gnostics, know that the soul is dressed with a marvelous garment. This is the astral body. We already know through our Gnostic studies that the astral body is a double of our physical organism and is endowed with marvelous internal senses. Great clairvoyants speak to us of the seven chakras,[87] and Mr. Leadbeater describes them in great detail. These chakras are really the senses of the astral body. Such magnetic centers are found in close correlation with the glands of internal secretions.

In the laboratory of the human organism, there are seven ingredients submitted to triple nerve control. These nerves control the glandular septenary as agents of the law of the triangle.[88] The three different nerve controls interact among themselves and are the following:

First: the cerebrospinal nervous system, agent of conscious functions.

Second: the grand sympathetic nervous system, agent of the unconscious, subconscious, and instinctive functions.

Third: the parasympathetic, or vagus, nervous system, that collaborates by restraining the instinctive functions under the commands of the mind.

The cerebrospinal system is the throne of the Divine Spirit.

The grand sympathetic system is the vehicle of the astral body. The vagus, or parasympathetic, obeys the commands of the mind.

---

87 Sanskrit चक्र "wheel, circle." In Asian traditions, the word chakra refers to any wheel or circle, and is often used to describe circular weapons used by the gods. Most people today associate the word with subtle centers of energetic transformation that are within our bodies. There are hundreds of chakras in our multi-dimensional physiology, but seven primary ones related to the awakening of consciousness.

88 The law of three creates. The law of seven organizes. Study the tree of life and its ten sephiroth.

Three rays and seven magnetic centers are the basis for any cosmos, in the infinitely large, as well as in the infinitely small. "As above, so below."

The seven most important glands of the human organism constitute the seven laboratories controlled by the law of the triangle. Each of these glands has an exponent in a chakra of the organism. Each of the seven chakras is found located in intimate correlation with the seven churches of the spinal medulla. The seven churches of the dorsal spine control the seven chakras of the grand sympathetic nervous system.

With the ascent of the Kundalini along the medullar canal, the seven churches become intensely active. The Kundalini dwells in the electrons. The sages meditate on it; devotees adore it, and in homes where the perfect matrimony reigns, it is worked with practically.

SEVEN CHAKRAS AND CHURCHES

The Kundalini is the solar fire enclosed in the seminal atoms. It is the ardent electronic substance of the Sun, which when liberated, transforms us into terrifically divine gods.

The fires of the heart control the ascension of the Kundalini through the medullar canal. The Kundalini develops, evolves, and progresses according to the merits of the heart.

THE COILED SERPENT: (LEFT) AZTEC SERPENT; (MIDDLE) GREEK
SERPENT; (RIGHT) THE BASKET OF ISIS, ROME, 1ST CENT

The Kundalini is the primordial energy enclosed within the Church of Ephesus. This church is found two fingers above the anus and two fingers behind the genitals. The divine serpent of fire sleeps coiled up three and a half times within its church. When the solar and lunar atoms make contact in the Triveni[89] near the coccyx, the Kundalini, the divine serpent of our magical powers, awakens. As the serpent rises through the medullar canal, it activates each of the seven churches.

The chakras of the gonads (sexual glands) are directed by Uranus, and the pineal gland (situated in the upper part of the brain) is controlled by Neptune. There is a close correlation between these two glands, and the Kundalini must connect them with the sacred fire in order to achieve profound Realization of the Self.

The Church of Ephesus is a lotus of four splendid petals. The brilliance of this church is that of ten million suns. The elemental earth of the sages is conquered with the power of this church.

CHURCH OF EPHESUS

The ascent of the Kundalini to the prostatic region activates the six petals of the Church of Smyrna. This church bestows upon us the power to dominate the elemental waters of life and the joy of creation.

CHURCH OF SMYRNA

89   "This junction of three Nadis at the Muladhara Chakra is known as Mukta Triveni." —Swami Sivananda

When the sacred serpent reaches the region of the umbilical cord, we can dominate the volcanoes because the elemental fire of the sages corresponds to the Church of Pergamos, situated in the solar plexus.

This center controls the spleen, the liver, the pancreas, etc. This center of Pergamos has ten petals.

CHURCH OF PERGAMOS

With the ascent of the Kundalini to the heart region, the Church of Thyatira with its twelve marvelous petals is activated. This church bestows upon us power over the elemental air of the sages. The development of this cardiac center confers inspiration, presentiment, intuition and powers for leaving our physical body consciously in the astral body as well as the power to place our body into a Jinn state.

CHURCH OF THYATIRA

The second chapter of Revelation deals with the four inferior churches of our organism. These are the four centers known as the fundamental or basic, the prostatic, umbilical, and cardiac. Now we shall study the three

CHURCH OF SARDIS

superior magnetic centers mentioned in Revelation, chapter three. These three superior churches are the Church of Sardis, the Church of Philadelphia and, lastly, the Church of Laodicea.

The ascent of the Kundalini to the region of the creative larynx bestows upon us the power to hear the voices of beings that live in the superior worlds. This chakra is related to pure Akasha. Akasha is the agent of sound. The larynx chakra is the Church of Sardis. When the Kundalini opens the Church of Sardis, it blossoms forth upon our fertile lips made Word. The laryngeal chakra has sixteen beautiful petals.

The complete development of this Akashic center allows us to keep our bodies alive even during the deep dark nights of the great Pralaya. The incarnation of the great Word is impossible without having awakened the sacred serpent. Precisely, the agent of the Word is Akasha. It is to the Word what wire is to electricity. The Word needs the Akasha to manifest itself. Akasha is the agent of sound. The Kundalini is Akasha.

Akasha is sexual. The Kundalini is sexual. The magnetic center where our Kundalini normally lives is absolutely sexual, as demonstrated by the fact that it is located two fingers above the anus and close to two fingers behind the genitals. The space where it is located is four fingers wide. The Kundalini can only be awakened and fully developed with Sexual Magic.

This is what the infrasexual people do not like. They feel themselves to be super-transcendental and mortally hate Sexual Magic. On one occasion, after listening to a conference that we gave about Sexual Magic, someone protested saying that that was how we Gnostics were corrupting women. This individual was an infrasexual. The man protested because we were teaching the science of regeneration. However, on the other hand, he did not protest against those of intermediate sex, against prostitutes, against the vice of masturbation, nor did he say that these people were corrupt. He protested against the doctrine of regeneration but did not protest against the doctrine of degeneration. That is how infrasexual people are. They feel highly superior to all people of normal sexuality. They protest against regeneration but defend degeneration. Infrasexual people can never incarnate the Word. They spit inside the sacred sanctuary of sex, and the law punishes them, hurling them into the Abyss forever. Sex is the sanctuary of the Holy Spirit.

When the Kundalini reaches the level of the middlebrow, the Church of Philadelphia is opened. This is the eye of wisdom. The Father who is in secret dwells in this magnetic center. The middlebrow chakra has two fundamental petals and many splendorous radiations. This center is the

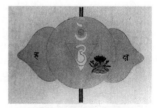

CHURCH OF PHILADELPHIA

throne of the mind. No true clairvoyant says that they are one. No true clairvoyant says: "I saw." The clairvoyant initiate says: "We have learned."

All clairvoyants need initiation. The clairvoyant without initiation is liable to make very serious mistakes. The clairvoyant who goes around telling his visions to the whole world is liable to lose their faculty. The charlatan clairvoyant who talks about their visions can also lose their mental equilibrium. The clairvoyant must be quiet, humble, modest. The clairvoyant must be like a child.

When the Kundalini reaches the level of the pineal gland, the Church of Laodicea is opened. This lotus flower has a thousand resplendent petals. The pineal gland is influenced by Neptune. When this church is opened we receive polyvision, intuition, etc. The pineal gland is intimately related to the chakras of the gonads or sexual glands. The greater the level of sexual potency, the greater the development of the pineal gland. The lesser the degree of sexual potency, the lesser the degree of development of the pineal gland. Uranus in the sexual organs and Neptune in the pineal gland unite to take us to total Realization of the Self. In the schools of regeneration (so mortally hated by infrasexual people) we are taught how to work practically with the science of Uranus and Neptune.

CHURCH OF LAODICEA, AS SEEN ON THE VIRGIN MOTHER OF CHRIST.

16TH CENTURY

The Tao path[90] includes three paths, and Tao itself is the fourth. Much has been said about the four paths. We Gnostics travel along the Fourth Path[91] in full consciousness. During

---

90 "The ineffable Chinese Tao [Dao] is the same Latin Deus, the French Dieu, the Greek Theos, the Spanish Dios, and also the Nahuatl Aztec Teotl... The Tao is the Being, the Tao is INRI, the Tao is the inner Christ." —Samael Aun Weor

91 "The school of the Fourth Way is very ancient; it comes from the archaic lands. It is the foundation of the great mysteries and is found alive in Gnosticism, and in the religions of the Egyptians, Lemurians, Atlanteans, Phoenicians, etc." See glossary for more.

the sexual act, we transmute the brutal instincts of our physical body into willpower, the passionate emotions of the astral body into love, and the mental impulses into comprehension. As Spirit, we perform the Great Work. This is how we travel along the four paths in practice. We do not need to become fakirs for the first path, neither monks for the second, nor scholars for the third. The path of the perfect matrimony permits us to travel the four paths during the sexual act itself.

From the first verse to the seventh, Revelation speaks about the coccygeal center. The Church of Ephesus is in this center. The igneous serpent is found coiled three and a half times within this creative center. Whosoever awakens the serpent and makes it rise through the spinal medulla receives the flaming sword and then enters Eden.

The redemption of the human being is found in the serpent, but we should be on guard against the astuteness of the serpent. We must contemplate the forbidden fruit and inhale its aroma, but remember what the Lord Jehovah said:

"Thou shalt not eat of it: for in the day that thou eatest thereof thou shalt surely die." —Torah/Bible, Bereshit/Genesis 2:17

Man must enjoy love's blessings and adore the woman. A good painting enraptures us; a beautiful piece of music brings us to the state of ecstasy. Nevertheless, an adorable, beautiful woman makes man to want to possess her in the act. Woman is the living representation of God-Mother.

The sexual act with one's beloved has indisputable delights. Sexual enjoyment is a legitimate right of humans. Enjoy love's blessing, but do not spill the semen. Do not commit this sacrilege. Be not a fornicator. Chastity turns us into gods. Fornication turns us into demons.

Krumm-Heller stated: "The Sethians adored the Great Light and said that the Sun in its emanations forms a nest in us. This constitutes the Serpent." The Nazarenes said: "All of you shall be gods, if you leave Egypt and cross the Red Sea." Krumm-Heller tells us in his book *The Gnostic Church* that this Gnostic sect also had as a sacred object, a chalice, from which they drank "the semen of Benjamin." This, according to Huiracocha, was a mixture of wine and water. The great Master

THE ARCANUM (ARK) OF THE COVENANT WAS ALWAYS KEPT SECRET.

Krumm-Heller tells us that the sacred symbol of the sexual serpent was never missing from the altars of the Nazarenes. In reality "the force, the power which accompanied Moses was the serpent on the staff, which later was turned into the staff itself. This serpent was certainly the one that spoke to the rest of the serpents and the one which tempted Eve."

The Master Huiracocha, in another paragraph of his immortal work entitled *The Gnostic Church,* said: "Moses in the wilderness showed his people the serpent on the staff and said to them that whosoever would make use of this serpent would not be harmed during his journey."

All of the marvelous powers of Moses resided in the sacred serpent Kundalini. Moses practiced Sexual Magic extensively in order to lift the serpent upon the staff. Moses had a wife.

In the terrifying darkness of centuries past, the sublime and austere hierophants of the great mysteries were the jealous guardians of the Great Arcanum. The great priests had sworn silence, and the key to the ark of science was hidden from the eyes of the people. Sexual Magic was only known and practiced by the great priests. The wisdom of the serpent is the basis of the great mysteries. This was cultivated in the mystery schools of Egypt, Greece, Rome, India, Persia, Troy, Aztec Mexico, Inca Peru, etc.

Krumm-Heller tells us that in the *Hymn to Demeter* by Homer (found in a Russian library) we can read that everything revolved around a physiological cosmic fact of great transcendence. In that ancient song of that Human-God who sang to old Troy and Achilles's wrath, we clearly see Sexual Magic serving as a cornerstone in the great Temple of Eleusis. The naked dance, delightful music in the temple, the enraptured kiss, the mysterious magic of the secret act made Eleusis a paradise of beloved gods and goddesses.

In those times nobody thought in "perversities" but only of holy and sublime things. It would never have occurred to anyone to profane the temple. The couples knew how to withdraw in time to avoid spilling the sacred wine.

In Egypt, Osiris appears as the masculine principle facing Isis, the eternal and beloved feminine principle. In this sunny country of Khem, the lord of all perfection also worked with the Great Arcanum A.Z.F., precisely when he was in the preparatory period for his initiation before beginning his mission. That is how it is written in the memoirs of Nature.

In Phoenicia, Hercules and Dagon loved each other intensely, as did Pluto and Persephone in Attica. Yet, as Dr. Krumm-Heller states, the phallus and uterus are clearly spoken of amongst themselves: this is the lingam-yoni of the Greek mysteries.

The great priests of Egypt, old inheritors of the archaic wisdom that was cultivated by the Atlanteans, represented the great god Ibis of Thoth with the virile member in a state of erection. Krumm-Heller states that over this erected phallus of the Ibis of Thoth a phrase was written which said: "Giver of reasoning." Next to the inscription, a lotus flower shone gloriously.

The ancient sages of sacred Egypt engraved the divine symbol of the sexual serpent upon their millenarian walls.

The secret of Sexual Magic was incommunicable. That is the Great Arcanum. Those unfortunate ones who divulged the unspeakable secret were sentenced to death. They were taken to a stone patio, and before a millenary wall covered with croco- dile skins and indecipherable hieroglyphics, their heads were cut off, their hearts were torn out, and their cursed ashes were flung to the four winds.

This brings to mind the great French poet Cazote, who died at the guillotine during the French Revolution. This man prophesied his own death at a famous banquet along with the fate that was awaiting a certain group of noble initiates who contemplated divulging the Great Arcanum. For some he prophesied the guillotine, for others the dagger, poison, jail, exile. His prophecies were fulfilled with absolute accuracy. In the Middle Ages, anyone who divulged the Great Arcanum died mysteriously, be it by shirts of Nessus, poisoned soaps that arrived as a birthday present at the door of the condemned, perfumed bouquets, or the dagger.

The Great Arcanum is the key to all powers and the key to all empires. The powers of Nature are unleashed upon those who dare attempt to dominate her. The great hierophants hide their secret, and divine kings do not entrust the secret key of their power to any mortal. Wretched, unfortunate is the mortal who, after receiving the secret of Sexual Magic, does not know how to use it to its full advantage. For him it would be better never to have been born or "to hang a rock from his neck and throw himself to the bottom of the sea." Nature is not inter- ested in the cosmic Realization of the Self of the human being, and this is even contrary to her own interests. That is the rea- son why Nature opposes with all her strength anyone daring to try and dominate her.

Conveniently, a curious anecdote comes to mind. Once upon a time, a poor customs-house guard was walking along the beach. Suddenly, in the sand he noticed a leather object being beaten by the waves of the Caribbean. The man came closer and with great surprise, found a small valise or black leather briefcase. He went immediately to the harbor master's office and turned the object over to his superior. Mission ac- complished, he went to his house. When he went to work on the following day, the superior officer, full of anger, gave the man a twenty cent coin saying, "Imbecile! This is what you deserve; take this coin, buy a rope and hang yourself; you do not deserve to live; so, buy a rope with these twenty cents and hang yourself from a tree. Luck came to you and you scorned it. The briefcase that you handed over to me had close to a million dollars in it. Go away. Get out of here imbecile! You do not deserve to live." This is truly the fate that awaits those who do not know how to take advantage of the precious treasure of the Great Arcanum. Those people do not deserve to live. The Great Arcanum of Sexual Magic has never before been taught in life, and now we are divulging it. Unfortunate are those who, after coming across the treasure of kings, scorn it as did the guard in the example! The treasure of the Great Arcanum is worth even more than the fortune found by the guard. To scorn this is to really be an imbecile.

In order to awaken the Kundalini, man needs a woman. Yet, we must warn that the initiate must practice Sexual Magic with only one woman. Those who practice Sexual Magic with different women commit the sin of adultery. They do not progress in these studies. Unfortunately, there are certain individuals who utilize Sexual Magic as a pretext for seducing women. They are profaners of the temple. Such men inevitably fall into black magic. We warn all women to guard against these sexually perverse characters.

There are also many women who, under the pretext of supposed profound Realization of the Self, unite with any male. What all these passionate women really want is to satiate their carnal desires.

The world is always the world, and since we have been divulging the Great Arcanum there have appeared, as one might expect, those swine who trample the doctrine and then die poisoned by the bread of wisdom. The sacrament[92] of Sexual Magic can only be practiced between husband and wife. We clarify this to avoid seduction, abduction, carnal orgies, and "sanctified lustful passion."

---

92 Samael Aun Weor had used the word "cult" in its original sense as "worship," but since the word is now used entirely negatively, we exchanged it for sacrament: a sacred act.

Sexual force is a terrible weapon. Scientists have not been able to find the origin of electricity. We affirm that the cause of electrical energy must be sought in the universal sexual force. This force not only resides in the sexual organs but also in all of the atoms and electrons of the universe. The light of the Sun is a product of sexuality. An atom of hydrogen unites sexually with an atom of carbon in order to produce solar light. Hydrogen is masculine. Carbon is feminine. Solar light results from the sexual union of these two elements. Studies on the processes of carbon are very interesting. These processes are the gestation of light.

The causa causorum [cause of causes] of electricity must be sought in the serpentine universal fire. This fire dwells in the electrons. The sages meditate on it, mystics adore it, and those who follow the path of the perfect matrimony work practically with it.

Sexual force is a terrific weapon in the hands of white magicians and black magicians. Thought attracts the sexual fluid to the dorsal spine in order to deposit it in its respective sack. With the spilling of this fluid, billions of solar atoms are lost. The contraction which follows the spilling of the semen gathers from the atomic infernos of the human being billions of satanic atoms which replace the lost solar atoms. This is how we form the devil within us. When we restrain the sexual impulse within us, the marvelous fluid returns to the astral body, multiplying its ineffable splendors. This is how we form the Christ within. Thus, with sexual energy, we can form the Christ or the Devil within us. The great master, in his rank as incarnated Cosmic Christ, said:

> "I am the bread of life. I am the living bread. If any man eat of this bread, he shall live forever. Who so eateth my flesh, and drinketh my blood, hath eternal life; and I will raise him up at the last day. He that eateth my flesh, and drinketh my blood, dwelleth in me, and I in him."

Christ is the solar soul, the living spirit of the Sun. He, with his life, makes the tassel of wheat grow. In the grain, the seed, all of the potency of the Solar Logos is retained. In all vegetable, animal, or human seed the Christonic substance of the Solar Logos is found enclosed as within a precious sheath.

Making the creative energy return inwards and upwards germinates and procreates within us a marvelous child, a Christified astral body. This vehicle bestows immortality upon us. This is our Chrestos mediator. With this vehicle we can go to the Father who is in secret. "No man cometh unto the Father but by me," said the lord of all perfection.

The astral phantasm possessed by mortals is nothing more than a sketch of man. It does not even have unity. This ghost-like facade is a den of demons and of dirty and loathsome foulness. Within this astral phantasm lives the "I" (the devil). This is the infernal legion.[93] The "I" is a legion. Just as the body is composed of millions of atoms, the "I" is composed of millions of "I's," diabolical intelligences, repugnant demons which quarrel amongst themselves.

When a person dies they become that "legion." The person becomes dust. Only the legion of "I's" remain alive. Clairvoyants often find the disincarnate people dressed distinctly and simultaneously in different places. The person seems to have become many people. This is legion. However, when we have given birth to the astral, Christic body, we continue after death living in that sidereal body. Then we are really immortal. Those who possess the Christified astral body find themselves in a conscious state after death. The run-of-the-mill disincarnate people live after death with their consciousness[94] asleep. Death is really a return to fetal conception. Death is the return to the seed. All those who die return to a new maternal womb totally unconscious, asleep.

People do not even have their soul incarnated. The souls of people are disincarnated. People have only incarnated an embryo of soul. Evil people do not even have this embryo of soul. We can incarnate the soul only when we possess a Christified

---

93 "And Jesus asked him, saying, What is thy name? And he said, Legion: because many devils were entered into him." See Christian Bible, Mark 5 and Luke 8.

94 See glossary.

astral body. Common, everyday people are solely the vehicle of many "I's." Therefore, the name of each mortal is Legion.

Only with Sexual Magic can we cause the astral Christ to be born within us. Temptation is fire. Triumph over temptation is light. "Refraining desire makes the astral liquid rise toward the pineal gland. Thus, the Adam Christ, the superhuman, is born within us."

Upon stimulation of the sexual organs (in order to perform the coitus) the semen multiplies. When it is not spilled, it is transmuted, and it transforms us into gods.

Sexual fire is the sword with which the inner God combats the tenebrous ones. All those who practice Sexual Magic open the seven churches.

Whosoever spills their semen after having worked with the Kundalini inevitably fails, because the Kundalini then descends one or more vertebrae in accordance with the magnitude of the fall. We should struggle until we reach perfect chastity, "or else I will come unto thee quickly, and I will remove the lampstand from its place, except thou repent." [Revelation 2:51]

The vapor that rises from the seminal system opens the inferior orifice of the medullar cord so that the sacred serpent can enter. In common, ordinary people this orifice is closed. The seminal vapor of black magicians is directed towards the abyss. The seminal vapor of white magicians is raised towards the heavens.

Opening the Church of Ephesus signifies the awakening of the Kundalini. The color of this center is a dirty red in the libertine, yellowish-red in the initiate, and purplish, blue-red in the initiated mystic.

Solar and lunar atoms rise up from the seminal system. The seminal vapors have the atoms of the Sun and of the Moon as their basis. Seminal vapors are transmuted into energy. This energy is bipolarized into positive and negative, solar and lunar.[95] These energies rise through the sympathetic canals of Ida and Pingala, up to the chalice. This chalice is the brain. The

---

95   Here, positive and negative are not "good and bad," but the polarities + and -, and when the kundalini awakens it is the third force (=), in the central column.

two sympathetic canals through which the semen rises (already completely converted into energy) are the two witnesses of Revelation, the two olives of the temple, the two candlesticks before the God of the Earth, the two serpents which are entwined on the rod of the Caduceus of Mercury.

When these two serpents touch tails, the solar and lunar atoms make contact in the coccyx, near the Triveni. Then, the Kundalini awakens.

The igneous serpent of our magical powers emerges from the membranous pocket where it was enclosed and rises through the spinal canal toward the chalice (the brain).

Certain nerve filaments that connect the seven chakras, or sympathetic plexus, with the spinal column, branch out from the medullar canal.

The sacred fire activates the seven magnetic centers. The Kundalini coordinates the activity of all seven chakras in a marvelous manner. We could illustrate all of this by a stalk with seven fragrant and beautiful roses. The stalk would represent the spinal column, and the seven roses would represent the seven chakras, or magnetic centers. The delicate stems of these seven roses of ardent fire are the fine threads which unite them to the spinal column.

The powers of light and the powers of darkness do battle within the semen.

The Advent of the Fire is the most magnificent event of the perfect matrimony.

The center where the serpent is coiled has four petals of which only two are active. The other two are activated with initiation.

The prostatic chakra is characterized by six beautiful colors: red, orange, yellow, green, blue and violet. This is the Church of Smyrna. This center is extremely important for the magician. We control the sexual act with this center. This is the magnetic center of practical magic.

The third center is the Church of Pergamos. This is the brain of emotions. Within the human organism we have a veritable wireless station. The receiver is the umbilical center. The transmitting antenna is the pineal gland. Mind waves of those who think about us reach the umbilical center, or brain of emotions, and later pass to the brain where we become consciously aware of these thoughts.

The Church of Thyatira, the fourth center, is worthy of total admiration. The cardiac plexus or cardiac center is closely related to the heart of the solar system. The human being is a universe in miniature. If we want to study the universe, we must study the human being. In the universe we discover the human being. Within the human being we discover the universe.

The solar system seen from far away truly seems like a glorious human being walking across the unalterable infinite. All time has been transformed there into a living form full of ineffable music, the music of the spheres. An instant of perception for this celestial man is eighty years. The heart of this celestial man is really found in the center of the solar disc. Those who know how to travel consciously and positively in the astral body are able to visit this temple.

A gigantic abyss, blacker than the night, leads to the sanctuary. Few are those brave enough to descend into this fatal abyss. In the frightening depths of that solar abyss, one can perceive terrible things, consuming flames, awesome mystery. Whosoever has the courage to descend there will find the vestibule of the sanctuary. An adept will bless them with an olive branch. Joyful are those who gain admittance to the secret place. A narrow passageway leads the beloved disciple to the secret place of the sanctuary. This is the cardia of the solar system. Seven saints live in this sacred place. They are the rulers of the seven solar rays. The most important ray is that of the Kundalini, or serpentine fire, that shimmers intensely in the aurora. Every perfect matrimony must practice Sexual Magic during the dawn.

The solar system is the body of a great being. That being is total perfection. The heart of this great being is the Sun.

The heart chakra has twelve petals. Six are active and six are inactive. All twelve petals are activated with the sacred fire. We must activate the heart through intense prayer.

The fifth center is the Church of Sardis. This is the center of the creative larynx. This is the lotus of sixteen petals. When the human being activates this lotus through the fire, he receives the magical ear.

The sacred fire becomes a creator in the throat. Angels create with the power of the Word. Fire blossoms as words on fecund lips. The initiate is capable of creating anything with thought and then materializing it with the Word. Hearing with the magical ear has not been well-defined by the esotericists. We should warn here that whoever has the magical ear can really hear internal sounds, perceive them almost physically, or more specifically, in a form similar to the physical. The magical ear permits us to hear the angels.

When the totality of the creative energy rises to the brain, we elevate ourselves to the angelic state. Then we can create with the power of the Word.

One does not reach these heights through the mechanical evolution of Nature. Evolution is the movement of universal life, but this does not take anyone to the angelic state. Nature is not interested in the superhuman. Nature contains all possibilities, but the superhuman is even contrary to her own vested interest. The most terrible forces of Nature oppose the birth of the superhuman. The angel, the superhuman, is the result of a tremendous revolution of consciousness. No one is obligated to help the individual in the revolution. This is a very intimate matter for each one of us. The problem is absolutely sexual.

The sword must be unsheathed, and we must combat the terrible forces of Nature which oppose the birth of the superhuman.

When the sacred fire opens the frontal chakra (the Church of Philadelphia with its marvelous petals and its innumerable splendors), we can see clairvoyantly. People are accustomed to theorizing in life and swearing to things that they have never seen. It is necessary to awaken clairvoyance in order to see the great inner realities. The frontal chakra is the throne of the mind. When study and clairvoyance move together in balance and harmony, we do, in fact, enter the temple of true knowledge.

Many are those who affirm what they have read, repeating borrowed learning. These people believe they know but have never seen what they have read about. They are repeating like parrots, that is all. These people know nothing. They are ignorant. They are learned ignoramuses.

In order to know, one must first be. Clairvoyance is the eye of the Being. The Being and knowing must be parallel and in balance. Those who have read much on esotericism feel they are wise. If these poor people have not seen what they have read, you can rest assured that they know absolutely nothing.

There are all types of seers in the world. The true clairvoyant never goes around saying that they are one. Every student of esotericism, upon having their first clairvoyant visions, has a tendency to tell the whole world. Then the others laugh at them, and since their vibrations are negative, the novice ends up losing their mind. Clairvoyance without intuition leads the student into error and the crime of insult and slander, sometimes even to homicide. Someone who has a flash of clairvoyance sees, for instance, their spouse in the astral committing adultery with their friend, and if the seer does not have initiation, and if they are jealous, they could then murder their spouse or friend, even though their unfortunate spouse might be a saint and their friend a true and loyal servant. Keep in mind that in the astral the human being is a legion, and each pluralized "I" repeats acts committed in a previous life.

The great masters of the White Lodge have been slandered by the seers. All masters have a double exactly like themselves. If the master preaches chastity, his double preaches fornication. If a master does good works, his double does evil ones. It is exactly his antithesis. Because of all this, we can only trust in those clairvoyants who have reached the fifth initiation of Major Mysteries. In addition, we must take into account that before the fifth initiation of Major Mysteries the human being does not have at their disposal solar vehicles to serve as the temple of their inner God. Neither the soul nor Christ can enter persons who do not have organized vehicles.

Whosoever has not incarnated their soul does not have real existence. They are a legion of "I's" that struggle to manifest through their body. Sometimes the drinking "I" acts out, other times the smoking "I," the killing "I," the stealing "I," the falling in love "I," etc. There is conflict between the "I's." That is why we see many who swear to belong to the Gnostic movement, and then they change their minds and declare that they are enemies of Gnosis. The "I" that swears loyalty to Gnosis is displaced by another "I" that hates Gnosis. The "I" that swears he adores his wife is replaced by another "I" that abhors her. The "I" is a legion of demons. How can we trust clairvoyants who have not yet incarnated their souls? The person who has not incarnated their soul is still not morally responsible. Could we possibly trust demons? Students of Gnosis should be very careful of those who go around declaring that they are seers and prophesying to people.

The true clairvoyant never claims to be one. The masters of the fifth initiation of Major Mysteries are very humble and quiet. No student of esotericism is a master. True masters are only those who have reached the fifth initiation of Major Mysteries. Before the fifth initiation nobody is a master.

The last flower of the lotus to open is the Church of Laodicea. This lotus flower has a thousand petals. This lotus flower shines gloriously on the heads of saints. When the Kundalini reaches the pineal gland this marvelous flower opens. This is the eye of polyvoyance, the diamond eye. With this faculty we can study the memories of Nature. This is the divine eye of the Spirit.

The first sacred serpent passes from the pineal gland up to the eye of wisdom, situated between the two eyebrows. Then it penetrates the magnetic field of the bridge of the nose. When it touches the atom of the Father situated there, the first initiation of Major Mysteries is attained. No one is a master by the mere fact of having received the first initiation of Major Mysteries. This only means that the initiate entered the current which leads to Nirvana.

The student should raise the seven serpents, one after the other. The second serpent belongs to the vital body, the third to the astral, the fourth to the mental, the fifth to the causal. The sixth and seventh serpents are of the Conscious Soul and Divine Spirit respectively. An initiation of the Major Mysteries corresponds to each one of the seven serpents. There are seven serpents: two groups of three with the sublime coronation of the seventh tongue of fire that unites us with the One, the Law, the Father.

We must open the seven churches on each plane of cosmic consciousness.

During the initiation, the devotee must receive the stigmas of Christ. Every one of our internal vehicles must be crucified and stigmatized. The stigmas are given to the human being according to our merits. Each stigma has its esoteric tests. The first stigmas received are those of the hands, and the tests to receive them are very painful. Precious stones also play an important part in the initiation. Revelation states:

BUDDHA WITH SEVEN
SERPENTS RAISED

> "And the foundations for the wall of the city were adorned with all precious stones. The first foundation was jasper, the second sapphire, the third agate, the fourth emerald, the fifth onyx, the sixth carnelian, the seventh chrysolite, the eighth beryl, the ninth topaz, the tenth chrysoprase, the eleventh jacinth, the twelfth amethyst. Revelation 21:19-20

> "I am the Alpha and the Omega, the beginning and the end. To he who thirsts I shall without price give to drink of the fountain of the water of life. Revelation 21:6

> "I am the Alpha and the Omega, blessed be those who wash their robes (the seven bodies), in the blood of the lamb (Christonic semen) that they may (have the right to the Tree of Life and that they may) enter the gates of the city." —Christian Bible, Revelation 22:14

Nevertheless, there are really so few who reach High Initiation. Very few are those who are capable of getting as far as kissing the whip of the executioners. It is very difficult to kiss the hand that beats us, yet for those who reach High Initiation it is urgent to do so. Christ said,

*"Of a thousand that seek me, one finds me; of
a thousand that find me, one follows me; of the
thousand that follow me, one is mine."*[96]

What is most grave is that those who have read much
about esotericism and have belonged to many schools are full
of platitudinous sanctity. They believe themselves to be very
saintly and wise even while they presume to be humble. These
poor brothers and sisters are farther from the altar of initiation than the profane. Whosoever wishes to reach High Initiation must begin by recognizing him or herself as perverse.
Anyone who admits his or her own wickedness is already on
the road to Realization of the Self. Remember that crime also
hides behind the incense of prayer. This is difficult for those
who have read a great deal. These people feel that they are full
of sanctity and wisdom. When they have flashes of clairvoyance
they are unbearable because they declare themselves to be masters of sapience. Naturally, people like this are sure candidates
for the Abyss and Second Death. The Abyss is full of sincerely
mistaken individuals and people with good intentions.

When the initiate has made part of their creative fire come
out of their head, they throw their crown to the feet of the
lamb. Saint John speaks of the twenty-four elders who hurled
their crowns to the feet of the Lord.

Revelation describes a rider with a sash on his thigh in
chapter nineteen. This sash has written on it in sacred characters the phrase, "King of kings and Lord of lords." [Revelation
19:11-16] Indeed, the king is not on the forehead, but in sex.
Rasputin, inebriated with wine, banged his sexual phallus on
the orgy tables saying, "This is the king of the world."

Fortunate are those couples who know how to love. With
the sexual act we open the seven churches of the Apocalypse,
and transform ourselves into gods.

---

96   This appears to be a rendition of a saying of Krishna, "Amongst
     thousands of persons, hardly one strives for perfection; and amongst
     those who have achieved perfection, hardly one knows Me in truth." —
     Bhagavad Gita 7:3

The seven chakras resound with the powerful Egyptian mantra[97] **FE... UIN... DAGJ**. The last word is guttural.

The perfect exercise of the seven churches, the complete priesthood, is performed with the body in Jinn state. Great magicians know how to put their bodies in Jinn state. This is how they exercise the full priesthood of their seven churches.

When Jesus walked upon the sea, he carried his physical body in the Jinn state. In this state we are omnipotent gods.

In the umbilical region, there is a mysterious chakra that the magician uses for Jinn states. If they utilize the power of this chakra, all magicians who are far away from their physical bodies in the astral body can beseech their inner God in this way: "My Lord, my God, I beg you to bring me my body." The inner God can bring the physical body to the magician in Jinn state; that is to say, submerged in the astral plane. The mysterious chakra of Jinn science spins at those moments.

Whosoever wants to learn the Jinn science can study *The Yellow Book*. We teach this mysterious science in *The Yellow Book*.

The seven churches bestow upon us power over fire, air, water, and earth.

---

97 (Sanskrit मन्त्रम्, literally "mind protection") A sacred word or sound. The use of sacred words and sounds is universal throughout all religions and mystical traditions, because the root of all creation is in the Great Breath or the Word, the Logos. "In the beginning was the Word..." Generally speaking, the sounds in mantras are pronounced using the ancient roots (Latin, Sanskrit, etc):
   - I: as the ee in "tree"
   - E: as the eh in "beg"
   - O: as the oh in "holy"
   - U: as the u in "true"
   - A: as the ah in "father"
   - M: extended as if humming, "mmmmm"
   - S: extended like a hiss, "sssss"
   - CH: if the word is Latin, pronounced as k. If the word is Hebrew, pronounced as a scrape in the back of the throat, as in "Bach"
   - G: in most mantras, G is pronounced as in "give"

Chapter 8

Happiness, Music, Dance, and the Kiss

Only love and wisdom should reign in the homes of Gnostic brothers and sisters. In reality, humanity confuses love with desire, and desire with love. Only great souls can and know how to love. In Eden, perfect men love ineffable women. In order to love, one must first be. Those who incarnate their soul truly know how to love. The "I" does not know how to love. The demon "I" that today swears love is replaced by the demon "I" that does not feel like loving. We already know that the "I" is plural. The pluralized "I" is really a legion. This whole succession of "I's" is in constant battle. It is stated that we have but one mind; nevertheless, we Gnostics affirm that we have many minds. Each phantasm of the pluralized "I" has its own mind. The "I" that kisses and adores his beloved wife is replaced by the "I" that hates her. One must first be in order to love. The present human being is not being. Whosoever has not incarnated their soul is not being. The present human being has no real existence yet. A legion of demons speak through the human's mouth. These are demons who swear love, demons who abandon their beloved, demons who hate, demons of jealousy, anger, resentment, etc.

Nevertheless, despite former statements, the intellectual animal mistakenly called human being has incarnated the Essence,[98] which is a fraction of the human soul, the Bud-

---

98   From the Chinese 體 ti, which literally means "substance, body" and is often translated as "essence," to indicate that which is always there throughout transformations. In gnosis, the term essence refers to our consciousness, which remains fundamentally the same, in spite of the many transformations it suffers, especially life, death, and being trapped in psychological defects. A common example given in Buddhism is a glass of water: even if filled with dirt and impurities, the water is still there. However, one would not want to drink it that way. Just so with the Essence (the consciousness): our Essence is trapped in impurities; to use it properly, it must be cleaned first. See glossary for more.

dhata.[99] The Essence knows how to love. The "I" does not know how to love. We must forgive the defects of our beloved because these defects are of the "I." Love is not to blame for disagreements. The "I" is the guilty one. The homes of Gnostic initiates must have a background of happiness, music, and ineffable kisses.

Dance, love, and the joy of loving strengthen the embryo of the soul that children have within. Thus, this is how Gnostic homes are a true paradise of love and wisdom.

Liquor and fornication must be banished from the bosom of Gnostic homes. However, we must not be fanatics. Whosoever is incapable of handling one drink at a social gathering is as weak as someone who cannot control his liquor and gets drunk. Fornication is something entirely different. Fornication is unforgivable. Whosoever ejaculates the seminal liquor is a fornicator. Thus, for those who reach orgasm, for fornicators, the Abyss and Second Death await.

The human being can be a part of everything but should not be the victim of anything. One must be the king, not the slave. Someone who has had a drink has not committed a crime, but the one who becomes a slave and victim of that drink has committed a crime. The true master is a king of the Heavens, of the Earth, and of the Infernos. The weak one is not king. The weak one is a slave.

The initiate only unites sexually with their spouse in order to practice Sexual Magic; wretched is the one who unites with their spouse in order to spill the semen. The initiate does not experience the feeling of death that fornicators feel when they lose their semen.

Man is one half and woman is the other half. During the sexual act they experience the joy of being complete. Those who do not spill the semen preserve this joy eternally.

---

99   Derived from buddhadhatu (Sanskrit), which means "essence of the Buddha," from बुद्ध buddha, "conscious, awakened" and धातु dhatu, "element, primary element, cause, mineral." The term buddhadhatu appeared in Mahayana scripture as a reference to tathagatagarbha, the "embryo of the Buddha," also called Buddha Nature. In general use, this describes that element in us that has the potential to become a Buddha, an "awakened one."

In order to create a child it is not necessary to spill the semen. The spermatozoon that escapes without spilling the semen is a selected spermatozoon, a superior kind of spermatozoon, a totally mature spermatozoon. The result of such a fertilization is truly a new creature of an extremely high order. This is how we can form a race of superhumans. It is not necessary to spill the semen in order to engender a child. Imbeciles like to spill the semen. Gnostics are not imbeciles.

When a couple is united sexually, clairvoyants often see a very bright light enveloping the couple. Precisely in that moment the creative forces of Nature serve as a medium for a new being. When the couple lets itself go in carnal passion, and later commits the crime of spilling the semen, these luminous forces withdraw, and in their place, satanic forces penetrate, luciferic forces of a bloody red color that bring quarrels, jealousy, adultery, weeping and desperation to the home. That is how homes that could be a heaven on Earth become true infernos. People who do not spill their semen retain and accumulate for themselves peace, abundance, wisdom, happiness, and love. Arguments within homes can be eliminated with the key of Sexual Magic; this is the key to true happiness.

During the act of Sexual Magic, couples charge themselves with magnetism; they mutually magnetize each other. In the woman the pelvis emanates feminine currents, while her breasts give off masculine ones. In the man the feminine current emanates from the mouth, and the masculine one from his virile member. All of these organs must be well excited through Sexual Magic in order to give off and receive, transmit and retrieve vital magnetic forces that increase extraordinarily in quantity and quality.

In the home of Gnostic initiates, the objective of delightful dances, joyful music, and ardent kisses, where couples come into intimate sexual contact, is the mutual magnetization of man and woman. The magnetic power is masculine and feminine at the same time. The man needs the fluids of his wife if he truly wishes to progress, and the woman inevitably needs the fluids of her husband in order to develop all of her powers.

When a couple mutually magnetizes each other, daily business progresses and happiness makes a nest in the home. When a man and woman unite, something is created. Scientific chastity allows the transmutation of the sexual secretions into light and fire.

Every religion that degenerates preaches celibacy. Every religion at its birth and its glorious splendor preaches the path of the perfect matrimony. Buddha was married and established the perfect matrimony. Unfortunately, after five hundred years, the prophecy made by the Lord Buddha that his Dharma would be exhausted and the Sangha would divide into dissident sects was precisely fulfilled. That was when Buddhist monasticism and hatred of the perfect matrimony was born.

Jesus the Divine Savior brought Christic esotericism to the world. The beloved one taught his disciples the path of the perfect matrimony. Peter, the first pontiff of the Church, was a married man. Peter was not celibate. Peter had a wife. Unfortunately, after six hundred years, the message of the beloved one was adulterated, and the Church of Rome returned to the dead forms of Buddhist monasticism, with its cloistered monks and nuns who mortally hate the path of the perfect matrimony. That is how after six hundred years of Christianity another message about the perfect matrimony became necessary.

Then came Mohammed, the great preacher of the perfect matrimony. Naturally, as always, Mohammed was violently rejected by infrasexual men who hate women.

This disgusting society of enemies of women believe that only by compulsory celibacy can one reach God. This is a crime.

Sexual abstinence as preached by infrasexual people is absolutely impossible. Nature rebels against that type of abstention. The outcome of celibacy is nocturnal emissions that inevitably ruin the organism. Every person who sexually abstains suffers nocturnal emissions. A cup that fills up will inevitably overflow. The luxury of sexual abstention is only possible for those who have already reached the kingdom of the superhuman. These people have already transformed their organisms into mechanisms of eternal sexual transmutation. They have already trained their glands with Sexual Magic. They are human-gods. They are the result of many years of Sexual Magic and of rigorous education in sexual physiology.

The initiate loves great classical music and feels repugnance for the infernal music of vulgar people. Afro-Cuban music awakens the lowest animal instincts of the human being. The initiate loves the music of the great composers. For example, *The Magic Flute* by Mozart reminds us of an Egyptian initiation. There is an intimate relationship between the Word and the sexual forces. The Word of the great Master Jesus had been Christified by drinking the wine of light of the alchemist in the chalice of sexuality. The soul communes with the music of the spheres when we listen to the nine symphonies of Beethoven, or the compositions of Chopin, or the divine Polonaise of Liszt. Music is the Word of the Eternal One.

Our words must be ineffable music; thus, we sublimate the creative energy to the heart. Disgusting, filthy, immodest, and vulgar words have the power to adulterate the creative energy, changing it into infernal powers.

In the mysteries of Eleusis, sacred dances, dances in the nude, ardent kisses, and sexual union made human beings into gods. At that time, it would not have occurred to anyone to think in perversities, but only in holy and profoundly religious matters.

Sacred dances are as ancient as the world itself and have their origin in the dawn of life on Earth. Sufi dances and Dervish dancers are tremendously marvelous. Music should awaken in the human organism so that the Word of Gold may be spoken.

The great rhythms of mahavan and chotavan,[100] with their three eternal tempos, sustain the steady motion of the universe. These are the rhythms of the fire. When the soul floats delightfully in sacred space, it must accompany us with its song because the universe is sustained by the Word.

The home of Gnostic initiates must be full of beauty. The flowers that perfume the air with their aroma, beautiful sculp-

---

100 Chotavan means "small rhythm" while Mahavan means "large rhythm". These refer to the rhythms of the fire of space, the rhythm of cosmos.

tures, perfect order and cleanliness make each home a true Gnostic sanctuary.

The mysteries of Eleusis still exist in secrecy. The great Baltic initiate, Von Uxkul, is one of the most exalted initiates of this school. This great initiate practices Sexual Magic intensely. We must clarify that Sexual Magic can only be practiced between husband and wife. The adulterer and the adulteress inevitably fail. You can only be married when there is love. Love is law, but it must be conscious love.

Those who use this knowledge of Sexual Magic in order to seduce women are black magicians who will fall into the Abyss, where wailing and the Second Death await them. The Second Death is thousands of times worse than the death of the physical body.

We call forth urgently to the virgins of the world, to the innocent women. We warn them that they can only practice Sexual Magic when they have their husband. They must guard themselves against all those sly foxes who go around seducing naive damsels with the pretext of Sexual Magic. We give you this warning so that you do not fall into temptation.

We also call forth a warning to the unredeemed fornicators who inhabit the Earth, that before the eyes of the Eternal it is useless to try to hide.

Those poor women who utilize this knowledge as a pretext in order to satisfy their lust and to lie in beds of pleasure will fall into the Abyss where all that awaits them is great weeping and the gnashing of teeth.

We speak clearly so that we will be understood. Go back, profane and profaners. Sexual Magic is a double-edged sword. It transforms the pure and virtuous into gods, and it injures and destroys the wicked and impure.

Chapter 9
Γαΐῳ (GAIO)

*"The ancient unto his well-beloved Gaio (Γαΐῳ),
whom I love in the truth."* —Christian Bible, 3 John 1:1

In the sanctum sanctorum of the Temple of Solomon, when the high priest chanted the terrific mantra IAΩ, the drums of the temple sounded in order to prevent the profane from hearing the sublime I.A.O.[101]

The great Master Huiracocha stated the following in *The Gnostic Church,*

> "Diodorus said, Know ye that among
> all gods the highest is Γ.A.I.O."[102]

---

101 "Diodorus Siculus, when enumerating the different legislators of antiquity, says, "Amongst the Jews Moses pretended that the god surnamed Iao gave him his laws" (i. 94). And this is elucidated by the remark of Clemens Alexandrinus, that the Hebrew Tetragrammaton, or Mystic Name, is pronounced IAOY, and signifies "He that is and shall be." Theodoret states that the same four letters were pronounced by the Samaritans as IABE (Jave); by the Jews as IAΩ. Jerome (upon Psalm viii. says, "The Name of the Lord" amongst the Hebrews is of four letters, יהוה Iod, He, Vau, He, which is properly the Name of God, and may be read as IAHO (Iaho) (that is in Latin characters), which is held by the Jews for unutterable. The author of the 'Treatise on Interpretations' says, "The Egyptians express the name of the Supreme Being by the seven Greek vowels IEHΩOYA": which sufficiently explains the mighty potency ascribed to this formula by the inspired author of the 'Pistis-Sophia... Rabbi Tarphon (Tryphon), who could remember the Second Temple, noticed that the Ineffable Name, though occurring a hundred times in the course of the daily service, was "rather warbled than pronounced." A precious hint this, as indicating how the Gnostic strings of boneless vowels give an approximation to the audible and yet unuttered sound. Since the destruction of the Temple, the Name has never been heard in prayer, or pronounced aloud. It is communicated, indeed, to every Rabbi, after his ordination, but not in full. One half of it is told; the rest he is left to make out for himself." —*The Gnostics and Their Remains,* by Charles William King, 1887

102 The Tetragrammaton (Four-lettered Name), the most holy name of God, which is Hebrew יהוה Iod, Hei, Vau, Hei.

"Gaio (Γαΐῳ) is Hades[103] in the winter, Zeus[104] in spring, Helios[105] in summer, and in autumn Gaio (Γαΐῳ) enters into activity, working constantly."

I.A.O. is Jovis Pater, Jupiter, whom the Jews unjustly call Javhe.[106]

I.A.O. offers the substantial wine of life, while Jupiter is a servant of the sun.

- I. Ignis (fire, soul)
- A. Aqua (water, substance)
- O. Origo (cause, air, origin)

Huiracocha stated, "Among Gnostics, I.A.O. is the name of God."

The Divine Spirit is symbolized by the vowel O, which is the eternal circle. The letter I symbolizes the Inner Being of each human being, but both are intermingled with the letter A, as a point of support. This is the powerful mantra or magic word that when practicing Sexual Magic the man must chant along with his priestess spouse.

The sound of the three powerful vowels must be prolonged like this, IIIIIIIII, AAAAAAA, OOOOOOHHHHH, that is to say, extending the sound of each vowel. The air is inhaled to fill the lungs, then one exhales it. One inhales counting to twenty, holds the air counting to twenty, and then exhales vocalizing the letter I. When exhaling one also counts to twenty. Repeat the same procedure for the letter A and then continue with the letter O. Do this seven times. After that, continue with the powerful archaic mantras: **Kawlakaw, Sawlasaw, Zeesar.**

Kawlakaw makes the human spirit vibrate.

Sawlasaw vibrates the earthly human personality.

---

103 Greek symbol of divinity as guide to the dead in the underworld. Sometimes his name is spelled Aïdōneús (Ἀϊδωνεύς) or Áïdos (Ἄϊδος), which have the three vowels I.A.O.

104 Derived from Dyēus ("daylight-sky-god"), also Dyēus ph₂tēr (lit. "father daylight-sky-god"), from Proto-Indo-European mythology.

105 Greek Ἥλιος , symbol of divinity as the Sun.

106 Often spelled Yahweh or Yahwe, and intentionally confused with Jehovah since they are both spelled the same way in Hebrew: יהוה. While יהוה Jehovah is a very positive and potent name of God, יהוה Yahve (Jahve) is the name of a demon who has been misleading humanity for ages.

Zeesar makes the astral body of the human being vibrate. These are very ancient mantras.

The Divine Savior of the world chanted the powerful sacred mantra of fire along with his priestess when practicing with her in the Pyramid of Kefren. This mantra is **INRI**. This is how the Lord of All Adoration practiced in Egypt with his Isis. He combined this mantra with the five vowels IEOUA.

INRI, ENRE, ONRO, UNRU, ANRA. The first is for clairvoyance. The second is for the magic ear. The third is for the heart chakra, the center of intuition. The fourth is for the solar plexus or the telepathic center. The fifth is for the pulmonary chakras that grant the power to remember past incarnations.

The mantra INRI and its four derivatives applicable to the chakras are vocalized by dividing them into two syllables and then pronouncing the sound of each one of its four magic letters. With these mantras we carry the sexual fire to the chakras during the practices of Sexual Magic.

Returning now to the I.A.O., which as we have already stated is the name of God among Gnostics, we would like to add the following:

The vowel I vibrates the pineal gland and the embryo of the soul that every human being has incarnated.

The vowel A places the physical vehicle in a high state of vibration.

The formidable O makes the gonads vibrate, marvelously transmuting the seminal liquor, until this is transformed into Christic energy that victoriously ascends up to the chalice (brain).

The Gospel of St. John commences praising the Word.

"In the beginning was the Word and the Word was with God, and the Word was God.

"The same was in the beginning with God.

"All things were made by Him and without Him was not anything made that was made.

"In him was life; and the life was the light of men.

"And the light shineth in darkness, and the darkness comprehended it not." —Christian Bible, John 1:1-5

The word John can be broken down into the five vowels in the following way: IEOUA, IEOUAN (John). The entire Gospel of John is the gospel of the Word.

There are people who want to disconnect the Divine Word from Sexual Magic. This is absurd. No one can incarnate the Word excluding Sexual Magic. Jesus, who is the incarnation of the Word itself, Jesus, who is the Word itself made flesh, taught Sexual Magic, precisely in the Gospel of Saint John. It is necessary to now study chapter 3 of the Gospel of Saint John from verse one to twenty-one. Behold...

> *"There was a man of the Pharisees named*
> *Nicodemus, a ruler of the Jews:*

> *"The same came to Jesus by night, and said unto Him, 'Rabbi,*
> *we know that thou art a teacher come from God: for no man*
> *can do these miracles that thou doest, except God be with him.*

> *"Jesus answered and said unto him, Verily, verily*
> *I say unto thee, Except a man be born again,*
> *he cannot see the Kingdom of God."*

Behold, dear reader, the former statement is a sexual problem. To be born has been and will always be a sexual problem. No one can be born of theories. We have never met a person born of a theory or a hypothesis. To be born is not a question of beliefs... If we could be born simply by believing in the gospels, then why have not all the students of the Bible been born? Being born is not a matter of believing or not believing. No child is born from beliefs. They are born through the sexual act. This is a sexual matter. Nicodemus did not know about the Great Arcanum. Therefore, he responded in his ignorance saying:

> *"How can man be born when he is old? Can he enter the*
> *second time into his mother's womb, and be born?*

> *"Jesus answered, Verily verily I say unto thee,*
> *Except a man be born of water and of the Spirit,*
> *he cannot enter into the Kingdom of God."*

It is necessary for you, dear reader, to know that the water of the gospel is the semen itself, and that the Spirit is the fire.

The Son of Man is born from the water and the fire. This is an absolutely sexual statement.

"That which is born of the flesh is flesh; and that which is born of the Spirit is spirit.

"Marvel not that I said unto thee, Ye must be born again."

It is necessary that the master be born within us.

"The wind bloweth where it listeth, and thou hearest the sound thereof, but canst not tell whence it cometh, and whither it goeth: so is every one who is born of the Spirit..."

Indeed, the one who is born of the Spirit shines for a moment and later disappears among the multitudes. The multitudes cannot see the superhuman. The superhuman becomes invisible to the multitudes. Just as the chrysalis cannot see the butterfly when it flies, likewise the common human being loses sight of the superhuman. Nicodemus did not understand any of this; thus, he answered to him and said:

"How can these things be?

"Jesus answered and said unto him, Art thou master of Israel, and knowest not these things?"

Indeed, Nicodemus knew the sacred scriptures because he was a rabbi. However, he did not know Sexual Magic because Nicodemus was not an initiate. Jesus continued, saying:

"Verily, verily, I say unto thee, We speak that we do know, and testify that we have seen; and ye receive not our witness."

Jesus gave testimony of what he knew, of what he had seen, and of what he had experienced in himself, because Jesus practiced Sexual Magic with a vestal of the Pyramid of Kefren. This is how he was born. This is how he prepared himself in order to incarnate the Christ. In this way he was able to incarnate the Christ in the Jordan River.

We all know that after leaving Egypt Jesus traveled to India, Tibet, Persia etc., and after returning to the Holy Land he received the Venustic Initiation in the Jordan River. When John baptized Master Jesus, then the Christ entered the soul of the master. The Christ became human. Jesus became divine. The outcome of this divine and human mixture is that which is called the Son of Man (the superhuman).

If Jesus had not practiced Sexual Magic in Egypt, he would not have been able to incarnate the Christ. He would have been a great master but not the living model of the superhuman.

"If I have told you earthly things, and ye believe not,
how shall ye believe, if I tell you of heavenly things?"

With this statement the great master emphasizes that he is talking about earthly things, about the practice of Sexual Magic. Without this one cannot be born. If people do not believe in earthly things, how can they believe in heavenly things?

"And no man hath ascended up to heaven, but He
that came down from heaven, even the Son of Man
which is in heaven." —Christian Bible, John 3

The "I" cannot ascend to heaven because it did not come down from heaven.

The "I" is Satan and must inevitably be dissolved. This is the law.

Speaking about the sacred serpent, the great master said:

"And as Moses lifted up the serpent in the wilderness, even
so must the Son of Man be lifted up." —Christian Bible, John 3

We must lift up the serpent on the staff as Moses did in the wilderness. This is a matter of Sexual Magic because the Kundalini can only be lifted up with Sexual Magic.

Thus, only in this way can we lift up the Son of Man, the superhuman within ourselves.

"...The Son of Man must be lifted up, that
whosoever believeth in Him should not perish but
have eternal life." —Christian Bible, John 3

The rational homunculus, mistakenly called human being, still does not have the authentic astral, mental, and causal vehicles. Therefore, he is really just a phantom.

It is necessary to practice Sexual Magic in order to live the path of the perfect matrimony in order to engender the Christ-astral, Christ-mind and the Christ-causal.

"For God so loved the world, that He gave His only
begotten Son, that whosoever believeth in Him
should not perish, but have everlasting life.

"For God sent not his Son into the world to condemn the
world; but that the world through him might be saved.

"He that believeth on Him is not condemned; he that believeth
not is condemned already, because he hath not believed in the
name of the only begotten Son of God." —Christian Bible, John 3

We affirm that true faith and belief is shown with facts. Anyone who does not believe in Sexual Magic cannot be born even though he says "I believe in the Son of God." Faith without deeds is dead. Anyone who does not believe in the Sexual Magic taught by Jesus to Nicodemus does not believe in the Son of God. These people are lost.

"And this is the condemnation, that the Light is come
into the world, and men loved Darkness rather
than Light; because their deeds were evil.

"For every one that doeth evil hateth the Light
(hates Sexual Magic), neither cometh to the Light,
lest his deeds should be reproved (discussed).

"But he who doeth Truth cometh to the Light,
that his deeds may be made manifest, that they
are brought in God." —Christian Bible, John 3

All of this is quoted from the Holy Gospel of John. One must be born in all the planes.

What does a poor man or woman filled with theories do when practicing exercises, etc., without having been born in the astral?

What good does it do to work with the mind if they still do not have the mental body?

Therefore, the first thing that a human being must do is to create their internal vehicles and then practice whatever they want and study whatever they want. Thus, we must first create the internal vehicles in order to have the right to incarnate the soul, and later the Word.

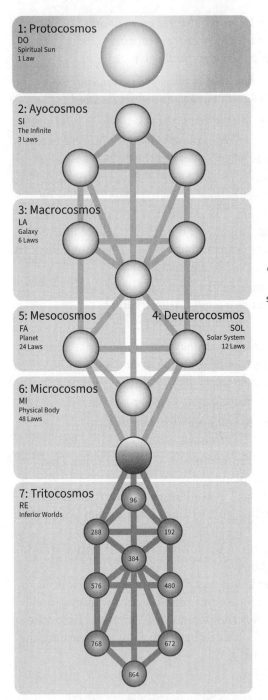

1: Protocosmos
DO
Spiritual Sun
1 Law

2: Ayocosmos
SI
The Infinite
3 Laws

3: Macrocosmos
LA
Galaxy
6 Laws

5: Mesocosmos
FA
Planet
24 Laws

4: Deuterocosmos
SOL
Solar System
12 Laws

6: Microcosmos
MI
Physical Body
48 Laws

7: Tritocosmos
RE
Inferior Worlds

96
288
192
384
576
480
768
672
864

LAWS ON THE TREE OF LIFE

Creation occurs by three forces, the law of three, symbolized by the trinity, trimurti, etc. Each level of existence is created by three laws, and is subject to the laws of the regions it is within. For example, when the astral world comes into existence by the law of three, it is within the worlds of 12, 6, and 3 laws, so: 3+12+6+3=24 laws. Those 24 laws are complications or elaborations of the law of three; they are not individual laws or features like gravity. Instead, the number of laws reflects the relative complication or density of that region. The fewer laws, the more freedom and happiness. The more laws, the more complicated, dense, compressed, and difficult life is.

When the legitimate astral body is born, we become immortal in the world of 24 laws (the lunar world).

When the authentic mental body is born, we immortalize ourselves in the world of 12 laws (the world of Mercury or of the mind).

When the true causal vehicle is born, we acquire immortality in the world of 6 laws (the causal world or world of Venus). We incarnate our human soul when we reach this height. Thus, we become true human beings.

These Christic vehicles are born through sex. This is a sexual matter. As above, so below. If the physical body is born through sex, also the superior vehicles are born through sex.

Whosoever engenders their Christic vehicles incarnates their soul and thus speaks the word of gold. This is the language of power that the human being spoke on the ancient Earth called Arcadia, where the Children of Fire were worshiped. This is the language that the entire universe speaks, a divine language of tremendous power. This was the mysterious language in which the angel of Babylon wrote, "Mene, Mene, Tehel Upharsin" at the famous banquet of Belshazzar. The same night the sentence was carried out, Babylon was destroyed, and the king died.

A great deal has been stated about the universal language. However, we can speak it only when we incarnate the soul, when the Kundalini flourishes on our fertile lips made Word. When humanity left paradise as a result of spilling the semen, it forgot the divine language that flows majestically under the Sun like a river of gold through the thick jungle. The roots of all languages correspond to the divine primitive language. Sexual Magic is the only path that exists in order to once again speak the golden language. There is a close relationship between the sexual organs and the creative larynx. In the old schools of mysteries, initiates were forbidden to tell of the antediluvian catastrophes for fear of evoking them and bringing them once again into manifestation. The old hierophants knew that there was an intimate relationship between the elements of Nature and the Word.

The book entitled *Logos Mantra Magic,* by the great Gnostic Rosicrucian Master Dr. Arnold Krumm-Heller, is a true jewel of esoteric wisdom. The great master concludes his book by saying the following:

> "In ancient times, a school of mysteries existed in which there was a ring, upon which the engraved image of Iris and Serapis united by a snake appeared."

Dr. Krumm-Heller continues:

> "Here I synthesize all that which I have stated in this book."

As well, in the eighth lesson of his *Zodiacal Course,* Dr. Krumm-Heller wrote a paragraph that scandalized many know-it-alls. After the master's death they tried to adulterate this paragraph in their own way, according to their own theories. Now lets transcribe the paragraph exactly as Master Huiracocha wrote it:

> "Instead of the coitus which reaches the orgasm, sweet caresses, amorous phrases and delicate touching should be lavished reflectively, keeping the mind constantly separated from animal sexuality, sustaining the purest spirituality as if the act were a true religious ceremony.

> "Nevertheless, the man can and should introduce the penis and keep it inside the feminine sex to bring about a divine sensation upon both, full of joy, that can last for hours, withdrawing it at the moment the orgasm is near to avoid the ejaculation of semen. In this way, they will have a greater desire to caress each other each time.

> "This may be repeated as many times as desired without ever becoming tiresome. On the contrary, it is the Magic Key to daily rejuvenation, keeping the body healthy and prolonging life, because this constant magnetization is a fountain of health.

"We know that in ordinary magnetism, the magnetizer communicates fluids to the subject and if the first has those forces developed, he can heal the second. The transmission of magnetic fluids is ordinarily done through the hands or through the eyes, but it is necessary to say that there is no greater and more powerful conductor, a thousand times more powerful, a thousand times superior to others, than the virile member and the vulva as receptive organs.

"If many people practice this, they spread force and success in their surroundings for all those who come into commercial or social contact with them. But in the act of sublime, divine magnetization to which we are referring, both man and woman reciprocally magnetize each other, the one being for the other as a musical instrument which, when plucked, gives off or emits prodigious sounds of mysterious and sweet harmonies. The strings of that instrument are spread all over the body, and it is the lips and fingers that make them vibrate, provided that the utmost purity presides over the act. This is what makes us magicians in that supreme moment."

This is the end of the statement of Dr. Krumm-Heller.

Thus, this is the path of initiation. One reaches the incarnation of the Word through this path.

We may be Rosicrucian, Theosophist, or Spiritualist students. We may practice Yoga, and there is no doubt that in all this there are marvelous works and magnificent esoteric practices; but if we do not practice Sexual Magic, we will not be able to create the Christ-astral, the Christ-mental and the Christ-will vehicles. Without Sexual Magic we cannot be born again. Practice what you will, study in any school that you like. Pray in the temple that pleases you the most, but practice Sexual Magic. Live the path of the perfect matrimony.

We are not against any holy religion, school, order, or sect. All of these sacred institutions are necessary. Nevertheless, we advise you to live the path of the perfect matrimony. The perfect matrimony is not opposed to any religious way of life or to the esoteric practices of holy yoga. The Gnostic movement is made up of people from all religions, schools, lodges, sects, orders, etc.

Beloved reader, remember the sacred jewel with its I.A.O. I.A.O. is hidden within GAIO (Gaius). Therefore, work with I.A.O.

The priest, the master of every lodge, the disciple of yoga, everyone will be able to be born, will be able to preserve their true chastity, if they practice Sexual Magic.

Blessed be I.A.O.; blessed be Sexual Magic; blessed be the perfect matrimony. Within Sexual Magic we find the synthesis of all the religions, schools, orders and yogas.

Every system for Realization of the Self without Sexual Magic is incomplete, therefore, it is useless.

Christ and Sexual Magic constitute the supreme practical synthesis of all religions.

Chapter 10

Direct Knowledge

Whosoever studies esotericism wants direct knowledge, yearns to know how they are doing, wants to know about their inner progress.

The greatest aspiration of every student is to become a conscious citizen of the superior worlds and study at the feet of the master. Unfortunately, esotericism is not as simple as it seems at first glance. The internal powers of the human race are completely damaged and atrophied. Human beings have lost not only their physical senses, but moreover, and what is worse, their internal faculties. This has been the karmic result of our bad habits. The student searches here and there, reads and rereads any book about esotericism and magic that falls into their hands and all the poor aspirant does is fill themselves with terrible doubts and intellectual confusion. There are thousands of authors and millions of theories. Some repeat the ideas of others; they in turn refute them, and it is all against one and one against all. Colleagues fight amongst themselves, ridiculing each other. Some writers advise devotees to be vegetarians; others say they should not be. Some advise them to practice breathing exercises, others say they should not practice them. The result is horrifying for the poor seeker.

Thus, the student does not know what to do. Longing for the light, they supplicate, beg, nonetheless, nothing, nothing, absolutely nothing happens.

What to do?

We have met highly mystical individuals, "group heroes," many of them are vegetarians, abstemious, virtuous, etc. They are usually very sincere and want the best for their followers; however, they sigh like everyone else, suffer, and weep in secrecy. These poor people have never seen what they preach.

They do not know their guru. They have never had the joy of speaking with him personally. They have never seen the planes of cosmic consciousness, the planes or superior worlds of which they make such pretty diagrams and such interesting descriptions. We, the brothers and sisters of the temple, feel true pity for them and we try to help them. That is what we attempt to do, but all is useless. They hate everything about sex, everything that seems like sex. When we speak to them about the perfect matrimony, they laugh and protest angrily, defending their sexual abstention. These poor blind ones who lead the blind need someone to guide them. They suffer a lot because they do not have the fortune of direct knowledge. They suffer in silence so as not to discourage or disappoint their followers. We, the brothers and sisters of the temple, frankly, love them and pity them.

It is necessary for them to stop theorizing. The opium of theories is more bitter than death. The only path for re-conquering the lost powers is Sexual Magic. The advantage of the Great Arcanum is that it regenerates the human being.

Human beings need to regenerate themselves, and this is not a matter of authors or libraries. We need to work with the grain, the seed. Just as the lizard and the worm can regenerate their tails, likewise humans can also regenerate their lost powers. These animals replace their lost tails with the sexual force they possess. Thus, with the same sexual force humans can replace, re-conquer, their internal powers. Therefore, this is the path on which those suffering pilgrims can reach direct knowledge. Thus, they can become true enlightened priests for their fraternal groups. The path is Sexual Magic.

Every guide must be clairvoyant and clairaudient. We will provide the following exercise to develop clairvoyance and the secret ear. After having acquired these faculties it is good to remain for periods of time within the deepest forests, away from urban life. Thus, within the peacefulness of Nature, the gods of fire, air, water, and earth teach us ineffable things. This is not a matter of living only in the forest. "What does a saint do in the forest?" However, what we must have is a good vacation within the woods, this is all.

Perfect mental equilibrium is of vital importance for those who want spiritual progress. Almost all the aspirants of esotericism easily lose their mental equilibrium and usually fall into the most absurd things. Whosoever yearns for direct knowledge must ensure that their minds are in perfect equilibrium.

Practice

The great Master Huiracocha teaches a very simple practice in order to see the tattvas (the vibration of the ether).[107] The exercise is as follows: the devotee puts their thumbs in their ears, closes their eyes and seals them with their index fingers, closes the nose with the middle fingers, and finally, seals the lips with the ring and little fingers. Under these conditions the student must try to see the tattvas with the sixth sense. This eye is found between the eyebrows.

Yogananda (who gives the same exercise as Krumm-Heller) advises to also chant the mantra **Om** (ॐ). Yogananda states that devotees must rest their elbows upon some cushions which should be placed on a table. The devotee will do this practice at a table facing East. Yogananda advises that the chair on which the devotee sits to do this practice should be wrapped in a wool covering. This reminds us of Apollonius of Tyana who wrapped himself in a wool cape to isolate himself totally from perturbing currents.

Many authors give this exercise and we consider it to be very good. We believe that with this practice clairvoyance and the magic ear are developed.

Initially the devotees will see only darkness. However, with more effort made in the practice, their clairvoyance and magic ear will develop slowly but surely.

In the beginning the devotees will hear nothing but physiological sounds, but little by little they will hear more and more delicate sounds during the practice. Thus, this is how they will awaken their magic ear.

Instead of giving oneself indigestion with so many contradictory theories, it is better that the reader practice and develop the internal faculties. The process of regeneration must

---

107 In general the word tattvas refers to the five elemental forces of nature: akash (which is the elemental force of the ether), tejas (fire), vayu (air), apas (water) and prithvi (earth).

proceed closely related with esoteric exercise. Science says that an organ that we do not use becomes atrophied. It is necessary to use the organs of clairvoyance and the magic ear. It is urgent that we train ourselves with these organs and regenerate them in order to attain inner Realization of the Self.

These practices are not against any religion, sect, school, or belief. All priests, guides, instructors of all the schools and orders can do these exercises to develop their faculties. Thus, they can guide their respective groups better.

Awakening internal faculties should run parallel with cultural, intellectual, and spiritual development.

The clairvoyant must also develop all the chakras so as not to make serious mistakes.

Most clairvoyants have made serious mistakes. Almost all famous clairvoyants have filled the world with tears. Almost all the great clairvoyants have slandered people. Badly used clairvoyance has led to divorces, assassinations, adultery, robbery, etc.

The clairvoyant needs logical thought and exact concepts. The clairvoyant must have perfect mental equilibrium. The clairvoyant must be powerfully analytical. The clairvoyant must be mathematical in investigation and demanding in expression.

Clairvoyance demands the perfect development of clairaudience, intuition, telepathy, premonition, and other faculties in order to function correctly.

Chapter 11

Grow and Multiply

Genesis 1:28 states,

"Be fruitful and multiply."

To be fruitful signifies to transmute and sublimate the sexual energy in order to grow spiritually. The word multiply refers to the procreation of the human species.

There are two types of children mentioned in the Bible: the children of God and the children of men. Children of God are the outcome of Sexual Magic, when there is no spilling of semen. Children of men are those who are the outcome of passionate pleasure by the spilling of semen.

We need to engender children of God and then to struggle for their spiritual growth.

The Education of Children

Children learn more by example than by precepts. If we want our children to grow spiritually we must be concerned with our own spiritual growth. To multiply our species is not enough, we also need to grow spiritually.

Sin

Our resplendent dragon of wisdom[108] has three aspects: the Father, the Son, and the Holy Spirit. The Father is the light and the life; the Son is the water and the blood that flowed from the wound of our Lord's side, made by the lance of

---

108 Whosoever attains the Venustic Initiation has the joy of incarnating the dragon of wisdom (the inner Christ)... One is the Father (Kether), two is the Son (Chokmah), three is the Holy Spirit (Binah): they are the resplendent dragon of wisdom within any human being that comes into the world. Anyone who achieves the dissolution of the psychological "I" (the Fool of the Tarot) incarnates one's resplendent dragon of wisdom. Whosoever incarnates the resplendent dragon of wisdom becomes a spirit of wisdom. —Samael Aun Weor, *Alchemy and Kabbalah in the Tarot*

Longinus. The Holy Spirit is the fire of Pentecost[109] or the fire of the Holy Spirit called Kundalini by the Hindus, the igneous serpent of our magical powers, holy fire symbolized by gold.

Whosoever lies sins against the Father. Whosoever feels hatred against someone sins against the Son. Whosoever fornicates, that is to say, whosoever spills the semen, sins against the Holy Spirit. The Father is the Truth, the Son is Love, the Holy Spirit is sexual fire.

Education

We must teach our children to tell the truth and nothing but the truth. We must teach our children the law of love.

Love is law, but conscious love. Around the age of fourteen we must teach our children the mysteries of sex. Therefore, based upon this triple aspect of sanctity and perfection, our children will grow spiritually. Thus, whosoever guides their children by this triple aspect of perfection will have established a foundation of steel for their happiness.

Nonetheless, it is necessary to teach them not only with precepts but also by example. We must show with deeds that which we preach.

Profession

Modern life demands that we prepare our children intellectually. It is right for them to have a profession in order to make a living. We must carefully observe the vocational aptitude of our children in order to guide them intellectually. We must never leave a daughter or son without a profession. Every human being needs to learn a profession in order to be able to live. It is a crime, and a very serious one, to leave a child abandoned and without a profession.

---

109 Read the Christian Bible, Acts 2.

Concerning Daughters

Modern times demands that our daughters receive solid spiritual and intellectual preparation. It is indispensable that mothers teach their daughters the mysteries of sex when they reach the age of about fourteen. It is upright for them to walk along the threefold path of truth, love, and chastity.

Thus, a modern woman must have a profession to make a living. It is necessary for fathers and mothers to understand that their daughters can procreate through the perfect matrimony and to also grow spiritually. Nevertheless, everything must be done properly and with order.

It is absurd for daughters to go alone in the streets, or in parks, or in cinemas, or dances with a boyfriend. Since they have not yet killed the animal ego, they are easily sexually seduced and fail miserably. Daughters should always be accompanied by their parents or family members and should never be alone with a boyfriend. Parents should never impede the marriage of their daughters. Nevertheless, I repeat, do everything with order and according to the Law. It is necessary to procreate with chastity and to grow spiritually. This is the path of the perfect matrimony.

THE LAST SUPPER. ENGRAVING BY GUSTAVE DORÉ

Chapter 12

Two Rituals

There are certain tenebrous rites that survive from the most remote epochs of history. The witches of Thessaly celebrated certain rituals in their cemeteries or pantheons in order to evoke the shadow of the dead. Thus, on the anniversary of the deaths of their loved ones, they congregated at the tombs of the cemetery and amidst the most terrifying shrieks they pierced their breasts so that blood might flow. This served as a vehicle for the shadows of the dead to materialize in the physical world.

The great initiate Homer narrates in his book *The Odyssey* something regarding a ritual celebrated by a sorcerer on the island of Calypso where the cruel goddess Circe reigned. The priest cut the throat of a beast within a pit, filling it with blood. At this point the priest invoked the soothsayer of Thebes. Homer says that the soothsayer answered the call and was able to totally materialize thanks to the blood. The soothsayer of Thebes spoke personally with Ulysses and predicted many things for him.

The wise author of *Thus Spoke Zarasthustra* stated, "Write with blood and you will discover that blood is Spirit."

Goethe exclaimed through his Mephistopheles, "Blood is a fluid of properties rare."

The Last Supper

The Last Supper is a magical ceremony with tremendous power, something very similar to the archaic ceremony of the blood brotherhood. The tradition of this brotherhood indicates that if two or more persons mix their blood in a cup and then drink of it, they remain brothers through the blood eternally. Thus, the astral vehicles of these people become intimately associated for all eternity. The Hebrew people assign very special characteristics to the blood. The Last Supper was a ceremony of blood. Each of the apostles brought drops of their own blood in their cups and they emptied them into the chalice of Jesus the Christ. The beloved had also placed his own royal blood in this chalice. Thus, this is how the blood of Jesus Christ was mixed within the Holy Grail with the blood of his disciples.

Tradition tells us that Jesus also gave infinitely small particles of his own flesh to his disciples to eat.

"And he took the bread, and gave thanks, and brake it, and gave unto them, saying: 'This is my body which is given for you, do this in remembrance of me.

"Likewise also the cup after supper saying, This cup is the new testament in my blood, which is shed for you." —Christian Bible, Luke 22:19-20

Thus, this is how the pact was signed. All pacts are signed in blood. The astral body of Jesus Christ remained associated, united with his disciples and with all of humanity, through the blood pact. The beloved is the savior of the world. This blood ceremony is as ancient as the infinite. All the great avatars have verified it since the most ancient times. The great Lord of Atlantis also had a Last Supper with his disciples.

This blood ceremony was not improvised by the divine master. This is a very ancient archaic ceremony, the blood ceremony of great avatars.

Every Gnostic Unction[110] in whatever tradition or belief, sect or religion, is associated, intimately united with the Last Supper of the beloved one through the blood pact. The holy, primeval, Christian Gnostic Church,[111] to which we have the

---

110 From Latin unctionem "anointing." The term unction generally refers to anointment, yet here refers to the rite in which blessed food and drink are prepared and consumed, such as Hindu prasad, Jewish kiddush קידוש, Buddhist ganapuja / tsog / tsok, and Christian communion, eucharist, unction, etc. Anyone can nourish themselves with blessed food and drink at home, even if they do not belong to a religion, church, or temple. Samael Aun Weor taught how to practice the Eucharist at home in *The Major Mysteries, Secret Notes of a Guru, The Seven Words,* and *Tarot and Kabbalah.*.

111 (Greek) From γνῶσις, knowledge, and ἐκκλησία, assembly. Thus, strictly defined, the Gnostic Church is a body or gathering of knowledge. The Gnostic Church is composed of all the perfect beings in existence,

privilege of belonging, preserves in secrecy the primeval rituals used by the apostles. These were the rituals of the Christians that met in the catacombs of Rome during the time of the Caesar Nero. These are the rituals of the Essenes, a humble cast of great initiates to which Jesus the Christ belonged. These are the primeval rituals of the ancient Christians.

These rituals have power. The whole of our secret science of the Great Arcanum is contained within them. When we ritualize, we vocalize certain mantras that have the power to sublimate the sexual energy up to the heart. The inner Christ lives in the heart temple. When the sexual energies are sublimated to the heart, they have the immense joy of mixing with the forces of the inner Christ to enter the superior worlds. Our rituals are repeated in all of the seven great cosmic planes. The ritual ceremony establishes the secret canal from the physical region, passes through all of the seven great planes to the world of the Solar Logos. The Christic atoms of the Solar Logos descend through this canal and thus accumulate in the bread and wine. That is how the bread and wine really change into the flesh and blood of the Christ through the work of transubstantiation. Upon eating the bread and drinking the wine, the Christic atoms fuse with our organism and pass to the internal bodies to awaken in us the powers of their solar nature.

The apostles drank the blood of the Christ and ate the flesh of the Christ.

Sexual Forces and Ritual

In the book *The Bush of Horeb* by Dr. Adoum (Magus Jefa) we have found the description of a black mass from Medieval times. Dr. Adoum transcribes a paragraph taken from a book

who are called gods, angels, buddhas, masters, etc. The Gnostic Church is not a physical entity, but exists in the internal worlds in the superior dimensions. The Gnostic Church utilizes whatever means are appropriate in the physical world in order to aid the elevation of humanity out of suffering. Throughout time, we have known that aid through the various religions, philosophies, teachers, etc.

by Huysmans. This is such an interesting description that we cannot but make it known to our readers. Let us see:

> "As a general rule a priest would officiate. He would completely undress, then put on an ordinary chasuble. On the altar there lay a naked woman, usually a petitioner. Two naked women served as acolytes, at times adolescents were used who would necessarily be naked. Those who attended the service would be dressed or naked according to the whim of the moment. The priest would carry out all the exercises of the ritual, and the audience present accompanied the representation with obscene gestures...

> "The atmosphere became more and more charged, the environment became fluid to a highest degree... Consecutively, everything, indeed, was joined unto it: the silence, darkness and the spiritual absorption... The fluid was attractive, that is to say, it put the participants in contact with the elementals. If during the ceremony the woman lying upon the altar concentrated her attention on a desire, it was not unusual to produce an absolutely real transmission of that desire, a transmission that converted that, the object of her desire, into a true obsession. This was the goal, finally achieved. Therefore that day or during the following days when the realization of the desired phenomenon occurred, it was attributed to the generosity of Satan. Nevertheless, this fluid ambience always had an inconvenience: to exacerbate the nerves and to produce in some member of the assembly a hysterical crisis which sometimes became collective.

> "It was not unusual to see the women at a given moment, out of their minds and pulling

off their clothes, and the men abandoning
themselves to wild gesticulations... Suddenly,
two or three women would even fall to the
ground, prey to violent convulsions... They
were simply mediums who entered into a
trance. It was said that they were possessed
and everyone seemed to be satisfied."

That is as far as we will go with the story told by Huysmans
transcribed by Dr. Adoum. Through this story we can realize
how rituals and sexual forces were misused for acts of terrible evil. Clearly, during a ritual of this type, the overexcited
nervous state, absolutely sexual and passional, violently deter-
mines a certain type of mental force saturated with creative
energy. The outcome of such a ritual is a magical phenomena.

All rituals have to do with blood and semen. Ritual is a
double-edged sword that defends and gives life to the pure and
virtuous, but hurts and destroys the impure and tenebrous.

Ritual is more powerful than dynamite and the knife.

One deals with nuclear forces in a ritual. Atomic energy is
a gift of God that can heal just as it can kill. Therefore, every
temple within which the Holy Gnostic Unction is celebrated, is
in fact and for this reason an atomic energy plant.

In Atlantis as well, black magicians used similar rituals
combined with sexual forces. The result of those abuses was
the sinking of this continent that had previously reached an
extremely high level of civilization.

Sexual forms are closely related to the four elements of
Nature. All black rituals, all black masses, have fatal coordinates in Nature. We now explain to ourselves the causes for
the sinking of Atlantis. Sexual energy is like electricity. It is
found everywhere. It is a force that is within electrons. This
force flows in the nucleus of each atom and in the center of
each nebula. Without this force, the worlds in infinite space
would not exist. This is the creative energy of the Third Logos.
White and black magicians work with this force. White magicians work with white rituals. Black magicians work with black
rituals. The Last Supper of the beloved savior of the world has
an extremely ancient tradition that is lost in the eternal night.

Black mass and all of the black ceremonies of tenebrous ones come from a very ancient lunar past. In every epoch, two rituals have always existed: one of light and one of darkness. Ritual is practical magic. Black magicians mortally hate the Holy Eucharist. Magicians of darkness justify their hatred for the rituals of bread and wine in many different ways. Sometimes they give the gospels the most whimsical interpretations based on their fantasy. Their own subconsciousness betrays them. They try to do away with the Last Supper in any way possible. They hate the Last Supper of the beloved one. Our disciples must be alert and vigilant for these types of dangerous subjects. Anyone who hates the rituals of the Last Supper is a black magician. Anyone who rejects the bread and wine of the Gnostic Unction rejects the flesh and blood of the Christ. These types of people are black magicians.

The Gnostic Church

There are four very important paths that every perfect matrimony must know:
- The path of the fakir
- The path of the monk
- The path of the yogi
- The path of the well-balanced human being

The universal Christian Gnostic movement has a school and a religion.

We experience the first path in practical matters, learning to live with rectitude.

The second path lies within our church. Our Gnostic Church has its sacraments, rituals, and its convent life.

The third path has to do with esoteric practices. We have our esoteric practices, special exercises for the development of the latent powers in the human being.

Within the Fourth Path, which is "the path of the astute," we live practically in the most complete equilibrium. We study Alchemy and Kabbalah. We work on the disintegration of the psychological "I."

We are not members of the Roman Catholic Church. That church only follows the path of the monk. We follow all four paths. We have the path of the monk in our Gnostic religion with its patriarch, archbishops, bishops, and priests. That is why we do not belong to the Church of Rome. We are not against any religion, school, or sect either. Many priests of the Roman Church have come to our ranks. People from all organizations have become affiliated with our Gnostic movement. Our Gnostic Church is one of the most complete ones. On the path of the fakir, we learn to live with rectitude. On the path of the monk, we develop emotion. On the path of the yogi, we practice esoteric exercises that activate our latent esoteric powers. On the path of the balanced human, we work with Alchemy and with Kabbalah, and we struggle disintegrating the "I."

Our Gnostic Church is the transcended church. This church is found in the superior worlds.

We also have many temples in the physical world. In addition, we have opened thousands of Gnostic lumisials[112] where holy rituals are celebrated and the secret doctrine of the beloved savior of the world is studied. We must not forget that our Gnostic movement has both a school and a religion.

It has already been decisively confirmed that Jesus the Christ was Gnostic. The savior of the world was an active member of the cast of Essenes, mystics who never cut their hair or their beards.

The Gnostic Church is the authentic primeval Christian Church whose first Pope was the Gnostic initiate called Peter. Paul of Tarsus belonged to that church. He was a Nazarene. The Nazarenes were another Gnostic sect.

The primeval Christian Church was the true main esoteric trunk from which many other Neo-Christian sects sprung forth, such as: Roman Catholicism, Protestantism, Adventism, the Armenian Church, etc. Frankly, we have made the resolution to make the root of Christianity, Gnosticism, publicly known. This is the primeval Christian Church. The Patriarch Basilides belonged to the Gnostic Church. He was the celebrated alchemist who left a seven page book of lead, which, ac-

---

112 "A place of light." A gnostic temple.

cording to Master Krumm-Heller, is preserved in the Kiercher Museum of the Vatican. This book cannot be understood by archaeologists because it is a book of esoteric science. Basilides was a disciple of Saint Matthias. Roman Catholicism of today is not true Catholicism. Legitimate, authentic, Catholicism is the primeval Christian Catholic Gnostic one. The current Roman Sect is only a deviation of primeval Gnostic Catholicism. Frankly, this is the basic reason why we have completely distanced ourselves from the Roman sect. Saints such as: Saturninus of Antioch, the celebrated Kabbalist, belonged to the primeval Christian Catholic Gnostic Church; Simon the Magician, who unfortunately deviated; Carpocrates, who founded several Gnostic convents in Spain; Marcion of Ponto, Saint Thomas, Saint Valentine; the great master of Major Mysteries called Saint Augustine; Tertullian; Saint Ambrose; Irenaeus; Hippolytus; Epiphanius; Clement of Alexandria; Mark, the great Gnostic who took care of the Holy Gnostic Unction and left us the extraordinary teachings about the path of sexual forces through the twelve zodiacal doors of the human organism. Also Cerdon, Empedocles, Saint Geronimo and many other saints were members of the primeval Christian Catholic Gnostic Church from which the current Roman sect deviated.

Sacraments

In our Gnostic Church, we have baptism, communion of bread and wine, matrimony, confession (friendly conversations between masters and disciples), and finally, extreme unction. The Gnostic matrimony becomes very interesting within the transcendent church. In this sacrament, the woman wears the vestment of the Gnostic priestess and her husband receives her as his wife. The holy masters officiate, and she is received as wife with the promise not to fornicate.

The Christ

The Gnostic Church adores the savior of the world, Jesus. The Gnostic Church knows that Jesus incarnated Christ, and that is why they adore him. Christ is not a human nor a divine individual. Christ is a title given to all fully Self-realized masters. Christ is the Army of the Voice.[113] Christ is the Word. The Word is far beyond the body, the soul, and the Spirit. Everyone who is able to incarnate the Word receives in fact the title of Christ. Christ is the Word itself. It is necessary for every one of us to incarnate the Word. When the Word becomes flesh in us, we speak with the Word of Light. In actuality, several masters have incarnated the Christ. In secret India, the Christ Yogi Babaji has lived for millions of years. Babaji is immortal. The great master of wisdom Kout Humi also incarnated the Christ. Sanat Kumara, the founder of the great College of Initiates of the White Lodge, is another living Christ. In the past, many incarnated the Christ. In the present, some have incarnated the Christ. In the future many will incarnate the Christ. John the Baptist also incarnated the Christ. John the Baptist is a living Christ. The difference between Jesus and the other masters that also incarnated the Christ has to do with hierarchy. Jesus is the highest solar initiate of the cosmos.

Resurrection

The supreme great Master Jesus lives today with the same physical body resurrected from among the dead. Presently, the great master lives in Shamballa. This is a secret country of oriental Tibet. Many other resurrected masters[114] live with the supreme, great master and collaborate with him in the Great Work of the Father.

---

113 A reference to Elohim Sabbaoth (Hebrew), the army or host of gods and goddesses. "...the Dhyan Chohans, called Devas (gods) in India, or the conscious intelligent powers in Nature... The "army of the Voice" is a term closely connected with the mystery of Sound and Speech, as an effect and corollary of the cause -- Divine Thought." —HP Blavatsky, *The Secret Doctrine*

114 See glossary.

Unction

The initiated priest, in a state of ecstasy, perceives the substance of Christ, and magically transmits his own influence on the bread and the wine, thus awakening the Christic substance that is found in these elements which can in turn perform miracles, awakening the Christic powers of our internal bodies.

Sacred Vestments

In great Gnostic cathedrals, Gnostic priests usually use the three vestments of all Catholic priests (cassock, rochet, and chasuble). These three vestments legitimately belong to the primeval Christian Catholic Gnostic Church. They also use the cap. The three vestments superimposed represent the body, the soul, and the spirit—the physical, astral, and spiritual worlds. The cap signifies that he is a man. When he preaches, he covers the head to signify that he only expresses personal opinions.

In Gnostic lumisials, the priest and Isis [priestess] use only a sky blue tunic with a white rope belt. They also wear sandals. The Isis of Gnostic lumisials covers her head with a white veil. That is all. At one point, we ordered the attendees to wear their own tunic, similar to the one that their own Innermost[115] wears internally, according to their esoteric level. Later on, we prohibited this custom due to the abuses of many attendees who believed themselves to be high initiates and dressed in beautiful tunics and took on sonorous names. Moreover, this lends itself to pride. Many of them saw themselves in tunics of certain degrees and were filled with vanity and pride during the rite, and they looked down with despise on those who were of a lower esoteric degree.

---

115 "That part of the Reality (God) within man that the Yogi seeks to attune himself to before attaining cosmic consciousness." - M, *The Dayspring of Youth*. "Our real Being is of a universal nature. Our real Being is neither a kind of superior nor inferior "I." Our real Being is impersonal, universal, divine. He transcends every concept of "I," me, myself, ego, etc., etc." —Samael Aun Weor, *The Perfect Matrimony*. Also known as Atman (the "self"), the Spirit, Chesed, our own individual interior divine Father.

The Officiating Altar

The altar for the holy service must be made out of stone. Remember that we work with the Philosophical Stone (sex). The altar also signifies the Philosophical Earth. The base of the chalice, the stem of the base, and the sacred cup, symbolize the flower. This means that the Christic substance of the sun penetrates the uterus of the Earth and makes the grain germinate, allowing the sprig of wheat to grow until the fruit appears (the seed). After the grain has been given, the rest dies. All of the power of the Sun Christ remains enclosed within the grain. The same thing happens with wine. The sun causes the grape to ripen. All of the power of the Sun Christ remains enclosed within the grape. With the Gnostic unction, all of the Christic solar powers are freed from the bread and the wine. Then they act within our organism, Christifying us.

Epiphany

Epiphany is the manifestation, or the revelation, or the ascension of the Christ within us. According to Krumm-Heller, Dietrich the great theologian stated, "To attain that which one is yearning for, that is the religare or union with divinity; it must be attained through these four ways:
- To receive God (the eucharist)
- Amorous union (Sexual Magic)
- Filial love (to feel that one is a child of God)
- Death and resurrection

The Gnostic lives these four paths.

The Praefor

In the superior worlds there is a Gnostic Church, the cathedral of the soul. In this cathedral, rituals are carried out Fridays and Sundays at dawn (or whenever necessary) for the good of humanity. Many devotees gather at the praefor[116] in

---

116 In the Spanish editions, the word praetor is used but seems to be a typo, since it is a title for a Roman administrative official. Praefor is Latin for "preliminary prayer."

their astral bodies. There are also some athletes of the Jinn science who take their physical body to the praefor. Thus, all of these devotees have the fortune of receiving the bread and wine.

The Key to Perform Conscious Astral Projection

The key to astral projection is very simple: all you have to do is fall asleep, mentally pronouncing the powerful mantra **FARAON**. This mantra is divided into three syllables: FA, RA, ON. When the devotees find themselves in this state of transition between vigil and sleep, they go deep within themselves by way of conscious self reflection and later jump gently from their bed, completely identified with their soft, fluidic spirit. The astral body of each devotee can join the praefor. Those who have not yet engendered their Christ-astral suffer greatly because they cannot learn to astral project without thousands of difficulties and after a tremendous amount of work. Those who in past reincarnations engendered the Christ-astral leave the physical body with great ease.

Key to Carry the Physical Body into the Jinn State

The disciple concentrates on Master Oguara. The disciple should fall asleep reciting this prayer:

> "I believe in the Christ, I believe in Oguara, Babaji, Mataji, and the Jinn masters. Take me from my bed with my physical body, take me to the Gnostic Church with my physical body in a Jinn state."

The devotee will say this prayer thousands of times. The devotee should fall asleep saying this prayer. When the devotee feels more asleep than awake, when one feels the body is weak and full of lassitude, when one feels drowsy with sleep, when one is already beginning to dream, one should get out of bed keeping sleep as a miser guards a treasure. All power is in sleep. In these moments, terribly powerful forces are at work that raise the vibration level of the physical body, accelerating the movement of the atom to astonishing speeds. Then the physical body enters the Jinn state, enters hyperspace.

If the student jumps with the intention of floating, one will notice with surprise that one can fly. In this state one is invisible to the physical world. In this state one can attend the praefor.

When the physical body is entering the Jinn state, it begins to inflate, beginning from the bottom (at the ankles) to the top. Properly stated, the physical body does not really inflate, rather, the astral forces fully interpenetrate it, giving it the appearance of being inflated.

General Aspects of the Gnostic Ritual

When a Catholic officiating priest goes from the Epistle to the Gospel, for the profane Romanists, this is the Christ going from Herod to Pilate; but for Gnostic priests, this is the passage from one world to another after death.

The Four Seasons

We, Gnostics, know of a different routine that occurs during the change of seasons. In the astral, there are angels who take seasonal turns helping humanity through their work: Raphael in the spring, Uriel in the summer, Michael in autumn, and Gabriel in winter. All of these angels attend the Gnostic rituals in order to help us.

The Pater Noster

Among all of the ritual prayers, the most powerful is the Pater Noster (Prayer of the Lord). This is a magical prayer of immense power.

> Our Father, Who art in heaven,
> hallowed be Thy name.
>
> Thy kingdom come.

Thy will be done on earth, as it is in heaven.

Give us this day our daily bread, and
forgive us our trespasses, as we forgive
those who trespass against us.

And lead us not into temptation,
but deliver us from evil.

[For Thine is the kingdom, the
power, and the glory forever.]

Amen. –Jesus, Christian Bible, Matthew 6:9–13 and Luke 11:2–4

Imagination, inspiration, and intuition are the three manda-
tory paths of initiation.

Master Huiracocha says the following.

"First, it is necessary to see spiritual things (God)
internally: "Our father who art in heaven,"

"Then one must listen to the Word, or the
divine Word, "Hallowed be thy name," in
other words, the divine Word, the magnificent
name of God, the creative Word.

"Lastly, we prepare our spiritual organism
for intuition, "Thy Kingdom come," that
is to say, with the pronunciation of the
Word, the mantras, the internal kingdom
of the holy masters comes to us.

"This trinity is found in the first three
supplications of the Pater Noster. The
union with God consists of performing all
of these. The rest remains resolved..."

With these three supplications, Krumm-Heller states, we ask
for an integral request, and if one day we achieve it, we will be
gods already, and therefore we will no longer need to ask.

The Gnostic Church preserves all of the secret doctrines
of the beloved savior of the world. The Gnostic Church is the
religion of happiness and beauty. The Gnostic Church is the

virginal trunk from which came forth Romanism and all of the other sects that adore Christ. The Gnostic Church is the only church that preserves, in secret, the doctrine that Christ taught from his lips to the ears of his disciples.

We are not against any religion. We invite people of all holy religions that adore the Lord to study our secret doctrine.

We must not forget that there are rituals of light and of darkness. We possess the secret rituals of the beloved savior of the world.

We neither scorn nor underestimate any religion. All religions are precious pearls linked on the golden thread of divinity. We only affirm that Gnosis is the flame from which come all religions of the universe. That is all.

THE DIVINE MOTHER AS DURGA UTILIZES THE POWER OF THE SERPENT
TO DEFEAT THE DEMONIC MULTIPLICITY OF THE EGO.

Chapter 13

The Two Marys

There are two serpents: one that ascends up the medullar canal, and one that descends. The serpent ascends within the white magicians because they do not spill the semen. The serpent descends within the black magicians because they spill the semen.

The serpent ascending in the medullar canal is the Virgin.[117] The serpent descending from the coccyx downwards towards the atomic infernos of Nature is the Santa Maria of black magic and witchcraft.[118] Behold, the two Marys: the white and the black.

White magicians abhor the black Santa Maria. Black magicians mortally hate the white Virgin Mary. Whosoever dares to name the Virgin is attacked immediately by the tenebrous ones.

When the initiate is performing the Great Work, one has to struggle terribly against the adepts of Santa Maria.

The creative forces are threefold: masculine, feminine, and neutral. These great forces flow from above to below. Whosoever wants to regenerate oneself has to change this movement and make these creative energies return inward and upward. This is contrary to Nature's interests. The tenebrous ones then feel offended and attack the initiate terribly. Adepts of the Black Hand assault the initiates in order to sexually discharge them. This happens especially during sleep. This is how wet dreams occur. The student dreams of beautiful people who sexually discharge them in order to impede the ascent of the fire through the medullar canal within them.

---

117 This refers to the virginal goddesses of all religions. One might assume this refers only to the Virgin Mary, yet she is not the only one. Many goddesses had virgin births: Hera, Semele, Danae, Rhea Silvia, Anahita, Aditi, Coatlicue, Dughdova, Dechtire, Ceridwyn, Kunti, and too many others to name here.

118 Again, this refers to the inverted aspect of the goddess, represented in all religions as Hekate, Proserpine, Kali Ma, etc.

The tenebrous ones adore Santa Maria within the Abyss, and they sing sublimely malignant verses to her.

The white magicians adore the Virgin who as a serpent of fire rises in the medullar canal, and upon her they rest their heads like children in the arms of their beloved mother.

In India, Kali the Divine Mother Kundalini is adored, but Kali in her black, fatal aspect is also adored. These are the two Marys, the white and the black, the two serpents: the serpent of brass which healed the Israelites in the wilderness, and the tempting serpent of Eden.

There are white initiations and black initiations, temples of light and temples of darkness. All degrees and all initiations are based on the serpent. When the serpent ascends, we become angels; when it descends we become devils.

We will now narrate a black initiation, exactly as we investigated it.

"While asleep, the devotee was taken out of his physical body. The festivity of the demons took place in the street. All the attendants were in their astral bodies. The neophyte practiced negative Sexual Magic with the loss of semen. This is how he progressed in the science of demons who presented themselves at the festival dressed in black tunics. That festivity was a true Witches' Sabbath. When the orgy had finished, the left-hand adepts escorted their beloved disciple towards a yellow temple. This was a cavern of black magic. Seen from the outside, this temple appeared to be a humble religious chapel. Inside, it was a magnificent palace. Inside the temple there were two floors (or levels) and magnificent corridors through which the tenebrous ones passed. The adepts of the shadows congratulated the candidate for his tenebrous triumphs. It was horrible to see the adepts of Santa Maria. The candidate was in compliance with it. The devil's tail was visible on those astral phantoms. The festivity of darkness was magnificent. A priest of the Abyss climbed on a rock to give a sermon. This phantom was a sincerely mistaken one, a man of good intentions but fatally lost. Thus, this adept of the shadows solemnly said, 'I shall be loyal to my religion; nothing will make me look back. This is sacred.'

"Then the tenebrous one continued with a long speech which everyone applauded.

"The guest of honor who had had the misfortune of awakening the Kundalini negatively was marked with a fatal seal. That mark was triangular and had black and grey lines. Before using it, this seal was placed into the fire. The mark of the seal was placed beneath his left lung.

"The tenebrous ones gave the disciple a fatal name which was engraved in black letters on his left forearm.

"The new black initiate was then led in front of a statue of terribly malignant beauty, which symbolizes the black goddess, the kingdom of Santa Maria. The disciple, sitting before this statue, crossed his legs in the Anagarika style (with the left over the right). He then placed his hands on his waist and concentrated on the fatal goddess. After everything finished, the tenebrous one returned into his physical body happy with his 'triumph.'"

That is as far as our investigation went in regard to the initiations of the Abyss.

All those who follow the path of the perfect matrimony must defend themselves against the tenebrous ones who try to take the devotees from the true path to make them a member of the Black Lodge. When they reach their goal, the student is taken to a banquet of demons.

The struggle is terrible: brain against sex; sex against brain, and what is even more terrible and the most painful is heart against heart. You know this.

We must crucify all human emotional attachments, abandon all that signifies carnal passion. This is extremely difficult. The past screams, implores, cries, begs... This is terribly painful.

The superhuman is the result of a tremendous revolution of consciousness. Those who believe that the mechanical evolution of Nature changes us into masters are absolutely mistaken. The master is the result of a tremendous revolution of consciousness.

We must fight against Nature and against the shadow of Nature.

Yama, the God of Death, grasps the Wheel of Samsara,
upon which all creatures revolve due to their karma.

Chapter 14

The Work on the Demon

The awakening of the Kundalini and the dissolution of the "I" precisely form the fundamental basis of all profound Realization of the Self.

In this chapter we shall deal with the theme of the dissolution of the "I." This is definitive for final liberation.

The "I" is the demon that we carry within. Concerning this affirmation, we can say that the work of the dissolution of the "I" is really the work on the demon. This work is very difficult. When we work on the demon, tenebrous entities usually launch terrible attacks against us. This is really the path of the astute, the famous Fourth Path, the path of Tao.

Origin of the "I"

The origin of the sinful "I" is in lust. The ego, Satan, is subject to the law of the eternal return of all things. It returns to new wombs in order to satisfy desires. In each one of its lives, the "I" repeats the same dramas, the same errors. The "I" complicates itself over time, each time becoming more and more perverse.

The Death of Satan

The Satan that we carry within is composed of atoms of the Secret Enemy.[119] Satan had a beginning; Satan has an end. We

---

119 "The Nous atom is sometimes called by the occultist the white or good principle of the heart. We will now speak of its opposite: the dark atom or Secret Enemy. In many ways its activities are similar to the Nous atom; for it has legions of atomic entities under its command; but they are destructive and not constructive. This Secret Enemy resides in the lower section of the spine, and its atoms oppose the student's attempts to unite himself to his Innermost. The Secret Enemy has so much power in the atmosphere of this world that they can limit our thoughts and imprison our minds... The Secret Enemy works in every way to deny us any intelligence that would illuminate our minds, and would seek to stamp man into a machine cursed with similarity and a mind lacking

need to dissolve Satan in order to return to the inner star that has always smiled upon us. This is true final liberation. Only by dissolving the "I" can we attain absolute liberation.

The Intimate Star

Within the unknowable depths of our divine Being we have a completely atomic internal star. This star is a super-divine atom. The Kabbalists denominate this star with the sacred name AIN SOPH.[120] This is the Being of our Being, the great Reality within ourselves.

God Does Not Evolve

God does not need to evolve because He is perfect. God does not need to perfect Himself. He is perfect. God is our inner Being.

Evolution and Devolution

We, the Gnostics have never denied the law of evolution; however, we do not accept that mechanical law as dogma.

The laws of evolution and devolution are the mechanical axis of Nature. For every ascent there follows a descent. For every evolution, there is a specific, corresponding devolution.

There is evolution in the seed which germinates, also in the shoot which grows and develops, consequently in the plant which bears fruit.

There is devolution in the tree that no longer grows, withers away, becomes old and dies.

---

all creative power... Man easily degenerates when in the power of the Secret Enemy; it preys upon the burning furnace of his desires, and when he weakens he is lost and sometimes cannot regain contact with his Innermost for two or three lives wherein he works out the karma of his evil desires." —M, *The Dayspring of Youth*

120 Hebrew אין סוף, "limitless."

Total Revolution

We need a tremendous revolution of consciousness to be able to return to the inner star that guides our Being. There is total revolution when we dissolve the "I."

Pain

Pain cannot make anyone perfect. If pain could perfect anyone, then all humanity would already be perfect. Pain is a result of our own errors. Satan commits many errors. Satan reaps the fruits of his errors. This fruit is pain. Therefore, pain is satanic. Satan cannot perfect himself, nor can he make anyone perfect. Pain cannot make anything perfect, because pain is of Satan. The great divine reality is happiness, peace, abundance, and perfection. The great reality cannot create pain. What is perfect cannot create pain. What is perfect can only engender happiness. Pain was created by the "I" (Satan).

Time

Time is Satan; Satan is memory. Satan is a bunch of memories. When a human being dies, only memories remain. These memories constitute the "I," the me, myself, the reincarnating ego. Those unsatisfied desires, those memories of yesterday, reincarnate. Thus, this is how we are slaves of the past.

Therefore, we can be sure that the past is what conditions our present life. We can affirm that Satan is time. We can also state, without fear of being mistaken, that time cannot liberate us from this valley of tears because time is Satanic. We have to learn to live from moment to moment. Life is an eternal now, an eternal present. Satan was the creator of time; those who think they will liberate themselves in a distant future, within some millions of years, with the passing of time and the ages, are sure candidates for the Abyss and the Second Death, because time is of Satan. Time does not liberate anyone. Satan enslaves. Satan does not liberate. We need to liberate ourselves right now. We need to live from moment to moment.

The Seven Fundamental Centers of the Human

All human beings have seven, basic fundamental centers.
  • the intellectual center, located within the brain
  • the motor center (or the center
    of movement), located in the
    upper part of the dorsal spine
  • the emotional center
    located in the solar plexus
    and in the specific nervous
    centers of the grand sym-
    pathetic nervous system
  • the instinctive center,
    located in the lower part
    of the dorsal spine
  • the sexual center, located
    in the genital organs
  • the superior emotional center
  • the superior intellectual center

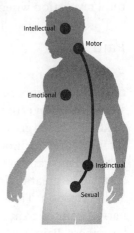

SEVEN CENTERS

These last two can only express themselves through the authentic astral body and the legitimate mental body.

Technique for the Dissolution of the "I"

The "I" exercises control over the five inferior centers of the human machine. These five centers are: intellectual, motor, emotional, instinctive, and sexual.

The two centers of the human being that correspond to Christ consciousness are known in esotericism as Christ-mind and Christ-astral. These two superior centers cannot be controlled by the "I." Unfortunately, the superior mind and the superior emotion still do not have these precious Christic vehicles at their disposal. When the superior mind is clothed in the Christ-mind, and when the superior emotion is invested with the Christ-astral, we are indeed elevated to the state of true human being.

Whosoever wants to dissolve the "I" must study its functionalism within the five inferior centers. We must not condemn the defects; we must not justify them either. What is important is to comprehend them. It is urgent to comprehend the actions and reactions of the human machine. Each one of these five inferior centers has a whole set of extremely complicated actions and reactions. The "I" works with each one of these five inferior centers. Therefore, by deeply comprehending the whole mechanism of each of these centers, we are on our way to dissolving the "I."

In everyday life, two people will react differently in front of any given representation. What is pleasant for one person can be unpleasant for the other. The difference could be that sometimes one person judges and sees with the intellect while the other might be touched emotionally. We must learn to differentiate between intellect and emotion. The intellect is one thing and emotion is another. Within the intellect there is a whole set of actions and reactions that must be comprehended. Within the emotional center there are attachments that must be crucified, emotions that must be carefully studied and, in general, a whole mechanism of actions and reactions that are easily confused with activities of the mind.

Intellectual Center

This center is useful within its own orbit. What is dangerous is to want to remove it from its gravitational field. The great realities of the Spirit can only be experienced with the consciousness. Therefore, those who attempt to investigate the transcendental truths of the Being based purely on reasoning make the same mistake as someone who ignores the use and management of modern scientific instruments, and attempts to study infinitely small life forms with a telescope and infinitely large life forms with a microscope.

Movement

We need to self-discover ourselves and to deeply comprehend all of our habits. We must not allow our life to continue to unfold mechanically. It seems incredible that, living within the patterns of our habits, we do not know the patterns that condition our lives. We need to study our habits; we need to comprehend them. These habits belong to the activities of the center of movement. It is necessary that we self-observe the way we live, act, dress, walk, etc. The center of movement has many activities. Sports also belong to the center of movement. When the intellect interferes with this center, it obstructs and causes damage to it, because the intellect is very slow and the center of movement is very fast. Any typist works with the center of movement and can naturally make mistakes at the keyboard if the intellect intervenes. A person driving an automobile could have an accident if the intellect intervenes.

Emotional Center

The human being stupidly wastes their sexual energy through the abuse of violent emotions, movies, television, football games, etc. We must learn to control our emotions; we must save our sexual energy.

Instinct

There are various instincts: the instinct of preservation, the sexual instinct, etc. There are also many perversions of instinct. Deep within every human being there are sub-human, instinctive, brutal forces that paralyze the true spirit of love and charity. These demonic forces must first be comprehended, then brought under control and eliminated. These bestial forces are: criminal instincts, lust, cowardliness, fear, sexual sadism, sexual bestialities, etc. Before we can dissolve and eliminate them, we must study and deeply comprehend these sub-human forces.

Sex

Sex is the fifth power of the human being. Sex can liberate or enslave the human being. No one can attain integrity, no one can be deeply Self-realized, without sexual energy. No celibate person can attain total Realization of the Self. Sex is the power of the soul. The integral human being is achieved with the absolute fusion of the masculine and feminine poles of the soul. Sexual force develops, evolves and progresses on seven levels (the seven levels of the soul). In the physical world, sex is a blind force of mutual attraction. In the astral world, sexual attraction is based on the affinity of types according to their polarities and essences. In the mental world, sexual attraction occurs according to the laws of mental polarity and affinity. In the causal plane, sexual attraction takes place on the basis of conscious will. It is precisely on this plane of natural causes where the complete union of the soul is consciously performed. Indeed, no one can attain the complete glory of the perfect matrimony without having attained this fourth state of human integration.

We need to deeply comprehend the sexual problem. We need to be integral. We must transcend the mechanization of sex. We need to know how to procreate children of wisdom. In the supreme moment of conception, human essences are completely open to all types of influences. The state of purity of the parents and their willpower used in order to not spill the Cup of Hermes is all that can protect the spermatozoon and the ovum from the danger of infiltration by the subhuman substances of the bestial egos which want to reincarnate.

The Absolute Death of Satan

We discover the whole process of the "I" by comprehending the intimate activities of each one of the five inferior centers. The result of this self-discovery is the absolute death of Satan (the tenebrous lunar "I").

Adultery

Since the woman's body is a passive and receptive element, it is clear that she collects and stores the results of the sexual acts with all those men who committed adultery with her. Those results are atomic substances from the men with whom she has had sexual intercourse. Therefore, when a man has sexual intercourse with a woman who has been with another man or other men, he then absorbs the atomic essences of the other men and poisons himself with them. This is a very grave problem for those brothers and sisters who are dissolving the "I" because then, not only do they have to fight against their own errors and defects, but moreover, against the errors and defects of those other men with whom the woman had sexual intercourse.

The Root of Pain

The "I" is the root of pain. The "I" is the root of ignorance and error. When the "I" is dissolved, the inner Christ is all that remains within us.

We need to dissolve the "I." Only by dissolving the "I" can ignorance and error disappear. When the "I" disappears, all that remains within us is that, which is called love.

When the "I" is dissolved, authentic and legitimate happiness comes to us.

Only by totally annihilating desire can we attain the dissolution of the "I." If we want to dissolve the "I," we must be sour like the lemon, to be displeased with the horrifying "I," the horrifying Satan, the horrible demon that has made our life so bitter and nauseating.

Chapter 15
Celibacy

Swami X stated the following in one of his lessons: "Unmarried people can unite spiritually within themselves the natural creative force of the soul by learning the correct method of meditation and its application to the physical life. Such people do not have to pass through the material experience of matrimony. They can learn to marry their feminine physical impulse with the masculine impulse of their inner soul."

If our beloved Gnostic disciples reflect on Swami X's words, they will reach the conclusion that they are manifestly absurd. This idea of marrying the feminine physical impulse with the masculine impulse of the inner soul is one hundred percent false. This type of utopian "marriage" is impossible because the human being has not yet incarnated the soul. With whom then is one going to marry the feminine physical impulse?

The intellectual animal still does not have a soul. Whosoever wishes to incarnate their soul, whosoever yearns to be a human with soul, must have the astral, mental, and causal bodies. The human being of this day and age still does not have these internal vehicles. The astral specter, the mental specter, and the causal specter are only specters. The majority of occultists believe that these inner specters are the true vehicles; nonetheless, they are very mistaken. We need to be born in the superior worlds. This subject matter about being born is a sexual problem.

No human being is born of theory. Not even a simple microbe can be born of theories. No one is born through the nostrils nor through the mouth. Every living being is born of sex. "As above, so below." If the human being is born of sex here in this physical world, it is logical that above, in the internal worlds, the process is analogous. Law is law and the law is fulfilled.

The Christ-astral is born in the same way as the body of flesh and bone is born. This is sexual. Only with Sexual Magic between husband and wife can one give birth to that marvelous body. We can say the same of the mental and causal.

We need to engender those internal bodies, and that is only possible with sexual contact because, as above so below and, as below so above. No celibate person can marry their feminine physical impulse with the masculine of their inner soul, because a single celibate person can not incarnate their soul. To incarnate the soul we must engender the internal bodies, and only through the sexual union of man and woman can they be engendered. No man or woman can engender or conceive on their own. The two poles are necessary to create. This is what life is.

It is necessary to engender the internal vehicles. It is necessary to be born in the superior worlds. Celibacy is an absolutely false path. We need the perfect matrimony.

After birth, each vehicle needs its special nourishment. Only with this special nourishment does it develop and strengthen itself totally. The nourishment of these vehicles is based on hydrogens.[121] The different types of hydrogens with which the

---

121 From Greek hydr-, stem of hydor "water" + French -gène "producing," from gen: generate, genes, genesis, genetic, etc. Hydrogen is the simplest element on the periodic table, and is the building block of all forms of matter. Hydrogen is a packet of solar light. The solar light (the light that comes from the sun) is the reflection of the cosmic solar intelligence, the Okidanok, the Cosmic Christ, which creates and sustains every world. Hydrogen is "fecundated water, generated water" (hydro). The water is the source of all life. Everything that we eat, breathe and all of the impressions that we receive are in the form of various structures of hydrogen. "It is urgent to know that there are twelve fundamental basic hydrogens in the universe. The twelve basic hydrogens are arranged in tiers in accordance with the twelve categories of matter. The twelve categories of matter exist in all creation; let us remember the twelve salts of the zodiac, the twelve spheres of cosmic vibration within which a solar humanity must be developed. All the secondary hydrogens, whose varied densities go from 6 to 12283, are derived from the twelve basic hydrogens. In Gnosticism, the term hydrogen has a very extensive significance. Indeed, any simple element is hydrogen of a certain density. Hydrogen 384 is found in water, 192 in the air, while 96 is wisely deposited in the animal magnetism, emanations of the human body, X-rays, hormones, vitamins, etc." —Samael Aun Weor, *Light from Darkness*

different internal bodies of the human being are nourished are produced within the physical organism.

Laws of the Bodies

- Physical body: This is governed by 48 laws. Its basic nourishment is Hydrogen 48.
- Astral body: This vehicle is subject to 24 laws. Its basic nourishment is Hydrogen 24.
- Mental body: This vehicle is subject to 12 laws. Its basic nourishment is Hydrogen 12.
- Causal body: This vehicle is governed by 6 laws. Its basic nourishment is Hydrogen 6.

Every substance is transformed into a specific type of hydrogen. Thus, just as the substances and life forms are infinite, likewise the hydrogens are infinite. The internal bodies have their special hydrogens, and with these they are nourished.

Swami X was only a monk. We have been told that soon this good monk will reincarnate in order to marry; thus, he will attain profound Realization of the Self. He is an excellent disciple of the White Lodge. In the superior worlds he thought himself to be Self-realized. However, in the temple he was greatly surprised when we had to make it known to him his mistake. Indeed, this good monk has not yet engendered his Christic bodies; he needs to engender them. This is a sexual problem. These marvelous internal bodies can only be engendered with Sexual Magic.

We give notice to our critics that we are not speaking against Swami X. His exercises are marvelous and very useful. But we do clarify that no one can achieve profound Realization of the Self with the system of the "bellows."[122]

There are many schools; all of them are necessary. All of them serve to help the human being, but it is good to warn that no theory can engender the internal bodies. We have never witnessed anyone being born from a theory. We have not yet met a human being who was born out of theories.

---

122 Breathing exercises, also called pranayama.

There are very respectable and venerable schools. These institutions have their courses of instruction and degrees. Some of them also have rituals of initiation. However, in the superior worlds the degrees and initiations from these schools are useless. The masters of the White Lodge are not interested in the degrees and hierarchies of the physical world. They are only interested in the Kundalini. They examine and measure the spinal medulla. If the candidate has not yet raised the serpent, for them, he is simply an ordinary being, like any other, even though he may occupy some high position in the physical world, or be a venerable person or some supreme hierarch in his school or lodge. If the Kundalini has risen three vertebrae, he is considered by the masters to be an initiate of the third degree, and if has risen it only one vertebra, an initiate of the first degree.

Thus, the masters are only interested in the Kundalini.

Indeed, those who abandon everything in order to work in their cave with their eagle and their serpent are very few.[123] This is something for heroes, and this present humanity does not abandon its lodges and schools to remain alone with its eagle and its serpent. The students of all organizations are not even loyal to their schools. They live flitting from lodge to lodge, from school to school. Thus, this is how they supposedly want to achieve profound Realization of the Self.

We feel infinite pain when we notice these capricious brothers and sisters. Many of them practice marvelous exercises. Certainly, there are many good practices in the schools. The practices of Yogananda, Vivekananda, Ramacharaka, etc., are admirable. Students practice them with very good intentions. These are very sincere students. We greatly value all those students and all those schools. Nonetheless, we feel great and unremediable pain for those who, with such yearning, seek for their final liberation. We know that they must engender their internal vehicles. We know they must practice Sexual Magic.

---

123 "The victorious adept becomes a child of the serpent, and into a serpent that must to be swallowed by the eagle of the Spirit (the Third Logos)."
    —*The Secret Doctrine of Anahuac*

We know that only with Sexual Magic will they be able to awaken their sacred fire and engender their internal vehicles to incarnate their soul. We know this through our own experience. Nonetheless, what can we do to convince them? We, the brothers and sisters, suffer greatly and without remedy...

In the former Earth-Moon,[124] millions of human beings evolved. However, from all of those millions, only a few hundred elevated themselves to the angelic state. The great majority of human beings were lost. The great majority sank themselves into the Abyss.

"Many are called, but few are chosen."
—Christian Bible, Matthew 22:14

If we observe Nature, we see that not all seeds germinate. Millions of seeds are lost, and millions of creatures perish daily. A sad truth it is, but it is the truth.

Every celibate person is a sure candidate for the Abyss and Second Death. Only those who have elevated themselves to the state of superhuman can give themselves the luxury of enjoying the delights of love without sexual contact. We enter then, the amphitheater of cosmic science. Nobody can attain the incarnation of the superhuman within themselves without Sexual Magic and the perfect matrimony.

---

124 Selene. Read *The Revolution of Beelzebub.*

DRAWING BY CAMILLE FLAMMARION, 1888

"We need to Self-remember in the
presence of every representation that
could fascinate us. Let us hold ourselves
while in front of any representation and
ask ourselves: Where am I? Am I in the
physical plane? Am I in the astral plane?"

Chapter 16

The Awakening of Consciousness

It is necessary to know that humanity lives with its consciousness asleep. People work asleep. People walk through the streets asleep. People live and die asleep. When we come to the conclusion that the entire world lives asleep, then we comprehend the necessity of awakening. We need the awakening of the consciousness. We want the awakening of the consciousness.

Fascination

The profound sleep in which humanity lives is caused by fascination.

People are fascinated by everything in life. People forget themselves because they are fascinated. The drunkard in the bar is fascinated with the alcohol, the place, the pleasures, his friends and the women. The vain woman in front of a mirror is fascinated with her glamor. The rich avaricious person is fascinated with money and possessions. The honest worker in the factory is fascinated with the hard work. The father of the family is fascinated with his children. All human beings are fascinated and sleep profoundly. When driving a car we are astonished when we see people dashing across the roads and streets without paying attention to the danger of the running cars. Others willfully throw themselves under the wheels of cars. Poor people... they walk asleep, they look like sleepwalkers. They walk asleep, endangering their own lives. Any clairvoyant can see their dreams. People dream with all that keeps them fascinated.

Sleep

During the physical body's sleep, the ego escapes from it. This departure of the ego is necessary so that the vital body can repair the physical body. However, in the internal worlds we can affirm that the ego takes its dreams into the internal worlds. Thus, while in the internal worlds the ego occupies itself with the same things which keep it fascinated in the physical world. Therefore, during a sound sleep we see the carpenter in his carpentry shop, the policeman guarding the streets, the barber in his barbershop, the blacksmith at his forge, the drunkard in the tavern or bar, the prostitute in the house of pleasures, absorbed in lust, etc. All these people live in the internal worlds as if they were in the physical world.

During their sleep, not a single living being has the inkling to ask themselves whether they are in the physical or astral world. However, those who have asked themselves such a question during sleep have awoken in the internal worlds. Then, with amazement, they have been able to study all the marvels of the superior worlds.

It is only possible for us to ask such a question of ourselves in the superior worlds (during those hours of sleep) if we accustom ourselves to ask this question from moment to moment during the so-called vigil state. Clearly, during our sleep we repeat everything that we do during the day. Therefore, if during the day we accustom ourselves to asking this question, then during our nocturnal sleep (while being outside of the body) we will consequently repeat the same question to ourselves. Thus, the outcome will be the awakening of the consciousness.

Remembering Oneself

The human being in their fascinated trance does not remember their Self. We must Self-remember from moment to moment. We need to Self-remember in the presence of every representation that could fascinate us. Let us hold ourselves while in front of any representation and ask ourselves: Where am I? Am I in the physical plane? Am I in the astral plane? Then, give a little jump with the intention of floating within the surrounding atmosphere. It is logical that if you float it is because you are outside the physical body. Thus, the outcome will be the awakening of consciousness.

The purpose of asking this question at every instant, at every moment, is with the intention of engraving it within the subconsciousness, so that it may manifest later during the hours given to sleep, hours when the ego is really outside the physical body. You must know that in the astral plane, things appear just as they are here in this physical plane. This is why during sleep and after death people see everything there in a form very similar to this physical world. This is why they do not even suspect that they are outside of their physical body. Therefore, no dead person ever believes themselves to have died, because they are fascinated and profoundly asleep.

If the dead had made a practice of remembering themselves from moment to moment when they were alive, if they had struggled against the fascination of the things of the world, the outcome would have been the awakening of their consciousness. They would not dream. They would walk in the internal worlds with awakened consciousness. Whosoever awakens the consciousness can study all the marvels of the superior worlds during the hours of sleep. Whosoever awakens the consciousness lives in the superior worlds as a totally awakened citizen of the cosmos. One then coexists with the great hierophants of the White Lodge. Whosoever awakens the consciousness can no longer dream here in this physical plane or in the internal worlds. Whosoever awakens the consciousness stops dreaming. Whosoever awakens the consciousness becomes a competent investigator of the superior worlds. Whosoever awakens consciousness is an illuminated one. Whosoever awakens the consciousness can study at the feet of the master. Whosoever awakens the consciousness can talk familiarly with the gods who initiated the dawn of creation. Whosoever awakens the consciousness can remember their innumerable reincarnations. Whosoever awakens the consciousness can consciously attend their own cosmic initiations. Whosoever awakens the consciousness can study in the temples of the great White Lodge. Whosoever awakens the consciousness can know in the superior worlds the evolution of their Kundalini. Every perfect matrimony must awaken the consciousness in order to receive guidance and direction from the White Lodge. In the superior worlds the masters will wisely guide all those who really love one another. In the superior worlds the masters give to each one that which one needs for their inner development.

Complementary Practice

Every Gnostic student, after waking from their normal sleep, must perform a retrospective exercise based on the process of their sleep, in order to remember all of those places they visited during the hours of sleep. We already know that the ego travels a great deal; it goes towards where we have physically been, repeating all that which we have seen and heard.

The masters instruct their disciples when they are out of the physical body.

Therefore, it is urgent to know how to profoundly meditate and then practice what we have learned during the hours of sleep. It is necessary not to physically move at the time of waking up, because with the movement, the astral is agitated and the memories are lost. It is urgent to combine the retrospective exercises with the following mantras: **RAOM GAOM**. Each word is divided into two syllables. One must accentuate the vowel O. These mantras are for the student what dynamite is for the miner. Thus, as the miner opens his way through the bowels of the earth with the aid of dynamite, similarly, the student also opens their way into the memories of their subconsciousness with the aid of these mantras.

Patience and Tenacity

The Gnostic student must be infinitely patient and tenacious because powers cost a great deal. Nothing is given to us for free. Everything has a price. These studies are not for inconsistent people, nor for people of fragile will. These studies demand infinite faith.

Skeptical people must not come to our studies because esoteric science is very demanding. The skeptics fail totally. Thus, skeptical people will not succeed in entering the Heavenly Jerusalem.

The Four States of Consciousness[125]

The first state of consciousness is called Eikasia.[126] The second state of consciousness is Pistis.[127] The third state of consciousness is Dianoia.[128] The fourth state of consciousness is Nous.[129]

Eikasia is ignorance, human cruelty, barbarism, exceedingly profound sleep, a brutal and instinctive world, an infrahuman state.

Pistis is the world of opinions and beliefs. Pistis is belief, prejudices, sectarianism, fanaticism, theories in which there is no type of direct perception of the truth. Pistis is that level of consciousness of the common humanity.

Dianoia is the intellectual revision of beliefs, analysis, conceptual synthesis, cultural-intellectual consciousness, scientific thought etc. Dianoetic thought studies phenomena and

---

125 There are two well known versions of this structure: the Greek is described in this chapter. They correspond to those of yoga: deep sleep (sushupti), dreaming (svapna), waking (jagrat), and superconscious (turiya).

126 Greek εἰκασία, "guess, suppose, conjecture." The lowest of the four states of consciousness. As you can see from the meaning of the word, eikasia is not based on facts, but is a projection of the mind, an illusion. This term is used by Plato to signify imagination that is focused exclusively on a temporal appearance or image; in other words, fantasy or illusion, one of the sources of suffering. This state of consciousness corresponds to the most unconscious and mechanical levels of the psyche, and relates also to the state of physical sleep (within which the consciousness is wandering within the subjective, inferior levels of the psyche, also called "dreaming").

127 Greek πίστις, literally "faith, trust" derived from Πειθώ peitho, meaning "to prevail," "to grow in confidence," or "persuasion." Has levels of meaning, both positive and negative.

128 Greek διάνοια from diá, "thoroughly, from side-to-side," which intensifies noiéō, "to use the mind," noús, "mind." Dianoia can be translated as understanding, discrimination. "Jesus said unto him, Thou shalt love the Lord thy God with all thy heart, and with all thy ψυχή psyche, and with all thy διάνοια dianoia." —Matthew 22:37

129 Greek νοῦς or νόος, "mind, perception, sense, thought, intelligence." Nous is a philosophical term for the faculty of perception of what is true or real. "And be not conformed to this aeon: but be ye transformed by the renewing of your nous, that ye may prove what [is] that good, and acceptable, and perfect, thelema of God." —Romans 12

establishes laws. Dianoetic thought studies the inductive and deductive systems with the purpose of using them profoundly and clearly.

Nous is perfect, awakened consciousness. Nous is the state of Turiya[130]: profound perfect inner illumination. Nous is legitimate objective clairvoyance. Nous is intuition. Nous is the world of the divine archetypes.[131] Noetic thought is synthetic, clear, objective, illuminated. Whosoever reaches the heights of Noetic thought totally awakens consciousness and becomes a Turiya.

The lowest part of a person is irrational and subjective and is related with the five ordinary senses.

The highest part of a person is the world of intuition and objective spiritual consciousness. In the world of intuition, the archetypes of all things in Nature develop.

Only those who have entered into the world of objective intuition, only those who have reached the solemn heights of Noetic thought, are truly awakened and illuminated.

A true Turiya cannot dream. The Turiya who has reached the heights of Noetic thought never goes about saying so, never presumes to be wise; they are extremely simple and humble, pure and perfect.

It is necessary to know that a Turiya is neither a medium, nor a pseudo-clairvoyant, nor a pseudo-mystic, unlike those who nowadays abound like weeds in all schools of spiritual, hermetic, occultist studies, etc.

The state of Turiya is most sublime and is only reached by those who work in the flaming forge of Vulcan[132] all of their lives. Only the Kundalini can elevate us to the state of Turiya.

---

130 (Sanskrit, literally "fourth") The fourth and highest of the four states of consciousness, transcending the states of vigil ("wakened"), dreaming, and deep sleep. The state of turiya is described in the Mandukya Upanishad as "Invisible, otherworldly, incomprehensible, without qualities, beyond all thoughts, indescribable, the unified soul in essence, peaceful, auspicious, without duality, is the fourth stage, that self, that is to be known."

131 In Kabbalah, the world of Atziluth.

132 The Latin or Roman name for the Greek god Ἥφαιστος Hephaestus, known by the Egyptians as Ptah. A god of fire with a deep and ancient mythology, commonly remembered as the blacksmith who forges

It is urgent to know how to meditate profoundly and then to practice Sexual Magic during the whole of our life in order to reach, after many difficult trials, the state of Turiya.

Meditation and Sexual Magic carry us to the heights of Noetic thought.

Neither dreamer nor medium, nor any of those who enter a school of esoteric teaching can instantaneously achieve the state of Turiya. Unfortunately, many believe that it is as easy as blowing glass to make bottles, or like smoking a cigarette, or like getting drunk. Thus we see many people hallucinating, mediums and dreamers, declaring themselves to be clairvoyant masters, illuminated ones. In all schools, including within the ranks of our Gnostic movement, those people who say that they are clairvoyant without really being so are never missing. These are the ones who, based upon their hallucinations and dreams, slander others saying that person is fallen, that fellow is a black magician, etc.

It is necessary to advise that the heights of Turiya require beforehand many years of mental exercise and Sexual Magic in the perfect matrimony. This means discipline, long and profound study, very strong and profound internal meditation, sacrifice for humanity, etc.

Impatience

As a rule, those who have recently entered Gnosis are full of impatience; they want immediate phenomenal manifestations, instantaneous astral projections, illumination, wisdom, etc.

The reality is another thing. Nothing is given to us for free. Everything has its price. Nothing is attained through curiosity, instantaneously, rapidly. Everything has its process and its development. Kundalini develops, evolves and progresses very slowly within the aura of the Maha-Chohan.[133] Kundalini has the power of awakening the consciousness. Neverthe-

---

weapons for gods and heroes. Vulcan is very important in the tradition of Alchemy. In Hinduism, he is symbolized by Tvastri, later called Visvakarma.

133 Sanskrit for "Chief Lord." A title or rank. Here, a reference to the Third Logos.

less, the process of awakening is slow, gradual, natural, without spectacular, sensational, emotional, and barbaric events. When the consciousness becomes completely awakened, it is not something sensational, or spectacular. It is simply a reality, as natural as a tree that grows slowly, unfolds and develops without sudden leaps or sensational events. Nature is Nature. The Gnostic student in the beginning says, "I am dreaming." Later they exclaim, "I am in the astral body, outside the physical body." Later still, they obtain Samadhi, ecstasy, and enter the Fields of Paradise. In the beginning, the manifestations are sporadic, discontinuous, followed by long periods of unconsciousness. Much later, the igneous wings give us continuous uninterrupted awakened consciousness.

Chapter 17

Dreams and Visions

Gnostic students must learn to differentiate between dreams and visions. To dream is one thing and to have visions, another. A truly "awakened" Gnostic cannot dream. Only those who have the consciousness asleep live dreaming.

The worst type of dreamer is the sexual dreamer. Those who live dreaming of carnal passions stupidly waste their creative energy in the satisfaction of their fantastic pleasures. Ordinarily, these people do not progress in their business. They fail in every sense. They end up in misery.

When we look at a pornographic image, it strikes the senses and then passes to the mind. The psychological "I" intervenes in these affairs by stealing the erotic image in order to reproduce it in the mental plane. Thus, in the world of the mind, that image is transformed into a living effigy. During sleep, the dreamer fornicates with that living effigy, which like an erotic demon tempts the dreamer for the satisfaction of lust. The outcome is wet dreams with all their horrible consequences. Therefore, the true devotees of the path must not visit cinemas because they are dens of black magic. The erotic figures of the screen give rise to mental effigies and erotic dreams. In addition, the cinemas are full of diabolic elementals created by the human mind. Those malignant elementaries[134] damage the minds of the spectators.

The subconscious mind creates fantastic dreams within the realm of dreams. The quality of dreams depends on the beliefs of the dreamer. When someone believes we are good, he dreams about us, seeing us as angels. When someone believes we are bad, he dreams about us, seeing us in the form of a devil.

---

134 Elementaries refers to various entities that we create through the misuse of our sexual energy. Examples include incubi, succubi, basilisks, etc. They abide in the fifth dimension where they pressure our mind with thoughts, desires, imaginations, and dreams to give them more energy, especially through masturbation, sexual fantasy, etc. Do not confuse with *elementals*, which are innocent creatures of nature.

Many things come into our memory whilst writing these lines. In the past when we, the brothers and sisters, worked in various countries, we were able to observe that whilst our Gnostic disciples believed in us, they dreamed seeing us as angels. It was sufficient for them to stop believing in us for them to then dream about us being demons. Those who swore before the altar to follow and obey us, admired us with great enthusiasm and dreamed seeing us as being angels. Many times it was enough for those students to have read a book or to have listened to some lecturer in order for them to become affiliated with a new school. Then, having stopped believing in us, having changed their concept and opinions, they dreamed about us, seeing us changed into devils. Then, which clairvoyance do these people possess? What became of their clairvoyant dreams? What type of clairvoyant is that which today sees us as gods and tomorrow affirms that we are devils? Where is the clairvoyance of these dreamers? Why do these people contradict themselves? Why do they swear today that we are gods and tomorrow swear that we are devils? What is this?

The subconsciousness is a screen upon which many internal films are projected. Sometimes the subconsciousness sometimes acts as a cameraman, other times as a director, and also as a projectionist who projects images onto the mental background. It is clear that our subconscious projector usually commits many errors. No one ignores that erroneous thoughts, groundless suspicions and also false dreams emerge on the screen of the mind.

We need to transform the subconsciousness into consciousness, to stop dreaming, to awaken the consciousness.

Whosoever awakens is incapable of dreaming. Thus, while their physical body sleeps within the bed, they live within the internal worlds in a state of intensified vigilance. Such people are authentic, illuminated seers.

We frankly cannot accept clairvoyants who have not awakened their consciousness. We cannot accept clairvoyants who have not engendered the Christ-astral, Christ-mind, and Christ-will. Those clairvoyants who have neither awakened consciousness nor possess their Christic vehicles can only see their own beliefs and concepts in the internal worlds. In short, they are useless.

Only those awakened clairvoyants, only those clairvoyants who already possess their Christic vehicles, are worthy of true credit. They are not dreamers. They do not make mistakes. They are true illuminates. Such people are in fact true masters of the White Lodge. The visions of this class of sublime humans are not simple dreams. These are the masters of perfection. This kind of master cannot dream any more. This class of master can investigate the memories of Nature and read in the sealed archives of creation all the history of the Earth and its races.

Everyone who follows the path of the perfect matrimony should live alert and vigilant as a watchman in the time of war, because during the hours of sleep the masters test their disciples. Yet, the tenebrous ones attack us during sleep when we are working in the Great Work. Thus, during sleep, we have to pass through many ordeals in the internal worlds.

When the masters are going to test the disciple in something, then they awaken the disciple's consciousness.

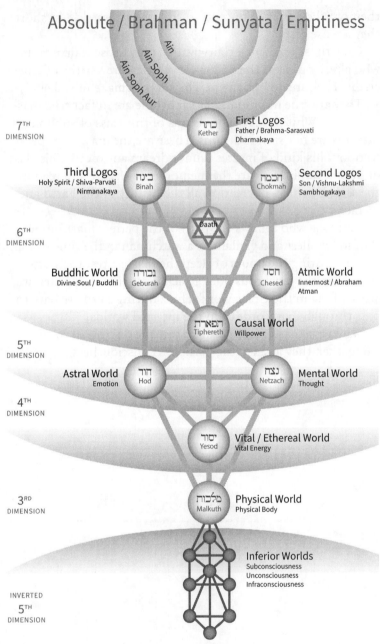

Absolute / Brahman / Sunyata / Emptiness

Ain
Ain Soph
Ain Soph Aur

7TH DIMENSION

כתר
Kether — **First Logos**
Father / Brahma-Sarasvati
Dharmakaya

Third Logos
Holy Spirit / Shiva-Parvati
Nirmanakaya — בינה Binah

חכמה Chokmah — **Second Logos**
Son / Vishnu-Lakshmi
Sambhogakaya

Daath

6TH DIMENSION

Buddhic World
Divine Soul / Buddhi — גבורה Geburah

חסד Chesed — **Atmic World**
Innermost / Abraham
Atman

תפארת Tiphereth — **Causal World**
Willpower

5TH DIMENSION

Astral World
Emotion — הוד Hod

נצח Netzach — **Mental World**
Thought

4TH DIMENSION

יסוד Yesod — **Vital / Ethereal World**
Vital Energy

3RD DIMENSION

מלכות Malkuth — **Physical World**
Physical Body

Inferior Worlds
Subconsciousness
Unconsciousness
Infraconsciousness

INVERTED 5TH DIMENSION

THE TREE OF LIFE AND THE DIMENSIONS OF NATURE

Beyond the sixth dimension is the Unknown,
the 7th or "0" dimension.

Chapter 18

Consciousness, Subconsciousness, Supraconsciousness,

Clairvoyant Consciousness

That which we call the ordinary vigil state of consciousness is profound sleep. The ordinary vigil state of consciousness is related with the five senses and the brain. People believe that they have an awakened consciousness, and that is absolutely false. Daily, people live in the most profound sleep.

Supraconsciousness

Supraconsciousness is an attribute of the Innermost (the Spirit). The faculty of supraconsciousness is intuition.

It becomes necessary to compel our supraconsciousness to work for intuition to become powerful. Let us remember that an organ that is not used becomes atrophied. The intuition of people who do not work with their supraconsciousness is atrophied. Polyvoyance is intuitive clairvoyance. It is divine omniscience. This eye is found in the pineal gland. The lotus of a thousand-petals resides there. Supraconsciousness resides there. The pineal gland is located in the upper part of the brain. Whosoever wants the development of the supraconsciousness must practice internal meditation. You must concentrate on the Divine Mother who resides in the depths of your Being. Meditate upon Her. Fall asleep while praying that She may put your supraconsciousness into activity. Meditate daily. Meditation is the daily bread of the wise. With meditation you will develop supraconsciousness.

Memory

You need memory in order to remember your internal experiences. Do not spill the semen. You must know that in the semen there are millions of microscopic brain cells. You must not lose those cells.

Special Nourishment to Develop the Power of the Memory

Prepare your breakfast with acidic fruits and ground almonds along with honey (bee honey). In this way you will provide the brain with the necessary atoms for memory.

Internal Experiences

The ego lives in the internal worlds and travels to different places while our physical body sleeps. There, within the internal worlds, we are repeatedly tested. It is within the temples of the internal worlds where we receive initiation. Therefore, it becomes necessary to remember everything that we do outside the body. Thus, with the instructions given in this book, every human being will be able to awaken their consciousness and remember their internal experiences.

It is painful to know that there are many initiates who work in the great temples of the White Lodge whilst their physical body sleeps; nonetheless, they do not remember anything because their memory is atrophied.

Here you have the exercises to develop the memory. Practice intensely. Enforce your subconsciousness to work. Awaken your consciousness, and put your supraconsciousness into activity.

Clairvoyance and Pseudo-clairvoyance

There is clairvoyance, and there is pseudo-clairvoyance. The Gnostic student must make a clear differentiation between these two forms of extrasensory perception.

Clairvoyance is based on objectivity.[135] However, pseudo-clairvoyance is based on subjectivity.[136]

---

135 "Impersonal, unbiased," from Latin object, which implies perceiving the reality or truth of an object.

136 "Existing in the mind" from Latin subiectivus "of the subject" from subiectus "lying under, below." Subjective indicates a mistaken

Understand that by objectivity we mean spiritual reality, the spiritual world. Understand that by subjectivity we mean the physical world, the world of illusion, that which has no reality. There is also an intermediate region. This is the astral world, which can be objective or subjective according to the degree of spiritual development of each person.

Pseudo-clairvoyance consists of imaginary perception, fantasy, artificially evoked hallucinations, absurd dreams, astral visions that do not coincide with concrete facts, the reading of one's own projected unconscious thoughts in the Astral Light, the unconscious creation of astral visions which are interpreted later as authentic realities, etc.

In like manner, within the field of pseudo-clairvoyance, we find subjective mysticism, false mysticism and the pseudo-mystical states which have no relation whatsoever with the intense and lucid sentiment. Most certainly, these states are related with stories and pseudo-magic, in other words, false religious influences which are projected unconsciously within the Astral Light. Thus, in general, pseudo-clairvoyance is related with all that which in the orthodox literature receives the name of "beauty" (seduction).

Objective Clairvoyance

There are four mental states that lead the neophyte to the ineffable summits of objective clairvoyance:
- First: To profoundly sleep
- Second: To sleep with dreams
- Third: Vigil state
- Fourth: Turiya or state of perfect illumination

Indeed, only a Turiya is an authentic clairvoyant. It is impossible to reach these heights without having been born in the causal world.[137] Whosoever wishes to reach the state of Turiya must thoroughly study the semi-unconscious psychic

---

perception, a mental interpretation.

137 This is to have completed the fifth initiation of Major Mysteries and created the causal body, giving one consciousness in the sixth dimension. Related to the sephirah Tiphereth.

processes which constitute the origin of many forms of self-deception, self-suggestion, and hypnosis.

- The Gnostic must first attain the ability to stop the course of thoughts, the capacity to not think. Indeed, only the one who achieves that capacity will hear the Voice of the Silence.
- When the Gnostic disciple attains the capacity to not think, then one must learn to concentrate thought on only one thing.
- The third step is correct meditation. This brings the first flashes of the new consciousness into the mind.
- The fourth step is contemplation, ecstasy, or Samadhi. This is the state of Turiya (perfect clairvoyance).

Clarification

Within the Gnostic movement, there are only a few Turiyas. To make this clarification is necessary, because with few and very rare exceptions, there are only pseudo-clairvoyants and subjective mystics.

In reality, all of the mystical schools and all of the spiritualist movements are full of misguided pseudo-clairvoyants who cause more harm than good. They are the ones who give themselves the title of master. Among them abound famous reincarnations, like the John the Baptists, of whom we know more than a dozen, the Mary Magdalenes, etc. This type of person believes that initiation is as easy as blowing glass in order to make bottles. Thus, based on their supposed mastery and their absurd visions created by their morbid mentality, they prophecy and excommunicate others at their whim, as they like, slandering people and denominating others black magicians, asserting that certain people are fallen, etc.

The Gnostic movement must cleanse itself of this evil and harmful plague. Therefore, we have begun with the expulsion of Mrs. X.

We are not willing to further tolerate the unhealthy morbidity of all those misguided pseudo-clairvoyants and all those subjective mystics.

We disseminate spiritual intellectual culture, decency, refinement, logical analysis, conceptual synthesis, academic culture, higher mathematics, philosophy, science, art, religion, etc. Therefore, in no way whatsoever are we willing to continue to accept the gossip of hallucinating people nor the madness of dreamers.

Indeed, the subjective clairvoyant transfers their dreaming type of consciousness to their vigil state of consciousness in order to see in others their own projected dreams. Thus, these projected dreams change according to the temperamental state of the dreamer. In the past, we have been able to confirm that when some pseudo-clairvoyant agreed with all our ideas and concepts, they would see us as angels or gods; thus, they would praise us and even adore us. Nevertheless, when they changed their concept, when the pseudo-clairvoyant became enthusiastic about some new school, when they read some book that appeared marvelous to them, when they listened to some lecturer who came to town, when they resolved to change organizations or schools, then they would accuse us of being black magicians and would see us as demons, etc. This demonstrates that these pseudo-clairvoyants are only dreamers who see their own dreams projected in the Astral Light.

The students who really want to reach the ineffable heights of true and legitimate clairvoyance must be extremely careful of the danger from those who deceive themselves. Thus, the students must submit themselves to authentic esoteric discipline.

Reality

The true and legitimate clairvoyant, the one who has achieved supraconsciousness, never presumes of being a clairvoyant, never goes about saying so. When they give advice, they do so without making others understand that they do it based on their clairvoyance.

All Gnostic sanctuaries must beware of those people who praise themselves and call themselves clairvoyant.

All Gnostic sanctuaries must exercise the greatest of vigilance to protect themselves against the spectacular pseudo-clairvoyants who, from time to time, appear on the scene to slander and discredit others, assuring us that such fellow is a sorcerer, that such a fellow is a black magician, that such a fellow is fallen, etc.

It is urgent to comprehend that no authentic Turiya has pride. Indeed, all those who say, "I am the reincarnation of Mary Magdalene, John the Baptist, Napoleon," etc., are proud fools, misguided pseudo-clairvoyants, stupid fools.

Before the terrible and glorious majesty of the Father, we are nothing but miserable particles of dust, horrible worms in the mud. What I am stating in this paragraph is neither an allegorical nor a symbolic matter. I am literally and bluntly asserting a terrible reality.

Indeed, it is the "I" that says, "I am the master such-and-such, the reincarnation of the prophet so-and-so," etc. Certainly the animal "I" is Satan. It is the "I," the ego-devil, who feels itself to be a master, mahatma, hierophant, prophet, etc.

Consciousness, Subconsciousness, and Supraconsciousness

Consciousness, subconsciousness, and supraconsciousness are summarized into only one thing: human consciousness. Therefore, we need to awaken the consciousness. Whosoever awakens the consciousness becomes supraconscious, reaches the heights of supraconsciousness. That one becomes a true illuminated clairvoyant, a Turiya. It is urgent to convert the subonsciousness into consciousness and totally awaken the consciousness.

It is necessary for the totality of the consciousness to become absolutely awakened. Only the person who has the totality of their consciousness awakened is a true clairvoyant, an illuminated one, a Turiya.

The so-called infraconsciousness, unconsciousness, and subconsciousness etc., are only different forms or zones of the sleeping consciousness. It is urgent to awaken the consciousness in order to become an illuminated one, a clairvoyant, a supraconscious one.

The Six Fundamental Dimensions

Beyond the three known dimensions—length, width, and height—is the fourth dimension; this dimension is Time. Beyond Time we have the fifth dimension; this dimension is Eternity. Moreover, we asseverate that beyond Eternity is a sixth dimension; this sixth dimension is beyond Eternity and Time. In this sixth fundamental dimension is where total liberation begins. Therefore, only the person who awakens in all the six fundamental dimensions of space is a true clairvoyant, a Turiya, a legitimate, enlightened one.

Venustic Initiations
SERPENTS OF LIGHT

8th Entrance into the Tomb
7th Crucifixion on Golgotha
6th Christification of the spiritual soul
5th Mount of Olives
4th Entrance into Jerusalem
3rd Transfiguration of Jesus
2nd The Baptism of John
1st Birth in the Manger

Initiation of Tiphereth

ENTRANCE INTO THE
STRAIGHT
PATH
PATH OF THE
BODHISATTVA

1 — INITIATION

NIRVANIC PARADISES

SPIRAL PATH

Major Mysteries
SERPENTS OF FIRE

7th Kundalini of Atmic Body
6th Kundalini of Buddhic Body
5th Creation of Causal Body
4th Creation of Mental Body
3rd Creation of Astral Body
2nd Kundalini of Vital Body
1st Kundalini of Physical Body

ENTRANCE INTO INITIATION

FORGE OF
HEPHAESTUS

PROBATIONARY TRIALS
Minor Mysteries

THE FIRST MOUNTAIN

Chapter 19
Initiation

Initiation is your own life. If you want initiation, write it upon a staff. Whosoever has understanding let them understand, because there is wisdom within. Initiation is neither bought nor sold. Avoid those schools that give initiations by correspondence. Avoid all those who sell initiations. Initiation is something very intimate to the soul. The "I" does not receive initiations. Therefore, those who say, "I have so many initiations," "I have such-and-such degrees," are liars and fakes, because the "I" does not receive initiations or degrees.

There are nine initiations of Minor Mysteries and five important initiations of Major Mysteries. The soul is the one who receives the initiations. This is a very intimate matter; something that one must not go about speaking of, nor something that must be told to anyone.

Indeed, all the initiations and degrees that many schools of the physical world confer have no value whatsoever in the superior worlds, because the masters of the White Lodge only recognize the legitimate initiations of the soul as genuine. These are completely internal.

The disciple can ascend the nine arcades, pass through all the nine initiations of Minor Mysteries, without having worked in the Arcanum A.Z.F. (Sexual Magic). Nevertheless, it is impossible to enter the Major Mysteries without Sexual Magic (the Arcanum A.Z.F.)

In Egypt, everyone who reached the Ninth Sphere would inevitably receive by word of mouth the terrific secret of the Great Arcanum (the most powerful arcanum, the Arcanum A.Z.F.).

The Guardian of the Threshold

The first ordeal that the candidate has to face is the trial of the Guardian of the Threshold. This Guardian is the reflection of the "I," the intimate depths of the "I." Many are they who fail this terrible ordeal.

In the internal worlds, the candidate has to invoke the Guardian of the Threshold. A terrifying electrical hurricane precedes the terrible apparition.

The larva of the threshold is armed with a terrible, hypnotic power. In fact, this monster has all the horrible ugliness of our own sins. It is the living mirror of our own evil deeds. The clash is terrible: it is a face to face and hand to hand battle. If the Guardian wins, the candidate becomes enslaved by the horrible monster. However, if the candidate is victorious, the monster of the threshold flees terrified. Then a metallic sound shakes the universe and the candidate is received in the Children's Chamber. This reminds us of that requisition uttered by the hierophant Jesus Christ who stated:

"Except ye become as little children, ye shall not enter into the kingdom of heaven." —Christian Bible, Matthew 18:3

In the Children's Chamber, the candidate is welcomed by the holy masters. The happiness is immense because a human being has entered the path of initiation. The entire College of Initiates (Children) congratulate the candidate. The candidate has defeated the first Guardian. This ordeal takes place in the astral world.

The Second Guardian

The Guardian of the Threshold has a second aspect, the mental aspect. We must know that the mind which the present human being possesses is still not a human mind. The present human being's mind is found in an animal stage.

Therefore, in the mental plane each person has the animal physiognomy that corresponds with his character. There, the cunning person is a real fox. The passionate person appears as a dog or a male goat, etc.

The encounter with the Guardian of the Threshold in the plane of the mind is even more frighteningly horrible than in the astral plane. Really, the second Guardian is the great Guardian of the Threshold of the World. The struggle with the second Guardian is usually very horrible. The candidate is the one who must invoke the second Guardian in the mental plane. The Guardian comes preceded by a horrifying electrical hurricane. If the candidate is victorious, they are received with a warm welcome in the Children's Chamber within the mental plane. However, if they fail, they remain enslaved by the horrible monster. All our mental crimes are personified in this larva.

The Third Guardian

The encounter with the third Guardian takes place in the world of the will. The Demon of Evil Will is the most terrible of the three. People do their personal will. The masters of the White Lodge do only the will of the Father, "on Earth as it is in Heaven."

When the candidate becomes victorious in the third ordeal, they are again welcomed in the Children's Chamber. The music is ineffable, the festivity solemn...

The Hall of Fire

After the candidate has triumphed in the three basic ordeals of the Guardian of the Immense Region, they must then enter into the Hall of Fire. There, the flames purify the candidate's internal vehicles.

The Ordeals of Fire, Air, Water, and Earth

In the ancient Egypt of the Pharaohs, these four ordeals had to be courageously faced in the physical world. Now the candidates have to pass these four ordeals in the suprasensible worlds.

The initiate must face his own defects and errors through the process of psychological tests. These tests come in the form of ordeals related to the elements (left) which push the defects and errors to the surface so they can be seen, comprehended, and eliminated. The initiate must battle against himself with the club of Heracles (willpower).

THE FOUR ORDEALS, FROM ATALANTA FUGIENS, BY MICHAEL MAIER, 1618

The Ordeal of Fire

The candidate is exposed to this ordeal in order to examine their serenity and sweetness. The wrathful and choleric inevitably fail this ordeal. The candidate experiences being persecuted, insulted, wronged etc. Many are those who react violently and return to the physical body having failed completely.

However, the victorious ones are received in the Children's Chamber and are welcomed with delightful music, the music of the spheres. The flames horrify the weak.

The Ordeal of Air

Those who despair because they lose something or someone, those who fear poverty, those who are not willing to lose what they love the most, fail in the ordeal of air. The candidate is thrown into the depths of a precipice. The weak ones cry out and return terrified to the physical body. However, the victorious ones are received in the Children's Chamber with festivities and greetings.

The Ordeal of Water

The great ordeal of water is really terrible. The candidate
is thrown into the ocean and they believe themselves to be
drowning. Those who do not know how to adapt themselves
to the various social conditions of life, those who do not know
how to live among the poor, those who after being shipwrecked
in the ocean of life reject the struggle and prefer to die, they,
the weak ones, inevitably fail in the ordeal of water. However,
the victorious ones are received in the Children's Chamber
with cosmic festivities.

The Ordeal of Earth

We must learn how to take advantage of the worst adversities. The worst adversities bring us the best opportunities. We
must learn to smile before all adversities. This is the law.

Those who succumb to pain before the adversities of existence cannot victoriously pass the ordeal of earth.

In the superior worlds the candidate finds themselves between two enormous mountains that menacingly close in upon
them. If the candidate screams with horror, they then return
as a failure into their physical body. However, if they are serene,
they become victorious and are received in the Children's
Chamber with great festivity and immense happiness.

The Initiations of Minor Mysteries

When the candidate becomes successful in all the introduc-
tory ordeals to the path, they have the absolute right to enter
into the Minor Mysteries. Each of the nine initiations of Minor
Mysteries are attained within the innermost consciousness.
Thus, if the student has a good memory, they then can bring
into their physical brain the memory of those initiations. However, when the candidate's memory is not good, then the poor
neophyte is unaware in the physical world of all that which
they learn and receive in the superior worlds. Therefore, those
who wish to be aware in the physical world of all that happens
to them during initiation have to develop their memory. It is

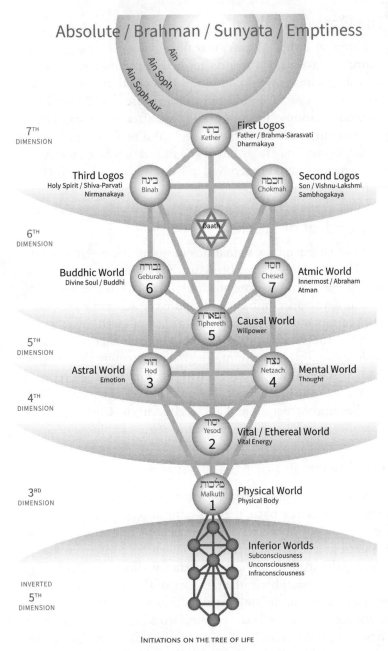

Absolute / Brahman / Sunyata / Emptiness

Ain
Ain Soph
Ain Soph Aur

7TH DIMENSION

First Logos
Father / Brahma-Sarasvati
Dharmakaya

בתר
Kether

Third Logos
Holy Spirit / Shiva-Parvati
Nirmanakaya

בינה
Binah

חכמה
Chokmah

Second Logos
Son / Vishnu-Lakshmi
Sambhogakaya

Daath

6TH DIMENSION

Buddhic World
Divine Soul / Buddhi

גבורה
Geburah
6

חסד
Chesed
7

Atmic World
Innermost / Abraham
Atman

הפארת
Tiphereth
5

Causal World
Willpower

5TH DIMENSION

Astral World
Emotion

הוד
Hod
3

נצח
Netzach
4

Mental World
Thought

4TH DIMENSION

יסוד
Yesod
2

Vital / Ethereal World
Vital Energy

3RD DIMENSION

מלכות
Malkuth
1

Physical World
Physical Body

Inferior Worlds
Subconsciousness
Unconsciousness
Infraconsciousness

INVERTED 5TH DIMENSION

INITIATIONS ON THE TREE OF LIFE

The nine Minor Mysteries correspond to the ninth regions
of the inferior worlds (hell realms). The Major Mysteries
correspond to the sephiroth of the Tree of Life.

urgent that the candidate develop their memory. It is urgent for the candidate to learn how to consciously depart within the astral body. It is urgent for the candidate to awaken their consciousness.

The nine initiations of Minor Mysteries constitute the probationary path. The nine initiations of Minor Mysteries are for the disciples who are on trial.

The married disciples who practice the Arcanum A.Z.F. pass these nine elementary initiations very rapidly. However, when the disciple is celibate and absolutely chaste, they can also pass the nine initiations, although more slowly. Fornicators cannot receive any initiation.

The Initiations of Major Mysteries

There are five great initiations of the Major Mysteries.[138] There are seven serpents: two groups of three, with the sublime coronation of the seventh tongue of fire that unites us with the One, with the Law, with the Father. We need to climb the septenary scale of fire.

The first initiation is related with the first serpent, the second initiation with the second serpent, the third initiation with the third serpent, the fourth initiation with the fourth serpent, the fifth initiation with the fifth serpent (the sixth and seventh belong to Buddhi, or soul consciousness, and to Atman, or the Innermost of the human being).

The First Initiation of Major Mysteries

The first serpent corresponds to the physical body. It is necessary to raise the first serpent through the medullar canal of the physical body. When the serpent reaches the magnetic field at the root of the nose, the candidate attains the first initiation of Major Mysteries. The soul and the Spirit come before the great White Lodge without the bodies of sin[139] and

---

138 "There are nine initiations of Minor Mysteries, and nine of Major Mysteries." —*Aztec Christic Magic*. In this book, the author is only addressing the initial initiations of Major Mysteries.

139 The lunar mental, astral, vital, and physical bodies. They were created by

in complete absence of the "I." They look at each other, they love and fuse as two flames which unite to form a single flame. Thus, this is how the divine hermaphrodite[140] is born, and receives a throne in order to command and a temple in order to officiate. We must transform ourselves into kings and priests of Nature according to the Order of Melchizedec.[141] Whosoever receives the first initiation of Major Mysteries, receives the flaming sword that gives them power over the four elements of Nature. We need to practice Sexual Magic intensely in order to raise the serpent upon the staff, as Moses did in the wilderness. Love is the basis and foundation of initiation. It is necessary to know how to love. The struggle in order to raise the serpent is very difficult. The serpent must rise slowly degree by degree. There are thirty-three vertebrae. There are thirty-three degrees. In each vertebra the tenebrous ones attack us terribly. The Kundalini rises very slowly in accordance with the merits of the heart. We need to terminate all of our sins.

It is urgent to tread the path of the most absolute sanctity.

It is indispensable to practice Sexual Magic without animal desire. Not only must we kill desire, but the very shadow of desire. We need to be like the lemon. The sexual act must become a true religious ceremony. Jealousy must be eliminated. You must know that passionate jealousy terminates household peace.

---

mechanical nature, belong to mechanical nature, and are thus perishable and unreliable.

140 (Greek) Hermaphrodite is from Hermes (male) + Aphrodite (female). Physically, hermaphrodite refers to the human being of the Lemurian epoch, who had both male and female sexual organs and characteristics in the physical body and reproduced the species without sexual intercourse. A true hermaphrodite produces both sperm and ovum, and reproduces by fecundating one egg with one sperm. Esoterically, the word hermaphrodite can refer to those who have developed spiritually to the point that they no longer require sexual cooperation, or to describe one who physically develops objective reasoning (Hermes) by means of the transmutation of the sexual power (Aphrodite).

141 "Malkhi-tzedek king of Salem brought forth bread and wine. He was a priest to God, the Most High. He blessed [Abram]..." —Genesis / Bereshit 14:18-20

The Second Initiation of Major Mysteries

The ascent of the second serpent through the medullar canal of the ethereal body[142] is very difficult. When the second serpent reaches the magnetic field at the root of the nose, the initiate then enters into the temple in order to receive the second initiation of Major Mysteries. It is good to emphasize that the human personality does not enter into the temple. The personality remains at the door putting its affairs in order with the Lords of Karma.[143]

The Innermost, together with his ethereal body, is crucified within the temple. That is to say, the Innermost clothes himself with the ethereal body for the crucifixion. This is how the ethereal body is Christified. To Soma Psuchikon,[144] the Wedding Garment[145] of the soul, the body of gold, is born in the second initiation. This vehicle is formed with the two superior ethers.[146] The ethereal body has four ethers, two superior and

---

142 Also known as the vital body. It is the subtle aspect of the physical body, composed of the energy or vital force that provides life to the physical body. In Tibetan Buddhism, the vital body is known as the subtle body (*lus phra-mo*). The ethereal / vital body corresponds to the fourth dimension, which in Kabbalah is called Yesod (foundation).

143 Causality, the law of cause and effect, is managed and balanced by awakened masters. Read *Hell, the Devil, and Karma* by Samael Aun Weor.

144 (Greek σῶμα ἡλιακόν) Literally, "The golden body of the solar man." A reference to the solar bodies, the soul, represented in various religions by the wedding garment, the chariot of Ezekiel, Krishna or Apollo, etc.

145 From a parable of Jesus: "Then saith he to his servants, The wedding is ready, but they which were bidden were not worthy. Go ye therefore into the highways, and as many as ye shall find, bid to the marriage. So those servants went out into the highways, and gathered together all as many as they found, both bad and good: and the wedding was furnished with guests. And when the king came in to see the guests, he saw there a man which had not on a wedding garment: And he saith unto him, Friend, how camest thou in hither not having a wedding garment? And he was speechless. Then said the king to the servants, Bind him hand and foot, and take him away, and cast him into outer darkness; there shall be weeping and gnashing of teeth. For many are called, but few are chosen." —Matthew 22

146 "It is written that the vital body or the foundation of organic life within each one of us has four ethers. The chemical ether and the ether of life are related with chemical processes and sexual reproduction. The chemical ether is a specific foundation for the organic chemical

two inferior. Thus, with the Wedding Garment of the soul we can enter all the regions of the Kingdom.

This initiation is very difficult. The student is severely tested. If they are victorious, the midnight sun shines, and from it descends the five-pointed star with its central eye. This star comes to rest above the head of the neophyte as a sign of approval. The result of the victory is the Initiation.

The Third Initiation of Major Mysteries

The third serpent rises through the medullar canal of the astral specter. The third serpent must reach the magnetic field at the root of the nose, and then from there descend to the heart through a secret passageway within which there are seven holy chambers.

When the third serpent reaches the heart, a most beautiful child, the Christ-astral is born. The outcome of all this is the initiation. The neophyte has to experience within their astral body the entire drama of the Passion of Christ. One has to be crucified, die and be buried. One has then to resurrect and must also descend to the Abyss and remain there for forty days before the Ascension.

The supreme ceremony of the third initiation is attained with the Christ-astral. Upon the altar appears Sanat Kumara,[147] the Ancient of Days, in order to grant us the initiation.

Everyone who attains the third initiation of Major Mysteries receives the Holy Spirit.

To attain this initiation, it is necessary to know how to love our spouse. The sexual union must be filled with immense

---

phenomena. The ether of life is the foundation of the reproductive and transformative sexual processes of the race. The two superior ethers, luminous and reflective, have more elevated functions. The luminous ether is related with the caloric, luminous, perceptive, etc., phenomena. The reflective ether serves as a medium of expression for willpower and imagination." —Samael Aun Weor, *The Gnostic Bible: The Pistis Sophia Unveiled*

147 Sanatkumar सनत्कुमार, "eternal youth." Founder of the College of Initiates of the White Lodge, a venerable elder mentioned in very ancient religions. Sanat Kumar is one of the four kumaras, the Four Thrones of which the Bible speaks. Three are gone and only he remains.

love. The phallus must always enter the vulva very gently, in order not to harm the organs of the woman. Each kiss, each word, each caress, must be totally free of desire. Animal desire is a very grave obstacle for the initiation. Upon reading these lines, many puritanical people will judge us as being immoral. Nonetheless, those people are never scandalized by brothels and prostitutes. They insult us, but they are incapable of going to the neighborhoods where the prostitutes live in order to preach the upright doctrine. They hate us, but they are incapable of abhorring their own sins. They condemn us because we preach the religion of sex, but they are incapable of condemning their own fornication. This is how humanity is.

The Fourth Initiation of Major Mysteries

When the fourth serpent has succeeded in the ascent through the medullar canal of the mental specter, then the fourth initiation of Major Mysteries is attained. The fourth serpent also reaches the space between the eyebrows and descends to the heart.

In the world of the mind, Sanat Kumara always welcomes the candidate saying, "You have liberated yourself from the four bodies of sin. You are a Buddha.[148] You have entered the world of the gods. You are a Buddha. Everyone who liberates themselves of the four bodies of sin is a Buddha. You are a Buddha. You are a Buddha."

The cosmic festivity of this initiation is grandiose. The entire world, the entire universe trembles with happiness, saying, "A new Buddha has been born." The Divine Mother Kundalini

---

148 "awakened one, enlightened, sage, knowledge, wise one." adj. "awake, conscious, wise, intelligent, expanded." Commonly used to refer simply to the Buddha Shakyamuni (the "founder" of Buddhism), the term Buddha is actually a title. There are a vast number of Buddhas, each at different levels of attainment. At the ultimate level, a Buddha is a being who has become totally free of suffering. The Inner Being (Hebrew: Chesed; Sanskrit: Atman) first becomes a Buddha when the Human Soul completes the work of the fourth initiation of Fire (related to Netzach, the mental body).

presents her child in the temple saying, "This is my beloved child. This is a new Buddha. This is a new Buddha. This is a new Buddha." The holy women congratulate the candidate with a sacred kiss. The festival is terribly divine. The great masters of the mind extract from within the mental specter the beautiful child of the Christ-mind. This child is born in the fourth initiation of Major Mysteries. Everyone who receives the fourth initiation gains Nirvana. Nirvana is the world of the holy gods.

Whosoever reaches the fourth initiation receives the globe of the imperator of the mind. The sign of the cross shines upon this globe.

The mind must be crucified and stigmatized in the initiation. The universal fire sparkles within the world of the mind. Each of the thirty-three chambers of the mind teaches us terrible truths.

The Fifth Initiation of Major Mysteries

The fifth serpent rises through the medullar canal of that embryo of the soul that we have incarnated. The fifth serpent must reach the eyebrows and then descend to the heart.

The body of conscious will is born in the fifth great initiation. Everyone who is born in the world of the conscious will inevitably incarnates their soul. Everyone who incarnates their soul becomes a true human being with soul. Every true complete and immortal human being is an authentic master. Before the fifth initiation of Major Mysteries no one must be called by the title of master.

In the fifth initiation we learn to do the will of the Father. We must learn to obey the Father. This is the law.

In the fifth initiation we must decide between two paths, which one to take to continue on: either to remain in Nirvana enjoying the infinite bliss of the boundless sacred space, sharing with the ineffable gods, or rather to renounce that immense bliss of Nirvana and remain living in this valley of tears in order to help the poor suffering humanity.

Renunciation, the long path of woe and bitterness is different. Whosoever renounces Nirvana in order to live to benefit mankind later attains the Venustic Initiation, this after Nirvanas gained and lost from boundless pity and compassion for humanity.

Everyone who receives the Venustic Initiation incarnates the inner Christ. There are millions of Buddhas in Nirvana who have not incarnated the Christ. It is better to renounce Nirvana for the love of humanity and have the joy of incarnating the Christ. The Christ-human has the right to enter into worlds of supernirvanic bliss, and later, the Absolute.

The Perfect Matrimony

The way to cosmic realization is the path of the perfect matrimony. Victor Hugo, the great initiate humanist, textually stated the following:

Man and Woman by Victor Hugo

Man is the most elevated of creatures,
Woman the most sublime of ideals.

God made for man a throne;
For woman an altar.
The throne exalts, the altar sanctifies.

Man is the brain,
Woman, the heart.
The brain creates light, the heart, love.
Light engenders, love resurrects.

Because of reason,
Man is strong,
Because of tears,
Woman is invincible.
Reason is convincing, tears moving.

Man is capable of all heroism,
Woman of all martyrdom.
Heroism ennobles, martyrdom sublimates.

Man has supremacy,
Woman, preference.
Supremacy is strength, preference is the right.

Man is a genius,
Woman, an angel.
Genius is immeasurable, the angel indefinable.

The aspiration of man is supreme glory.
The aspiration of woman is extreme virtue.
Glory creates all that is great;
virtue, all that is divine.

Man is a code,
Woman a gospel.
A code corrects; the gospel perfects.

Man thinks,
Woman dreams.
To think is to have a worm in the brain,
to dream is to have a halo on the brow.

Man is an ocean,
Woman a lake.
The ocean has the adorning pearl,
the lake, dazzling poetry.

Man is the flying eagle,
Woman, the singing nightingale.
To fly is to conquer space.
To sing is to conquer the soul.

Man is a temple,
Woman a shrine.
Before the temple we discover ourselves,
before the shrine we kneel.

In short, man is found where earth finishes,
Woman where heaven begins.

These sublime phrases of the great initiate humanist Victor Hugo invite us to live the path of the perfect matrimony. Blessed be love. Blessed are the beings who adore each other.

The Food of the Serpent

The entire path of initiation is based on the serpent. This has its special cosmic food. There are five known basic elements with which the serpent is nourished, namely the philosophical earth, the elemental water of the wise, the elemental fire, the elemental air, and the ether. In these elements live the elementals of Nature. The gnomes inhabit the philosophical earth, the undines live in the water, the sylphs in the air, etc.

The gnomes work in the entrails of the great mountain range. This is the spinal column. The work carried out by the gnomes consists of the transmutation of the lead of the personality into the gold of the Spirit. The raw matter is the seminal fluid. The furnace of the laboratory is the coccygeal chakra. The water is the seminal fluid and the sympathetic cords form the great chimney through which the seminal vapors ascend to the distillery of the brain. All the work of the gnomes is alchemical. The metallic transmutation is the basis of initiation. The raw matter must be transmuted into Philosophical Gold.

THE KUNDLAINI IS NOURSHED BY SEXUAL ENERGY. LEFT: PERU. RIGHT: GREECE.

The gnomes need the fire of the salamanders and the water of the undines. The gnomes also need the vital air and the friendly sylphs of the mind, to move the seminal vapors inward and upward. The outcome is the transmutation of lead into gold. When the aura of the initiate is pure gold, the work has been completely performed.

The region of the earth extends from the feet to the knees. Its mantra is **LA** (ल).

The region of the water is from the knees to the anus. Its mantra is **VA** (व).

The region of the fire is from the anus to the heart. Its mantra is **RA** (र).

The region of the air encompasses the area from the heart to the space between the eyebrows. Its fundamental mantra is **YA** (य).

The region of the ether extends from the space between the eyebrows to the top of the head and the mantra is **HA** (ह).

The serpent of fire is nourished with these five basic elements. Now we can understand why the neophyte has to pass the ordeals of earth, water, fire, and air. The purifications and sanctifications related with these elements of Nature nourish the serpent and permit its ascent through the sacred mountain range of the spinal column. The ascent of the serpent is impossible without the purifications and sanctifications of these four elements.

THE TATTVAS & THE ELEMENTS

TATTVA	Akash	Vayu	Tejas	Apas	Prithvi
ELEMENT	Ether	Air	Fire	Water	Earth
COLOR	Black	Blue	Red	White	Yellow
MANTRA	ह Ha	य Ya	र Ra	व Va	ल La
PLANET	Saturn	Mercury	Mars	Venus, Moon	Sun
REGENT	Sadashiva	Ishvara	Rudra	Narayana	Brahma
ELEMENT	A.Z.F.	Grape juice	Meat	Fish	Cereals
ELEMENTAL	Punctas	Sylphs, fairies	Salamanders	Ondines, mermaids	Gnomes, pygmies

Brahma[149] is the god of the earth. Narayana[150] is the god of the water. Rudra[151] is the god of the fire. Ishvara[152] is the god of the air. Sadashiva[153] is the god of the ether.[154]

By meditating upon these ineffable gods, we can obtain their assistance for the awakening of the chakras, wheels, or discs of the vital body. It is advisable to make these magnetic centers vibrate in order to prepare them for the advent of the fire. Meditate and vocalize the mantra for each element. Concentrate your attention on each of these elemental gods and beg them to help you with the awakening of the chakras. In this way you will become a practical esotericist.

The Laboratory of the Third Logos

The Earth has nine strata; in the ninth is the laboratory of the Third Logos. Actually, the ninth stratum of the Earth lies exactly in the center of the planetary mass. There the Holy Eight resides. This is the divine symbol of the infinite (∞). In this symbol the brain, heart and sex of the planetary genie is represented. The name of this genie is Chamgam. The center of the Holy Eight corresponds to the heart and its upper and lower extremities to the brain and sex, respectively. All beings of the Earth are structured on this basis. The struggle is terrible:

---

149 The first aspect of the Hindu trimurti (trinity), the other two being Vishnu and Shiva. Brahma is a symbol of eternity, the immutable, the origin of creation, and the ultimate root of self.

150 A name of Vishnu. "The waters are called नार narah, (for) the waters are, indeed, the offspring of Nara; as they were his first residence (ayana), he thence is named Narayana." —Laws of Manu 1:10

151 A name of Shiva.

152 "Ishvara (the supreme master) is a very special Purusha who is exempted from sufferings, actions with results, and desires. Imagine the Universal Spirit of Life as an ocean without beaches, without shores. Think for a moment of a wave that emerges in order to get lost anew within its liquid element. Then, this diamantine wave would be Ishvara. Brahma, the ocean of the Spirit, manifests itself as Ishvara, who is the master of masters, the governor of the universe. Within Him, that omniscience (which in others only exists as a germ) becomes infinite." —Samael Aun Weor, *Magic of the Runes*

153 A Hindu symbol of the Absolute.

154 All of these details are from Yoga Tattva Upanishad 84-102

brain against sex, sex against brain, and that which is most terrible, that which is most grave and painful: heart against heart.

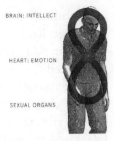

BRAIN: INTELLECT

HEART: EMOTION

SEXUAL ORGANS

THE HOLY EIGHT

The sacred serpent is coiled in the heart of the Earth, precisely in the Ninth Sphere. She is septuple in her constitution, and each of her seven igneous aspects corresponds to one of the seven serpents of the human being.

The creative energy of the Third Logos elaborates the chemical elements of the Earth, with all its multifaceted complexity of form. When this creative energy withdraws from the center of the Earth, our world will then become a cadaver; this is how worlds die.

The serpentine fire of the human being emanates from the serpentine fire of the Earth. The terrific serpent profoundly sleeps within its mysterious nest of strange hollow spheres, similar in fact to a true Chinese puzzle. These are subtle concentric astral spheres. Indeed, just as the Earth has nine concentric spheres in the depths of which is the terrific serpent, so too does the human being, because we are the microcosm of the macrocosm.

The human being is a universe in miniature. The infinitely small is analogous to the infinitely large.

Hydrogen, carbon, nitrogen, and oxygen are the four basic elements with which the Third Logos works. The chemical elements are placed in order of their atomic weights. The lightest is hydrogen, whose atomic weight is 1, ending up with uranium, whose atomic weight is 238.5 and which is in fact the heaviest of the known elements.

The electrons constitute a bridge between Spirit and matter. Hydrogen in itself is the most rarefied element known, the primary manifestation of the serpent. Every element, every food, every organism is synthesized into a specific type of hydrogen. Sexual energy corresponds to Hydrogen 12 and its musical note is Si.

The electronic solar matter is the sacred fire of Kundalini.

When we free this energy, we enter the path of authentic initiation.

Chac Mool

The Chac Mool of Aztec Mexico is marvelous. Chac Mool in fact existed. He was an incarnated adept, one of the great initiates of the powerful serpentine civilization of ancient Mexico and of the great Tenochtitlan. The tomb of Chac Mool was located and his remains found. Therefore, there can be no doubt that Chac Mool really existed.

CHAC MOOL

If one observes the manner in which Chac Mool is reclining, one sees that he is resting in the same position that the Egyptian initiates assumed when they wanted to leave in the astral body while pronouncing the mantra **FA-RA-ON**.

Nevertheless, something curious appears in the umbilical region of Chac Mool. It is a wide bowl or receptacle, as if to receive something. In fact, the solar plexus is marvelous. Chac Mool left humanity a great teaching.

The Kundalini or igneous serpent of our magical powers has a great deposit of solar energy in the umbilical region within the solar plexus chakra. This magnetic center is very important in initiation because it is the one that receives the primary energy which is subdivided into ten splendorous radiations. This primary energy circulates through the secondary nervous canals, animating and nourishing all the chakras. The solar plexus is governed by the Sun. If the student wants to have really vigorous objective clairvoyance in the most complete sense of the word, the student must learn to take the solar energy from its deposit in the solar plexus to the frontal chakra. The mantra **SUI-RA** is the key that permits us to extract solar energy from the plexus of the Sun in order to carry it to the frontal chakra. Vocalize in this way: SUIII RAAA. When practiced for one hour daily, the result will be the positive awakening of the frontal chakra. If we want solar strength for the laryngeal chakra, we must vocalize the mantra SUE-RA in this way: SUEEE RAAA. If we need solar energy for the lotus of the heart, we must vocalize the mantra SUO-RA in this way: SUOOO RAAA.

Everything is summarized in the great SUA-RA, where according to the Vedas and the Shastras the silent gandharva (heavenly musician) is found. It is necessary to know how to use the solar energy deposited in the solar plexus. It is good for the aspirants of initiation to lie down in the decubitus-dorsal position, feet on the bed, knees raised (see the graphic of Chac Mool). It is evident that by putting the soles of the feet on the bed, the knees are lifted, directed towards the sky, towards Urania.

While in the Chac Mool position the aspirant imagines that the energy of the Sun enters through the solar plexus making it vibrate and rotate from left to right, like the needles of a clock when we look at it from the front. This exercise can be done for one hour daily. The basic mantra of this magnetic center is the vowel **U**. This vowel can be vocalized by elongating the sound in this way: UUUUUU. A well awakened solar plexus marvelously animates all the chakras of the organism. Thus, this is how we prepare ourselves for initiation.

Chac Mool was venerated in serpentine Mexico. Two warrior castes worshiped him. Chac Mool was carried in great processions and entered the Aztec temples, worshiped by the multitudes. They also made supplications unto him asking for rain for the Earth. This great master helps those who invoke him. Tiny sculptures of Chac Mool can be made, or amulets of the figure of Chac Mool, in order to wear around the neck as a medallion.

Serpentine Civilizations

Authentic initiation was received in the great mystery temples of the serpentine civilizations. Only serpentine civilizations are true civilizations.

It is necessary that the vanguard of human civilization, made up of our beloved brothers and sisters—Theosophists, Rosicrucians, Hermetic yogis, Spiritualists, etc.—abandon their old prejudices and fears and unite together to create a new serpentine civilization. It is urgent to know that this barbarian populace of this day and age (wrongly called a civilization) is approaching its final catastrophe. The present world is struggling within a frightful chaos; if we really want to save it, we all need to be united in order to create a serpentine civilization, the civilization of Aquarius. We need to make a supreme and desperate effort in order to save the world, because right now everything is lost.

The universal Christian Gnostic movement is non-sectarian. The Gnostic movement is made up of the army of world salvation, of all spiritual schools, of all lodges, religions, and sects.

The Exoteric and Esoteric Circles

Humanity develops in two circles: the exoteric and the esoteric. The exoteric is public. The esoteric is secret. The multitudes live in the exoteric circle. However, the adepts of the great White Brotherhood live in the esoteric circle. It is an obligation for all the initiated brothers and sisters to help those who are within the public circle. It is necessary to bring as many people as possible into the secret circle of the White Brotherhood.

The initiatic path is a true revolution of the consciousness.

This revolution has three perfectly defined aspects: first, to be born, second, to die and third, to sacrifice ourselves for humanity, to give our life for humanity, to struggle in order to bring others to the secret path.

To be born is an absolutely sexual problem. To die is the work of the dissolution of the "I," the ego. Sacrifice for others is love.

In the public circle there are thousands of schools, books, sects, contradictions, theories, etc., a labyrinth which only the strongest leave. Really, all of those schools are useful. We find grains of truth in all of them. All religions are holy and divine, all of them are necessary. Nevertheless, the secret path is only found by the strongest. Infrasexual people mortally hate this path. They feel more perfect than the Third Logos. These people will never be able to find the secret path, the path of the razor's edge. The secret path is sex. Through this straight, narrow, and difficult path we reach the esoteric circle, the sanctum regnum Dei, magis regnum.[155]

The Chakras and the Plexuses

The candidate for initiation must profoundly know the position of the chakras and plexuses.

The fundamental is at the base of the spine, the fourth sacral vertebra, the coccygeal plexus.

The splenic is on the spleen, the first lumbar vertebra, the splenic plexus. This center obeys the solar plexus.

Nevertheless, we have to recognize that the true second center is the prostatic, or uterine, and not the splenic.

The umbilical is above the navel, the eighth thoracic vertebra, the solar plexus.

The cardiac is in the heart, the eighth cervical vertebra, the cardiac plexus.

The laryngeal is in the throat, the thyroid gland, the third cervical vertebra, the pharyngeal plexus.

The frontal is between the eyebrows, the first cervical vertebra, the carotid plexus.

It is urgent to know that the chakras and the plexuses are connected by means of nerve filaments.

As the serpent rises through the spinal column, the spinal chakras are put into activity, and by induction, the plexuses are also activated. The chakras are in the cerebrospinal nervous system and the plexuses in the sympathetic nervous system.

As the serpent rises through the medullar canal, it puts into full activity the spinal chakras or churches in successive order. These in turn make the corresponding sympathetic plexuses vibrate by electric induction. It is urgent to know that each spinal chakra and each sympathetic plexus is septuple in its internal constitution, just as the igneous serpent of our magical powers is.

The first serpent opens the chakras in the physical world, the second in the ethereal, the third in the astral, the fourth in the mental, the fifth in the causal, the sixth in the Buddhic

---

155 Latin, "holy kingdom of God, the greatest kingdom."

and the seventh in the Innermost. This process is the same for the plexuses, because the chakras or churches are connected to the plexuses by their nerve branches.

Then, the initiate should not despair because they have not opened the astral chakras with the first serpent. They are only opened by the third serpent, that of the astral. With the first, only counterparts of the physical are opened in the Innermost.

Bear in mind that the Innermost is the counterpart of the physical body.

Clarifications

Initiation cannot be bought with money or sent by mail. Initiation is neither bought nor sold. Initiation is your own life accompanied by the festivals of the temples.

It is necessary to avoid all those impostors who sell initiations. It is urgent to keep away from all those who send initiations by mail.

Initiation is something very intimate, very secret, very divine. Avoid all those who say, "I have so many initiations, so many degrees."

Avoid all those who say, "I am a master of Major Mysteries; I have received so many initiations."

Remember, dear reader, that the "I," that the personality does not receive initiations.

Initiation is a matter for the Innermost; it has to do with the consciousness, with the very delicate things of the soul. One must not go about speaking of these things. No true adept would ever use phrases like, "I am a master of the White Lodge," "I have such-and-such degree," "I have so many initiations," "I have these powers," etc.

The Problem of Internal Illumination

Many students of esotericism want internal illumination and suffer horribly because in spite of many years of study and esoteric practices, they remain as blind and unconscious as when they first began to read the first books. We, the brothers and sisters of the temple, know through our own experience that the cardiac chakra is definitive for internal illumination. The *Shiva Samhita*, a great Hindustani book, speaks at great length about the benefits obtained by the yogi on meditating on the chakra of the tranquil heart:

> *"The yogi acquires immense knowledge, knows the past, the present and the future; he has clairaudience and clairvoyance and can go through the air wherever he pleases. He sees the adepts and the yogini goddesses; he obtains the faculty called kheckari (to move through the air) and bhuchari (to go at will to all corners of the world)."*

Those who want to learn how to leave in the astral body at will, those who want to enter into the Jinn science, to learn how to place themselves within the fourth dimension with the physical body and travel with their physical body to any distant place in the world without the necessity of an airplane; those who urgently need to awaken their clairvoyance and clairaudience must concentrate their mind daily on the cardiac chakra and meditate profoundly on that marvelous center. To meditate on this center for one hour daily is marvelous. The mantra of this chakra is the vowel **O**, which is vocalized by prolonging the sound like this: OOOOOOOOOOOOOOOO.

During the former indicated practice, one must pray to Christ, asking him to awaken the heart chakra.

Summary of the Five Great Initiations

First Initiation. The Innermost and the Conscious Soul (Buddhi) are fused, thus creating a new initiate, one more who enters the stream.

Second Initiation. The ethereal body called Soma Psuchikon is born.

Third Initiation. The chakras of the astral body are opened and the Christ-astral is born as a beautiful child.

Fourth Initiation. The Christ-mind is born as a very precious child. The initiate has been born as a new Buddha.

Fifth Initiation. The Human Soul (causal body, body of will) is fused with the inner master, who is Atman-Buddhi (the

Innermost and Divine Consciousness). Thus, the three flames are one. This is a new and legitimate master of the Major Mysteries of the White Lodge. Whosoever reaches the fifth initiation can enter Nirvana. Whosoever reaches the fifth initiation is born in the causal world. Whosoever reaches the fifth initiation incarnates the soul. Only the person who reaches the fifth initiation is a human being with soul, that is to say, a true human.

The Vehicles of Fire

The authentic and legitimate astral, mental, and causal vehicles are born of Sexual Magic. It is obvious that during the copula between man and woman, the aura of the husband and wife is totally opened. Then, within our own depths, marvelous psychic fertilizations can be performed. The final outcome becomes precisely the birth of our legitimate astral, and later the birth of the other bodies in successive order.

Patience and Tenacity

Powers are not obtained by playing around. This is a question of much patience. The inconsistent people, those who go about looking for results, those who after a few months of practices are already demanding signs, indeed are not ready for esotericism. Such people are not good for these studies. Such people are not mature. We advise these people to become members of some religion and to wait a while until they mature. To tread the path of the razor's edge, one needs the patience of Saint Job. To tread the path of the razor's edge, we need the tenacity of very well-tempered steel.

Conscious Faith

Those people who enter practical esotericism, that are full of doubt, totally fail. Whosoever doubts our teachings is not prepared for the path of the razor's edge. For people like this it is best that they join some religion and beg the great Reality for the solar power of conscious faith.[156] Thus, when they have gained conscious faith, they are then ready to enter this strait, narrow, and difficult path. Whosoever doubts esotericism must not walk this difficult path, until the moment that they receive the power of conscious faith. The esotercist who doubts can become easily demented. Faith is a marvelous solar power.

Religions and Schools

All the religions and spiritual schools in the world are very necessary and serve as an antechamber to entry into the vestibule of wisdom. Therefore, we must never speak against these schools and religions because all are necessary for the world. In these schools and religions we receive the first light of spirituality. The worst would be a people without religion, a people who persecute those dedicated to spiritual studies.

In fact, a people without religion is monstrous. Each human group needs its school, its religion, its sect, its instructors, etc. Each human group is different, and therefore the different schools and religions are necessary.

Whosoever treads the path of initiation must know how to respect the beliefs of others.

Charity

Whosoever follows the path of the perfect matrimony must develop charity. Cruel and pitiless people do not progress in this path. It is urgent to learn how to love and always be willing to give even to the last drop of blood for others.

The warmth of charity opens all the doors of the heart. The warmth of charity brings solar faith to the mind. Char-

---

156 The modern use of the word faith is mistaken. Faith is not "belief," but actually means "confidence, trust, integrity." The modern interpretation as "belief" started in the 13th-16th centuries when the Christians were attempting to spread their teachings, and changed the meaning to "belief." In reality, faith is not equal to belief. From the same root are fid-el-i-ty, af-fi-ance, con-fide, de-fy, dif-fid-ent, per-fid-y, fiducial, faith, confidense, fiance, fiancee. Thus, we can now see why we still say an adulterer is "unfaithful."

ity is conscious love. The fire of charity develops the chakra of the heart. The fire of charity permits the sexual serpent to rise rapidly through the medullar canal. Whosoever wants to advance rapidly on the path of the razor's edge must practice Sexual Magic intensely and give themselves totally to the great universal charity. Thus, by sacrificing ourselves absolutely for our fellowmen and giving our blood and life for them, we will be rapidly Christified.

Psychic Development

Every sensation is an elemental change in the state of the psyche. There are sensations in each of the six basic dimensions of Nature and the human being, and they are all accompanied by elemental changes of the psyche.

Sensations that we experience always leave a trace in our memory. We have two types of memory: spiritual and animal. The first conserves the memories of sensations experienced in the superior dimensions of space; the second conserves the memory of the physical sensations. Memories of sensations constitute the perceptions.

Every physical or psychic perception is really the memory of a sensation.

The memories of sensations are organized into groups that associate or dissociate, attract or repel.

Sensations are bipolarized into two perfectly defined currents. The first obeys the character of the sensations. The second obeys the time of reception of the sensations.

The sum total of various sensations, converted into a common cause, is projected externally as an object. Then we say, this tree is green, high, low, has an agreeable smell, disagreeable, etc. When the perception is in the astral or in the mental world, we say, this object or subject has these qualities, this color etc. In this last case, the sum total of sensations is internal and its projection is also internal; it belongs to the fourth, fifth, or sixth dimensions, etc. We perceive physical perceptions with the physical apparatus, and the psychic with the psychic apparatus. In the same way that we have physical senses of perception, we also have psychic senses of perception. Everyone who follows the path of initiation has to develop these psychic senses.

Concepts are always formed with the memories of perceptions. Thus, the concepts transmitted by the great adept founders of religions are due to the transcendental memories of their psychic perceptions.

The formation of perceptions leads to the formation of words, and the appearance of language. The formation of internal perceptions leads to the formation of the mantric language, and the appearance of the Language of Gold spoken by adepts and angels.

The existence of language is impossible when there are no concepts, and there are no concepts when there are no perceptions. Those who toss about concepts of the internal worlds without ever having perceived them, as a rule falsify reality, although they do so with good intentions.

In the elemental levels of psychic life, many sensations are expressed with screams, howls, sounds etc., which reveal joy or terror, pleasure or pain. This happens in the physical world and also in the internal worlds.

The appearance of language represents a change in consciousness. Thus also, when the disciple has already begun to speak in the universal cosmic language, a change in consciousness has been made. Only the universal fire of the serpent and the dissolution of the reincarnating ego can bring about such a change.

Concept and word are one and the same substance. The concept is internal and the word is external. This process is similar in all the levels of consciousness and in all dimensions of space. Ideas are only abstract concepts. Ideas are much larger concepts and belong to the world of spiritual archetypes.[157] Every existing thing in the physical world is a copy of those archetypes. During Samadhi, the initiate can visit the world of spiritual archetypes in astral or super-astral journeys.

The mystical content of the transcendental sensations and emotions cannot be expressed in common language. Words

---

157 In Kabbalah, the world of Atziluth.

can only suggest them, indicate them. Actually, only the royal art of nature can define these superlative and transcendental emotions. Royal art was known in every serpentine civilization. The pyramids of Egypt and Mexico, the millenarian sphinx, the ancient monoliths, the sacred hieroglyphs, the sculptures of the gods etc., are archaic testimony of the royal art that only speaks to the consciousness and to the ears of initiates. The initiate learns this royal art during mystical ecstasy.

Space, with its properties, is a form of our sentient receptivity. We can verify this when through the development of the chakras we are able to perceive all space in four-dimensional form instead of the three-dimensional form to which we were previously accustomed.

The characteristics of the world change when the psychic apparatus changes. The development of the chakras makes the world change for the initiate. With the development of the chakras, we eliminate from our mind the subjective element of perceptions. "Subjective" is that which does not have reality. "Objective" is that which is spiritual, the reality.

With the awakening of the chakras by means of internal discipline comes an increase in psychic characteristics. The novelty in the psychic field obscures the changes taking place simultaneously in the perception of the physical world. The new is felt, but the initiate is not capable of logically defining and axiomatically the scientific difference between the old and the new. The result of such incapacity is the lack of perfect conceptual equilibrium. It is thus urgent to achieve conceptual equilibrium, so that the doctrinary exposition of the initiates may correctly fulfill its intention.

The change of consciousness is the true objective of esoteric discipline.

We need cosmic consciousness; this is the sense of consciousness of the cosmos; this is the life and order of the universe.

Cosmic consciousness brings into existence a new type of intellectualism: illuminated intellection. This faculty is a characteristic of the superhuman. There are three types of consciousness: first, simple consciousness, second, individual self-consciousness, and third, cosmic consciousness. The animals have the first, the intellectual animal called a human being, the second. The gods have the third. When cosmic consciousness is born in the human being, we feel internally as if the fire of the serpent were consuming us. The flash of Brahmanic[158] splendor penetrates our mind and consciousness, and from that moment, we are initiated into a new and superior order of ideas. The Brahmanic delight has the flavor of Nirvana.

When the initiate has been illuminated by the Brahmanic fire, we enter the esoteric or secret circle of humanity. In that circle we find an ineffable family made up of those ancient hierophants who are known in the world as avatars, prophets, gods, etc. The members of this distinguished family are found in all of the advanced races of the human species. These beings are the founders of Buddhism, Taoism, Christianity, Sufism, etc. Actually, these beings are few, but despite being so few they are in truth the directors and leaders of the human species.

Cosmic consciousness has infinite degrees of development. The cosmic consciousness of a new initiate is inferior to that of an angel and that of the angel is not the same as the development of an archangel. In this there are degrees and degrees. This is Jacob's ladder.[159]

It is impossible to achieve cosmic consciousness without sanctity. It is impossible to obtain sanctity without love. Love is the path of sanctity. The most grandiose manifestation of love is found during Sexual Magic. In these moments the man and woman are a single, terribly divine hermaphroditic being.

Sexual Magic offers us all the internal conditions that are needed to receive the Brahmanic splendor.

Sexual Magic gives the devotee all the igneous elements necessary for the birth of cosmic consciousness.

For cosmic consciousness to appear, a certain degree of culture is required: the education of elements in affinity with cosmic consciousness and the elimination of those elements which are opposing the cosmic consciousness.

---

158 From Sanskrit Brahman, the Absolute; the Supreme Reality of non-dualistic Vedanta.

159 Judeo-Christian Bible, Bereshit / Genesis 28

The most characteristic features of those individuals who are prepared in order to receive the cosmic consciousness is that they look at the world as Maya (illusion).[160] They have the feeling that the world as people perceive it is only an illusion, and they search for the great reality, the spiritual, the truth, that which is beyond illusion. For the birth of cosmic consciousness, it is necessary for the human being to surrender themselves completely to the spiritual, to the internal.

Sexual Magic offers the initiate all the possibilities required to obtain Brahmanic splendor and the birth of the cosmic consciousness. It is urgent that Sexual Magic be combined with internal meditation and sanctity. In this way, we prepare ourselves to receive the Brahmanic splendor.

In reality, angels are perfect human beings. Therefore, whosoever reaches the perfect state of human being becomes an angel. Those who claim that an angel is inferior to humans are falsifying the truth. No one can achieve the angelic state if they have not previously reached the state of perfect human being. No one can achieve the state of perfect human being if they have not previously incarnated their soul. This is a sexual problem. The angel is born only within the true human beings. Cosmic consciousness is born only within the true human being.

---

160 Sanskrit माया literally "not That," meaning "not Truth." Here used to mean the illusory nature of appearances.

THE RESURRECTION BY CARL HEINRICH BLOCH, 1873

Chapter 20

Resurrection and Reincarnation

The beings who love each other can become immortal like the gods. Blissful is the one who can already eat the delicious fruits of the Tree of Life.[161] You must know, beloved ones, that there are two exquisite trees in Eden that even share the same roots. One is the Tree of Knowledge.[162] The other is the Tree of Life. The first gives you wisdom. The second makes you immortal.

Everyone who has worked in the Great Work has the right to eat of the delicious fruits of the Tree of Life. Indeed, love is the summum of wisdom.

Those men and women who follow the path of the perfect matrimony finally gain the bliss of entering Nirvana, which is to be oblivious of the world and people forever... It is impossible to describe the bliss of Nirvana. There, every tear has disappeared forever. There, the soul, divested of the four bodies of sin, submerges herself within the infinite joy of the music of the spheres. Nirvana is a sacred, star-filled space.

The masters of compassion, moved by human pain, renounce the great bliss of Nirvana and resolve to stay with us in this valley of great bitterness.

Every perfect matrimony inevitably reaches adepthood. Every adept can renounce Nirvana for the love of the great orphan.[163] When the adept renounces the supreme bliss of

---

161 "The fruit of the righteous [צדיק tsadik] is a tree of life... - Proverbs 11:30. Every religion is founded upon a mathematical, scientific basis, which in the Judeo-Christian is symbolized by the Tree of Life. Religions around the world also have a Tree of Life, though the means of representing it vary. In the Western religions, the Tree of Life is most known from the story of Genesis / Bereshit: "And out of the ground made יהוה אלהים [Jehovah Elohim] to grow every tree that is pleasant to the sight, and good for food; עץ החיים [the tree of lives] also in the midst of the garden, and the tree of knowledge of good and evil." —Genesis 2:9

162 Hebrew עץ הדעת טוב ורע, usually translated as "the tree of knowledge of good and evil." דעת Daath means "knowledge." טוב means "goodness." רע means "pollution" or "impurity."

163 Humanity.

Nirvana, the adept can then ask for the Elixir of Long Life. The blessed ones who receive this marvelous elixir die but do not die. On the third day they rise. This has already been demonstrated by the beloved one.

On the third day, the adept comes before the sepulcher accompanied by holy women who bring medicine and aromatic unguents. The angels of death and other ineffable hierarchies also accompany the adept.

The adept calls out in a great voice, invoking the physical body which sleeps within the holy sepulcher. The body is raised and can escape from the sepulcher taking advantage of the existence of hyperspace. In the superior worlds, the physical body is treated by the holy women with medicines and aromatic unguents. After the body has returned to life (obeying supreme orders), it enters the sidereal head of the Soul-Master. Thus, this is how the master regains possession of his glorified body. This is the precious gift of Cupid.

Every resurrected body normally lives within the superior worlds. Nevertheless, we must clarify that the resurrected masters can make themselves instantaneously visible and tangible in any place and then disappear. In this regard, the Count Cagliostro comes into our memory. This great master fulfilled a remarkable political mission in Europe and astounded the whole of humanity. This great master was really the one who provoked the fall of the kings of Europe. In fact, we owe the republic to him. He lived during the time of Jesus Christ, was a personal friend to Cleopatra, and worked for Catherine de Medici. He was known during various centuries in Europe. He used various names such as Giuseppe Balsamo, Count Cagliostro, etc.

The immortal Babaji, the yogi Christ of India, still lives in India. This master was the instructor of the great masters who lived through the terrifying night of time. Nevertheless, this sublime elder looks like a young man of twenty-five years.

Let us remember Count Zanoni, a youth despite his thousands of years. Unfortunately, this Chaldean sage failed completely because he fell in love with an actress from Naples. He committed the mistake of uniting with her and spilling the

Cup of Hermes. The result was horrible. Zanoni died on the guillotine during the French Revolution.

Resurrected masters travel from one place to another utilizing hyperspace. This can be demonstrated with hypergeometry. Astrophysics will soon discover the existence of hyperspace.

Sometimes after fulfilling a particular mission in a country, the resurrected masters allow themselves the luxury of passing for dead. On the third day, they repeat their resurrection and leave for another country in order to work under a different name. Thus, in this way, two years after his death, Cagliostro appeared in other cities using a different name in order to continue his work.

The perfect matrimony converts us into gods. Great is the bliss of love. In fact, only love confers upon us immortality.

Blessed be love; blessed be the beings who adore each other.

Resurrection and Reincarnation

Many students of esotericism confuse resurrection with reincarnation. The gospels have always been very poorly interpreted by esotericist students. There are various types of resurrection, just as there are various types of reincarnation. This is what we shall clarify in this chapter.

Every true adept has a body of paradise. This body is of flesh and bone. However, this is flesh that does not come from Adam. The body of paradise is formed from the best atoms of the physical organism.

Many adepts resurrect with this body of paradise within the superior worlds after death. Resurrected masters can visit the physical world and make themselves visible and tangible at will with this body of paradise. This is a type of ineffable resurrection. Nevertheless, we affirm that the resurrection with the mortal body of Adam, though more painful due to the return into this valley of bitterness, is because of this more glorious. All the adepts of the secret path who form the Guardian Wall have resurrected with the body of Adam.

There are also initiatic resurrections. The third initiation of Fire signifies the resurrection in the astral world. Everyone

who passes through the third initiation of Fire has to live the
drama of Christ within the astral world: his life, passion, death,
and resurrection.

Reincarnation of the Personality

The personality[164] is time. The personality lives in its own
time and does not reincarnate. After death, the personality also
goes to the grave. For the personality there is no tomorrow.
The personality lives in the cemetery, wanders about the cemetery or goes down into its grave. It is neither the astral body
nor the ethereal double. It is not the soul. It is time. It is energetic and it disintegrates very slowly. The personality can never
reincarnate. It does not ever reincarnate. There is no tomorrow
for the human personality.

That which continues, that which reincarnates, is not the
soul either because the human being still does not have soul.
In fact it is the ego that reincarnates, the "I," the reincarnating principle. The ghost of the defunct, the remembrance, the
memory, the error that is perpetuated.

Life-span

The unit of life of any living creature is equivalent to one
beat of its heart. Every living thing has a defined period of
time. The life of a planet is 2,700,000,000 beats. That same
quantity corresponds to the ant, the worm, the eagle, the
microbe, to humans and in general to all creatures. The life
span of each world and each creature is proportionally the
same. Indeed, the beat of a world occurs every 27,000 years, but
the heart of an insect beats more rapidly. An insect that lives
for only one summer evening has had in its heart the same

---

164 Latin personae: mask. We create a new personality in each physical
      body, in accordance with three influences: genotype, phenotype and
      paratype. Genotype is the influence of the genes, or in other words,
      karma, our inheritance from past actions. Phenotype is the education we
      receive from our family, friends, teachers, etc. Paratype is related to the
      circumstances of life (language, country, religion, etc).

number of beats as a planet, except that those beats were more rapid.

Time is not a straight line as the learned ignoramuses believe. Time is a closed curve.

Eternity is another thing. Eternity has nothing to do with time, and what is beyond eternity and time is known only by the great illuminated adepts, the masters of humanity.

There are three known dimensions and three unknown dimensions, a total of six fundamental dimensions. The three known dimensions are length, width, and depth. The three unknown dimensions are time, eternity, and what is beyond time and eternity. This is the spiral of six curves.

Time belongs to the fourth dimension. Eternity to the fifth dimension. That which is beyond eternity and time, to the sixth dimension.

The personality lives in a closed curve of time. Personality is a child of its time and ends with its time. Time cannot reincarnate. There is no tomorrow for the human personality.

The circle of time revolves within the circle of eternity. In eternity there is no time; however, time revolves within the circle of eternity. The serpent always bites its own tail. A time and a personality end, but with the turning of the wheel, a new time and a new personality appear upon the Earth. The ego is reincarnated and everything is repeated. All the sexual sensations and all the amorous drama which gives rise to a new physical body are caused by the last realizations, sentiments, preoccupations, affections and words. Therefore, all the romances of married couples and lovers are related to the defunct one's last agonizing moments. "The path of life is formed by the hoofprints of the horse of death." At death, time is closed and eternity is opened. The circle of eternity first opens and then closes when the ego returns to the circle of time.

Recurrence

The initiates of the Fourth Way define recurrence as the repetition of acts, scenes, and events.

Everything is repeated. The law of recurrence is a tremendous reality. In each incarnation the same events are repeated. The repetition of acts is accompanied by its corresponding karma. This is the law that reconciles effects to the causes which gave rise to them. Every repetition of acts carries karma and sometimes dharma (reward).

Those who work with the Great Arcanum, those who tread the straight, narrow and difficult path of the perfect matrimony, are liberated little by little from the law of recurrence. This law has a limit. Beyond that limit we become angels or devils. With White Sexual Magic we become angels. With Black Sexual Magic we become devils.

The Question of Personality

This subject matter about the personality, which is a child of its time and which dies in its time, deserves our attention. Indeed, it is completely evident that if the personality were to reincarnate, time then would also reincarnate, and this is absurd because time is a closed curve. An ancient Roman man reincarnated in these modern times of the twentieth century, with his Roman personality of that time of the Caesars, would in fact be intolerable. We would have to treat this Roman man as a delinquent because his customs would in no way correspond to those that we have today.

The Returns of the Ego

The symbol of Jesus expelling the merchants from the temple with a whip in hand is concerned with a tremendous reality of death and horror. We have already said that the "I" is pluralized. The "I," the ego, is a legion of devils. Many readers will not like this assertion; nonetheless, it is the truth, and we must utter this assertion even though we may not like it.

During the work on the demon, during the work of the dissolution of the ego, parts of the subhuman entities that possess part of our consciousness and our life are eliminated, cast out of our inner temple. Sometimes these entities reincarnate in animal bodies. While at the zoo, we could meet forms that have been discarded from ourselves, now living in animal bodies. There are people so animalistic that if everything animal was removed from them, nothing would remain. This class of people are lost cases. The law of recurrence has ended for these people. The law of reincarnation has ended for them. This type of person can incarnate into animal bodies or enter definitively into the Abyss. There they disintegrate slowly.

Advantages of Resurrection

Whosoever renounces Nirvana because of love for humanity is able to conserve their physical body for millions of years. Without resurrection, the adepts would find themselves with the necessity of changing bodies constantly. This would be an evident disadvantage. With the resurrection, the adept does not need to change the body. One can conserve the vehicle for millions of years.

The body of a resurrected adept is totally transformed. The soul within the body transforms it totally, converting it also into soul, until the adept totally becomes soul.

A resurrected body has its fundamental seat in the internal worlds. It lives in the internal worlds and only makes itself visible in the physical world by means of willpower. Thus, a resurrected master can instantaneously appear or disappear wherever they wish. No one can apprehend or incarcerate them. They travel within the astral plane to wherever they want.

The most interesting thing for the resurrected adept is "the great leap." When the time comes, the resurrected master can take their body to another planet. The resurrected master can live with their resurrected body on another planet. This is one of the great advantages.

Every resurrected adept is able to make the things of the astral world visible and tangible by transferring them into the physical plane. This can be explained because a master has their fundamental seat in the astral world even though they can manifest themselves physically. Cagliostro, the enigmatic Count Cagliostro, after his departure from the Bastille, invited his friends to a banquet. There, in the midst of the feast, he invoked many deceased spirits, who also sat at the table to the amazement of the guests.

On another occasion, as if by magic, Cagliostro made a precious golden dinner service appear from which his guests ate. The powerful Count Cagliostro transmuted lead into gold and made pure diamonds of the highest quality through the vivification of carbon.

The powers of every resurrected master are a true advantage.

A great friend, a resurrected adept who currently lives in the Great Tartary, told me the following: "Before swallowing soil, one is nothing but a fool. One thinks one knows a lot but knows nothing. One only really comes to be good when one has already swallowed soil; before this, one knows nothing." He also said to me, "The masters fall because of sex." This reminds us of Count Zanoni. He fell when he ejaculated the semen. Zanoni was a resurrected master. He fell in love with an actress from Naples and he fell. Zanoni died on the guillotine during the French Revolution.

Whosoever wants to achieve resurrection has to follow the path of the perfect matrimony. There is no other path. Only with Sexual Magic can we attain resurrection.

Only with Sexual Magic can we liberate ourselves from the wheel of reincarnations in a positive and transcendental manner.

The Loss of the Soul

In the preceding chapters, we have already said that the human being still has not incarnated the soul. Only with Sexual Magic can we engender the internal vehicles. These vehicles, as with plants, sleep latent within the hard darkness of the grain, the seed that is deposited in the seminal system. When the human being has the Christic vehicles, they can incarnate their soul. Whosoever does not work with the grain, whosoever does not practice Sexual Magic, cannot germinate their Christic bodies. Whosoever does not have Christic bodies cannot incarnate their soul. They lose their soul, and in the long term are submerged within the Abyss where they disintegrate slowly. Jesus, the great master, said:

For what is a man profited, if he shall gain the whole world, and lose his own soul? Or what shall a man give in exchange for his soul?

Whosoever does not incarnate their soul loses it. The one who does not have Christic vehicles does not incarnate soul. Whosoever does not work with the grain does not have Christic vehicles. Whosoever does not practice Sexual Magic does not work with the grain. The resurrection of the dead is only for humans with souls. In fact only humans with souls are true human beings in the complete sense of the word. Only true humans can achieve the great resurrection. Only humans with souls can endure the funeral trials of the Thirteenth Arcanum. These trials are more horrifying than death itself.

Those who do not have a soul are mere sketches of human beings, phantoms of death. That is all. The vehicles of humans without soul are ghostly vehicles; they are not the authentic vehicles of fire. In reality, humans without souls are not true human beings. In fact the human being is still a non-realized being. Very few are those who have soul. The great majority of beings who are called humans still do not have their souls. Of what use is it for man to accumulate all the riches of the world if he loses his soul?

The resurrection of the dead is only for humans with souls. Real immortality is only for humans with souls.

Love and Death

To many readers, it may seem strange that we relate love with death and resurrection. In Hindustani mythology, love and death are the two faces of the one deity. Shiva, the god of the universal sexual creative force, is at the same time the god of violent death and destruction. The wife of Shiva also has two faces. She is at one and the same time Parvati and Kali. As Parvati, she is supreme beauty, love, and happiness. As Kali or Durga, she can transform herself into death, disgrace, and bitterness.

Shiva and Kali together symbolize the Tree of Knowledge, the Tree of the Science of Good and Evil.

Love and death are twin brothers who never separate. The path of life is formed by the hoofprints of the horse of death.

The error of many cults and schools lies in being unilateral. They study death but do not want to study love, when in fact these are the two faces of the deity.

The diverse doctrines of the Orient and the Occident really believe that they know love, when in fact they do not. Love is a cosmic phenomenon in which the history of the Earth and its races are simple accidents.

Love is the mysterious magnetic and hidden force which the alchemist needs to fabricate the Philosophical Stone and the Elixir of Long Life, without which resurrection is impossible.

Love is a force that the "I" can never subordinate, because Satan can never subjugate God.

The learned ignoramuses are mistaken about the origin of love. The foolish are mistaken about its effect. It is stupid to suppose that the only objective of love is the reproduction of the species. In fact, love unfolds and develops in a very different plane, which the swine of materialism radically ignore.

Only an infinitesimal force of love is used for the perpetuation of the species. What happens to the rest of the force? Where does it go? Where does it develop? This is what the learned ignoramuses ignore.

Love is energy, and cannot be lost. The surplus of energy has other uses and purposes which people ignore.

The surplus of the energy of love is intimately related with thought, feeling, and will. Without sexual energy these faculties could not develop. The creative energy is transformed into beauty, thought, feeling, harmony, poetry, art, wisdom, etc.

The supreme transformation of creative energy produces, as a result, the awakening of consciousness and the death and resurrection of the initiate.

Indeed, all the creative activity of humanity comes from the marvelous force of love. Love is the marvelous force that awakens the mystical powers of the human being. Without love, the resurrection of the dead is impossible.

It is urgent to once again open the temples of love, to celebrate again the mystical festivals of love. The serpent of fire only awakens with the enchantments of love. If we want the resurrection of the dead, we first need to be devoured by the serpent. Whosoever has not yet been devoured by the serpent has no value whatsoever. If we want the Word to become flesh within us, we need to practice Sexual Magic intensely. The Word is in the sex. The lingam and yoni are the basis of all power.

First, we need to raise the serpent upon the staff, and then we need to be swallowed by the serpent. Thus, we become serpents. In India, the adepts are called nagas, serpents. The marvelous temple of the serpents is in Teotihuacan, Mexico. Only the serpents of fire can resurrect from the dead.

An inhabitant of a two-dimensional world with their two-dimensional psychology would believe that all the phenomena occurring in that plane would have their cause and effect, their birth and death only there. Such phenomena would for these beings be identical. All phenomena which originated from the third dimension would be taken by these two-dimensional beings as unique facts of their two-dimensional world; they would not accept being told of a third dimension, because for them, only their flat, two-dimensional world would exist. Nevertheless, if these flat beings would resolve to abandon their two-dimensional psychology in order to deeply comprehend the causes of all the phenomena of their world, they could then depart from it and discover with astonishment a great unknown world, the three-dimensional world. The same thing happens with the question of love. People believe that love is only to perpetuate the species. People believe that love is only vulgarity, carnal pleasure, violent desire, satisfaction, etc. Only the person who can see beyond these animal passions, only the person who renounces this type of animal psychology can discover in other worlds and dimensions the grandeur and majesty of that which is called love. People sleep profoundly.

People live sleeping, and dream about love, but they have not awakened themselves to love. They sing about love and believe that love is that which they dream about. When a human being awakens to love, they make themselves conscious of love, and recognize that they were dreaming. Then and only then do we discover the true meaning of love. Only then do we discover that which before we only dreamed of. Only then do we come to know that which is called love. This awakening is similar to that of the man who, being far away from the physical body in the astral body, realizes that he has awakened consciousness. People walk asleep in the astral. When someone realizes that he is dreaming and then says, "This is a dream. I am dreaming. I am in the astral body. I am outside of my physical body," the dream then disappears as if by magic, and the individual awakens within the astral world. A new and marvelous world appears before the one who before was dreaming: his consciousness has awakened. Now he can know all the marvels of Nature. Similarly is the awakening of love. Therefore, before that awakening, we only dream about love. We take those dreams as reality, believing that we are loving. Thus, we live in a world of passions, romances which are occasionally delectable, disillusions, vain oaths, carnal desires, jealousies, etc., and believe that this is love. We are dreaming, and we ignore it.

The resurrection of the dead is impossible without love, because love and death are the two faces of the same deity. It is necessary to awaken to love to attain resurrection.

It is urgent to renounce our three-dimensional psychology and the mundane facts in order to discover the meaning of love in the fourth, fifth, and sixth dimensions.

Love comes from the superior dimensions. Whosoever does not renounce their three-dimensional psychology will never discover the true meaning of love, because love does not have its origin in the three-dimensional world. The flat being who does not renounce their two-dimensional psychology would believe that the only reality in the universe is lines, the changes of color of the lines in the plane, etc. A flat being would ignore that the lines and the change of color in certain lines could be the result of the turning of a wheel with multicolored spokes, perhaps that of a carriage. The two-dimensional being would ignore the existence of such a carriage, and with their two-dimensional psychology would not believe in such a carriage.

They would only believe in the lines and the changes of color seen in their world without knowing that these are only effects of superior causes. Similarly are they who believe that love is only from this three-dimensional world and who only accept the mundane facts as the only true meaning of love. People like this cannot discover the true meaning of love. People like this cannot be devoured by the serpent of fire. People like this cannot resurrect from the dead.

All poets, all lovers, have sung of love; however, none of them really know that which is called love. People only dream about that which is called love. People have not awakened to love.

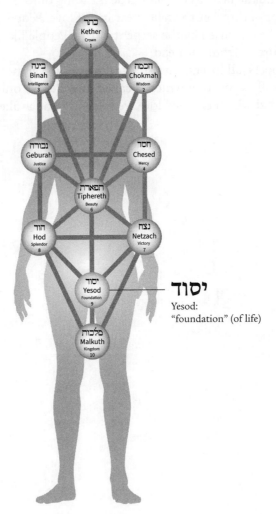

יסוד

Yesod:
"foundation" (of life)

THE NINTH SPHERE OF KABBALAH

Chapter 21

The Ninth Sphere

In the great ancient civilizations which have preceded us in the course of history, the descent into the Ninth Sphere was the greatest ordeal for the supreme dignity of the hierophant. Hermes, Buddha, Jesus, Dante, Zoroaster and many other great masters had to pass through that difficult ordeal.

Remember, most beloved disciples, that the Ninth Sphere is sex. Many are those who enter the Ninth Sphere; however, it is very rare to find anyone who can victoriously pass that difficult ordeal. Most students of esotericism live fluttering from school to school, from lodge to lodge, always curious, always in search of novelties, on the lookout for any new lecturer who arrives in the city. When any of those students resolve to work with the Arcanum A.Z.F., when any of those students resolve to descend to the Ninth Sphere in order to work with the fire and the water they do it as always, "searching," always curious, always "foolish." The student of esotericism turns everything into "little schools and theories." If they enter the Ninth Sphere, they do so as if they entered into another "little school," always an imbecile, always curious, always foolish. It is difficult to find a serious and determined aspirant of the truth on the path of the perfect matrimony. Sometimes students appear who appear very mature and serious; however, in the long run, they show what they are really made of. It is a sad truth, but a fact of life.

The ordeals of the Ninth Sphere are very fine and subtle. The doctor advises the devotee to fornicate, because otherwise, the doctor says, he will become ill. Tattling women stir up fear in the wife; the so-called brothers of different organizations frighten the student. The magicians of darkness, disguised as saints, advise the devotee to spill the semen in a saintly manner. The so-called sages teach the aspirant negative Sexual Magic with the spilling of the semen. The manner of teaching, the sublime and mystic tinge that the tenebrous ones (disguised as saints) give to their doctrine succeeds in misleading the devotee and keeps them away from the path of the razor's edge. Then the student falls into black magic.

When the student goes astray, they believe they are wiser than the masters of Gnosis. Indeed, the failures of the Ninth Sphere, those who do not succeed in passing the very long and hard ordeals of this arcanum, in fact become terribly perverse demons. Worst of all is that no demon believes themselves to be bad or perverse. Every demon believes themselves to be saintly and wise.

In the beginning, the practices of Sexual Magic affect the organism. Sometimes the sexual and parathyroid glands become inflamed, the head aches, one feels a certain dizziness, etc. This frightens the curious butterflies of the "little schools," who then flee terrified, looking as always for refuge in some new "little school." This is how these poor "fools" spend their lives, always moving from flower to flower. The day comes when these poor fools die, having achieved nothing. They have miserably wasted their time. Thus, when death arrives, these fools continue as a legion of demons.

The Ninth Sphere is definitive for the aspirant to the realization of the Self. It is impossible to intimately realize the Self without having incarnated the soul. No one can incarnate the soul if one has not engendered the Christ-astral, the Christ-mind, and the Christ-will. The present internal vehicles of the human being referred to by Theosophy are only simple mental forms that every human being must dissolve when they try to achieve intimate Realization of the Self.

We need to be born, and being born is, has been, and will always be an absolutely sexual problem. It is necessary to be born, and for that, one must descend to the Ninth Sphere. That is the greatest ordeal for the supreme dignity of the hierophant. That is the most difficult ordeal. It is very rare to find someone who can pass that difficult ordeal. As a rule, everybody fails in the Ninth Sphere.

It is necessary that husband and wife love each other deeply. People confuse desire with love. The whole world sings of desire, and this is confused with that which is called love. Only those who have incarnated their souls know what love is. The "I" does not know what love is. The "I" is desire.

Everyone who incarnates their soul becomes, as an outcome of that fact, a Buddha. Every Buddha must work in the Ninth Sphere to incarnate the Inner Christ. The Buddha is born within the Ninth Sphere. The Christ is born within the Ninth Sphere. First we must be born as Buddhas and then as Christs.

Blessed be love. Blessed are the beings who truly love one another. Blessed are those who become victorious in the Ninth Sphere.

Fear-mongers

Many pseudo-esotericists have committed unspeakable genocides. When fear-mongers act against the Kundalini, indeed, it is a true genocide. It is an indescribable crime against humanity to tell people in published books that the awakening of the Kundalini is dangerous. Those who spread fear against the Kundalini are worse than war criminals. The latter committed crimes against people; however, the pseudo-esotericists who spread fear commit crimes against the soul. Whosoever does not awaken the Kundalini cannot incarnate their soul. Whosoever does not awaken their Kundalini remains without soul; they lose their soul.

It is false to state that the Kundalini can awaken without moral progress, and due to this, one must wait until such progress is made. The development of the Kundalini is controlled by the merits of the heart. We give concrete instructions about the Kundalini, and every true serpentine culture knows the path in depth. It is false to state that when white Sexual Magic is practiced the Kundalini may flow through different channels. It is only when black Sexual Magic is practiced that the Kundalini descends to the atomic infernos of the human being and becomes the Tail of Satan. Therefore, that absurd affirmation of the fear-mongers is false that the Kundalini can leave the medullar canal, tear tissue, produce terrible pains and cause death. These affirmations of the assassins of souls are false, because each of the seven serpents has its specialized masters who watch over the student. The student is not abandoned in the work. When the student awakens the first serpent, they are attended by a specialist, and when the second serpent is awakened, they are helped by another, and so on. These specialists take the serpent through the medullar canal. No student is abandoned. The specialists have to answer for the student. The specialists live in the astral world.

The Kundalini awakens negatively only when the semen is spilled. Whosoever practices Sexual Magic without spilling the semen has nothing to fear.

Nobody can actualize the superior aspects of the Kundalini without perfect sanctity. It is then false to say that there are disastrous possibilities in the premature actualization of the Kundalini. This affirmation is false because the premature actualization of fire cannot occur. The Kundalini can only be actualized based on sanctification. The Kundalini does not rise even one vertebra if the conditions of sanctity required for that vertebra have not been conquered. Each vertebra has its moral conditions of sanctity. It is false and stupid to say that the Kundalini can awaken ambition or pride, or intensify all of the coarse qualities and animal passions of the animal ego. Whosoever uses these fear mongering tactics to keep students from the real path is truly ignorant, because the Kundalini awakened with white Sexual Magic cannot progress even one degree without true sanctity.

The Kundalini is not a blind force. The Kundalini is not a mechanical force. The Kundalini is controlled by the fires of the heart and can only be developed based on Sexual Magic and sanctity.

We have to recognize that in Mexico, the serpentine culture was and continues to be formidable. Every Aztec sculpture is a marvelous book of esoteric science. We have been enraptured contemplating Quetzalcoatl with the serpent entwined about his body and the lingam-yoni in his hands. We have been amazed contemplating the giant serpent devouring the magician. We have been filled with singular veneration to see the tiger with a phallus hanging about its neck. Indeed, the Word is in the phallus.

In the Aztec culture, there are no fear-mongers. Each book of stone, each indigenous lamen invites us to awaken the Kundalini. It is urgent to first awaken the Kundalini and then to be devoured by the Kundalini. We need to be swallowed by the snake. We need the Kundalini to swallow us. We need to be devoured by the serpent. When one is devoured by the serpent, one also becomes a serpent. Only the human serpent can incarnate the Christ. Without the snake, Christ cannot do anything.

The authentic Aztec and Mayan cultures, the Egyptian and Chaldean, etc. are serpentine cultures that cannot be understood without Sexual Magic and the Kundalini.

Every archaic culture is serpentine. Every authentic and true civilization is serpentine. A civilization without the wisdom of the serpent is not a real civilization.

The Ascent and Descent of the Kundalini

Those pseudo-esotericists who affirm that the Kundalini descends once again into the Church of Ephesus or coccygeal center (after having ascended to the crown chakra or lotus of a thousand petals) and remains stored there, are lying terribly. The Kundalini only descends when the initiate lets themselves fall. The initiate falls when they spill the semen. The work to raise the serpent after having fallen is very difficult and arduous. The Lord of Perfection said,

> "The disciples must never let themselves fall, because whosoever falls then has to struggle a great deal to regain what was lost."

The Hindus state that within the medullar canal there is a channel called Sushumna, and within this channel is another called Vajrini and within this a third called Citrini, which is "as fine as a spider's thread on which the chakras are threaded, like the knots on a bamboo pole." Thus, this is what the sacred

KRISHNA (CHRIST) DANCING
WITH A SERPENT

books of India state, and we know that the Kundalini rises through the Citrini solely and exclusively with the Maithuna, Sexual Magic, Arcanum A.Z.F.

We practice internal meditation to achieve ecstasy; however, we know very well that the Kundalini does not awaken with meditation, because the Kundalini is sexual. It is false to affirm that the awakening of the Kundalini is achieved through meditation. Meditation is a technique to receive information. Meditation is not a technique for awakening the Kundalini. The pseudo-esotericists have done much damage with their ignorance.

In India there are seven fundamental schools of yoga and all speak of the Kundalini. These schools of yoga are of no use if Tantra[165] is not studied. Tantra is the best of the East.

Maithuna (Sexual Magic) is practiced in every authentic school of esoteric yoga. This is Tantra. The Tantras give fundamental value to yoga.

In the center of the lotus of the heart is a marvelous triangle. This triangle also exists in the coccygeal chakra and in the chakra located between the eyebrows. In each of these chakras is a mysterious knot. These are the three knots.

These knots enclose a profound meaning. Here we have the three fundamental changes in the work with the serpent. In the first knot (Church of Ephesus), we abandon the system of spilling the semen. In the second knot (Church of Thyatira), we learn to truly love. In the third knot (Church of Philadelphia), we gain true wisdom and we see clairvoyantly.

---

165 Sanskrit for "continuum" or "unbroken stream." from Sanskrit tantram, lit. "loom, warp," hence "groundwork, system, doctrine," from tan "to stretch, extend." Tantra refers first (1) to the continuum of vital energy that sustains all existence, and second (2) to the class of knowledge and practices that harnesses that vital energy, thereby transforming the practitioner. There are many schools of Tantra, primarily in Hindu and Buddhist traditions. Tantra has long been known in the West as Alchemy. In Asian religions, there is a corresponding class of books called Tantras. "In the view of Tantra, the body's vital energies are the vehicles of the mind. When the vital energies are pure and subtle, one's state of mind will be accordingly affected. By transforming these bodily energies we transform the state of consciousness." —The 14th Dalai Lama

The Kundalini in its ascent must untie these three mysterious knots.

The pseudo-esotericists marvel that the primeval Hindu yogis hardly mention the ethereal chakras or plexuses, but instead concentrate all of their attention on the chakras of the spine and the Kundalini. In fact, the primeval Hindu yogis were Tantric and practiced Maithuna. They were true initiates of the wisdom of the serpent. They knew very well that the key to our redemption is found in the spinal medulla and in the semen. They understood that the awakened Kundalini opens the spinal chakras and that these in turn activate the chakras of the plexuses. Therefore, the foremost are the spinal chakras and the serpent. All the great sages and patriarchs of the ancient serpentine civilizations knew this very well.

In the three triangles—base, cardiac, and frontal—the Deity is represented as a sexual lingam. This symbol reveals all; however, the learned ignoramuses always search for evasions and excuses in order to alter the truth. It is not fair that pseudo-esotericists continue to deceive this poor suffering humanity consciously or unconsciously. We have studied the great serpentine civilizations in depth, and therefore we speak clearly so that those who want to be saved can truly save themselves. We are here to utter the truth, and we utter it even though pseudo-occultists and infrasexual people declare themselves to be our worst enemies. The truth must be uttered, and we utter it with great pleasure.

It is necessary to work with the Kundalini and untie the three knots. Those three knots are the three triangles which transform our lives with chastity, love, and wisdom.

The Sexual Spasm

The White Lodge has totally and absolutely prohibited the sexual spasm [orgasm]. It is absurd to reach the sexual spasm. Those who practice Sexual Magic must never reach the spasm.

Those who attempt to avoid seminal ejaculation without giving up the pleasure of the spasm may suffer disastrous consequences to the organism. The spasm is very violent, and if the organism is violated, the results come right away: impotence, damage to the nervous system, etc. Therefore, those who practice Sexual Magic must withdraw from the act long before the sexual spasm. Doctors know very well the reasons why those who practice Sexual Magic must withdraw before the spasm.

Sexual Magic must be practiced only once a day. One must never practice twice a day.

Never in our lives must we spill the semen.[166] Never. Never. Never.

One has to know how to understand this order of the White Lodge, because if by misfortune, the spasm comes against our will, the disciple will then withdraw from the act and immediately lie down in decubitus-dorsal (face up) and will then quickly refrain with the following movements:

Instructions

- Execute a supreme effort (one like that of a woman who is giving birth) sending the nervous current towards the sexual organs while also making an effort to close the sphincters or exits through which the seminal fluid usually escapes. This is a supreme effort.
- Inhale as if you were pumping, or making the seminal fluid rise with the respiration towards the brain. As you inhale, vocalize the mantra **HAM** (हं). Imagine this energy rising to the brain and then passing to the heart.
- Now exhale the breath, imagining the sexual energy being fixed in the heart. While exhaling, vocalize the mantra **SAH** (स).
- If the spasm is very strong, refrain, refrain, and continue inhaling and exhaling with the help

166 Remember, the Latin word semen literally means "seed of plants, animals, or people; race, inborn characteristic; posterity, progeny, offspring," figuratively "origin, essence, principle, cause." Semen refers to the sexual energy of both masculine and feminine bodies.

of the mantra HAM-SAH. HAM is masculine. SAH is feminine. HAM is solar. SAH is lunar.

One must expel the air rapidly through the mouth producing the sound SAH in a soft and delightful way. One must inhale with the mouth half open, mentally chanting the mantra HAM.

The basic idea of this esoteric exercise is to invert the respiratory process, making it truly positive, since in the present state the negative lunar aspect SAH predominates, which leads to seminal discharge. By inverting the respiratory process through this breathing exercise, the centrifugal force becomes centripetal and the semen then flows inwards and upwards.

Amplification

The instructions that we have given in the former paragraphs can also be applied in the case of spasm and, in general, to every practice of Sexual Magic.

Every practice of Sexual Magic can be concluded with this marvelous exercise.

The work in the Ninth Sphere means struggle, sacrifice, effort, and willpower. The weak ones flee from the Ninth Sphere, horrified, terrified, frightened. Those who are devoured by the serpent become serpents, gods.

In very grave cases, when the sexual spasm occurs suddenly, with imminent danger of seminal ejaculation, the initiate must immediately withdraw from the act and lie on their back on the floor, holding their breath. To do this they must seal the nasal passages, pressing them with the index finger and thumb. This effort must be accompanied by concentration of thought. The neophyte must concentrate intensely on the pulsations of the sexual organ, which are a repetition of the cardiac pulse. One must try to restrain these sexual pulsations to avoid spilling the semen, and if one is forced to inhale oxygen, this must be done with a very short and rapid inhalation, continuing with the maximum retention of breath.

PADMASAMBHAVA AND YESHE TSOGYAL

Chapter 22
Sexual Yoga

There are three types of Tantra in India: first, White Tantra, second, Black Tantra, and third, Grey Tantra. In White Tantra, Sexual Magic is practiced without the spilling of semen. In Black Tantra there is spilling of semen. In Grey Tantra, the semen is and is not spilled; sometimes the semen is spilled, and sometimes it is not spilled. This type of Tantra leads the devotee to Black Tantra.

Within Black Tantra we find the Bons and Drukpas of the "Red Cap," terrible and perverse black magicians. These malignant people have disgusting procedures in order to reabsorb the semen through the urethra after having miserably spilled it. The outcome is fatal because the semen, after having been spilled, is charged with satanic atoms, which upon re-entering the body acquire the power to awaken the Kundalini negatively. It then descends to the atomic infernos of the human being and becomes the Tail of Satan. This is how the human being separates themselves permanently from their Divine Being and sinks forever into the Abyss. Everyone who spills the Cup of Hermes is properly recognized as a black magician.

In Hindustan, Sexual Magic is known as Maithuna.[167] It is also known as Oordhvareta Yoga[168] and those who practice it are called Oordhvareta yogis.

In all truly serious and responsible yoga schools, Sexual Magic is practiced in an extremely secret manner. When a yogi couple, man and woman, have been well prepared, they are taken to a secret place where they are instructed about the Maithuna (Sexual Magic).

---

167 The Sanskrit word मिथुन maithuna is used in Hindu Tantras (esoteric scriptures) to refer to the sacrament (sacred ritual) of sexual union between husband and wife. See glossary.

168 Sanskrit; urdhva ,"upwards" + reta, "seed" thus literally meaning to send the seed upwards. "An Oordhvareta Yogi is one in whom the seminal energy has flown upwards into the brain as Ojas Sakti. There is now no possibility of the semen going downwards by sexual excitement." - Swami Sivananda

The couples unite sexually to work in the Great Work under the supervision of a guru (master). The man, seated on a rug on the floor in the Buddhic position, with his legs crossed in oriental style, enters into sexual contact with the woman. She sits upon the legs of the man so that her legs encircle the male's trunk. It is evident that the woman absorbs the phallus by sitting upon the man in this way. Thus, the man and woman are sexually united. The yogi couple remains in this state for hours without spilling the semen. It is the obligation of the yogi not to think during the practice of Sexual Magic. In those moments both man and woman are found in a state of ecstasy. Thus, in this way, the couple become deeply in love. The creative energies rise victoriously through their respective canals to the chalice of the brain. Animal desire is rejected. Then, the couple withdraws from the act without having spilled the semen.

The way Sexual Magic is practiced in the oriental style may be very uncomfortable for Westerners. Nevertheless, it is recommended for those people who are not capable of avoiding the spilling of the Cup of Hermes. Gnostics can sexually train themselves with this practice in order to learn how to refrain and avoid the spilling of semen. Gnostic couples do not need the physical supervision of a master; however, they could invoke the masters of the astral to help them (the couple must be alone.)

It is necessary that animal desire does not prevail during the practice of Sexual Magic. Remember that desire is diabolic. The "I" is desire. The "I" is diabolic. Where there is desire, there cannot be love, because love and desire are incompatible. It is necessary to know that desire produces illusion.

Whosoever desires believes themselves to be in love, feels themselves to be in love, could swear they are in love. This is the illusion of desire. How many times have we seen couples who claim that they adore each other? After marriage, the castle of cards falls down and what remains is the sad reality. Thus, those who believed they were truly in love in reality hate each other. Once desire is satisfied, failure is inevitable. Then we only hear complaints and regrets, reproaches and tears.

Where was love? What happened to love? It is impossible to love when there is desire. Only those who have already incarnated their soul truly know how to love. The "I" does not know how to love. Only the soul knows how to love. Love has its own atmosphere, its flavor, its happiness. It is only known to the one who has already killed animal desire. It is only known and experienced by the one who has already incarnated their soul.

Love in no way resembles that which people call love. What people believe love to be is only deceiving desire. Desire is an illusory substance that is combined astonishingly in the mind and in the heart to make us feel something that, though not love, makes us firmly believe that it is love. Only the horrible reality that appears after the consummation of the act and the satisfaction of desire shows us clearly that we were the victims of illusion. We believed we were in love, and really we were not.

The human being does not yet know that which is called love. Actually, only the soul knows and is able to love. The human beings still have not incarnated their souls. The human beings still do not know what it is to love. Satan does not know what love is. The only thing that the human being presently has incarnated is Satan (the "I"). The human being does not know how to love.

Love can only exist from heart to heart, from soul to soul. Whosoever has not incarnated their soul does not know how to love. Satan cannot love, and this is what the human being has incarnated. The perfect matrimony is the union of two beings, one who loves more, and the other who loves better. Love is the best religion that the human being can profess.

Desire is a substance that separates into many substances. These substances of desire manage to deceive the mind and the heart. The man who despairs because his wife has left him for another man was not actually in love. True love demands nothing, asks nothing, desires nothing, thinks nothing, only wants one thing: the happiness of the beloved. That is all. The man who loses the one he loves only says, "I am happy that you have found your happiness. If it is with another man that you have found it, I feel happy that you have found it."

Desire is another thing. The passionate man who has lost the woman he loved because she left him for another, may even go so far as to kill and also kill himself. He falls into the most horrible desperation. He has lost the instrument of his pleasure. That is all.

Really, true love is only known by those who have already incarnated their soul. Humanity still does not know that which is called love. Indeed, love is like an innocent child; it is like the white plumed swan. Love is like the first games of childhood. Love does not know anything, because it is innocent.

When we dissolve that horrible phantom that continues after death (the "I"), then that which is called love is born within us. When we reach that state, we recover our lost innocence.

The human being of this day and age has only incarnated an embryo of the soul. At times this emits some sparks of love. The mother who adores her child is a very good example of that which is called love. The embryo of the soul can be strengthened with the blessed flame of love.

Sometimes man and woman feel the radiations of love which flow from the embryo of the soul, but they are immediately suffocated by the violent and terrible passions that Satan gives to both man and woman.

If we cultivate those divine vibrations of love, we can then fortify and strengthen the embryo of the soul, so that later we may live that which we call love intensely.

Love strengthens the embryo of the soul. When the embryo grows stronger, then we achieve the incarnation of the soul.

Rare are those human beings who come to feel the divine loving vibrations that radiate from the embryo of the soul. What humanity normally feels are the forces of desire. Desire also sings, becomes romantic and infinitely tender. Desire is the most deceptive poison in the entire cosmos. Anyone who is a victim of the great deceiver would swear that they are in love.

Men and women, I invite you to love. Follow the footprints of those few in the world who have known how to love.

Gods and goddesses make love in the nuptial enchantment of Paradise. Blessed are the beings who truly love. Only love can make us gods.

Endocrinology

Although it may appear incredible, it is true, and factually certain, that science is closer to transmutation and sexual yoga than many students of yoga. Endocrinology is bound to produce a true creative revolution. Already the people of science know that the sexual glands are not sealed capsules. They absorb and secrete hormones. The hormones of secretion are called "conserving," because they perpetuate the species; the hormones of absorption are called "vitalizing," because they vitalize the human organism. This process of hormonal absorption is transmutation, the transformation of one type of energy-matter into another type of energy-matter. Maithuna, Sexual Magic, is intensified sexual transmutation. The Gnostic absorbs, transmutes and sublimates the totality of the sexual energy-matter. The rich and abundant sexual hormones inundate the circulatory system of the blood and reach the different glands of internal secretion, stimulating and inciting them to work intensely. Thus, with intensified sexual transmutation, the endocrine glands are super-stimulated, producing (as is natural) a greater number of hormones which animate and modify the entire liquid nervous system.

Already, science recognizes sexual transmutation in every individual of normal sexuality. Now it is only a question of advancing a little further to recognize the intensified sexual transmutation of suprasexual individuals. Whosoever studies the thirty-two capital signs of Buddhahood biologically will reach the conclusion that the secondary sexual characteristics of Buddha were really those of a superhuman. These secondary sexual characteristics of Buddha indicate, point to, a very intense sexual transmutation. There can be no doubt that Buddha practiced Maithuna, Sexual Yoga, Sexual Magic, the Arcanum A.Z.F. Buddha taught White Tantra (Sexual Magic); however, he taught these teachings in secrecy to his disciples. Zen and Chan Buddhism teach Maithuna and couples practice this Sexual Yoga.

Secondary Sexual Characteristics

There are primary sexual characteristics and there are secondary sexual characteristics. The primary are related to the sexual functions of the creative organs, and the secondary to the distribution of fats, the formation of muscle, hair, speech, body shape, etc. Obviously, the body of a woman is a different shape from that of a man and vice versa. It is also very true that any damage to the sexual organs modifies the human organism. The secondary sexual characteristics of a eunuch are those of degeneration. The secondary sexual characteristics of an individual of intermediate sex, or sodomite, reveal someone who is inverted, an infrasexual person. What could we deduce from an effeminate man or from a manly woman? What kind of primary characteristics would correspond to people with secondary sexual characteristics opposite to those of their own sex? There is no doubt that there is infrasexuality in such people.

Sexual Yoga, Maithuna, the Arcanum A.Z.F. (Sexual Magic) is a type of suprasexual function that in fact modifies the secondary sexual characteristics producing a new type of human, a superhuman. It is absurd to suppose that the superhuman is the outcome of beliefs, theories, sectarianism, fanaticism, schools, etc. Really, the superhuman does not come from what one believes or ceases to believe, or from the school with which we are affiliated, or from the school that we cease to belong to. The secondary sexual characteristics are only modified by changing the primary characteristics. With sexual yoga, with Maithuna, the authentic yogi initiates are able to modify the secondary sexual characteristics in a positive, transcendental and divine manner.

Psychology and Endocrinology

Psychology appeared to be stagnant. Fortunately, the science of endocrinology appeared. Now, psychology has taken on a new life. There have already been various attempts to study the lives of the great sages based on their biological types. It is said, for example, that the decline of Napoleon coincided with a retrograde process of his pituitary gland. Psychological characteristics are determined by the endocrine glands and the primary sexual characteristics. The psychological bio-type is definitive and can no longer be denied. This depends on the primary sexual characteristics. Indeed, the psychological bio-type belongs to the secondary sexual characteristics, and it is totally determined by the primary sexual characteristics. On this basis, we can affirm that if we want a psychological bio-type being, we must work with the primary sexual characteristics. Only with Sexual Magic, Maithuna, or Sexual Yoga, do we succeed in producing the psychological bio-type of the master, the superhuman, the mahatma.

Infrasexuality

In this chapter we have made statements that infrasexual people mortally hate. They in fact really consider themselves to be suprasexual, super-transcendent. Infrasexual people believe themselves to be more perfect than the Third Logos, and they have no trouble affirming that sex is something gross, filthy, materialistic. Infrasexual people ignore that sex is the creative force of the Holy Spirit, without which they will never reach intimate Realization of the Self. Unfortunately, they insult the Third Logos and its marvelous sexual force. For the infrasexual person, the divine sexual force of the Holy Spirit is something sinful, gross and material.

Infrasexual people have the vain illusion of attaining Realization of the Self by means of lectures, philosophies, beliefs, respiratory exercises, the "bellow system," etc. It is clear that with these things they will never transform their secondary sexual characteristics, and the result is failure.

Evolution and Devolution

In this day and age, as much in the oriental as in the occidental world, many philosophical doctrines based on the dogma of evolution are being disseminated. Evolution and devolution are mechanical forces that simultaneously process themselves in all of Nature. We do not deny the reality of these two forces; we explain them.

Nobody can deny the creative and destructive processes, evolving and devolving, generative and degenerative. What occurs is that things are attributed to the mechanical force of evolution that it does not have. Neither evolution nor devolution can liberate anyone. This idea that with evolution everybody will achieve liberation, the goal, is a fantasy of deluded people. Jesus the Christ spoke clearly and never promised salvation to everyone. The great master emphasizes the tremendous and terrible difficulty implied by the struggle to enter the sanctum regnum, the kingdom of magic and esotericism.

"For many are called, but few are chosen."

—Christian Bible, Matthew 22:14

"Of thousands that search for me, one finds me;
of a thousand that find me, one follows me; of
a thousand that follow me, one is mine."

Here, we are not dealing with a matter of believing or disbelieving, of considering oneself chosen, or of belonging to such-and-such sect. This question of salvation is very serious. One must work with the grain, with the sexual seed. From nothing comes nothing. It is necessary to work with the grain. From the grain itself an effort is required, a total revolution. Only from the sexual grain is the inner angel born. Only the inner angel is admitted into the kingdom of esotericism. Maithuna, Sexual Yoga, Sexual Magic, is imperative. The forces of devolution and evolution are simply mechanical forces, forces which liberate no one, which save no one. That is all.

Many organisms are the result of devolution and many others of evolution. The indigenous and anthropophagus races are not evolving; really they are undergoing devolution. They are the degenerated products of powerful civilizations that preceded them in the course of history. All these tribes say that they descend from gods, demigods, titans etc. All these races conserve traditions that tell of the wonders of their glorious pasts.

The lizard is a degenerated crocodile. The archaic ancestors of ants and bees were titans who existed before mankind.

The humanity of this day and age is a degenerated product of preceding races, as the secondary sexual characteristics of the people show.

Manly women who fly airplanes and fight wars are infra-sexual women. Effeminate men who perm their hair and who manicure their nails in beauty salons are infrasexuals.

Those writers who consider the former statement to be evolution, the return to a divine hermaphroditic state, etc., are mistaken. The authentic hermaphrodite is not of intermediate sex. The hermaphrodite of the submerged continent of Lemuria[169] was complete, having both sexes totally developed and evolved. They were not infrasexual people. They were not of intermediate sex. Today it is only possible to find the divine hermaphrodite in the Spirit and soul that is fused and perfect. The completely feminine soul and the completely masculine Spirit are fused in initiation. An angel is a divine hermaphrodite. No angel is of intermediate sex.

It is necessary to place ourselves upon the path of the revolution of the consciousness. This path is apart from the laws of evolution and devolution. Indeed, this is the straight, narrow and difficult path of which the great Kabir Jesus spoke.

Yoga Exercises

We do not condemn yoga exercises. These are very useful and contribute to inner development. Nevertheless, every yoga that does not teach the Maithuna and the White Tantric sadhanas is incomplete. The great yogis of the east and the west attained Realization of the Self with Sexual Yoga. The yogis of the new era, the Agni yogis, will have to make a profound study of endocrinology, and give public teachings about Sexual Yoga.

The Tantric postures of the *Kama Kalpa*[170] are very exaggerated and many of them degenerate into Black Tantra. We only recommend the Tantric posture of this chapter.

---

169 The ancient people of the third root race, previous to Atlantis. Their story is symbolized by Adam and Eve in the Judeo-Christian scriptures: before the division of sexes they were hermaphrodites.
170 A book about love and sex in India written by a European.

KUKULCAN, THE FEATHERED SERPENT

MEXICO

Chapter 23

The Flying Serpent

With tears in my eyes (it tears at my heart to have to reveal things that should not be revealed because it is like casting pearls before swine) I must reveal something about the flying serpent for this poor suffering humanity that needs them, even though it is distressing to do so.

The Serpent Bird

In the *Popol Vuh* of the Mayans, the bird and the serpent are featured as the sexual creators of the universe. Tepeu and Gucumatz sent a sparrow hawk to the immense ocean of great life to bring the serpent, whose marvelous blood they kneaded into yellow and white maize. The *Popol Vuh* states that with this dough of white and yellow maize mixed with the blood of the serpent, the god Tzacol formed the flesh of people. The bird represents the universal spirit of life. The serpent represents the sexual fire of the Third Logos. The blood of the serpent represents the waters of Genesis, the great universal sperm, the ens seminis[171] or Christonic semen, in whose waters is the germ of all life. These waters are the blood of the earth, according to the Mayan philosopher. The goddess Coatlicue is the mother of life and death (the ens seminis).

Indeed, the sexual fire of the Third Logos makes the waters of life fertile in order for the universe to emerge.

In the Mayan theogony, two gods intervened in creation: one who gives life and form to people, and the other who gives them consciousness. The Third Logos makes the waters of life fertile, and when these have been fertilized, the Second Logos intervenes, infusing consciousness into every organism. The ineffable gods are the vehicles of action for all the Logoic forces.

The sparrow hawk H'ch'uuy, the macaw Mo, the kestrel X'Cen Cen Bac, the tapir Tzimink Aax, and the serpent Can are the basic components of the Mayan geogenetic myths. These

---

171 Latin, "the entity of semen." A term used by Paracelsus.

symbols are used exoterically and esoterically. In the exoteric or public field they symbolize tribal facts, historical incidents, etc. In the esoteric or secret aspect, this matter is highly scientific, profoundly philosophical, sublimely artistic, and tremendously religious.

Amongst the Maya, the terrestrial paradise is Tamoanchan, the sacred place of the serpent bird. Tamoanchans are in fact the initiates of the serpent. The myth of the Tamoanchans is the myth of the serpent bird. The Tamoanchans are descended from the Toltec, Olmec, and Maya.

Quetzalcoatl within the Feathered Serpent, which is coiled three and one half times.

The Aztecs, after much hardship, reached the lake of Texcoco, symbol of the Christonic semen, where they found the bird and the serpent, the eagle and the snake. The Aztecs are the ones who have the high honor of having founded the great Tenochtitlan based on the wisdom of the serpent.

The feathered serpent clearly represents the serpent bird. The feathered serpent was identified with Quetzalcoatl, the Mexican Christ. Quetzalcoatl is always accompanied by the sacred symbols of the eagle and serpent. The feathered serpent discloses everything. The eagle of the Spirit and the serpent of fire transform us into gods.

The Quetzal of the Mayans is the feathered serpent, the serpent bird.

The Caduceus of Mercury

The Caduceus of Mercury symbolizes the spinal medulla with its two serpents representing the canals of Ida[172] and

---

172 Sanskrit इडा feminine noun, "vital spirit, libation, refreshment, goddess, heaven, earth, food, offering, comfort, refreshing draught, cow." The lunar conduit along the spinal column, symbolized in the bible by Eve. Ida is also called Chandra Nadi (moon). Ida is cooling and is related to procreation. In Kabbalah, it is called Obd.

ENTWINED SERPENTS BORN FROM THE FIRE. AZTEC

Pingala[173] through which solar and lunar atoms ascend to the brain. These are the musical sharps and flats of the great FA that resounds in all creation.

The Akasha ascends like flaming fire through the medullar canal, and its two poles of energy flow through Ida and Pingala. From the medullar canal and its two canals, (which are entwined like serpents around the dorsal spine) a circulation begins, which departing from the central duct, is then distributed throughout the whole organism.

Ida and Pingala depart from the sexual organs. In men, Ida is to the left of the medullar canal and Pingala to the right. In women this order is reversed. The canals terminate in the medulla oblongata. This pair of cords are semi-ethereal, semi-physical, and correspond to the superior dimensions of space.

The Igneous Wings

When the solar and lunar atoms unite at the base of the spinal column, the igneous serpent of our magical powers awakens. The serpent ascends slowly amidst the ineffable delights of the perfect matrimony. The serpent enjoys the enchantment of love.

When the serpent reaches the height of the heart, we receive the igneous wings, the wings of the Caduceus of Mercury.

---

173 Sanskrit पिनाल-नदि "reddish conduit." The solar channel of energy that entwines up the spinal column, symbolized in the bible by Adam. Also called Surya Nadi (sun) and Od (Kabbalah).

Then, the serpent has feathers. This is the Quetzal, the serpent bird, the feathered serpent.

Every initiate who transforms themselves into the serpent bird can fly to the superior worlds. They can enter the different regions of the kingdom, travel in the astral body at will, travel with the super-astral vehicles, travel with their physical body within the fourth dimension. They are a serpent bird.

The serpent bird can escape from a sealed tomb, walk upon the waters (as was demonstrated by Jesus the Christ), pass through a rock from one side to the other without injury (as was proven by the disciples of Buddha), can fly with their physical body through the air, etc.

FARAON

Ida is feminine and Pingala is masculine. Here are the sharps and flats of the great FA that resounds in Nature. FA corresponds to the solar atoms, RA to the lunar atoms, ON to the flaming fire that ascends through the central canal. It is necessary to learn how to sound these sharps and flats with the powerful mantra **FARAON** in order to go out in the astral body consciously and positively. With the mantra of these sharps and flats we can travel in the astral body.

In Egypt, when the initiate received the igneous wings, they were decorated in the temple with a pair of wings fixed to their tunic at the level of the heart. When Jesus of Nazareth spread his igneous wings, he was personally decorated by the Pharaoh of Egypt.

The position in which Jesus lay down to go into the astral was like that of Chac Mool, but with the head very low and without pillows, the soles of the feet upon the bed, the legs bent and the knees raised. In this way, the great hierophant would fall asleep playing on his marvelous lyre, the dorsal spine. The whole mantra FARAON is divided into three syllables, as follows: FA RA ON. The FA is that of the musical scale. The RA is a deep sound; it must be vocalized with a rolling R. ON reminds us of the mantra OM of India, but the only difference is that here, instead of having the consonant M, it has

the consonant N; ON. In general, we can give to the mantra
FARAON all the intonation which resounds in all creation
with the great FA.

We advise you to vocalize mentally. The disciple must fall
asleep singing this mantra with the imagination and willpower
concentrated upon the pyramids of Egypt. It requires practice
and much patience.

The Flying Serpent

White magicians and black magicians use the flying serpent
to travel in the astral body or with the physical body in the Jinn
state.

In profound meditation, white magicians know how to pray
and to supplicate the serpent of brass to be transported to any
place on Earth or in the cosmos and the flying serpent trans-
ports them.

Black magicians pray to the tempting serpent of Eden, and
it takes them to the Abyss or to the salons of witchcraft or to
the Witches' Sabbath, etc.

The serpent of brass rises through the medullar canal.

The tempting serpent descends from the coccyx downwards
towards the atomic infernos of Nature. This is the tail of Satan.
Devils have their power in the tail.

Blessed be the Divine Mother Kundalini. Blessed be they
who fly with the power of the beloved mother.

Wretched be they who move with the power of Santa Maria
(the tempting serpent of Eden, the descending Kundalini).

Unhappy are they who fly with the tenebrous power of
Santa Maria. The Abyss and the Second Death are for them.

The Jinn State

A point is a cross section of a line. A line is a cross section
of a plane. A plane is a cross section of a body. A body is the
cross section of a tetra-dimensional body, that is to say, of four
dimensions.

Every body is tetra-dimensional, has four dimensions. The
fourth coordinate or fourth vertical is the basic foundation of

all mechanics. Intermolecular space corresponds to the fourth dimension.

In this three-dimensional world of length, width, and height we never see a complete body. We only see sides, planes, angles, etc. Therefore, perception is incomplete and subjective.

In the fourth dimension, perception is objective. There we see bodies from the front, from the back, from above, from below, from within, from without, that is to say, completely. In the fourth dimension, all objects appear simultaneously complete. There, perception is objective.

With the power of the flying serpent we can take the physical body out of the world of three dimensions and pass it into the fourth dimension. In more advanced states we can take the physical body to the fifth or the sixth dimension.

Serpents That Fly

When we visited the region of Magdalena, in the Republic of Colombia, we were surprised to discover flying serpents. In the jungles of this region there are sorcerers who know how to send flying serpents to their hated victims. The procedures used by these sorcerers are very uncommon. Generally, these sorcerers are a type of witch doctor who dedicate themselves to the practice of curing victims of venomous snake bites, which is so common in the tropics. There are many sorcerers who heal people bitten by snakes. Also, there is much competition in the craft, and the mysterious war between these sorcerers is tremendous. They live at war because of matters of their craft. Witch doctors usually use the fourth dimension to teletransport certain types of artificial serpents to the abode of their enemies. The procedure is simple and marvelous at the same time. The element that the witch doctor utilizes to make the serpents is vegetable fiber from the exterior bark of the trunk of the plantain tree or banana plant. This fiber when made into a small cord about one to two meters in length becomes an artificial snake. The witch doctor makes seven knots in the vegetable fiber from this trunk, to symbolize the seven churches of the snake, and then he walks about reciting his secret magical prayers. The final climax of the magical operation is the instant in which the sorcerer, full of frenzy, flings the vegetable fiber into space. It is transformed into a serpent upon entering the fourth dimension. The worst thing is that this flying serpent falls back into the third dimension, but inside the distant home of the hated enemy. Usually, the person is a competitor in the craft. If the victim has his body well prepared, clearly the serpent can do no harm to it, but if the victim's body is not prepared, the serpent will precisely bite the heart of the victim, and he will immediately be struck dead. Normally, the witch-doctors prepare the body with special herbs to defend themselves against their enemies. The vegetable fiber that they use for those criminal acts is called by the indigenous name of majagua de platano. There is no doubt that these sorcerers use the power of the tempting serpent of Eden (the snake that descends) to commit these criminal acts.

If those sorcerers can do such remarkable things like transforming a vegetable fiber into a flying serpent, how much more can the white magician do with his flying serpent? The flying serpent of the white magician is the Kundalini. The white magician is really the serpent bird, the serpent who flies.

The seven centers of the snake are omnipotent. The serpent with wings is something formidable. With the power of the serpent bird, the magician can become invisible at will, can transport themselves through the air within the fourth dimension, appear and disappear before the astonished people. They can unleash thunder and hurricanes, calm tempests, resurrect the dead, transmute lead into gold, cure the sick by the laying on of hands, raise themselves from the tomb on the third day and conserve their body for millions of years. The serpent bird is immortal, omnipotent, wise, amorous, and terribly divine.

The guardians of the temples of the mysteries are serpents of fire. With the power of the serpent bird we can transport ourselves to the other planets of the infinite.

The Doubles

In all of our books, we have taught different systems to go out in the astral body. Many people have learned to go out and many have not learned. Some have read a key from our books, have understood it, put it into practice and then have immediately learned how to go out in the astral body. Many others have practiced with one system or another without having obtained anything.

In practice, we have been able to prove that people who are very intellectual, full of bookish culture (the library bookworms), do not manage to go out at will in the astral body. On the other hand, people who are very simple—humble peasants, poor servants of families—can do so perfectly. This has made us think a great deal about the matter and we have carefully investigated the problem. The fact is that travel in the astral body is not something intellectual. Rather, astral travel is more aligned with feelings and superior emotions. These qualities are related to the heart, not to the brain.

The intellectuals polarize themselves in the brain in an exaggerated fashion, and abandon, in fact, the world of the heart. The result of their lack of equilibrium is the loss of the psychic powers of the soul. Unfortunately, a faculty cannot be acquired without the loss of another. Whosoever wants to develop the intellect does it at the expense of the psychic faculties. This problem is serious, because in no way can we approve ignorance and illiteracy. It is logical that an intellectual culture is necessary. Ignorance leads to very serious errors. An illiterate and ignorant esotericist can become a mythomaniac or slanderer, and in the worst cases, an assassin.

In the astral world we find the perverse doubles of saintly people. Facing the angel Anael is his perverse double, the terrible demon Lilith. Facing Elohim Gibor is the terrible demon Andrameleck. Facing every good citizen is a citizen of evil. The worst of this matter is that the appearance of the double is exactly the same as the model of light. If an adept teaches White Magic, his double, the black adept, besides having a similar physiognomy, manners, posture, etc., teaches black magic. This is very serious, because like any illiterate who mistakes, for example, "gymnasium" for "magnesium," the ignorant esotericist can very easily, in fact, become a slanderer of good people, and we restate, even an assassin. If an ignorant esotericist finds their spouse in the astral world having sex with one of his friends, and if unfortunately they are a schizophrenic or neurasthenic, they can assassinate their friend and spouse. Their ignorance does not allow them to understand what they have seen is a pair of doubles cohabiting, or a fact from a past reincarnation, etc. Somebody who is jealous and supposes that their spouse is unfaithful with some known or unknown person can then project their thought forms and see them in the astral world. If the subject is a neurasthenic, or an ignorant schizophrenic, but knows how to go out in the astral body, they can take everything that they saw seriously, and then commit murder, confused by their jealousy and visions. Because they are ignorant, they do not understand that they have seen their own mental forms projected unconsciously. All this leads us to the conclusion that intellectual culture is necessary.

Now the interesting thing is to know how to re-conquer the lost psychic faculties. A person with a brilliant, illuminated intellect and with all their psychic faculties in full activity, is really in fact and by their own right, a true, illuminated one.

The esotericist needs to establish perfect equilibrium between mind and heart. When the mind has become excessively frozen in the brain, leaving at will in the astral body becomes completely impossible because there is imbalance. It is urgent then for the intellectual esotericists to re-establish equilibrium between mind and heart. Fortunately, there is a technique to re-establish the lost equilibrium. This technique is inner meditation.

For those intellectuals who write to us alleging that they have not been able to leave in the astral body with the clues that we have taught, we prescribe a good daily dose of inner meditation. It is urgent that they drink the wine of meditation from the cup of perfect concentration.

The Cardiac Plexus

The cardiac plexus is the magnetic center of the heart. This center is marvelously described in verses 22 to 27 of the *Shatchakra-nirupana*; let us read:

> "...in the heart is the charming Lotus, of the shining colour of the Bandhūka flower, with the twelve letters beginning with Ka [to Tha], of the colour of vermilion, placed therein. It is known by its name of Anāhata, and is like the celestial wishing-tree [Kalpa-taru], bestowing even more than is desired. The Region of Vāyu [Vayu-Mandala], beautiful and with six corners, which is like unto the smoke in colour, is here.

> "Meditate within it on the sweet and excellent Pavana Bīja [mantra Yam], grey as a mass of smoke, with four arms, and seated on a black antelope. And within it also (meditate) upon the Abode of Mercy, the Stainless Lord who is lustrous like the Sun [Surya], and whose two hands make the gestures which grant boons and dispel the fears of the three worlds.

> "Here dwells Kākinī, who in colour is yellow like unto new lightning, exhilarated and auspicious; three-eyed and the benefactress of all. She wears all kinds of ornaments, and in Her four hands She carries the noose and the skull, and makes the sign of blessing and the sign which dispels fear. Her heart is softened with the drinking of nectar.

> "The Śakti whose tender body is like ten million flashes of lightning is in the pericarp of this Lotus in the form of a triangle (Trikona). Inside the triangle is the Śiva-Linga known by the name of Bāna. This Linga is like shining gold, and on his head is an orifice minute as that in a gem. He is the resplendent abode of Lakshmī.

> "Whoever meditates on this Heart Lotus becomes (like) the Lord of Speech, and (like) Īśvara is able to protect and destroy the worlds. This Lotus, is like the celestial wishing-tree, the abode and seat of Śarva. It is beautified by the Hamsa, which is like unto the steady tapering flame of a lamp in a windless place. The filaments which surround and adorn its pericarp, illumined by the solar region, charm.

Foremost among Yogīs, one ever is dearer than the dearest to
women, one is pre-eminently wise and full of noble deeds. One's
senses are completely under control. One's mind in its intense
concentration is engrossed in thoughts of the Brahman. One's
inspired speech flows like a stream of (clear) water. One is like
the Devatā who is the beloved of Lakshmī... [The red lotus in
this quotation is Ānanda-kanda below the pericarp of the heart
lotus; it has its head turned upwards, and has eight petals. It is in
this lotus that mental worship (Mānasa-pūjā) should be made.]"

The Hindu description of this chakra is marvelous. The
number of its petals is mentioned, the principle of air (Vayu),
Shiva, the sexual force, with its lingam and the crescent moon,
etc., indicating the heart as an altar of mental worship, the
marvelous center of meditation. Upon these Hindu paragraph,
many a volume could be written.

The cardiac plexus is the magnetic center related to astral
journeys. Whoever wants to conquer the power to leave in the
astral body at will must change their vibratory type. This is
only possible by developing the cardiac plexus.

Astral projection is rather emotive and sentimental. The
cold intellect has nothing to do with voyages in the astral body.
The brain is lunar. The heart is solar.

Superior emotion is needed to leave at will in the astral
body: a certain type of emotive nature, of sentiment, a very
special supra-sensitivity, and sleep combined with meditation.
These qualities are only achieved with the development of the
cardiac plexus.

Regarding the cardiac plexus, the *Shiva Samhita* states,

"They acquire immeasurable knowledge, know the past,
present, and future, acquire clairaudience, clairvoyance,
and can travel the airs whenever they please.

"They see the adepts, and the yogini goddesses, obtains the
faculty called Khechari, and conquer all who move in the air.

"Whoever meditates daily on the hidden Banalinga undoubtedly
obtains the psychic powers called Khechari [moving in the
air in the astral body, or to acquire also the power of putting

the physical body in the Jinn state] and Bhuchari [to go at will anywhere in the world]." —Shiva Samhita 5:87-88

Practice

The devotee must concentrate on their heart, imagining there thunder, lightning, and fast moving clouds that are lost in the twilight, blown by strong hurricanes. The Gnostic must imagine many eagles flying in that infinite space which is within, very deep within their heart. Imagine the profound forests of Nature, filled with sun and life, the song of birds and the sweet and peaceful chirping of the crickets in the forest. The disciple must fall asleep imagining all of this.

Imagine now that in the forest there is a throne of gold, upon which is seated the goddess Kakini, a very divine woman.

The Gnostic must fall asleep meditating on this, imagining all of this. The Gnostic must practice for one hour daily, but if they practice two, three or more hours daily, that is even better. You can practice seated in a comfortable armchair, lying on the floor, or on your bed, with your arms and legs stretched out to your sides like a five-pointed star. Sleep must be combined with meditation.

One must have much patience. These marvelous faculties of the cardiac plexus are obtained with infinite patience. For the impatient ones who want everything right away, who do not know how to persevere their whole life through, it is better for them to leave, because they are of no use. Powers are not obtained by playing around; everything has a price. Nothing is given to us for free.

The Temple of the Serpent Bird

The heart is the temple of the serpent bird. It is necessary to know how to love. The serpent bird officiates in the temple of the tranquil heart. It is urgent to be devoured by the serpent. Whosoever is devoured by the serpent becomes in fact a serpent bird. Only with Sexual Magic and the love of the heart is the serpent awakened, which will later devour us. When the

"The serpent bird officiates in the temple of the tranquil heart."
EGYPTIAN

serpent reaches the level of the heart, it receives the igneous wings. It is then transformed into a serpent bird.

It is urgent to know how to lead a married life. The quarrels between husband and wife are of Satan. Thus, Satan fights against the serpent bird. He wants to damage the Great Work. Therefore, we need to understand how to tolerate the defects of our spouse, because no one is perfect.

The work in the flaming forge of Vulcan is more valuable than all the defects of our spouse. It is stupid to throw away all the work, to give Satan his pleasure. In the heart is the temple of the feathered serpent, and we must not profane it by sinning against love. The path of the perfect matrimony is wisdom and love.

We must love consciously. We must love our worst enemies, returning good for bad. In this way, by knowing how to love, we prepare ourselves for the festival of the tranquil heart.

Hermes Trismegistus said, "I give you love within which the whole summum of wisdom is contained."

Another Type of Fear-monger

There are many pseudo-occultists and pseudo-esotericists who spread fear-mongering rumors against the voluntary projection of the astral body. It is false and harmful to the Great

Work of the Father to make people fearful of projecting the astral body. Indeed, projecting the astral body is not dangerous, because every human being projects the astral body during the hours of normal sleep. Unfortunately, all human beings project themselves in their astral body with their consciousness asleep. People do not know how to project their astral bodies at will. There is no danger whatsoever in becoming conscious of one's own natural functions, which are eating, drinking, marrying, and projecting the astral body. These functions are completely natural. If traveling in the astral body were dangerous as the fear-mongers state, then by now there would be no one living on Earth, because everybody projects the astral body, and still worse, they do so with their consciousness asleep. Nevertheless, nothing happens. And so...?

At this moment, the planet Mercury is coming out of a cosmic night. As it leaves its state of rest, the hierarchies of this planet will become more and more active. The lords of Mercury propose to teach the inhabitants of the Earth (in a practical way) the art of entering and leaving the physical body at will. In the future, all humans must consciously project the astral body. This then is a law of Nature, a cosmic commandment, and everything opposed to this law is a crime. Indeed, those who spread this kind of fear are unconsciously acting as black magicians when they do so.

The special objective of the Universal Spirit of Life[174] is to become conscious of itself in all the dimensions of space. In principle, the Universal Spirit of Life is unknowable to itself. It is happy, but it does not have consciousness of its own happiness. Happiness without consciousness of it is not happiness. The Universal Spirit of Life descends into matter to become conscious of itself. The Great Reality arises from its own bosom in the dawn of the whole universe and contemplates itself in the living mirror of Nature. That is how it comes to know itself. In this way a vibratory mental activity is created through which the Great Reality contemplates its infinite images on the cosmic stage. This activity, moving from the periphery

---

174 Also called the Absolute, the Ain Soph, Adi Buddha, Brahman, Shunyata, etc.

to the center, is called Universal Mind. We all live submerged
in the infinite ocean of the Universal Mind. The intellectual
activity of the Universal Mind springs from a centripetal force.
Every action is followed by a reaction. The centripetal force (on
finding its resistance in the center) logically reacts and creates
a centrifugal activity called cosmic soul. This vibratory soul
becomes a mediator between the center and the periphery,
between the Universal Spirit of Life and matter, between the
Great Reality and its cosmic images. The great Master Paracelsus stated, "The soul is the product of the centrifugal action
of universal activity, impelled by the centripetal action of the
imagination of the universe."

In this day and age, human beings have only an embryo
of a soul within their astral ghost, and this embryo must be
strengthened and self-awakened. The awakening of cosmic
consciousness within a human being is the most grandiose
event in the universe.

In these moments, the great White Lodge is intensely occupied with the awakening of human consciousness. The adepts
struggle intensely to teach the human being to leave at will
in the astral body. They want people to awaken; therefore, all
that goes against this great law is a crime. The whole objective of the descent of Spirit into matter is to create soul and to
become self-conscious of itself. When we direct mental power
towards the interior of our own intimate center, the resistance
that we will find internally will cause a reaction, and the more
vigorous the centripetal force that we apply, the more vigorous will be the resulting centrifugal force. Thus, we create soul.
Thus, we invigorate the embryo of the soul, and finally one
day, when we have already been born as serpent birds, we will
completely absorb and assimilate the totality of the soul within
our astral body.

The awakening of the consciousness is urgent. Whosoever
learns to project the astral body at will can study at the feet of
the great masters of wisdom. In the astral world we find our
guru who will instruct us in the great mysteries.

We need to abandon fear to have the joy of visiting the lands
of paradise. We need to abandon fear to have the joy of enter-

ing the temples of the Land of the Golden Light. There we shall sit at the feet of the great masters of the White Lodge. There we shall gain strength for the difficult path. It is necessary that we strengthen ourselves on the path; to take a break and receive direct instruction from the lips of our guru, who like a loving parent, always waits for us in the astral body to console us. The adepts are true flying serpents.

Chapter 24
Secret Egypt

The great mysteries of Gnosis existed in ancient Egypt,
yonder, in the sunny land of Khem. In those days, after having
been submitted to the most difficult trials, whoever was admitted to the initiatic colleges received the terrific secret of the
Great Arcanum (the key of Sexual Magic) by word of mouth.

Everyone who received this secret had to take an oath of
silence. Whosoever swore and then later violated their oath was
taken to a rocky, paved courtyard of death. There, before a wall
covered with strange hieroglyphs, they were inevitably put to
death. Their head was cut off, their heart was torn out, their
body was burned and their ashes thrown to the four winds.

In fact, everyone who received the Great Arcanum during
the sacred ceremony immediately moved to work with the
vestal of the temple. There were many vestals ready to work in
the Great Work with the celibate initiates. The married initiates practiced in their homes with their priestly spouses. The
vestals were duly prepared for the priesthood of love. They had
great masters who prepared them, and they were submitted
to great ordeals and penances. These were precisely the sacred
prostitutes about which many authors speak. Today it would
be impossible to have vestals of this type in the lumisial. The
world has become so corrupted that the result would be to
further corrupt that which is already corrupted. We would in
fact become abject accomplices to crime.

All the celibate initiates who have shone throughout the
history of the centuries practiced Sexual Magic inside the pyramids with the vestals. Jesus also practiced Sexual Magic in the
pyramid of Kefren. There he recapitulated all of his initiations.
Many will be shocked by our statement. We cannot criticize
these puritans. Actually, it was the Roman Catholic priesthood
that dehumanized Jesus. Unfortunately, this has been so deeply
ingrained into peoples' minds, that even esotericists continue
with the false idea of a castrated, mutilated Jesus. The reality

is that Jesus was a complete man in the full sense of the word: fully a man.

In the esoteric Masonry of the ancient Egypt of the Pharaohs, there were three basic degrees:

1. Apprentice
2. Journeyman
3. Master

These three degrees are related to the ethereal forces that flow through and around the spinal column of each human being.

Madame Blavatsky refers to them as follows:

> "The Trans-Himâlayan school... locates
> Sushumna, the chief seat of these three Nâdis, in
> the central tube of the spinal cord, and Idâ and
> Pingala [the two Witnesses of the Apocalypse]
> on its left and right sides.... Idâ and Pingala
> are simply the sharp and flat of that Fa (of
> human nature), the keynote and the middle
> key in the scale of the septenary harmony of
> the principles--which, when struck in a proper
> way, awakens the sentries on both sides, the
> spiritual Manas and the physical Kâma, and
> subdues the lower through the higher."

> "The pure Akasha passes through Sushumna
> (the medullar canal). Its two aspects flow in
> Ida and Pingala (the pair of sympathetic cords
> that are entwined around the spinal medulla).
> These are the three vital airs, symbolized by the
> Brahmanic thread and are ruled by the will.
> Will and desire are the superior and inferior
> aspects of one and the same thing. Hence, the
> importance of purifying the channels... from
> these three a circulation is established which from
> the central canal penetrates the whole body.

> "Ida and Pingala function in the curved wall
> of the vertebral column in which is found

Sushumna (the medullar canal). They are
semi-material, positive and negative, Sun
and Moon, and put into activity the free and
spiritual igneous current of Sushumna. Each
has its own particular path, then, if this were
not so, they would irradiate the whole body."

In that ancient, elemental Egypt (which grew and matured
under the protective wings of the elemental sphinx of Nature)
the ceremony of initiation was something terribly divine.

When the venerable master wielded the sword in the act of
admission, the canals of Ida and Pingala (the Two Witnesses)
and the canal of Sushumna (along with the forces which
circulated through them) received a tremendous stimulus. In
the first degree, this stimulus only affected the feminine lunar
current of Ida; in the second degree, Pingala, the masculine
current; and in the third, the igneous current of Kundalini
(that flows ardently through the medullar canal of Sushumna)
received the stimulus. With this third degree, the Kundalini
remained awakened. We want to clarify that these three stimuli
were related with the work of Sexual Magic that the initiate
performed with the vestal of the temple. Such stimuli would be
useless if the candidate was a fornicator. This is for people who
are practicing Sexual Magic intensely.

In men, Ida rises from the base of the spinal column to the
left of Sushumna, and Pingala to the right. These positions are
reversed in women. The cords end in the medulla oblongata.
All this is symbolized by the Caduceus of Mercury with its two
spread wings. The two wings of the Caduceus of Mercury signify the power to travel in the astral body, the power to travel in
the mental body, the power to travel in the causal, conscious,
and spiritual vehicles. The fire gives those who follow the path
of the razor's edge the power to leave the physical body at will.

Kundalini has the power of awakening the consciousness of
the human being. With the fire, we remain completely awakened in the superior worlds. All those who have awakened in
the superior worlds live absolutely conscious outside of the
physical body during the hours of sleep. Whosoever awakens
the consciousness can never again dream. They become in fact,

and rightfully, absolutely conscious citizens of the superior worlds. They work with the White Lodge while their physical body sleeps. They are the collaborators of the great White Universal Fraternity.

We clarify: Ida and Pingala are not physical. A physician could not find them with a scalpel. Ida and Pingala are semi-ethereal, semi-physical.

The great mysteries of ancient Egypt, as well as the mysteries of Mexico, Yucatan, Eleusis, Jerusalem, Mithra, Samothrace, etc., are all intimately related and are in fact absolutely sexual.

"Ask, and it shall be given you. Knock, and it shall be opened unto you." —Christian Bible, Matthew 7:7

The great initiates always answer. The guardians of the elemental sphinx of Nature always respond.

Everyone who practices Sexual Magic must ask for the fire, beg the guardians of the sphinx, and invoke the god Agni.[175] This god restores the igneous power in each of the seven bodies.

There are five great initiations of sacred fire. The first means the departure of the one who has already entered the current leading to Nirvana. The fifth means the entry into the temple raised upon the summit of the mountain. With the first we leave the well-trodden path; with the fifth we enter the secret temple.

---

175 (Sanskrit) One of the most ancient symbols in the world, representing the source and power of the sun, lightning, and fire. The Rig Veda states that all the gods are centered in Agni (fire).

Chapter 25
Fatality

When the dark age arrived, the colleges of initiation were closed. This was a fatality. Henceforth, as a matter of fact, the great black lodges, which were born during the archaic darkness of the ancient times, became more active. The limit of light is darkness. Next to every temple of light is another of darkness, and where the light more brightly shines, there darkness becomes more dense.

The colleges of initiation from Egypt, Greece, India, China, Mexico, Yucatan, Peru, Troy, Rome, Carthage, Chaldea, etc., had their dangerous antipodes, their fatal antitheses, tenebrous schools of black magic, fatal shadows of the light. Those schools of black magic were the shadows of the colleges of initiation. Thus, when the colleges were closed, these fatal schools became very active.

Therefore, it is not strange to find among these dens of the black lodge terms, sciences, and rituals similar to those that were used within the colleges of initiation. This confuses the devotees of the path. By nature, the devotee is a lover of the "strange," of the "exotic," of the "distant," and of the "impossible." Therefore, when the devotees find a black magician of this type, speaking of the Egyptian, Mayan, Aztec, Inca, Greek, Chaldean, Persian mysteries, etc., they then believe they have ingeniously caught God by the beard, and place themselves in the hands of the black magician, believing him to be white.

These magicians of darkness abound wherever there were colleges of initiation. They are the antitheses of those colleges, and they speak like masters, always boasting about being initiates of those colleges. They never say anything that could arouse suspicion. They show that they are kind and humble, defend the good and the truth, adopt tremendously mystical attitudes, etc. Clearly, under such conditions, the naive and inexperienced devotee abandons the path of the razor's edge and entrusts themselves fully to those wolves in sheep's clothing. That is a fatality.

Those schools of black magic are everywhere. We remember the dissident sect of the Mayans. Their adepts were expelled from the white Mayan lodge. They are black magicians. They established a school between the Yucatan and Guatemala. Presently, this school of Mayan black magic has active agents in Mexico and Guatemala. Nonetheless, who would dare to doubt these tenebrous people who say they are Mayan princes and great priests? These people still speak with much reverence about Teoti, the supreme God, creator and maintainer of the world. They become ecstatic when remembering Bacabes, the Mayan trinity, and Camaxtli, punisher of the evil ones, etc. Under these circumstances it is very difficult to detect such tenebrous people. When devotees entrust themselves to them, they take them to their temples where they initiate them. Clearly the devotees naively become black magicians. A devotee under these circumstances would never accept that they should be classified as a black magician. The Abyss is full of sincerely mistaken people and people of very good intentions.

Thus, on the banks of the Nile, as well as in the sacred land of the Vedas, there are many tenebrous people like this. Indeed, they are now very active, struggling to increase their numbers.

If the student wants a key in order to discover these people in the shadows, we shall give it to them with great pleasure.

Speak to the person about White Sexual Magic without the spilling of the semen. Mention scientific chastity to them. Tell them that you never spill your semen. This is the key. You can be sure that if the suspected person is really a black magician, he will try every means to convince you that Sexual Magic is bad for the health, that it is harmful, and will suggest to you the idea of spilling the semen.

Be careful, good disciple, of people who advise you to spill the Cup of Hermes. They are black magicians. Do not let them seduce you with sweet words, exotic manners, or strange names.

Every devotee who spills the Cup of Hermes inevitably falls into the abyss of fatality. Be vigilant. Remember that the path of the perfect matrimony is the path of the razor's edge. This path is full of dangers, both within and without. Many are those who begin, but it is very difficult to find someone who does not leave the path.

The case of an initiate in the time of Count Cagliostro comes into my memory. This student practiced Sexual Magic intensely with his wife, and of course, naturally acquired degrees, powers, initiation, etc. Everything went very well until the day he had the weak misfortune to reveal his intimate matters to an occultist friend. That friend was shocked, and armed with great erudition, advised the initiate to abandon his practice of Sexual Magic in which the semen was not ejaculated. The teachings of his mistaken friend misguided the initiate. Henceforth, he dedicated himself to practice Sexual Magic with the spilling of the Cup of Hermes. The outcome was disastrous. The Kundalini of the initiate descended to the magnetic center of the coccyx. This is how he lost his degrees and powers, sword and cape, sacred tunics and mantles. This was a true disaster. This was a fatality.

It is good to know that black magicians love to strengthen the mind. They asseverate that only through the mind can someone resemble God. The magicians from darkness mortally hate chastity.

The devotees of the path who abandoned the path of the perfect matrimony in order to become disciples of the black lodge can be found in the millions. It happens that the devotees of esotericism are attracted by the "unusual," by the novel and mysterious, and when they find an "interesting" magician they immediately place themselves in his hands, like any vulgar prostitute of the mind. This is a fatality.

Whosoever wants to be born as a cosmic angel, whosoever wants to transform themselves into an angel with power over fire, air, water and earth, whosoever wants to transform themselves into a god, must in fact not let themselves become trapped by all of these dangerous temptations.

It is very difficult to find people who are sufficiently firm and constant in order to never abandon the path of the perfect matrimony. The human being is extremely weak. This is a fatality.

"For many are called, but few are chosen."
—Christian Bible, Matthew 22:14

Therefore, if through our doctrine we achieve the elevation of a few beings to an angelic state, then we will consider our job done.

Love: the Only Path of Salvation

The enemies of love are called fornicators. They confuse love with desire. Any magician who teaches the ejaculation of the semen is a black magician. Every person who spills the seminal fluid is a fornicator. It is impossible to attain the intimate Realization of the Self whilst one has not yet killed animal desire. Those who spill the Cup of Hermes are incapable of loving. Love and desire are incompatible. Whosoever spills the Cup of Hermes is a victim of animal desire. Love is incompatible with desire and fornication.

Sufism

The most ineffable part of Mohammedan mysticism is Persian Sufism. It has the merit of struggling against materialism and fanaticism and against the literal interpretation of the Koran. The Sufis interpret the Koran from the esoteric point of view as we, the Gnostics, interpret the New Testament.

What is most disconcerting to Westerners is the strange and mysterious mixture of the erotic with the mystical in the oriental religions and Sufi mysticism. Christian theology considers the flesh to be hostile to the Spirit. However, in the Muslim religion, the flesh and the Spirit are two substances of the same energy, two substances that must help each other. This subject-matter is only understood by those who practice positive Sexual Magic. In the East, religion, science, art, and philosophy are taught in an erotic and exquisite sexual language. "Mohammed fell in love with God," state the mystic Arabs. "Select a new wife for yourself each spring of the new year, because last year's calendar is no good," says a Persian poet and philosopher.

Those who have carefully studied the Song of Songs by the sage Solomon find that delicate mixture of the mystical and the erotic, which scandalizes infrasexual people a great deal.

A true religion cannot renounce the erotic because it would be its death. Many myths and ancient legends are based on the erotic. In fact, love and death form the base of every authentic religion.

The Sufis, Persian poets, wrote about the love of God in expressions applicable to beautiful women. These scandalize the infrasexual, fanatic people. The idea of Sufism is the amorous union of the soul with God.

Indeed, nothing can better explain the amorous union of the soul with God than the delectable sexual union of man and woman. That is the brilliant idea of Sufism. If we want to talk about the union of God with the soul, we must do so in the erotic language of love and sex. Only in this way can we express what we have to say.

The symbolic language of the Sufis has marvelous expressions. Among them, sleep signifies meditation. Actually, meditation without sleep damages the mind. This is known by every true initiate. One must combine sleep with meditation. This is known by the Sufis.

The word 'perfume' symbolizes the hope of divine favor; 'kisses' and 'embraces' amongst other things, signify the rapture of piety; 'wine' means spiritual knowledge, etc.

The Sufi poets sang of love, of women, of roses and of wine, and nonetheless many of them lived the lives of hermits.

The seven mystical states described by the Sufis are something extraordinary. There are certain chemical substances closely related with these mystical states. Nitrous oxide and ether (especially nitrous oxide when it is dissolved sufficiently in air) stimulate the mystical consciousness to an extraordinary degree.

We have to acknowledge that this present humanity is subconscious. People like this are incapable of knowing the superior dimensions of space. Therefore, it is urgent to awaken the consciousness, and this is only possible during ecstasy. If we analyze ecstasy with dialectic logic, we discover that it is sexual. The same sexual energies that are expressed in erotic pleasure, when transmuted and sublimated, awaken the consciousness and then produce ecstasy.

Fatality is the loss of ecstasy, it is the fall again into subconsciousness. This happens when we spill the Cup of Hermes.

A great master stated: "With the sexual impulse, the human being finds themselves in the most personal relationship with Nature. The comparison of the sensation which a man experiences with a woman or vice versa, with the consent of Nature, is indeed the same sensation as that offered by the forest, the prairie, the sea, the mountains; save that in this case it is even more intense, since it awakens more internal voices, provokes the sound of more intimate chords." This is how we reach ecstasy.

Ecstasy, the mystical experience, has its principles based on dialectic logic. This logic can never be violated. Let us reflect for example on the unity of experience. This principle exists among the mystics of the East as well as those of the West, among the hierophants of Egypt, as well as the Sufi sages, or among the Aztec magicians. During ecstasy, the mystics speak in the same universal language, use the same words and feel united with all creation. The sacred scriptures of all religions show the same principles. This is dialectic logic, superior logic. This proves that the mystics of all countries of the world drink from the same fountain of life. The conditions of the causes of the world (another of the principles of dialectic logic) show with exactitude, precision, and complete agreement of facts the reality and truth of ecstasy. The mystics of all religions of the world totally agree in their affirmations about the conditions of the causes of the world; the concordance is therefore perfect.

The unity of life is another principle of dialectic logic. Every mystic in ecstasy perceives and feels the unity of life. The mathematics of the infinite and of dialectic logic can never fail.

Whosoever spills the Cup of Hermes loses the state of ecstasy. Their visions are then no longer within dialectic logic. Nonetheless, they believe themselves to be super-transcendent. They violate the principles of dialectic logic and fall into dementia from absurdity. That is fatality.

Every Gnostic student must avoid Black Tantra and those who teach black Sexual Magic if they do not want to fall into the abyss of fatality.

During this Kali Yuga,[176] the dissidents of the ancient archaic schools are very active.

In this day and age, the black magicians are carrying out a tremendous campaign with the purpose of imposing their false knowledge on the epoch which is commencing. They want the black lodge to triumph.

Infrasex in Yoga

The seven schools of yoga are archaic and grandiose, but they could not escape the goals of the tenebrous ones. At the present time, there are many infrasexual people who look for proselytes by establishing schools of yoga. These individuals mortally hate the path of the perfect matrimony, abhor White Sexual Magic. Some of them teach Black Tantra. That is a fatality.

True yoga is based on White Sexual Magic. Yoga without Sexual Magic is an infrasexual doctrine, proper for infrasexual people.

In the *Kama Kalpa* and Tantric Buddhism one finds the legitimate foundations of yoga. Ahamkara[177] and Maithuna are in fact the bases of true yoga: ahamkara (dissolution of the "I") and Maithuna (Sexual Magic)—behold the true synthesis of yoga.

---

176 Literally, "the black era." Sanskrit काली kali, "black, night, discord, strife" and युग yuga, "age, era, period of time." Tibetan: snigs-ma'i dus, literally "the degenerate age."

177 (Sanskrit अहंङ्कार, also ahankara) Literally, "pride, egotism, conception of one's individuality, individualization, arrogance, etc." From अहम् aham, "I." Hindu philosophies use the word ahankara in varying ways, not always negative. At its base, ahankara is simply the perception of being "separate." Yet this perception quickly develops into egotism. "From desire spring cupidity and delusion and vanity and pride and ahankara (selfishness)." —Mahabharata. "You are born to conquer nature and thereby realise Atman. Try to know the ways and habits of this Ahankara. It thirsts for self-aggrandisement or self-advancement, power, possession of objects and enjoyment. Kill this Ahankara or egoism and selfishness. Be disinterested. Pin your faith to the opposite virtues, spirit of sacrifice and selflessness. Accept sacrifice and service as guiding principles of life. At once you will have a rich, expanded spiritual life." —Swami Sivananda

Those who have been members of a monastery of Zen Buddhism know very well that the fundamentals are the Maithuna and the dissolution of the reincarnating ego. In the Self-Yoga of Babaji, he was not celibate. Those who believe that Mataji is his physical sister are mistaken. Mataji is his priestess wife. With her he attained intimate Realization of the Self.

Indian Buddhism, like Zen and Chan Buddhism, is Tantric. Without White Tantra, Yoga is a failure. That is a fatality. Chinese and Japanese Buddhism are completely Tantric.

There is no doubt that Chan and Zen Buddhism really are on the path of the intimate Realization of the Self.

In secret Tibet, Sexual Yoga is grandiose. The great masters of Tibet practice Sexual Magic.

A great friend of mine wrote to me from India saying,

> "In Hindu and Tibetan Tantra, positive sexual yoga (Maithuna) is practiced without seminal ejaculation. After a preparation in which the couple learn to perform the practices of Laya Kriya[178] together, under the direction of an expert guru, they then proceed to the Tantra sadhana during which the husband must introduce the virile member into the vagina. This operation takes place after an exchange of caresses between the couple. The male sits with his legs crossed in an asana (posture) and the woman absorbs the phallus. The couple remain in this union for a long time without moving, trying to prevent their ego and their analytic consciousness from intervening; thus, leaving Nature to act without interference. Then, without expectation of orgasm, the erotic currents enter into activity, provoking the ecstasy. In this instant, the ego dissolves (withdraws);

---

178 From Sanskrit लय laya, "mental inactivity, rest, repose, dissolution." "Laya Yoga is Kundalini Yoga. Concentration on the sound emanating from the heart-lotus is Laya Yoga. Laya is dissolution. The mind is dissolved in God just as a lump of ice is dissolved in a tumbler of soda-water." —Swami Sivananda

thus, desire is transmuted into love. Intense currents similar to electromagnetism, which produce static effects, traverse both bodies. A sensation of ineffable bliss possesses the entire organism, and the couple experiences the ecstasy of love and cosmic communion."

Here ends the statement of my friend whose name I do not mention. This former quoted statement is hated by the infra-sexual people who are involved in yoga. They want to work with yoga in order to use it to increase the number of infra-sexual fanatics. That is a fatality.

Yoga without Sexual Magic is like a garden without water or a car without gasoline or a body without blood; it is a fatality.

Aztec Magic

In the rocky paved courtyards of the Aztecs, naked men and women spent long periods of time kissing and caressing each other and practicing Sexual Magic. However, if the initiate committed the crime of spilling the Cup of Hermes, they were condemned to death for having profaned the temple. The delinquent was beheaded. That is a fatality.

Totem Pole in Bella Coola, British Columbia, Canada

Chapter 26
Totemism

The ignorant swine of dialectic materialism criticize Totemism;[179] they laugh at it without comprehending it. We, the Gnostics, comprehend the grandeur of Totemism and know that its doctrine rests on the basic principles of esotericism.

The Totemists profoundly know the law of reincarnation, as well as the laws which govern the evolution of all living species. They know that karma is the law of cause and effect. They comprehend that all that lives is subject to karma.

The great initiates of Totemism have investigated (with their clairvoyant powers) the intimate life of all creation, and they based the principles of their doctrine on these scientific investigations. These principles are totally unknown for the ignorant swine of materialism.

The Totemists scientifically know that every mineral atom is the physical body of an intelligent elemental.[180] The Totemists know that this mineral elemental evolves until later becoming the anima of a plant. The animas of vegetables are the vegetable elementals which Paracelsus knows how to manage for his healing purposes. One can provoke tempests and earthquakes with

179 Or Animism. "*Totem* comes to us from Ojibwa, an Algonquian language spoken by an American Indian people from the regions around Lake Superior. The most basic form of the word in Ojibwa is believed to be *ote*, but 18th-century English speakers encountered it as *ototeman* (meaning "his totem"), which became our word *totem*. In its most specific sense, *totem* refers to an emblematic depiction of an animal or plant that gives a family or clan its name and that often serves as a reminder of its ancestry." -Merriam-Webster Dictionary

180 Strictly defined, elementals are creatures who have not yet created the soul; in other words, they have consciousness ("anima," raw, unformed soul) as given by nature, and have evolved mechanically through the lower kingdoms. Their physical bodies are the minerals, plants, animals, and humanoids (intellectual animals); internally they have the appearance of people (gnomes, sprites, elves, fairies, mermaids, dwarves). However, in common usage the term elementals refers to the creatures of the three lower kingdoms: mineral, plant and animal, and out of politeness we call the intellectual animals "human," even though they have not become human yet.

the help of plants. We can cure sick people from a distance with plants. The plant elementals are omnipotent because they have developed their Kundalini due to the fact that they never fornicate.[181]

The Totemists know that through evolution the plant elementals later become animal elementals.

The great magicians know about animal elemental magic. Thus, they frequently perform marvels with the animal elementals.

The Totemists know that when the animal elementals are very evolved, they then become human beings. Every well advanced animal elemental reincarnates within a human body.

The Totemist priests wisely state that if the human being does evil, they may devolve, regress, to once again become an animal. This is true. Every perverse human being regresses to the animal state. Often they may reincarnate as an animal; however, they become or are transformed into an animal within the astral plane. Therefore, this affirmation of Totemism is true. It is also very true that perverse people may indeed reincarnate within the bodies of ferocious animals.

There are other cases in which the most pure soul of a saint reincarnates into some species of animal. This is in order to help this species and elevate it to a superior level of consciousness. Therefore, the principles of Totemism are exact.

The Totemists profoundly know the law of karma and know that the fate of every human being is the outcome of their karma from past lives.

In the tribes where Totemism reigns, traditionally they venerate a particular plant or mineral elemental which they know through direct experience. As a rule, this elemental has given great service to the tribe. When the Totem is a tree, they carve human figures into the trunk of that species. Now we have an explanation of all those myths and strange fables that speak of strange beings, half-man, half-animal, like the centaurs, the minotaurs, the sphinx, etc. Those strange images of Totemism are true treasure-troves containing gems of wisdom that are totally unknown to the swine of materialism. Those swine of materi-

---

181 Read *Esoteric Medicine and Practical Magic* by Samael Aun Weor.

alism only know how to laugh. Victor Hugo stated: "The one who laughs at what he does not know is an ignoramus who walks on the path of idiocy."

In Totemism, it is forbidden to kill the animal that is considered a Totem. This animal has been anointed from among those of its species, because it reunites determined secret characteristics which only clairvoyants can recognize. The wise Totemist priests venerate the animal or plant elemental who serves as a vehicle for divinity. This creature is much cared for, and its death is only possible with a very sacred liturgy and several days of common lamentation. Civilized ignorant people do not understand this because they have divorced themselves from great Nature. Nevertheless, the Totem priests do understand it.

We find traces of Totemism in all religious cults. The Hindus venerate the white cow; the Chaldeans, the humble lamb; the Egyptians, the ox; the Arabs, the camel; the Inca, the llama; the Mexicans, the dog and the hummingbird; the primeval Gnostic Christians worshiped the lamb, the fish, and the white dove as symbols of the Holy Spirit.

Specific plant or animal elementals have always been revered. We have to recognize that these elemental creatures are omnipotent, because they have not left Eden.

The great plant elementals are true angels[182] who work for all humanity in the ethereal plane or region of the magnetic fields.

The plant elementals reproduce by means of Sexual Magic. There is sacred copula among the vegetable elementals, and the seed passes to the womb without the necessity of ejaculating the semen.

Each animal is the body of an elemental. Each plant is the physical body of an elemental. These elementals are sacred and perform marvels in Eden. The most powerful elementals are venerated by the Totem.

---

182 "There are two types of angels: innocent angels and virtuous angels. The innocent angels are the elementals of plants, and the virtuous angels are perfect human beings." —Samael Aun Weor, *Esoteric Medicine and Practical Magic*

When the human being learns how to procreate without spilling the semen, they enter Eden. There they know the elemental Totem creatures. These creatures are innocent.

Within themselves, animal elementals are innocent. Some waste the semen stupidly; nonetheless, they are not to be blamed since their divine spark is still innocent. That spark is not yet reincorporated; it is a creature that does not have consciousness of its Self, which still has not taken possession of its vehicles. It retains its fires. It is only its shadow, its ego (the protoplasmic bodies) in a potential state, which reincorporates into animal bodies.

The plant elemental is more pure, more beautiful. They reproduce like the gods. The perfect matrimony is among them.

We also find the perfect matrimony among the mineral elementals. They love each other and procreate, have children, have their own language and customs. They do not waste the seminal fluid; they are complete. They are more perfect than the animal elementals, because unlike the latter, they never waste their seminal fluid.

In Eden, the elementals live happily. Everyone who follows the path of the perfect matrimony, in fact, enters into Eden.

In fact, whosoever has completely developed the sacred fire enters into Eden.

The complete development of the Kundalini allows us to visit Eden with the ethereal body.

Eden is an ethereal plane, a region of an intensely blue color where only happiness reigns. Those who have learned to love live in Eden.

The Totem Gods

The gods exist, and Christianity worships them with the names of Angels, Archangels, Seraphim, Virtues, Thrones, etc.

The ignorant swine of materialism believe that the human being created the gods of fire, air, water, and earth out of fear. This concept of the learned ignoramuses of materialism is totally false. Soon there will appear a special lens through which we will be able to see the aura, the astral body, the astral world, the disincarnate egos, and the gods of the astral world. Then all the stupid statements of the learned ignoramuses will be reduced to dust. The human being will once again adore and revere the ineffable gods. They existed even before the world appeared.

Elementals

Paracelsus states that we need to harness the elementals of Nature to the chariot of science in order to fly through the air, to ride the eagle, to walk on water, to travel to the most distant places of the Earth within a few moments.

There are elementals that can help us with astral travel. Let us remember the elemental of the datura arborea tree that is known in different countries as borrachero, angel's trumpet, flower of the night. This elemental can take any human being out in their astral body into the astral world. It is enough for the Gnostic student to always have one of these trees in their home. It is necessary to gain the affection of the elemental of the tree. During the night the Gnostic student concentrates on the elemental of the tree. They will vocalize the syllable KAM many times and then fall asleep begging the elemental of the tree to take them from the physical body into the astral body to whatever remote part of the world of the infinite cosmos. This plant elemental will help all those who in truth know how to ask with faith and love. The datura arborea tree is known as floripondio in Peru; higanton in Bolivar, Colombia. Many people triumph with these practices immediately because they are hypersensitive; yet on the other hand, there are people who are not hypersensitive. These people need to practice a great deal in order to attain victory.

SHIVA, THE CREATOR AND DESTROYER

INDIA

Chapter 27
Sacred Phallicism

Every religion has a sexual origin. The veneration of the lingam-yoni and pudenda is common in Africa and Asia. Secret Buddhism is sexual. Sexual Magic is taught practically in Zen Buddhism. Buddha taught Sexual Magic in secrecy.

There are many phallic divinities. Shiva, Agni, and Shakti in India are phallic divinities. Legba in Africa, Venus, Bacchus, Priapus, and Dionysus in Greece and Rome were phallic divinities.

The Jews had phallic gods and sacred forests consecrated to the sexual sacrament. Sometimes the priests of these phallic religions allowed themselves to fall miserably and descended to wild bacchanalian orgies. Herodotus quotes the following: "All the women of Babylon had to prostitute themselves with the priests of the temple of Milita."

Meanwhile, in Greece and Rome, in the temples of Vesta, Venus, Aphrodite, Isis etc., the priestesses exercised their holy sexual priesthood. In Cappadocia, Antioch, Pamplos, Cyprus, and Bylos, with infinite veneration and mystic exaltation, the priestesses celebrated great processions carrying a great phallus, as god or the generative body of life and of the seed.

The Bible also has many allusions to the phallic religion. The oath from the time of the Patriarch Abraham was taken by the Jews by placing their hand beneath the thigh, that is, on the sacred member.

The Feast of the Tabernacles was an orgy similar to the famous Saturnalia of the Romans.

The rite of circumcision is totally phallic.

The history of all religions is filled with symbols and phallic amulets, such as the Hebrew mitzvah, the maypole of the Christians, etc.

In ancient times, sacred stones with a phallic form were profoundly venerated. Some of those stones resembled the virile member and others the vulva. Flint stones and silica were taken as sacred stones, because fire was produced with them, fire which esoterically was developed as a divine privilege in the spinal column of the Pagan priests.

In Christianity we find a great deal of phallicism. The circumcision of Jesus, the feast of the three wise men (Epiphany), the Corpus Christi, etc., are phallic festivals inherited from the holy Pagan religions.

The dove, symbol of the Holy Spirit and of the voluptuous Venus Aphrodite, is always represented as the phallic instrument used by the Holy Spirit to impregnate the Virgin Mary. The very word "sacrosanct" is derived from sacral,[183] and therefore its origin is phallic.

The phallic religion is terribly divine. The phallic religion is scientifically transcendental and profoundly philosophical. The era of Aquarius is at hand, and in it the laboratories will discover the energetic and mystical principles of the phallus and uterus.

The sexual glands are governed by Uranus, and enclose tremendous forces that laboratory science will discover in the new era. The scientific value of the ancient phallic cults will then be publicly recognized.

The entire potential of universal life is within the seed. The materialist science of this day and age does not know anything but to criticize sardonically that which it does not know.

In the rocky paved courtyards of the Aztec temples, men and women used to sexually unite to awaken the Kundalini. The couples remained in the temples for months and years, loving and caressing each other, practicing Sexual Magic without the spilling of the semen. However, those who reached the ejaculation of the semen were condemned to death. Their heads were cut off with an axe. Thus, this is how they paid their sacrilege.

In the Eleusinian Mysteries, naked dances and Sexual Magic were the very foundation of the mysteries. Phallicism is the foundation of profound Realization of the Self.

---

183 "of or pertaining to the sacrum," compound bone at the base of the spine, from Latin os sacrum "sacred bone," from Latin sacrum "sacred thing, rite"

All the principal tools of Masonry serve in order to work with the stone. Every Master Mason must chisel his Philosophical Stone well. This stone is the sex. We must build the temple of the Eternal One upon the living stone.

Sex and Serpent

A certain initiate, whose name I do not mention, states the following textually:

"With complete dominion of the serpent force anything can be achieved. One can move mountains or walk on water, fly, or be buried under the earth in a sealed casket from which one can emerge at any determined time.

"The ancient priests knew that under certain conditions the aura can be seen, they knew that the Kundalini can be awakened through sex.

"The force of the Kundalini coiled below is a terrific force; it resembles the spring of a clock in the manner in which it is coiled. Like the spring of the clock which suddenly jumps, uncoiling itself, it can cause damage (to those who commit the crime of spilling the semen).

"This particular force is found at the base of the spinal column; however, in the present day and age, part of it abides within the generative organs. The Orientals recognize this. Certain Hindus use sex in their religious ceremonies. They use a different form of sexual manifestation (Sexual Magic) and a different sexual position to obtain specific results, and they have been successful. Many centuries and centuries ago, the ancients worshiped sex. They accomplished the phallic religion. There were certain ceremonies within the temples which aroused the

Kundalini, which in turn produced clairvoyance, telepathy and many other esoteric powers."

Sex, used properly and with love, can attain particular vibrations. It can bring about that which the Orientals call the opening of the lotus flower, and it can embrace the world of the spirits. It can promote the arousal of Kundalini and the awakening of certain centers. However, sex and the Kundalini must never be abused. Each must complement and help the other. Those religions that say that there must be no sex between husband and wife are tragically mistaken.

"Those religions which state that there must be no sexual experiences try to suffocate individual evolution and the evolution of the race. Let us look at an example: in magnetism, we obtain magnetic power by aligning the molecules of a substance directed towards a specific point. That is to say, normally in a piece of iron the molecules are randomly positioned like an undisciplined multitude. They may join by chance, but when a certain force is applied (in the case of iron, a magnetic force) all the molecules face in one direction and thus, magnetic power is obtained, without which there would not be radio or electricity; without which we would not have road, rail or even aerial transport.

"When the human being awakens the Kundalini, when the serpent of fire begins to live, the molecules of the body are aligned in one direction, because the force of the Kundalini has this effect when awakened. Then the human body begins to vibrate with health, becomes powerful in knowledge, and can see everything.

"There are various methods (Tantric positions) to fully awaken the Kundalini (the *Kama Kalpa* contains all those sexual positions). Nevertheless this must not be done except by those who are

truly trained for it, because of the immense
power and control that this awakening gives over
others, and because this power can be abused
and used for evil. But the Kundalini can awaken
partially (and completely) within the married
couple, and can vivify certain centers through
love. With true intimate ecstasy, the molecules
of the body are aligned in such a way that many
of them face the same direction. Consequently,
these people develop a great dynamic power.

"When false modesty and all the false
teachings about sex are changed, the human
being will again reach his true Being. Once
again the human being will be able to
regain his place as an astral traveler."

The phallic religion is as ancient as the world. Sex must
help the Kundalini and the Kundalini must help sex. Neither
sex nor the Kundalini must be abused. Sexual Magic must be
practiced only once a day.

"Man and woman are not simply a mass of
protoplasm, flesh attached to a frame of bones.
The human being is, or can be, something
more than that. Here on Earth we are simple
puppets of our Spirit. That Spirit which
resides temporarily in the astral accumulates
experience through its body of flesh, which
is the puppet, the instrument of the astral.

"Physiologists and others have analyzed the body
of the human being, and have reduced it to a
mass of flesh and bones. They can talk about this
or that bone, about different organs, but these
are material things. They have not discovered,
nor have they tried to discover the most secret
things, the intangible things, the things that
the Hindus, the Chinese and the Tibetans knew
centuries and centuries before Christianity.

"The dorsal spine is indeed a very important structure. It contains the spinal medulla, without which one would be paralyzed, without which one is useless as a human being. Nevertheless, the dorsal spine is even more important than all that. Exactly in the center of the spinal nerve, the spinal medulla, is a passage that extends to other dimensions (fourth, fifth, sixth dimensions, etc.), a passage through which the force known as the Kundalini can travel through when it is awakened. At the base of the dorsal spine is what the Orientals call the serpent of fire. This is the seat of life itself.

"In Western people, this great force is inactive, asleep, almost paralyzed for lack of use. At the present time it is like a serpent coiled upon itself, a serpent of immense power, but for various reasons (that is, because of filthy fornication), it cannot escape from its confines at this time. This mystical representation of the serpent is known as the Kundalini, and in those Orientals in whom it is awake, the serpent force can advance through the passage of the spinal nerve, passing straight to the brain and beyond, far beyond, to the astral. As this potent active force advances, each of the chakras or centers of power, such as the umbilical, the throat and others, are awakened and the person becomes a vital, powerful, dominant individual."

Phallicism, the awakening of the Kundalini, Sexual Magic, is not dangerous when practiced with uprightness and with love.

Sexual Magic should only be practiced between husband and wife. Those men who abuse and practice with other women outside the home inevitably fail.

Infrasexual Schools

There are many infrasexual schools in the world that mortally hate the phallic religion and Sexual Magic. Lovers of wisdom must avoid these schools if they do not also want to become infrasexual.

It is necessary to remember that infrasexuality hates normal sex and suprasex. In all ages, infrasexual ones have blasphemed against the Third Logos, considering sex to be taboo, a sin, a cause for shame, clandestine, etc. Infrasexual people have schools where they teach people to hate sex. Infrasexual people consider themselves to be mahatmas, hierophants, etc.

Lovers of wisdom are often confused by infrasexual people. They assume certain attitudes, so mystical and ineffable, so anchorite-like and pious that if one does not have a certain degree of comprehension, one can very easily be led astray onto the path of infrasexuality.

Initiation and the Serpent

It is impossible to receive the initiations of Major Mysteries without the phallic religion and without Sexual Magic.

Many single students receive the initiations of the Minor Mysteries in their superlative and transcendental consciousness when they are chaste. Nevertheless, the Initiations of Major Mysteries cannot be attained without Sexual Magic and the Kundalini.

The Minor Mysteries are none other than the probationary path, a chain that has to be broken, the kindergarten of esoteric studies, the first reader. The phallic religion is the only one that can lead the human being to intimate Realization of the Self.

Ahura Mazda

Chapter 28

The Religion of Fire

The religion of fire from ancient Persia was grandiose. The religion of fire is very ancient. It is said that this religion preceded the Achaemenid dynasty and Zoroaster's epoch. The Persian priests possessed a very rich esoteric liturgy related with the religion of the fire. The ancient Persian sages were never careless with the fire. They had the mission of always keeping it alight. The secret doctrine of Avesta states that there are different types of fires: the fire of the lightning that flashes in the terrifying night, the fire that works inside the human organism producing calories and directing the processes of digestion, the fire that is concentrated in the innocent plants of Nature, the fire that smolders within the mountains, and which is spewed out by the volcanoes of the Earth, the fire that is in the presence of Ahura Mazda and forms his divine halo, and the everyday fire that the profane use in order to cook their food. The Persians used to say that when boiling water is spilled or when a living being is burnt, in those cases, God stops all the benefits he has granted unto his privileged people.

Indeed, fire has many modifications, but among all the fires, the most powerful is the one that blazes in the presence of Ahura Mazda (the Solar Logos), forming his divine halo.

This fire is the outcome of the transmutation of the sexual secretions. This fire is the Kundalini, the igneous serpent of our magical powers, the fire of the Holy Spirit.

Whoever wants to find the fire of Ahura Mazda must search for it within the interior of their philosophical earth. This earth is the human organism itself. The Persian priests cultivated this fire in places of complete darkness, subterranean temples, and secret places. The altar was always an enormous metal chalice with its base upon the Philosophical Stone. The fire was always nourished with fragrant and dry wood, especially the delectable branches of sandalwood. The old priests always blew upon the fire with bellows, so as not to profane it with the sinful breath of the human mouth.

Fill your chalice with the sacred wine of light. Remember, dear reader, that the secret and philosophical living fire blazes within your own philosophical earth. Now you will comprehend the esoteric mystery of the ritual of fire.

Two priests always tended the fire. Behold the binary. They each used tongs to place the pieces of wood and a spoon to scatter in it the perfumes. There were, then, two tongs and two spoons. In all this we can see the binary. The binary enables us to understand that only the number two can tend the fire. It is necessary that man and woman in perfect binary light watch over the divine fire of Ahura Mazda.

In the Bundahishn,[184] a kind of ritual gospel, it is stated that a well of sacred water was within a special chamber where the priest performed ablutions before presenting himself before the altar of fire. Only the one who drinks the pure water of life can light the fire. Only the one who washes his feet in the waters of renunciation can light the fire. Only the one who conserves the water can ritualize with the fire. That water symbolizes the ens seminis.

Everywhere in Persia there are rchaeological ruins of complex temples and antechambers where the fire was worshiped. These ruins can be found today in Persepolis, Isfahan, Yazd, Palmyra, Susa, etc.

The fire is terribly divine. Therefore, the fire must never be absent from within the homes of those who follow the path of the perfect matrimony. A flame lit with profound devotion is always equal to a prayer; thus, it attracts from above a tremendous flow of divine energy. Every prayer to the Logos must be accompanied by fire. Thus the prayer is powerful.

The time in order to return to the religion of fire has arrived. Gnostics must journey to the mountains. Thus there, within the profound bosom of mother Nature, ignite a bonfire, light the fire, and pray and meditate. In this way we can attract powerful currents of divine energy from above that will help us in the Great Work of the Father.

The human being must light their forty-nine fires by means of Sexual Magic. Thus, when our thoughts are aflame we can

---

184 Pahlavi, "Original Creation," Zoroastrian account of creation.

create like the ineffable gods of the cosmos. The holy gods are true ministers of fire. The holy gods are tongues of flaming fire.

The Whirling Dervishes

In Persia, as well as in Turkey, etc., the sacred dances of the whirling dervishes are in essence a religion to the fire. It is a shame that the authorities of Ankara, boasting of being very civilized, have prohibited these public dances of the whirling dervishes.

The dervishes marvelously imitate the movement of the planets of the solar system around the Sun. The dances of the dervishes are intimately related with the dorsal spine and the sexual fires. We must never forget that the serpent enjoys music and dance, as the snake charmers from Egypt and India have already demonstrated. They play their marvelous flutes and the enchanted serpents dance.

It is now opportune to remember the ritual dances of the fire from all the ancient temples. Let us remember the naked dances of the Eleusinian Mysteries, the sacred dancers of India, Egypt, Mexico, Yucatan, etc. When the Akashic Records fall into the hands of scientists and the world will be able to watch the fire dances of archaic times on television, then we will return to these dances, which will inevitably replace the profane dances.

Egyptian Darkness

Some years ago several monks with wicked faith from the Athos monastery, famous in Greece and Russia, undertook the business of selling "Egyptian Darkness" in bottles, making thus a great deal of money. It is absurd to sell Egyptian Darkness as a black powder in bottles. The reality of the Egyptian Darkness cannot be sold as a black powder. "Egyptian Darkness" is an allegorical, archaic phrase. The Egyptians, when they covered themselves with their mantle and closed their eyes to the physical world, remained in darkness to the world, but in splendorous light to the Spirit.

At the present time, there are many sages within the Egyptian Darkness. Nevertheless they shine with the sacred fire in Amen-Ra.

Many Egyptian sages who were buried alive exist in a state of catalepsy. They sleep deeply in their tombs until the day and the hour when they must awaken according to the plans of the White Lodge. There is one, whose body has been asleep since three thousand years before the time of Jesus the Christ. Another has been sleeping since ten thousand years before Jesus Christ, and all of them sleep in this manner; their bodies lie in Egyptian Darkness, nevertheless, their souls live consciously in the superior worlds working intensely for humanity.

When the right day and hour arrives, each of these adepts will be assisted by their brothers and sisters; they will be taken out from within their sepulchral home and awakened. These Egyptian adepts will initiate a new era of spiritual activity.

They conserve within their memory all the archaic knowledge.

It is interesting to know that the bodies of these adepts, duly bandaged and protected in their funeral coffins, sleep without eating or drinking. All their organic functions are suspended. Strange and mysterious chemical substances protect them. Terrible, elemental guardians guard their tombs; therefore, no archaeologist will ever find them.

To leave the tomb, after thousands of years, to maintain oneself without eating and without drinking for so many centuries, is only possible with the religion of the fire, with the power of the fire. All these adepts practiced Sexual Magic intensely. Only the serpent of fire can give the adept this kind of tremendous power.

Javhe יהוה

In the Hall of Memories (the Akasha), the history of that angel named יהוה Javhe is written. Saturnine of Antioch, the great Kabbalist, states that Javhe is a fallen angel, the genius of evil, the Devil. Javhe is a terribly perverse demon.

Javhe is that demon who tempted Christ in the wilderness when he took him to a high mountain and showed him all the kingdoms of the world and the glory of them. Thus, when tempting Christ, Javhe said, "ITABABO. All these things will I give thee, if thou wilt fall down and worship me."

Javhe called the Jewish people "my chosen people." The Jews intentionally mingled יהוה Javhe with the Lord יהוה Jehovah.

Javhe was a Lemurian hierophant. Javhe had a priestess wife. Javhe was an angel with a human body. The Master Javhe was a warrior of the light, a great priest of the ray of might, and due to his high priestly dignity, had the legitimate right to wear a helmet and armor, shield, and sword made of pure gold.

The priestess wife of Javhe was by all means a lady-adept.

In archaic times, the warrior and priestly castes developed independently of each other. Nevertheless, there were exceptions as in the case of Javhe who was both priest and warrior.

The Lucifers of the ancient Earth-Moon floated within the Lemurian atmosphere. These Lucifers were searching for proselytes and they enrolled many. Javhe was one of their proselytes. Javhe became a disciple of these tenebrous sub-lunar beings; thus, he practiced black Sexual Magic with the spilling of the Cup of Hermes. This is the science of the Bons and Drukpas of the "Red Cap." The result was fatal. His igneous serpent fell; it descended downwards towards the atomic infernos of the human being. This is how Javhe became a terribly perverse demon.

This history is described in the Akasha. Javhe became a member of a Lemurian temple of Black Tantra. His priestess-wife never accepted Sexual Magic with the spilling of the Hermetic cup. Javhe fell with another woman. The efforts that Javhe made in order to convince his priestess wife were useless. She refused to enter the black temple. That marriage ended. The lady-adept did not want to enter the black path. Now, this lady-adept is an ineffable angel of the superior worlds.

The religion of fire is very delicate. The gods of fire help to protect all those who follow the path of the perfect matrimony.

The Ages of the World

The division of the history of humanity into the Golden, Silver, Copper, and Iron Ages is a tremendous reality. The planetary fire devolves and evolves, passing through these stages. There is no doubt that the fire of our planet Earth produced very little profit in the three preceding rounds and in the ancient Earth-Moon;[185] therefore, the fire is full of karma. This is the cause of the failure of humanity on the planet Earth.

The cycles unfold alternately. An age of great mystical inspiration and of unconscious productivity is followed by another of tremendous critique and of self-consciousness. One provides the material for the analysis and criticism of the other. In the field of spiritual conquests, Buddha and Jesus represent the highest conquests of the Spirit. Alexander of Macedonia and Napoleon the Great represent the conquests in the physical world. These figures were reproductions made by the fire, reproductions of human types that had existed ten thousand years before. Reflected images from the tenth former millennium were reproduced by the mysterious powers of fire.

As above, so below. What has been shall again be. In the same way as things are in Heaven so they are also on Earth.

In this moment, the life of our planet Earth would be a true paradise, if the fire of our planet Earth had totally evolved in the ancient Earth-Moon and in the three preceding rounds. Unfortunately, our planetary fire is full of cosmic karma.

The Great Problem

The whole of humanity, the sum total of all human units, is Adam Kadmon,[186] the human race, homo sapiens, the sphinx, which is the being with the body of an animal and the head of a human being.

---

185 Read *The Revolution of Beelzebub* by Samael Aun Weor.

186 Hebrew אָדָם קַדְמוֹן, "primordial man." Adam Kadmon has many applications, including the first manifestation of the Abstract Space; The Archetypal Man; Humanity; The Heavenly Man, not fallen into sin.

The human being participates as a component part in many lives, great and small. The family, populace, religion, country, are living beings of which we form a part.

Within us there are many unknown lives, many "I's" that quarrel amongst themselves, and many "I's" that do not know they live among one other. All of them live within the human being, just as a human and all humans live within the great spiritual body of Adam Kadmon.

These "I's" live within the human being, just as a human and all humans live within cities, towns, and religious congregations, etc. In the same way that the inhabitants of a city do not know each other, likewise, not all the "I's" which live within the city of nine gates (the human being) are known to each other. This is the great problem.

The so-called "human being" does not yet have a true existence. The human being is still an unrealized being.

The human being is similar to a house occupied by many people. The human being is like a ship in which many passengers travel (many "I's"). Each "I" has its own ideals, its own projects, desires, etc.

The "I" that becomes enthusiastic with the work in the magisterium of fire is later displaced by another "I" that hates that work, and if the aspirant began to work in the forge of Vulcan with much enthusiasm, we later see him disillusioned, leaving the work and seeking refuge in any little school that offers him consolation. Then, even later, another "I" intervenes in order to take him out of there also. This is the greatest problem.

Furthermore, there are many tenebrous visitors. Just as many people enter a city, including unwelcome people, individuals with bad habits, this unfortunate tragedy is also repeated in the city of nine gates (the human being).[187] Tenebrous inhabitants who suggest evil ideas and stimulate animal desires enter into this city. Unfortunately, the human being is ninety-seven percent subconscious, and indeed they ignore all that

---

187 In the Bhagavad-gita, Krishna describes the human body as a city of nine gates or openings: two openings each for the eyes, ears, and nose; and one each for the mouth, anus, and urethra.

happens in their interior. When these tenebrous inhabitants totally control the human brain, the human being then does things that they would not normally do, even for all the money in the world. Therefore, it is not strange that in one of those fatal moments even saints may have raped and murdered.

The magisterium of fire is extremely difficult because of the number of invisible people who inhabit and visit the city of nine gates. Each of these mysterious people, each of these "I's" thinks differently and has his own customs. Now we can explain to ourselves the cause of many problems in the home. The man who today is enthusiastic about his wife, abandons her tomorrow. The woman who today is loyal to her husband, goes off with another man tomorrow. This is the great problem.

Within the psyche of the human being there is a continuous change of perspective from one object to another. A continuous film of impressions, occurrences, feelings, desires, etc., occurs within the mind. Each of these things perfectly defines the "I" in any given moment.

Many people live within the city of the nine gates. This is a serious thing. This is a great problem. The fire religion is very difficult because within the city of nine gates live many people who hate that religion.

The physical body is only one section of the tetra-dimensional body, the linga sharira or vital body. The human personality is in like manner another tetra-dimensional section of the human body. Beyond this is the ego (the pluralized "I") like an upper part of the human personality. The personality dies; however, its memory remains within the ego.

The poor intellectual animals still do not know anything about the soul and Spirit. This is still very far from the common level of humanity.

The body, the personality, and the ego are still unknown to each other, because the human being is subconscious. The common level human being has even less knowledge about the soul and the Spirit.

In fact, the three inferior aspects of the human being—the body, the personality, and the ego—can only know each other under the influence of narcotics, or in a trance, or in medium-istic or hypnotic states, or during sleep, or through ecstasy.

The mystery of the sphinx is the human being. The animal with a human head is the human being. Whilst one has not yet resolved the problem of the sphinx, one can fall into the abyss of perdition.

Everyone who is working in the magisterium of fire must beg daily to their Father who is in secret for an abundance of assistance. It is urgent to appeal to our inner God to repeat within our inner consciousness the miracle accomplished by Jesus when he expelled the merchants from the temple with the terrible whip of willpower. Only the Beloved One can expel these intrusive "I's" from the temple of our consciousness.

These merchants of the temple sabotage the Great Work. These evil ones are the ones who extinguish the fires of the temple. This is the great problem.

Indeed, this is the path of the razor's edge. This path is full of dangers, both within and without.

"For many are called, but few are chosen."
—Christian Bible, Matthew 22:14

The Four Gospels

The four gospels[188] are intimately related with the magisterium of fire. It is absurd to interpret the four gospels literally. The gospels are completely symbolic. The birth in the manger of Bethlehem symbolizes the Venustic Initiation. Christ is always born among the animals of desire within the stable of the human being in order to save the world.

The star that the wise men saw is seen by all mystics during ecstasy. This star is the central Sun, the Christ Sun, formed by the Army of the Voice. This is the star that announces initiation. This is the star that guides the devotees of the fire.

---

188 The first four books of the Christian New Testament: Matthew, Mark, Luke, and John, which tell the story of Jesus.

Initiation always begins with the miracle of Cana,[189] transmuting the water of life into the wine of light of the alchemists. This miracle is performed within the perfect matrimony.

We have to raise the igneous serpent of our magical powers up to the Golgotha[190] of the Father (the brain).

In the magisterium of fire, the true devotee has to live the whole drama of initiation. The four gospels are written in code, and only the initiates can understand them. The hierophant Jesus was not the first who lived this drama of the Passion,[191] nor was he the last. This drama has been lived by all those who have Christified themselves. Whosoever investigates the sacred scriptures of all the archaic religions will discover with astonishment that this drama existed many millions of years before Jesus Christ. All the great avatars have lived the same drama of the Passion, have also been in the same position as Jesus.

The great master of perfection lived the whole drama as it is written, but we must not interpret the four gospels literally. Let us remember that the town of Bethlehem did not even exist in the time of Jesus.

The four gospels constitute a practical guide for the devotees of the religion of the fire. Whosoever does not know the Arcanum A.Z.F. cannot comprehend the four gospels of fire.

The Mother Kundalini

Christ is always the son of the Divine Mother Kundalini. She always conceives her son through the work and grace of the Third Logos. She is always virginal, before the birth, during the birth, and after the birth. Among the Egyptians, the virgin is Isis; among the Hindu, Kali (in her positive aspect); among

---

189 The first miracle performed by Jesus was at a wedding, where he transmuted water into wine. Note that Cana means "cane, reed," a symbol of the spinal column. Read the Christian Bible, John 2.

190 Aramaic, literally "pile of skulls." Hebrew גלגלת (Num 1:2; Ch1 23:3, Ch1 23:24; Kg2 9:35). Also called Calvary from Latin calva "bald head" or "skull." A skull-shaped hill in Jerusalem, the site of Jesus' Crucifixion.

191 "sufferings of Christ on the Cross," from O.Fr. passion, from L.L. passionem (nom. passio) "suffering, enduring."

the Aztecs, Tonantzin. She is Rhea, Cybele, Maria, Adonia, Insoberta, etc.

It is impossible to incarnate the Word without the development, evolution, and progress of Kundalini.

This prayer is written in a Gnostic ritual:

Oh Hadit, winged serpent of light, be thou the Gnostic secret of my Being, the central point of my connection; the sacred sphere and the blue of the sky are mine.

O AO KAKOF NA KHONSA.

The worshippers of the fire, priest and priestess, can chant this prayer during the practice of Sexual Magic.

The mantras of this prayer have the power to sublimate the sexual energies, the Hyle[192] of the Gnostics, to the heart.

When the initiate invokes the Divine Mother Kundalini, either to help place the physical body into Jinn state or for any other miracle of high magic, she appears as a most pure virgin, as a most beloved mother. All of our most beloved mothers of all our reincarnations are represented by her.

Mother Kundalini is the serpent of fire that rises through the medullar canal. We need to be swallowed by the snake. We need to be transformed into the snake itself.

Those pseudo-esotericists who suppose that the serpent awakens totally and completely developed are very mistaken. The Kundalini needs to develop, evolve, and progress until it reaches its complete development. Sex must help the Kundalini. The Kundalini must help sex. We must neither abuse sex nor the Kundalini.

The seven serpents have their marvelous double in the seven serpents of light. First the fire, then the Brahmic splendor of the Venustic Initiation. We first need to climb the septenary scale of fire and then the septenary scale of light.

We first need to resurrect in the fire and then in the light. The Divine Mother Kundalini, with the golden child of sexual

---

192 Primordial matter. "The elements are made out of hyle and every element is converted into the nature of another element." —Roger Bacon

alchemy in her loving arms, guides us along the terrible path of the razor's edge.

Our beloved Isis, whose veil no mortal has ever lifted, can forgive all of our past karma if we really repent for all of our errors.

The serpent of fire totally transforms us. The serpent transforms us into tremendously divine gods of the cosmos.

Chapter 29

The Edda

We can consider the German *Edda*[193] to be the Germanic
Bible. This archaic book contains the esoteric knowledge of the
Nordics. The narratives concerning the genesis of the world
described in the *Edda* are as follows:

> *"In the beginning there were two unique regions: one of fire
> and light where the absolute and eternal being, Alfadur ruled,
> and the other, a region of darkness and cold called Niffleheim,
> ruled by Surtur (the Dark One). Between one region and the
> other there was chaos. The sparks that escaped from Alfadur
> fertilized the cold vapors of Niffleheim, and Ymir, father of
> the race of giants was born. To nourish him, and in the same
> manner, the cow Audhumbla was created, from whose udder
> flowed the four rivers of milk. Satiated, Ymir fell asleep, and
> from the sweat of his hands a giant couple was born, male and
> female; and from one of his feet, a monster with six heads."*

In this genesis of creation we discover sexual alchemy. The
fire fecundated the cold waters of chaos. The masculine principle Alfadur fecundated the feminine principle Niffleheim,
dominated by Surtur (the darkness), to bring forth life. That
is how Ymir is born, the father of the giants, the inner God of
every human being, the master. He is nourished with the raw
matter of the Great Work. This substance is the milk of the
cow Audhumbla, the sacred white cow of India. In Genesis,
written by Moses, the four rivers of Eden are mentioned, the
four rivers of milk. These four are the flaming fire, the pure
water of life, the impetuous air, and the perfumed elemental
earth of the sages (the four tattvas). In every alchemical operation, the four elements come into activity. These cannot be
absent from the sexual alchemy of creation.

Ymir sleeps and from his sweat a giant couple is born, male
and female, the sublime and giant primeval divine hermaph-

---

193 Documents that compiled fragments of medieval skaldic tradition in
Iceland and Norse mythology.

rodite of the sacred island. In the Genesis written by Moses, Adam falls asleep and God takes Eve from one of his ribs. Before this moment, Eve was inside of Adam; thus, Eve and Adam were one being. This being was an hermaphrodite (the polar race).

From the feet of this giant hermaphrodite (the polar race), the six headed monster was born, the star of Solomon, the sexual alchemy of the human being, which after many centuries ends up in the separation or division of the giants, transforming them into human beings of separate sexes. The division into opposite sexes is the beginning of the great tragedy. Thus, from the hermaphroditic giant, the six headed monster is born.

The human being will again become a divine hermaphrodite. Accompanied by his divine Eve, Adam will return to Eden. When man and woman are sexually united, in those moments they are a single hermaphroditic being. Indeed, during those moments of supreme sexual voluptuousness we are gods. This is the supreme moment the initiate knows how to take advantage of in order to execute magical phenomena.

The birth of the human being in separate sexes was a grandiose event of anthropogenesis (which was accomplished over many millions of years).

After giving this marvelous description of the creation of the world, the Germanic *Edda* describes the separation into opposite sexes as follows:

> *"Immediately the gods decided to create the first human pair. The man was formed from an ash tree, and they called him Aske. The woman was formed from an alder, and they called her Embla. Odin gave them the soul; Vili gave them understanding; Ve gave them beauty and the senses. And the gods, satisfied with their work, retired to rest and to enjoy themselves in their mansion at Asgard, located in the center of the universe."*

The Germanic apocalypse is shown in the narratives of the Edda, the destruction of the world is as follows:

> *"Nature itself starts to become disordered; the seasons cease to alternate; the terrible Fimbulvetr [winter] dominates and lasts*

*for three years because the Sun has lost its strength; there is no
faith among men; peace between brothers, relatives and children
of the same tribe is not observed; the sacred duty of the Germans
to respect the dead, of cutting their nails and of burning them
is neglected. At the consummation of the centuries, Hrimer the
frost giant and his innumerable companions have to embark
on a colossal ship in order to destroy the gods, and their happy
and resplendent abode Valhalla, and the universe. This terrible
reproachful ship, which is made only of the nails of the dead,
never cut by any merciful soul, advances and grows in spite
of the smallness of the material, until the corruption reaches
its limit. Then the monsters, whom the gods had managed to
enchain, break the chains which bind them. The mountains
sink, the jungles are uprooted, the wolves, who since the
beginning of the world have howled at the Sun and Moon,
trying to devour these two stars, and who have sometimes
almost had them within their claws, now reach them and
consume them once and for all. The wolf Fernis breaks his
bonds and assails the world with open jaws, reaching the sky
with one jaw and the Earth with the other, and would open
them even wider, but there is no space. The serpent of Midgard
floods all the Earth (because the human being has become
a fornicator); the frost giants come from the Levant in their
ship of nails. At high-noon the powers of the destructive fire
draw nearer. Loki, the Surda, and the sons of Mitspellheim
come to fight the final decisive battle of the Ases. The divinities
of Valhalla prepare to receive the enemy. Their watchman
Heimdall, posted at the entrance to the bridge that leads to
their dwelling, sounds the clarion, and the gods, in union with
the souls of the heroes who have died in battle, go out to receive
the giants. The battle begins, and ends with the destruction
of both armies; with the death of the gods and the giants. The
incandescence of those of the fire spreads over the world, so
that all is consumed in an immense purifying holocaust."*

A wise analysis of the Edda's genesis and apocalypse reveals
to us that the key point (in one as well as in the other) is the
sexual subject matter. The world is sexually created. The primeval hermaphrodite becomes sexually divided. He is a god when

he does not spill the semen. He becomes a demon when he spills the semen. The world is created sexually, and this world is destroyed when human beings become terrible fornicators, when the Great Whore (humanity) has reached the breaking point of her corruption, that is, when the serpent of Midgard floods the entire Earth.

Indeed, the Great Whore whose number is six hundred and sixty-six[194] is born when the human being becomes accustomed to ejaculating the semen. Fornication is what corrupts the human being. It is through fornication that the human being becomes terribly perverse and then the world is destroyed.

The unknown monsters of Nature, which are elements that the human being does not know, and which the gods have enchained, are unleashed through the atomic weapons. The jungles are uprooted, the wolves of karma howl horribly. The wolf Fenrir breaks his bonds and attacks the world with an open mouth, touching the sky and the earth with his jaws.

Karma is indeed terrifying; thus, a collision of worlds will occur. In archaic times a similar collision already occurred. Then, the Earth was closer to the Sun, yet it was hurled to its present distance. Now the same cataclysm will be repeated because of the law of karma. At that moment, as the Germanic *Edda* states, all shall be consumed in an immense purifying holocaust.

There can be no genesis without sexual alchemy. There can be no apocalypse without sexual degeneration. Every genesis and every apocalypse is based on the phallus and the uterus. The fire creates and the fire destroys. Indeed, the destructive powers of the fire are already in movement. Atomic wars will definitively unleash powers that will consume the Earth. This race will soon be destroyed by fire.

The hour has arrived to comprehend the necessity of totally entering the path of the perfect matrimony. Only those who resolve to follow this path can save themselves from the Abyss and the Second Death.

God shines upon the perfect couple.

---

194 From the Christian Bible, Revelation 13.

Human Salvation

In the name of truth, we have to recognize that the problem of human salvation is a true Chinese puzzle, very difficult to solve. Jesus emphasizes the tremendous difficulty of entering into the kingdom of esotericism and attaining eternal salvation.

If we truly want to save ourselves, it is urgent to fabricate the soul. We have already stated the human being only has an embryo of soul incarnated. We have also stated that we need to fortify this embryo and later incarnate the cosmic soul. Now it is good to clarify that to incarnate the soul essentially means to be assimilated, devoured by the tiger of wisdom. We need the tiger of wisdom to devour us. This tiger is the Innermost, our real Being.

The Aztecs state that the first root race[195] that existed in the world was devoured by tigers. The Temple of the Tigers was in the Yucatan. Quetzalcoatl snatches the human heart with his tiger claws. The tiger cult was never absent in any of the temples of mysteries of America. The Order of the Tiger Knights was very sacred in Aztec Mexico.

It is interesting to remember that during human sacrifice, the hearts of virgins were offered to the gods. All this contains an esoteric meaning which the learned ignoramuses of this century do not understand. Obviously, we do not approve of human sacrifices. Those sacrifices were barbaric; millions of children and virgins were sacrificed to the gods. These were horrifying scenes of pain. This is abominable. Despite this, we are only reflecting upon the fact of offering the bleeding heart to the gods. This fact is tremendous. The Innermost needs to swallow the heart of the human being, that is to say to assimilate it, absorb it, devour the human personality who has fabricated that which is called soul.

---

195 "The Aztecs state that the human beings of the first root race were extraordinary, dark-colored giants. This was a very civilized, androgynous, asexual, semi-physical, semi-ethereal root race... The first root race lived on the sacred island situated in the north polar cap. That island still exists, yet it is in a Jinn state within the fourth vertical." — Samael Aun Weor, *The Kabbalah of the Mayan Mysteries*

The fact is tremendously true that the Innermost is like a tree with many leaves. Each leaf is a human personality. The Innermost does not have a single personality, as pseudo-esotericists believe. The Innermost has various personalities, and what is most astonishing is that he can have them incarnated in different parts of the world. When a human person does not fabricate their soul, it is logical that they are lost and descend into the Abyss. However, this matter has no importance for the Innermost. This is like a leaf that falls from the Tree of Life, one leaf without any importance. The Innermost continues attending to his other personalities, struggling for them so that they may fabricate their soul, so he can devour them like a tiger of wisdom.

Therefore, the value of the human person (which is the intellectual animal called a human being) is less than the ash of a cigarette. However, fools feel themselves to be giants.

Unfortunately, within all the pseudo-esoteric currents there are a great number of mythomaniacs, individuals who feel themselves to be masters, people who enjoy when others call them masters, individuals who believe themselves to be gods, individuals who presume to be saints. The only one who is truly great is the Spirit, the Innermost. We, the intellectual animals, are leaves that the wind tosses about, leaves of the Tree of Life, that is all.

"The present human being is a hybrid mixture of plant and phantom, a poor shadow that can only achieve immortality if it fabricates that which is called soul."

Humanity has failed. Most of humanity, almost all of it, still does not have a soul. The great majority of humans are dead leaves that the hurricane of fatality drags to the Abyss. They are leaves fallen from the Tree of Life.

The Germanic *Edda* states that the wolf Fenrir breaks his terrible bonds. That is, karma falls upon the whole of humanity. The divinities of Valhalla will fight the enemy. The serpent of Midgard floods the entire Earth; thus, this world is a failure.

Germanic mythology is Nordic. The knowledge comes from the north. The first root race was devoured by the tigers of wisdom. That was an immortal race. The second root race[196] was swept away by strong hurricanes. The third root race[197] was converted into birds. The fourth[198] into men-fish. The fifth[199] into goats.

The cradle of humanity is in the north. The Germanic *Edda* is Nordic wisdom. The forefathers of the Aztecs lived on the sacred island of the north.[200]

Esoteric wisdom came from the north to Lemuria, and from Lemuria it passed to Atlantis. After the Atlantean submersion, the wisdom remained on those surviving lands that once formed part of the Atlantean continent. India never formed part of the Atlantean continent. It is absurd to think that all ancient wisdom comes from India. If we want to find the wisdom of the serpent, we shall then find it in Mexico, Egypt, the Yucatan, etc. Indeed, these countries formed part of Atlantis.

It is urgent to study the Germanic *Edda*. It is urgent to know how to read it between the lines; then afterwards, one must investigate Easter Island, Mexico, the Yucatan, etc.

The Germanic *Edda*, with its genesis and its apocalypse, is pure Sexual Magic. The root of our Being is found within sex.

We need to be devoured by the serpent. We need to be devoured by the tiger. First, the serpent devours us, then afterwards the tiger.

---

196 The Hyperboreans, a nation mentioned in Greek mythology. The name means "beyond the North Wind," thus they are supposed to have been somewhere north of Greece, but the name also means "beyond the mountains" and "those who carry across." Apollo was said to spend the winter months among them, and his mother Leto was presumed to have been born in their land. Perseus went there searching for the Gorgon, and Heracles chased the Cerynitian hind to their country. The writer Pindar represented them as a blessed people untouched by human afflictions. H. P. Blavatsky places their country around the North Pole, saying it was "The Land of the Eternal Sun," beyond Boreas, the god of winter. She asserts that this land was of a near tropical climate.

197 On the continent called Lemuria or Mu, which was in the Pacific Ocean, and the setting of the symbolic story of Adam and Eve.

198 The Atlantean continent, which was in the Atlantic Ocean.

199 Modern humanity.

200 The Aztecs called it Tula. The Nordics called it Thule. It was the ancient land of Polaris, the continent inhabited by the polar race, the first human race on this planet, many millions of years ago.

THE PENTAGRAM

Chapter 30

The Five-pointed Star

The pentagram expresses the dominion of the Spirit over the elements of Nature. With this magical sign we can command the elemental creatures which inhabit the regions of fire, air, water, and earth.

In the presence of this terrific symbol, demons tremble and run away terrified.

The pentagram, with its superior ray aiming up, forces the tenebrous ones to scatter.

The pentagram, with its superior ray aiming down, serves in order to call upon the tenebrous ones.

When the pentagram is placed on the floor of the threshold (entrance) of the room, with its superior ray aiming towards the interior and its two inferior rays aiming towards the outside of the room, it prevents the entrance of black magicians.

The pentagram is the flaming star. The pentagram is the sign of the Word made flesh, and according to the direction of its rays, it can represent God or the Devil, the immolated lamb or the male goat of Mendes.

When the superior ray of the pentagram is aiming up towards the sky, it represents Christ.

When the two inferior points of the pentagram are aiming up towards the sky, it represents Satan.

The pentagram represents the human being in its entirety. The pentagram with its superior ray aiming upwards represents a master. The pentagram with its superior ray aiming down and its two inferior angles aiming up represents a fallen angel. Thus, every fallen bodhisattva[201] is the inverted flaming

---

201 Sanskrit बोधिसत्त्व from bodhi "enlightened, wisdom, perfect knowledge," and sattva "essence, goodness." Therefore, the term bodhisattva literally means "essence of wisdom." A bodhisattva is a human soul (consciousness) who is on the direct path. A bodhisattva is the messenger or servant of their inner Being / Buddha. The inner Being or Buddha resides in the superior worlds, and sends the bodhisattva into the lower worlds to work for others.

star. As a matter of fact, every initiate who allows themselves to fall becomes an inverted flaming star.

The best electrum is a flaming star composed of the seven metals which correspond to the seven planets. These are the following: silver for the Moon, quicksilver for Mercury, copper for Venus, gold for the Sun, iron for Mars, tin for Jupiter, and lead for Saturn. Pentagram medallions (for wearing around the neck) and rings (for wearing on the ring finger) can be manufactured.

The flaming star may also be drawn on a very white lambskin to be kept inside the bedroom. It can also be used at the threshold of the nuptial chamber. Thus, this is how we can prevent the tenebrous ones from entering our bedroom.

We may also draw the pentagram on glass, for this terrorizes ghosts and demons.

The pentagram is the symbol of the Universal Word of Life.

The pentagram can be made to shine instantaneously when uttering certain secret mantras.

Within the *Gopalatapani* and *Krishna Upanishads*, we have found mantras that have the power to instantaneously form the terrible flaming star within the astral plane, the sight of which makes demons scatter in terror. These mantras are five, namely:

**Klim Krishnaya Govindaya
Gopi-jana-vallabhaya Swaha.**[202]

The tenebrous ones of the Eighteenth Arcanum[203] scatter in terror, because the flaming star is instantaneously formed when vocalizing these mantras. These demons violently attack the initiate who is working in the Great Work. Thus, the devotees of the perfect matrimony have to wage tremendous battles against the tenebrous ones. Each vertebra of the spinal column represents terrible battles against the black magicians. They

---

202 This is the mahamantra of Krishna. "Then the goddess of learning Sarasvatī, the divine consort of the Supreme Lord, said thus to Brahmā who saw nothing but gloom in all directions, "O Brahmā, this mantra, viz., klīm krishnāya govindāya gopī-jana-vallabhāya svāhā, will assuredly fulfill your heart's desire." —Brahma-samhitā 5:24

203 The eighteenth Tarot card, Twilight, which is related to black magic.

struggle in order to deviate the student away from the path of the razor's edge.

The powerful mantra mentioned above has three perfectly defined stages. On chanting **KLIM** (क्लीं),[204] which the esotericists of India call the "seed of attraction," we provoke a flow of Christic energy which instantaneously descends from the world of the Solar Logos in order to protect us; thus, a mysterious door is then downwardly opened. Afterwards, by chanting the three following parts of the mantra, the Christic energy is infused within the one who chants them. Finally, by means of the fifth part, the one who has received the Christic energy can radiate it with tremendous force in order to defend themselves from the tenebrous ones. They then scatter away in terror.

The word always crystallizes in geometric lines. This is demonstrated by magnetic tapes. When speech is recorded on a cassette tape, each letter crystallizes into geometrical figures. Afterwards, it is sufficient to make the tape vibrate in the tape recorder in order for the speech to be repeated. God geometrizes. The word is shaped with geometric forms. The mantras cited here by us have the power to instantaneously form the flaming star within the suprasensible worlds. This kind of star is a vehicle of Christic force. This kind of star represents the Word.

Everyone who works in the flaming forge of Vulcan can defend themselves with these powerful mantras. These mantras must be chanted syllable by syllable. One can conjure the demons who control the possessed ones with these mantras.

It is urgent to learn how to instantaneously create the flaming star. With these mantras we can create that star in order to combat the tenebrous ones.

---

204 "Kling [क्लीं klim] is the Beeja Akshara of Lord Krishna. It is a powerful Mantra. It produces a powerful vibration in the mental stuff and transforms the Rajasic nature of the mind. It produces certain kind of powerful spiritual idea in the mind which greatly helps purification of mind, concentration and contemplation. It induces Vairagya and Antarmukha Vritti and attenuates the force of Vasanas and Samskaras. It completely checks the thought-force. It produces rhythmical vibrations of the five sheaths [bodies]." —Swami Sivananda, *Lord Krishna and His Teachings*

The Word

The learned ignoramuses who are so numerous in this century may laugh like idiots at what they do not know. These people suppose that our mantras are words without any value whatsoever and that their energy is lost in space. They ignore the internal value of words. The principle substance of the word is unknown to them. This is why they laugh at our mantras.

In every word there is an external and an internal value. It is precisely the internal value that is the principle substance of the word. The internal element of the word is not in tridimensional space. The internal element of the word must be sought in superior space with dimensions superior to ours. The physical space that appears before us is only a part of the superior space. Therefore, in conclusion, we do not know space in its entirety. Presently, humans only know a small part, which can be measured in terms of longitude, latitude, and height.

The internal element of the word is formed geometrically within the superior dimensions of space. This is how, with the mantras given in this chapter, we can undoubtedly form a pentagonal star, invisible to the physical eyes, but perfectly visible to the sixth sense.[205]

Scientists do not know anything about the fourth dimension of matter in space. They do not know anything about the hypergeometry of that type of fourth-dimensional space. To define space as "the form of matter in the universe" is to suffer the most grave conceptual deficiency, which is to introduce the concept of matter, that is to say, the unknown, because indeed, matter continues to be unknown. All of the attempts in order to attain a physical definition of matter only leads to a dead end: X = Y, and Y = X. This is the physicists' blind alley.

The psychological definitions of matter also lead to the same dead end. A sage said, "Matter (as a force) does not present us any difficulty at all. We understand all about it, because of the very simple reason that we have invented it... When we speak of matter we think of sensible objects. However, what is

---

205 Clairvoyance, the perception of non-physical imagery.

difficult for us to deal with is the mental variation of concrete but complex facts...

> "Therefore, strictly speaking, matter exists only as a concept... to tell the truth, the character of matter, (even when treated just as a concept) is so obscure, that the majority of people are unable to tell us exactly what they mean by it."

Indeed, no one really knows what "matter" is. Nonetheless, the conservative and reactionary school of materialistic positivism is founded on that concept.[206]

Even though physicists may not like the following assertion, we have to state that "matter" and "energy" are words which are officially accepted in order to designate a long series of complicated facts, even when the substantial origins of them are unknown to present science. Who has seen matter? Who has seen energy? We only see phenomena. No one has seen matter independent of substance. No one has seen energy separate from movement. Therefore, this factually demonstrates to us that matter and energy are only abstract concepts. No one sees matter separated from objects. No one sees energy separated from movement. Matter and energy separated from things and phenomena are a mystery for the human being. The human being is ninety-seven percent subconscious and only three percent conscious. The human being dreams of the phenomena of Nature and calls them matter, energy, etc.

Before the existence of the universe, before the existence of all phenomena, there was the Word. Indeed, the Logos (the Word) sounds.

---

206 "Physicalism is, in slogan form, the thesis that everything is physical...
The general idea is that the nature of the actual world (i.e. the universe and everything in it) conforms to a certain condition, the condition of being physical. Of course, physicalists don't deny that the world might contain many items that at first glance don't seem physical — items of a biological, or psychological, or moral, or social, or mathematical nature. But they insist nevertheless that at the end of the day such items are physical, or at least bear an important relation to the physical." — Stanford Encyclopedia of Philosophy

At the dawn of life, the Army of the Voice celebrated the rituals of fire by singing in the sacred language. The Great Word crystallized into geometrical figures that were condensed by means of the raw matter of the Great Work, thus originating all the phenomena of Nature.

The world and the consciousness are indeed the result of the Word. Tridimensional space is a property of our material perception. When we improve the quality of representations, the quality of perceptions also improves. Then, we enter into the superior dimensions of space where the tridimensional world no longer exists. This remains in our memory only as a dream.

Indeed, the world that is presented to our consciousness is only the mechanical aspect of all those combined causes which give origin to a definite series of sensations.

The principle cause of all existence is found beyond the world and the consciousness. This principle is the Word. It is the Word that creates worlds.

"In the beginning was the Word, and the Word was with God, and the Word was God.

"The same was in the beginning with God.

"All things were made by him; and without him was not anything made that was made.

"In him was life; and the life was the light of men.

"And the light shineth in darkness; and the darkness comprehended it not." —Christian Bible, John 1

The Word is completely symbolized by the five-pointed star. This is the flaming star. We can defend ourselves against the tenebrous ones with it. The columns of angels and demons tremble in the presence of this marvelous star.

Chapter 31
The Inuit of the North

Some traditions state that the Inuit of Greenland and Alaska have their origin in distant Thule. It is stated that the Inuit are mixed with invaders from Polynesia, Tunguska, and Dene.

The great Gnostic Rosicrucian Master Arnold Krumm-Heller speaks sublimely about distant Thule, the sacred island. Don Mario Rosso de Luna states that this island still exists, however, it is found in the Jinn state. We know that the first human root race existed on this island.

The polar root race was developed within an environment totally different from the present one. In that age, which dates back in time more than three hundred million years,[207] the planet Earth was really semi-ethereal, semi-physical. It appeared like a curved blue ocean, like the firmament at night.

In those times, human beings could float within the atmosphere. The human bodies were androgynous and ethereal. These bodies were elastic and subtle. They could maintain the form of their gigantic bodies (of ten or twenty meters in stature). As well, they could reduce their size at will, thus adopting a pygmy-like stature, or they could take on the size of the present human body.

We cannot say that those people were hermaphrodites. This first root race was androgynous. The sexual energy operated differently, and they reproduced through the fissiparous sexual act. In a determined moment, the original organism divided into exact halves. This is similar to multiplying by cellular division. Each time this occurred, there was prayer and profound veneration of the divine.

Although it may seem incredible, the first human root race reached a very high degree in its civilization. Houses, palaces, cities and grandiose temples were built with the flexible and ethereal matter of this primeval Earth. Naturally, the swine of materialism from this day and age will laugh at our assertions,

---

207 Read *Gnostic Anthropology* by Samael Aun Weor.

because they have never found the remains of such a civilization. It is impossible to find the remains of such an ancient
civilization, because in that age the Earth was ethereal, that is
to say, it was made of protoplasmic matter. Only in the memories of Nature can the great clairvoyants find all of the living
history of the first root race.

This was the protoplasmic root race. This was the human
race's legitimate protoplasm. The great clairvoyants can laugh
at any time at the theoretical protoplasm of the followers of
Darwin and Haeckel.

The fossil remains of the human beings found in the subterranean caverns of the Earth have nothing to do with the protoplasmic root race. Those remains belong to degenerated tribes,
descendants of the submerged Atlantis.

In the culture of the polar root race, religion, science, and
philosophy were totally united. The inhabitants of distant
Thule were bodhisattvas of masters from other mahamanvan-
taras.[208]

At that time, Adam and Eve were a single being. In this day
and age, Adam and Eve are separated and suffer; thus, they
search for each other with an insatiable thirst to unite. Only
during the sexual act are the man and woman one single being.
In those moments of sexual voluptuousness, man and woman
have the immense joy of being a single being.

The cosmic rituals of that age are very interesting. The
trained clairvoyant can discover pure esoteric Masonry within
their temples. Nevertheless, those rituals differ so greatly from
the rituals that currently exist in the world, that it would be impossible for a modern Mason to admit that these rituals were
Masonic.

The lights of the temple were not fixed. As soon as a venerable master would occupy the throne, just as quickly he would
leave it. Sometimes the first vigilant would occupy a throne,
then suddenly he would leave it in order to switch it to the
throne of the second vigilant. The high dignitaries levitated
in order to switch thrones amongst themselves. The colors
black and white were combined on their vestments in order

---

208 Sanskrit, "great cosmic era."

to represent the struggle between the Spirit and matter. The construction of the temple was perfect. The symbols and the tools of work were inverted in order to represent the drama projected through the centuries, that is, the descent of the Spirit into matter. Thus, we may contemplate with amazement the inverted scepters, chalice, etc.—all inverted. At that time, life was descending towards matter; therefore, it was then necessary to give a symbolic expression to this. Their sacred processions were grandiose. These sacred processions made the great mysteries and the supreme descent of the Spirit into matter understandable. This descent was an awaited grandiose event that was going to be fulfilled through the downward course of the centuries. This grandiose event was awaited with much yearning, like how in this day and age the human being is awaiting for our return into the superior worlds.

The language of the protoplasmic root race was the Word of Gold, a universal and cosmic language whose combinations of sounds produced cosmic phenomena of all kinds. Those who follow the path of the perfect matrimony come to discover that primeval language again within themselves. When the sacred fire reaches the level of the throat, we then begin to speak in the very pure rising of the divine language, which flows majestically under the Sun like a river of gold through the thick jungle. The cosmic laws of Nature were taught to the gods by their inner Fathers by chanting in this language.

The script of the first root race was with the runes. The mallet of Masonry comes from the arrow of the Egyptian god Ra, and this is a rune. In that epoch, the rituals of the polar temple were all runic. The movements of the officials were runic. This is the divine script. Let us remember that the swastika is a rune. The Hebrew letters are but modifications of runic letters.

The cradle of esoteric wisdom was not Asia as many believe. The true cradle of esoteric wisdom was the sacred island, the distant Thule, about which Huiracocha said so many beautiful things.

In that age, the protoplasmic root race, the sacred island, was not in the north. Indeed, that island was a continent whose exact position was on the equatorial line. However, much later, with the revolution of the axis of the Earth, that island remained in the north. The revolution of the axis of the Earth has already been demonstrated by contemporary science. Presently, the poles are gradually diverging toward the equator.

The present Inuit, although mixed with other races, are not descendants of the first root race. Rather, they are degenerated Atlanteans; nevertheless, they preserve some very interesting traditions. These people have a family bond that unites them among themselves. Each patriarch uses a special amulet consisting of a sign, totem mark, or the name of a species of a sacred animal which he passes onto his descendants. Many thinkers may feel inclined to believe that the Inuit race could have its origin in the primeval Nordics of the first age, because of the fact that they live near the North Pole. It is interesting to know that among the ancient Inuit there was no special authority, cacique, or king. They were ruled by a council of elders. The young males married women from other clans in a perfect matrimony; however, the amulet served as a distinguishing sign in order to avoid marriages among relatives. In other times, there was polyandry. They killed every female child that was born before a male child. Fortunately, they have now abandoned that barbaric custom.

In his book entitled *History of Matrimony*, R. Westermarch states that the Inuit lend or exchange their wife to another man. Indeed, this is an adulterous custom, a horrible custom incompatible with the doctrine preached by our beloved savior Jesus Christ. Nevertheless, every rule has its exception and we cannot believe that all Inuit have this same barbaric custom. There is a bit of everything within the garden of the Lord.

It is a custom for the Inuit to wrap their dead in skins and bury them beneath a tumulus surrounded by a fence. In the Aleutian Islands they were tied up with cords and buried within the crevices of cliffs.

The Inuit know the law of eternal return. They know that the ego returns into a new womb. The fetishes or diminutive dolls of the Inuit symbolize the Essence. They believe that the Essence is tiny and minute, however, their priests do not ignore that the soul is built with it.

Pregnancy, the birth of children, puberty, and death are celebrated with special esoteric practices.

The Inuit worship the feminine principle of God. They love their sublime elder Sedna who lives in the depths of the ocean and sends marine animals for their nourishment.

Naturally, the learned ignoramuses who do not know anything about esoteric science laugh at the divine religion of the Inuit.

The best canticles and rituals of the Inuit are for the Divine Mother. The symbolic journeys of the shaman (priest) in search of the ancient Sedna (in order to console her when she becomes angered) and the processions that the community perform in order to reconcile her, remind us of the symbolic journeys of the Masonic candidate around the lodge. The journeys are the external symbols of the elevation of the candidate's consciousness through the superior worlds. Esoteric Masonry's five symbolic journeys are intimately related with the five initiations of Major Mysteries. When the profaned ignoramuses see these journeys of the Inuit, they do nothing but laugh, and laugh at what they do not know. They laugh like idiots; they laugh at what they do not know.

The Inuit know with perfect exactitude (like a true initiate who has awakened their sixth sense also knows) that genies, elves, gnomes, giants, salamanders of fire, undines etc., exist. Fortunately, after official science accepted hypnotism and baptized it with the new name of hypnology, it has to accept clairvoyance as a logical consequence. Only in this way is it possible to explain to ourselves how a subject in a hypnotic state can see through a wall or can inform about events which sometimes are happening thousands of kilometers away.

What science rejects today, it accepts tomorrow. Today those who laugh at Paracelsus and the Inuit because of the elementals, gnomes, pygmies, salamanders, genies, undines, sylphs, etc., will have to laugh at themselves and blush in shame when these creatures are rediscovered by science.

Who would have believed only five years ago in the glass snake? Now, in 1961, a famous scientist, one of those who previously described himself as incredulous, has just discovered the famous glass snake. This snake has the power to drop its tail at will in cases of danger, easily being able to regenerate it afterwards. When the glass snake finds itself in danger, attacked by some animal, it coils up, becomes rigid and throws itself over the animal. It then instantly abandons its tail and its head escapes in a flash. The animal is distracted by the snake's tail while the snake's head saves itself. Later a new tail grows from the head. Thus, this is how everything is; Nature has many marvels.

Therefore, it is necessary to learn how to respect all religions, because they are but forms of a single universal religion. Tremendous truths and cosmic sciences are contained within every religion; these are unknown by the learned ignoramuses of this barbaric age.

All those who want to attain in depth Realization of the Self must work in their laboratory with sulphur (fire), azoth (air), the human being (water), and the bull (earth). These four elements form a cross. The alchemist who follows the path of the perfect matrimony must transmute the lead into gold within the profound caverns of the great mountain range (the dorsal spine). In this great mountain range live the gnomes, the guardians of all the treasures of the earth, the great alchemists who transmute lead into gold. The gnomes work with the salamanders of fire, with the sylphs of the air, and with the voluptuous undines of the pure waters of life. The ardent salamanders fertilize the boisterous undines, and the happy and playful sylphs animate the fire of the laboratory's furnace (the chakra called the Church of Ephesus) so that the water (semen) evaporates from within its container (sex). The seminal vapors rise through the chimney to the distillery (the brain). There, the gnomes perform the great distillation, perfectly transmuting the remaining lead into gold.

It is necessary to transmute the lead of the personality into the gold of the Spirit. Only in this way can we again utter the very pure rising of the divine language. Our motto is Thelema (willpower).[209]

---

209 (Greek θέλημα) Willpower. "Father, if thou be willing, remove this cup from me: nevertheless not my will (Thelema), but thine, be done." —Luke

We need to pass through the five great initiations of fire, symbolized by the three degrees of esoteric Masonry.

We need to return, to go back to the divine wisdom of distant Thule. Much has been said about this distant Thule, the land of the gods. The forefathers of the Inuit and the Aztecs are inhabited there. Quetzalcoatl lives there. From Thule he came, and to Thule he returned. The Emperor Monteczuma sent a group of ambassador magicians to that mysterious Thule. They went in Jinn state, that is to say, they traveled within the fourth dimension.

Distant Thule is the sacred land, the sacred island, the first continent which existed and the last which shall cease to exist. That continent is found in the polar ice cap of the north, within the fourth dimension. The Aztec magicians sent by Monteczuma arrived there in Jinn state, carrying presents for the forefathers of the Aztecs. On their return, they brought a message for Monteczuma and the Aztecs, which we could synthesize as follows, "If you do not stop your passions, cruelties and vices, you will be punished. White men will come from the sea and will conquer you and destroy you." All this was fulfilled with the arrival of the Spaniards in Mexico.

The subject matter about the fourth dimension and a sacred land within this fourth dimension at the North Pole may make the learned ignoramuses laugh. Indeed, they have not studied all the dimensions of space. It is unfortunate that mathematics cannot define the dimensions of space. "Every mathematical expression always corresponds to a realization of realities." This is how one thinks with formal logic. Fortunately though, there is a dialectic logic that permits us to use mathematics in order to define the six fundamental dimensions of the universe.

22: 42. So (Father), "do what thou wilt (Thelema), shall be the whole of the Law." And what is the whole of the law? "Jesus said unto him, Thou shalt love the Lord thy God with all thy heart, and with all thy soul, and with all thy mind. This is the first and great commandment. And the second is like unto it, Thou shalt love thy neighbour as thyself (who is thy Father, thy true Self)." —Matthew 22: 37-39. On these two commandments hang the whole of the law and the prophets.

Generally, the dimensions are represented by powers: the first, second, third, fourth, etc. It was precisely this that provided a base for Hinton to construct his famous theory of tesseracts, or tetra-dimensional solids [(A^4), a raised to the fourth power]. This is the representation of dimensions in the form of powers. Many authors consider that mathematics have nothing to do with dimensions, because there is no difference between the dimensions. This concept appears false to us. We believe that the difference between dimensions is obvious, and that the entire universe is made up according to the law of numbers, measure, and weight. What happens is that whilst the mind is bottled up in formal logic, we will limit the use of mathematics to the three dimensional world. We urgently need dialectic logic in order to be able to consider the representation of dimensions by powers as something logical. This is only possible dialectically with dialectic logic.

Metageometry studies "superior space." Metageometry is destined to totally replace Euclidean geometry. Indeed, Euclidean geometry only serves to investigate the properties of a particular physical space. However, if we want to abandon the study of the fourth vertical, it is obvious that physics will be halted in its progress.

The vital secret of all mechanics is found in the fourth coordinate.

Metageometry has the merit of considering the three dimensional world as a section of a superior space. A point from the tridimensional space is only a section or slice of a metageometrical line. With formal logic, it is impossible to consider metageometric lines as distances between points in our space. Thus, it is impossible to represent them by forming figures in our space. Nevertheless, with dialectic logic, metageometric lines have distances between points of our space, and we can represent them with figures and qualities. Therefore, it is not absurd to state that the continent of the North Pole belongs to the fourth dimension. Neither would it be an absurdity in the light of the dialectic logic thought to affirm that this continent is inhabited by people who have physical bodies. We can even design a map of this continent and this would be accepted by dialectic logic. Formal logic on the other hand, besides considering our affirmations an absurdity, would veritably lead us into error.

Indeed, the tridimensionality of the world is in our psyche, in our receptive apparatus. It is also in our psyche where we can all find the marvels of the supradimensional, if we develop clairvoyance, clairaudience, etc., that is to say, if we perfect our psychic apparatus. We can study the superior dimensions of Nature only through the development of our powers of inner perception.

Comparable to the Great Wall of China, materialistic positivism has built a great wall around free investigations. Now, the learned ignoramuses condemn all that which delves in contradiction against that wall as anti-scientific.

Materialistic positivism is conservative and reactionary. We, the Gnostics, are revolutionaries and we totally reject reactionary and conservative ideas.

Emmanuel Kant, the great German philosopher, considers space to be a property of the receptivity of the world through our consciousness.

"We carry within ourselves the conditions
of our space, and therefore, within
ourselves we will find the conditions
that allow us to establish correlations
between our space and superior space."

When the microscope was invented, the world of the infinitely small was opened up to us. In the same way the world of the fourth dimension will be opened to us with the awakening of the sixth sense.

Those who have developed the sixth sense can study the Akashic Records of Nature and discover for themselves the reality of the northern polar continent.

The first root race that existed in the world was of a dark color. This was the protoplasmic root race, the androgynous race who reproduced themselves through the fissiparous sexual act (similar to reproduction by cellular division).

The first root race lived within the fourth dimension of space. The planet Earth itself was then submerged within the fourth dimension. That root race had a gigantic civilization; the language of gold was spoken and they wrote with runic letters. These letters are of great esoteric power. In that epoch, the angel Uriel wrote a precious cosmic book with runic letters. We can only study this book in the Akashic Records.

The kind of perception and representation that the people of the first root race had was not as subjective as the perception and representation that this present humanity has. The polar people had clear and perfect objective representations and perceptions. They could see bodies completely and exactly. The people of this day and age can only see sides, angles, faces, surfaces, etc. Presently, nobody sees complete bodies. People of this day and age are degenerated; therefore, they only have incomplete, subjective perceptions and representations that are completely degenerated and subjective.

In order to re-conquer objective representations and perceptions, we need to return to the point of departure and regenerate our psychic apparatus through Sexual Magic and internal meditation.

It is urgent to eliminate all those subjective elements from our representations and perceptions. This is possible by improving the quality of the representations with the technique of meditation and by regenerating the psychic apparatus with Sexual Magic.

The cradle of esoteric wisdom is in the north and not in the orient as some orientalists suppose.

The Inuit conserve many religious traditions that are worth investigating seriously.

Archimedes stated, "Give me a fulcrum strong enough and a lever long enough and I shall move the world." Archimedes searched for a lever in order to move the universe. This lever exists. Eliphas Levi states that this lever is the Astral Light. We prefer to speak more clearly and declare that the lever of Archimedes is the Kundalini.

Whosoever develops the Kundalini can place their body of flesh and bone into the fourth dimension in order to transport themselves to distant Thule, the land of the gods.

Whosoever knows how to pray and ask the Mother Kundalini could sincerely beg her to put them within the fourth dimension and transport them to the sacred island. The Kundalini is the lever of Archimedes, the lever with which we can place ourselves inside the fourth dimension in order to travel with our physical bodies.

The invention of the lever immediately differentiated primitive humans from the animal, and in fact, was linked with the real appearance of concepts. If we psychically comprehend the action of the lever in depth, we then discover with amazement that it consists of the construction of a correct syllogism.[210] Whosoever does not know how to correctly construct a syllogism, cannot totally comprehend the action of a lever. The syllogism in the psychic sphere is literally the same thing as the lever in the physical sphere. Indeed, we can asseverate that the beings who live on Earth are divided into two groups: those who know the action of the lever and those who do not know this action.

The human being needs the lever of Archimedes, the superastral serpent, in order to place themselves inside the fourth dimension and transport themselves with their body to the land of the gods.

The path that leads us to a superior order of things in the superior dimensions of space is found when mathematics has renounced the fundamental axioms of identity and difference.

The great writer P. O. stated, "In the world of the infinite and variable magnitudes, a magnitude may not be equal to itself. One part can be equal to the whole, and of two equal magnitudes, one can be infinitely greater than the other."

Indeed, the former statement can seem a complete absurdity when we study this matter in the light of mathematics of constant and finite numbers. Nevertheless, it is true, the plain truth, and nothing but the truth, that the mathematics of

---

210 "A form of deductive reasoning consisting of a major premise, a minor premise, and a conclusion; for example, *All humans are mortal,* the major premise, *I am a human,* the minor premise, *therefore, I am mortal,* the conclusion." —The American Heritage® Dictionary of the English Language, 5th Edition

constant and finite numbers is in itself the calculus of the relations that exist between nonexistent magnitudes, that is, the calculus of the absurd. Therefore, we can completely asseverate that what appears as absurd from the point of view of these mathematics may indeed be true, even though people do not believe it.

On one occasion, a famous penologist stated, "To discover truth we have to renounce logic." In part, this lawyer spoke the truth, but partially he did not. Indeed, we have to renounce formal logic, but not logic, because logic is the art of correct thinking. If we stop thinking correctly, clearly we fall into the absurd. In his *Critique of Pure Reasoning*, Emmanuel Kant showed us the path of transcendental logic. Prior to Bacon and the famous Aristotle, formulae for a superior logic were already given in the archaic scriptures of the sacred land of the Vedas. These formulae were written in very ancient books. This logic is dialectic logic. This is intuitive logic, the logic of ecstasy, the logic of the infinite. This logic existed long before deductive or inductive logic were formulated. When the human being dominates this marvelous key of the mind called dialectic logic, we can then open the mysterious door of the world of natural causes without the risk of falling into error.

The axioms of dialectic logic can only be formulated during ecstasy.

If, indeed we want to deeply comprehend the multidimensional world and visit the sacred land of the gods situated in the northern polar cap, we urgently need to hurl everything out of the temple of our mind, hurl out all the intellectual idols that have become axioms. We need to emancipate the mind, to liberate it from formal logic, which is only good for Molière[211] and his caricatures.

When we find the lever of Archimedes, the Jinn lands, the marvels hidden within *A Thousand and One Nights,* the golden countries inhabited by the ineffable gods of dawn, become a tremendous reality. We leap into the fourth dimension supported by this mysterious lever.

---

211 French writer of comedies.

The hour has arrived to liberate the mind and to awaken the Kundalini. The moment has arrived for the human being to learn how to pass into the fourth dimension at will, any time they wish to do so. If someone who has awakened the Kundalini would supplicate their Kundalini in the moments of falling asleep, asking to be placed into the fourth dimension and to be transported towards the sacred island of the North Pole, you could be sure, dear reader, that the miracle would inevitably occur. The only thing that the initiate needs is to know how to get up from bed whilst conserving sleep. The snake will help them with everything when they also know how to help themselves.

"Help thyself so that I can help thee."

LAKSHMI, PARVATI, AND SARASVATI

Chapter 32

The Divine Trinity

The sacred scriptures of India affirm that the navel, the heart, and the throat are igneous centers of the human organism. They also affirm that by meditating on these centers, we experience the presence of the Masters Sarasvati,[212] Lakshmi,[213] and Parvati / Gauri[214] in successive hierarchical order.

These three masters work with the three profundities of our resplendent Dragon of Wisdom. These three masters direct the forces that come from the three aspects of the Solar Logos. Sarasvati works with the forces of the Father. Lakshmi works with the forces of the Son, and Parvati with the forces of the Holy Spirit.

Sarasvati exerts control over the human mind. Lakshmi exerts control over the astral body. Parvati exerts control over the physical body.

---

212 Sarasvati represents the Divine Mother as goddess of knowledge. Her name literally refers to an abundance of water (from सरस् saras, "anything flowing or liquid, lake, pool") which symbolically is central to her importance, especially in esotericism. Her male counterpart is Brahma. While they are symbolized as god and goddess, the reality is that these are formless intelligences, aspects of cosmic beingness. Sarasvati is the power, energy, shakti of Brahma. Without Sarasvati, Brahma would be powerless. Brahma is the Hindu equivalent of the sephirah Kether, thus Sarasvati is the shakti (power) of Kether.

213 Sanskrit लक्ष्मी, "success, splendor, wealth, fortune, majesty, glory, power." In Hinduism, one of the three primary aspects of the Divine Mother, alongside Sarasvati and Parvati. Lakshmi is the wife / feminine aspect — meaning the shakti, power — of Vishnu, the preserver or restorer. He is the Second Logos, the Son of Christianity, the sephirah Chokmah ("wisdom") in Kabbalah. Thus, Lakshmi is the power of Chokmah, "wisdom."

214 Sanskrit पार्वती "She of the mountain." Also called Uma. In Hinduism, one of the three primary aspects of the Divine Mother. Parvati is the wife / feminine aspect — meaning the shakti, power — of Shiva, the creator and destroyer; He is the Third Logos, the Holy Spirit, the sephirah Binah in Kabbalah; thus, Parvati is the power of Binah, and is thus the goddess of creation, fertility, destruction, and mother of all. She also manifests as Durga and Kali.

The Apprentice[215] has to perfect their physical body by accustoming it to the practice of Sexual Magic with their priestly spouse. This work is very arduous and difficult.

The Companion needs to perfect their astral body until it becomes a useful instrument.

The Master needs to perfect their mental body with the power of fire that blazes in universal orchestration.

The Apprentice must invoke the Master Parvati to help them control the sexual organs during the practice of Sexual Magic.

The Companion must invoke Lakshmi to teach them how to project the astral body. It is urgent to learn how to consciously and positively travel with the astral body.

The Master must invoke Sarasvati to help them to Christify the mind.

These invocations are made during Sexual Magic.

It is necessary to invoke the forces of the Holy Spirit during Sexual Magic. It is urgent to call the forces of the Christ so that they give rise to the birth of the Christ-astral in the depths of our internal universe. It is indispensable to ask for assistance from the forces of the Father with our mind. We need to engender the Christ-mind.

The physical, astral, and mental vehicles must become fine instruments of the Spirit.

It is indispensable to learn how to depart consciously in the astral body. Let us remember that the mind is within the astral. It is urgent to consciously visit the temples of the White Lodge. We can study at the feet of the master in the astral world.

We are going to teach the mantras for astral projection as taught by a sage in one of his books. These mantras are in the Sanskrit language. The yogis from India chant them in order to project themselves in their astral body. They are as follows:

---

215 Here the author is referring to the three symbolic degrees of spiritual development represented in all religions: 1. Apprentices, 2. Companions / Workers / Journeymen, 3. Masters. See Chapter 24, Secret Egypt.

Mantras for Astral Projection

**Hare Rama Hare Rama, Rama Rama
Hare Hare, Hare Krishna Hare Krishna,
Krishna Krishna Hare Hare.**[216]

**Hare murare madhu kaita bhare,
gopala govinda mukunda shaure.**[217]

**Mēm prage yōdī kolpī basi parvot tullo
hiro no dāna en bai de nam.**[218]

Sri Govind,[219] **Sri Govind. Sri Govind.
Sri Govind. Ganesha Namah.**[220]

The devotee must fall asleep with the head towards the north or towards the east. First of all, it is necessary for the devotee to learn by heart these mantras from India. Thus, while the devotee is laying down dorsal decubitus (face up), they beg, call and invoke, with all their soul, the Master Lakshmi in order for the master to take them out consciously and positively

---

216 From *Kali-Santarana Upanishad*, हरे राम हरे राम , राम राम हरे हरे | हरे कृष्ण हरे कृष्ण , कृष्ण कृष्ण हरे हर "Hare Rama Hare Rama, Rama Rama Hare Hare, Hare Krishna Hare Krishna, Krishna Krishna Hare Hare." This is the mahamantra of Krishna. "Hare Rama" has many deep meanings, significantly as names of Radha and Krishna. In Spanish, instead of Krishna Samael Aun Weor wrote "Cristo," which is appropriate, but when translated to English as "Christ," the mantra loses the ending vowel and thus the mantra loses its beauty when pronounced, so here we used Krishna as it occurs in the original scripture. Each of these words call upon the same force, the Cosmic Christ, so use whichever you prefer.

217 हरे मुरारे मधुकैटभारे गोपाल गोविंद मुकुंद शौरि, meaning "Vishnu (remover of illusions), killer of the demons Mura, Madhu, and Kaitabha, warrior, protector of cows (symbol of the Divine Mother), lord of the Earth (our body), quicksilver (mercury, sexual power), son of the Sun!"

218 From *Bhaktirasbodhini*, *Bhaktirasamrat*, and *Bhaktirasasudharnava*, में પ્રાગે ચોદી કોલ્પી બસિ પરવોત ટુલ્લો હીરો નો દાણ એન બાઇ દે નમ, meaning "If the basis to achieve perfection is in my heart, may the grace of God guide me."

219 गोविन्द is usually translated as "cowherd" as a reference to Vishnu / Krishna, but also means "pleasant to the senses" and "lord of the Earth."

220 "Hail Ganesh." Ganesha symbolizes the aspect of divinity that removes obstacles.

in the astral body. It is necessary to call Lakshmi in the name
of Christ.

Invocation

**In the name of Christ, by the glory of
Christ, by the power of Christ, I call upon
you, Lakshmi, Lakshmi, Lakshmi, Amen.**

This invocation is repeated thousands of times, supplicating
the Master Lakshmi to take you consciously out of the physical
body and to teach you how to travel consciously in the astral
body. After making this invocation, recite the Sanskrit mantras
thousands of times with the mind concentrated on Christ.
Calmly fall asleep while making the invocation. When you
wake up, practice a retrospective exercise to remember where
you were, where you walked, with whom you were speaking,
etc.

It is necessary to ask Lakshmi to teach you how to go into
the astral world consciously.

To learn how to go out consciously in the astral body, it is
necessary to have patience as great as that of Saint Job.[221] Let
us remember that the degree of Apprentice is seven years long,
and that only after seven years do the first flashes of illumination begin. We give this caution so that the student knows
what to expect. It is best for the curious, the profane, and the
profaners of the temple to withdraw. This science is not for the
curious.

The splendors and powers of the Innermost (the Spirit)
begin to reflect in their astral body and mind according to how
the devotee practices Sexual Magic with their priestly spouse,
according to how their conduct becomes more and more
upright, according to their continuing sanctification. Then
comes illumination.

This is the path; however, such illumination is attained only
after the degree of Apprentice (we are speaking in the termi-
nology of esoteric Masonry). Every true candidate prepared for

---

221 From the Judeo-Christian scriptures. Job was tested very severely.

illumination will be able to be recognized and verified with the
square and the compass. The devotee is prepared for illumination when the Spirit and the human personality act in an or-
derly manner and in full harmony. Those who complain of not
being illuminated cannot withstand the ordeal of the square
and the compass. When the inferior quaternary[222] loyally obeys
the Spirit, the result is illumination. As long as the inferior
quaternary does not obey the Spirit, that is to say, while the
human personality does not know how to obey the Spirit, illumination is impossible.

The devotee must purify their bedroom daily with the
smoke of special aromatic substances. Incense purifies the
astral body. A good incense attracts the great masters whom
we need for our work. We can mix incense with gum benzoin.
Benzoin purifies the astral body and dispels gross and sensual
thoughts. Benzoin can be mixed with incense in a perfume
censer, or all can be burned within a brazier. This is the most
practical way. The essence of roses can also be mixed with these
perfumes to purify the environment. It is good to remember
that roses have great power. The rose is the queen of flowers. It
is necessary for the rose of the Spirit to open its fragrant and
delicious bud upon the cross of our body. We also recommend
olibanum (frankincense) to create a devotional atmosphere
in the nuptial chamber. Husband and wife should live in the
midst of perfume and love. Incense and perfume burn delightfully in all Hindu, Parsi, Jain, Shinto temples, etc. Incense and
perfumes were never absent from the temples of Greece, Rome,
Persia, etc.

The devotee needs much purification and sanctification in
order to reach illumination.

Special Indication

Jesus, the great hierophant said, "Help thyself so that I
can help thee." Therefore, the Gnostic student must take into
account these words of the master. The mantras in order to
travel in the astral body (as we have taught in this chapter)

---

222 The "four bodies of sin": physical, vital, emotional, and mental.

are marvelous. The invocation of the Master Lakshmi is magnificent, marvelous; however the Gnostic students must help themselves, must concentrate on the navel. They must fall asleep by chanting the mantras mentally; thus, when they find themselves somnolent, when they feel that lassitude characteristic of sleep, they should imagine themselves to be a breeze, a gas, something subtle, to feel that they are completely aerial and gaseous. Thus, feeling themselves in that state, aerial and subtle, they forget the heaviness of the physical body, and think that they can fly anywhere because they no longer have weight of any kind. Thus, forgetting their physical body, and feeling like a cloud, aroma, breeze, divine breath, they must leap up from bed. Do not try to leap mentally, it is urgent for all of this to be translated as action, as concrete acts. Once outside of the physical body, leave your house and direct yourself (in your astral body) towards the Gnostic Church or towards whichever place you want. One can travel to other planets with the astral body. One can visit the most distant places of the cosmos, the temples of mysteries, etc., with the astral body.

The devotee will be able to study the Akashic Records of Nature with the astral body and know all past, present and future events. There is an oriental prophecy which states that by the end of the twentieth century, scientists will have special radio-television apparatuses to study the Akashic Records of Nature. Then all of humanity will be able to see the whole history of the Earth and its races on a screen. The whole living history of great people like Jesus, Mohammed, Buddha, Hermes, Quetzalcoatl will then be seen. Present technology struggles to perfect the radio in order to receive the discourses of Christ, Cicero, Orpheus, etc. These waves exist because nothing stops vibrating in Nature. Therefore, it is only a matter of perfecting the radio and the radio television. Likewise, the day when humans will invent certain special lenses in order to see the astral body and the astral plane is not too far in the distance. The great White Lodge is initiating these types of scientific inventions and discoveries.

Chapter 33
The Christ

The beloved God Kristos (Christ) comes from archaic cults of the fire god. The letters P (pyre) and
X (cross) are the hieroglyph which represent the
generation of the sacred fire.

Christ was worshiped in the mysteries of Mithra,
Apollo, Aphrodite, Jupiter, Janus, Vesta, Bacchus, Astarte,
Demeter, Quetzalcoatl, etc. The Christic principle has never
been absent from any religion.

All religions are one. Religion is as inherent to life as humidity is to water. The great cosmic universal religion becomes
modified into thousands of religious forms. Thus, the priests
from all religious forms are completely identifiable with one
another through the fundamental principles of the great cosmic universal religion. Therefore, there is no fundamental difference between the Mohammedan priest and the Jewish priest,
or between the Pagan priest and the legitimate Christian one.
Religion is one. Religion is singular and absolutely universal.
The ceremonies of the Shinto priest of Japan or of the Mongol
Lamas are similar to those ceremonies of the shamans and
sorcerers from Africa and Oceania.

When a religious form degenerates, it disappears; yet, the
universal life creates new religious forms in order to replace it.

Authentic primeval Gnostic Christianity comes from Paganism. Prior to Paganism, the Cosmic Christ was worshiped in all
religions. In Egypt, Christ was Osiris, and whosoever incarnated him was an Osirified one. In all ages there have been
masters who have assimilated the infinite universal Christic
principle. In Egypt, Hermes was the Christ. In Mexico, the
Christ was Quetzalcoatl. In sacred India, Krishna is Christ.

In the Holy Land, the great Gnostic Jesus (who was edu-
cated in the land of Egypt) was the one who had the bliss of as-
similating the universal Christic principle, and because of this,
he was worthy of being rebaptized with the seity of fire and of
the cross, Kristos. The Nazarene, Jesus-Iesus-Zeus, is the mod-

THE UNIQUE AND AUTHENTIC IMAGE OF OUR LORD JESUS CHRIST.

Taken from an emerald cutting sent to be engraved by order of the Roman Emperor Tiberius. It comes from the treasure of Constantinople and was surrendered by the Sultan of Turkey to Pope Innocent VIII as ransom payment for his brother, held captive by the Christians. This image has been taken directly from the priceless emerald, belonging to the Vatican Treasury.

ern man who totally incarnates the universal Christic principle. Prior to Jesus, many masters incarnated this Christic principle of fire. The Rabbi of Galilee is a god, because he totally incarnated the Cosmic Christ. Hermes, Quetzalcoatl, Krishna are gods because they also incarnated the Cosmic Christ.

It is necessary to worship the gods; they help their devotees.

"Ask, and it shall be given you... Knock, and it shall be opened unto you." —Christian Bible, Matthew 7:7

Sexual Magic is the art of producing fire. We can produce fire, develop it, and incarnate the Christ only with the perfect matrimony. This is how we become gods.

The Christic principle is always the same. The masters who incarnate it are living buddhas. Among them there are always hierarchies. The Buddha Jesus is the most exalted initiate of the universal White Fraternity.

When a religious form has fulfilled its mission, it disintegrates. Jesus the Christ was in fact the initiator of a new era.
Jesus was a religious necessity of that epoch. At the end of the
Roman Empire, the Pagan priestly caste had fallen into the
most complete disrepute. The multitudes no longer respected
the priests, and the artists satirized the divine rituals in comedies, sarcastically nicknaming the divinities of Olympus and
Avernus. It is painful to see how these people depicted the god
Bacchus as a drunken woman, and at other times caricatured
him as a pot-bellied drunkard mounted upon a donkey. They
represented the ineffable and blessed goddess Venus as an
adulterous woman who went in search of orgiastic pleasure,
followed by nymphs who were chased by satyrs in front of Pan
and Bacchus. During that epoch of religious decadence, the
people of Greece and Rome did not even respect Mars, the god
of war. They sarcastically represented him trapped by Vulcan's
invisible net, in the moment of committing adultery with
his wife, the beautiful Venus. The way that they ridiculed the
offended one, along with the sarcasm, the irony, etc., clearly
shows the decadence of Paganism. Not even Jupiter-Olympus,
the father of the gods, escaped profanation for he was sarcastically represented in many satires busily seducing goddesses,
nymphs, and mortals. Priapus became the terror of husbands,
and Olympus, the ancient abode of the gods, became a licen-
tious bacchanal. The terrible Avernus (inferno) ruled by Pluto,
source of terror for innumerable centuries, no longer frightened anybody and became a subject of comedy with intrigues
of all kinds, sarcasm and ridicule that made everybody laugh.
The anathemas and the excommunications performed by
priests, pontiffs, bishops, etc., did not have any effect, because
the people no longer respected them. The religious form had
fulfilled its mission and its death was inevitable. Most of the
priests and priestesses degenerated and prostituted themselves
in the already degenerated temples of Vesta, Venus-Aphrodite,
and Apollo. During that epoch, many Pagan priests became
vagrants, comedians, puppeteers, beggars. The common people
mocked them and ran after them throwing stones. This is how
the religious form of Roman Paganism ended. That form had

already completed its mission and at that point all that remained was for it to die.

The world needed something new. The universal religion needed to manifest in a new form. Jesus was the initiator of that new era. Indeed, Jesus the Christ was the divine hero of the new age.

The Nicene Council held in the year 325 A.D. did not create a new hero, as the materialistic swine suppose. In the Nicene Council, a doctrine and a man were officially recognized. The doctrine was primeval Christianity, today disfigured by the Roman Catholic sect. The man was Jesus. Many people had declared themselves avatars of the new era; however, none of them except for Jesus had taught the doctrine of the new era. The facts speak for themselves, and Jesus spoke with facts; this is why he was recognized as the initiator of the new era.

The doctrine of Jesus is Christic esotericism, the solar religion of all ages and centuries. The Gnosticism taught by Jesus is the religion of the Sun, the primeval Christianity of the gods of the dawn.

Indeed, the Nicene Council gave legal status to a new religious form that had long endured terrifying persecution and martyrdom. It is enough to remember the circus of lions (in the times of Nero), when the Christians were thrown into the arena to be devoured by those wild animals. Let us remember the epoch of the catacombs and the suffering of all those Gnostics. It was only just that the Nicene Council should definitively, officially recognize a Ssolar doctrine and a man who had incarnated the Cosmic Christ.

We clarify that the holy gods of the Egyptian, Greek, Roman, Iberian, Scandinavian, Gaelic, Germanic, Assyrian, Aramaic, Babylonian, Persian religions, etc., have not died. Those gods fulfilled their mission and thereafter they withdrew; that is all. In a future mahamanvantara those ineffable gods and their divine religions will return at the right day and hour for a new manifestation.

When a religious form disappears, it commends its ecumenical universal principles to the religious form that follows it. This is the law of life.

Jesus has the divine attributes of Krishna, Buddha, Zeus-Jupiter, Apollo. All of them were born of a virgin. Indeed, Christ is always born from the virgin mother of the world. Every master practices Sexual Magic; thus, speaking symbolically, we can assert that Christ is born within the womb of the priestess-wife.

The emblems, symbols, and dramas of the birth of the gods are always the same. The god Mithra was born on the 24th of December at midnight, just as Jesus was. The birthplace of Jesus was Bethlehem. This name comes from the name of the god of the Babylonian and Germanic people, who named their Sun god Bel or Beleno. Therefore, the birth in Belen or Bethlehem was in order to make the reality of a man who had incarnated the Christ-Sun understandable.

Thus, the goddesses Isis, Juno, Demeter, Ceres, Vesta, Maia, were personified in the mother of the hierophant Jesus. The Hebrew maiden Mary was a great initiate. Every esotericist knows this. All these goddess mothers can rightly represent the Divine Mother Kundalini from whom the Universal Word of Life is always born.

All the martyred Saints, Virgins, Angels, Cherubim, Seraphim, Archangels, Powers, Virtues, and Thrones are the same Demigods, Titans, Goddesses, Sylphs, Cyclops, and Messengers of the gods, yet now with new names. The religious principles are always the same. The religious forms may change, however, the principles do not change because there is only one religion, the universal religion.

The ancient convents of nuns reappeared in a new form. Nonetheless, it was a misfortune, because the medieval priests only used the priestesses to fornicate, because of the fact of not knowing the great arcanum. If they had known the great arcanum, the priestesses would have fulfilled a great mission, and the priests would have attained profound Realization of the Self. Then the Roman Catholic form would not have degenerated, and Christic esotericism would now be resplendent in all temples.

In the new age of Aquarius, Gnostic Christic esotericism will replace the Catholic form; then the human being will venerate the ineffable gods. The perfect matrimony is the religious path of the new age.

It is impossible to incarnate the Cosmic Christ without Sexual Magic. Love is the highest religion. God is love. The hour has arrived to understand in depth the profound meaning of that which is called love. Indeed, love is the only type of energy that can totally Christify us.

Sex is the stone of the Sun. Sex is the cornerstone upon which we have to build the temple for the Lord.

> *"The stone which the builders disallowed, the same is become the head of the corner; this is the Lord's doing, and it is marvelous in our eyes."*

Precisely, this stone is rejected by infrasexual people who presume of being perfect. It is indeed something marvelous that this stone, considered taboo, or sinful, or simply an instrument of pleasure, be placed at the head of the corner of the temple.

> *"Therefore I say unto you, the kingdom of God (the magis regnum or kingdom of magic) shall be taken from you and given to a nation bringing forth the fruits thereof.*
>
> *"And whosoever shall fall on this stone shall be broken, but on whomsoever it shall fall, it will grind him to powder."* —Christian Bible, Matthew 21: 42-45

Sex is the foundation stone of the family, because without it, the family could not exist. Sex is the foundation stone of the human being, because without it, the human being could not come into existence. Sex is the foundation stone of the universe, because without it the universe could not exist.

The sexual energy of the Third Logos flows from the center of every nebula and from the vortex of every atom. When this energy stops flowing from the center of the Earth, this planet will become a corpse.

The sexual energy of the Third Logos has three modes of expression:

- Reproduction of the species
- Evolution of the human race
- Spiritual development

The Kundalini is the very same type of energy with which the Third Logos elaborates all the elements of Earth.

In Nature, there are three types of energy: first, the energy of the Father, second, the energy of the Son, third, the energy of the Holy Spirit. In India, the Father is Brahma, the Son is Vishnu, and the Holy Spirit is Shiva.

The force of the Holy Spirit must return inwards and upwards. It is urgent that the sexual forces are sublimated to the heart. In this magnetic center, these forces are mixed with the forces of the Son in order to ascend to the superior worlds. Only the one who attains the complete development of the Kundalini is totally Christified. Only the one who is Christified can incarnate the Father.

The Son is one with the Father and the Father is one with the Son. No one reaches the Father but through the Son. So it is written.

The forces of the Father, the Son and the Holy Spirit descend to later return inwards and upwards. This is the law.

The energies of the Holy Spirit descend into the sexual organs. The energies of the Son descend into the heart, and the energies of the Father into the mind. We return by means of the energies of the Holy Spirit, and on this return marvelous encounters occur. Thus, in the heart we meet the Christ and in the mind the Father. An inward and upward return is what these encounters signify. This is how we pass beyond the fourth, fifth, and sixth dimensions of space. This is how we liberate ourselves completely.

Much has been stated about the hierophant Jesus, however, the fact is that nobody knows his personal biography. There is a tendency to castrate the hierophant Jesus. The Christian sects depict an infrasexual Jesus, effeminate, weak, yet at times angry, like a whimsical woman. Naturally, all of this is absurd. The fact is that nobody knows the personal life of Jesus, because we do not have his biography. Only with the faculties of objective clairvoyance can we study the life of Jesus in the Akashic Records of Nature. The Akasha is a subtle agent that penetrates and permeates the whole space. All the events of the Earth and its races, the life of Jesus etc., are depicted as an eternal and living film within the Akasha. This medium even permeates the air. Radio-television science will have instruments adequate enough to see the Akashic records at the end of this century. Then, people will study the personal life of the hierophant Jesus with this equipment.

We already know that all movement is relative and that there is only one constant. This one is the velocity of light. Light travels at a certain constant velocity. With their lenses astronomers perceive stars that have already ceased to exist. What they see and even photograph of these stars is the memory, the Akasha. Many of these stars are so distant, that the light coming from them could have begun its journey before the formation of the world. This slowness of light, this constant, may in reality make possible the invention of certain special instruments with which the past can be seen. None of this is impossible. Thus, with a very special telescope, with a very special radio-television apparatus, it is possible to capture sounds and light, events and happenings that have occurred on our Earth since the formation of the world. Science will achieve this very soon, at the end of this century. Then it will be possible to write the biography of Jesus.[223]

In the astral body, the Gnostics study the Akashic records whenever it is necessary. We know the life of the great master and we know that Jesus was really a complete man in the full sense of the word. Jesus had a priestess wife, because he was not an infrasexual. The wife of Jesus was obviously a complete lady-adept, endowed with great secret powers. Jesus traveled through Europe and was a member of a Mediterranean mystery school. Jesus studied in Egypt and practiced Sexual Magic with his priestess in one of the pyramids. That is how he recapitulated the initiations and later achieved the Venustic Initiation. Jesus traveled through Persia, India, etc. Thus, the great master was a master in the most complete sense of the word.

---

223 Readers have asked if this has come to pass; our answer is to consider if such a powerful technology were available in the current social and political circumstances, do you believe the public would be informed, or given access to it? Or would it be kept secret among a certain elite?

The four gospels are indeed four texts of Alchemy and White Magic. Initiation begins with the transmutation of the water of life (semen) into the wine of light of the alchemist. This miracle is performed at the wedding of Cana, a miracle always in wedlock. With this miracle one begins to traverse the path of initiation.

All the drama of the life, passion, and death of Jesus is as ancient as the world. This drama comes from the past, from ancient archaic religions, and is known in every corner of the world. This drama is applicable to Jesus, and in general to all those who traverse the path of the razor's edge. That drama is not the personal life of one man. That drama is the esoteric life of all those who follow the secret path. That drama can be applied to Jesus, as well as to any other Christified initiate. Indeed, the drama of the life, passion, death and resurrection of Jesus is a cosmic drama that existed long before the existence of the world. That drama is known in all the worlds of infinite space.

The four gospels can only be understood with the key of Sexual Magic and the perfect matrimony. The four gospels were only written to serve as a guide to the few who follow the path of the razor's edge. The four gospels were never written for the multitudes. The work of adapting the cosmic drama to the new age was marvelous. Secret groups of initiates took part in this work. They did a splendid job. When profane people study the gospels, they misinterpret them.

Jesus had the heroism to assimilate the Christic substance in all his internal vehicles. He achieved this by working with INRI (fire). This is how the hierophant was able to be one with the Father. Jesus became a Christ and ascended to the Father. Everyone who assimilates the Christic substance in the physiological, biological, psychic, and spiritual Self becomes a Christ. Therefore, Christ is not some kind of human or divine individual. Christ is a cosmic substance that is found in the whole infinite space. We need to form Christ within us. This is only possible with INRI (fire).

Christ cannot do anything without the snake. The snake only develops, evolves, and progresses by practicing Sexual Magic.

Whosoever forms Christ becomes Christ. Only Christ can ascend to the Father. The Father is neither a human nor a divine individual. The Father, the Son, and Holy Spirit are substances, forces, transcendental, and terrifically divine energies. That is all. What happens is that unfortunately, people have a marked tendency to anthropomorphize these superior forces.

Jesus lived the drama of the Passion; nonetheless, he was not the only one who has lived it. Prior to him, some initiates like Hermes, Quetzalcoatl, Krishna, Orpheus, Buddha etc., lived it. After him, a few others have lived it. The drama of the Passion is cosmic.

Christ and Sexual Magic are the synthesis of all religions, schools, and beliefs. The perfect matrimony does not harm anyone. All the priests of all religions, teachers of all schools, the worshippers of Christ, the lovers of wisdom, can traverse the path of the perfect matrimony. The synthesis does not harm anyone, rather it benefits all. This is the doctrine of the synthesis. This is the doctrine of the new era.

We, the members of all schools, religions, sects, orders, etc., would do well to agree on the basis of the perfect matrimony as the foundation for a new civilization based on the wisdom of the serpent. We need a new civilization based on the perfect matrimony. The entire world is in crisis and only with love can we save ourselves.

We, the Gnostics, are not against any religion, because this would be an absurdity. All religions are needed. All religions are diverse manifestations of the universal infinite cosmic religion. People without religion would be a serious and lamentable thing. We believe that all schools and sects fulfill their mission teaching, studying, discussing, etc. What is important, and indeed fundamental, is that people follow the path of the perfect matrimony. Love does not harm or hurt anyone. Gnosis is the flame from which all religions, schools, and beliefs come. Gnosis is wisdom and love.

Those who believe they will achieve Christification in time, by means of evolution, reincarnating, and gaining many experiences, are in fact mistaken. Those who think in that way are delaying the error from century to century, from life to life; however, the reality is that in the end, they will be lost in the Abyss. We, the Gnostics, do not deny the law of evolution. We only state that this law does not Christify anyone. The laws of evolution and devolution are purely mechanical laws of Nature that proceed simultaneously in the entire great laboratory of Nature. Many organisms, many species are a product of devolution and many other organisms and species are a product of evolution. The grave problem lies in attributing to evolution aspects, virtues, and qualities that it does not possess. Evolution does not Christify anybody. Whosoever wants Christification needs the revolution of the consciousness. This is only possible by working with the grain.

We must clarify that the work with the grain has three completely defined lines.

- First: to be born.
- Second: to die.
- Third: to sacrifice for poor, suffering humanity.

To be born is a completely sexual problem. To die is a matter of sanctity. Sacrifice for humanity is Christ-centrism.

The angel must be born within us. This angel is born from our sexual seed. Satan must die; this is a matter of sanctity. We must give our life so that others may live. This is Christ-centrism.

The hierophant Jesus really lived out all the drama of the Passion, just as it is written. Even though we are really miserable worms of the Earth, we also need to live all the drama of the Passion.

Jesus was the son of a Roman soldier and a Hebrew woman. The great hierophant was of medium stature and with fair skin, lightly tanned by the rays of the Sun. The great master had black hair and a beard of the same color. His eyes were like two ineffable nights. The word Nazarene comes from nazar, meaning "a man with a straight nose." Jesus did not have the hooked, Jewish type nose. The great master had a straight nose.

This is typical of the white European race. Jesus was only Jewish on the side of the Hebrew Mary; however, on his father's side he was of the white Celtic race. His father was a Roman soldier.

The priestess-wife of the Master Jesus was also of the white race and had great esoteric powers, as she demonstrated when traveling with the Nazarene through the countries of the Mediterranean in the lands of Europe.

Jesus was a complete man. Jesus was not the castrated one that many religions depict. Jesus followed the path of the perfect matrimony. Jesus formed the Christ within himself by practicing Sexual Magic with his wife. What we are stating will shock fanatics. Nevertheless, when scientists have the Akashic Records of Nature in their power, then these people will see that we were right, because they will be able to see for themselves the life of Jesus by means of ultramodern television (it does not matter what name will be given to those devices in that age).

The whole history of the world will be known through the Akashic Records, the lives of all the great beings, the complete history of Cleopatra and Mark Antony, etc. Time is passing and the facts will confirm our statements.

When completing these thirty-three chapters of *The Perfect Matrimony*, we were informed that the great Master Jesus is in the western United States. The great master walks the streets anonymously and unknown; he dresses as any citizen and nobody knows him. A tremendous flow of Christic energy comes from him and is dispersed to all America. The great master still maintains the same body that he had in the Holy Land. Indeed, the great hierophant Jesus resurrected on the third day from among the dead, and still lives with his physical body. Jesus achieved resurrection through the Elixir of Long Life. Jesus received the Elixir of Long Life because he was Christified. Jesus was Christified. Jesus was Christified because he followed the path of the perfect matrimony.

We close these thirty-three chapters by stating that in the center of the four ways called religion, science, art, and philosophy is found the supreme synthesis. This is the perfect matrimony.

Conclusion

"My beloved brothers and sisters of the Gnostic movement: We have concluded this course of esoteric teaching. I was thinking about ending these meetings in order to enter into a recess for a while; however, I see that these meetings are a spiritual necessity for all of us. Therefore, I believe that it would be better if we were to continue meeting on the 27th of each month."

This is what I said on the 27th of July, 1961, in the home of a distinguished man of science. At that time I had finished *The Perfect Matrimony* and at the same time concluded a course of sexual-esoteric teaching that I had been lecturing about to a group of Gnostic Rosicrucian students.

The reason I thought of terminating the esoteric meetings in Mexico was that I was disappointed. In the beginning, the meeting room was full of people. Everyone enjoyed studying the mysteries of sex and the path of the perfect matrimony. Afterwards, as time passed, the people were no longer interested in the perfect matrimony or in Sexual Magic.

After two years, the esotericists attending these meetings could be counted on the fingers of one hand. Therefore, under such circumstances, I considered that it was useless to continue giving lectures. My intention was to end the lectures and meetings that night. Nevertheless, something remarkable occurred that night. I was filled with an immense, grandiose, and sublime love. My heart was filled with pain upon remembering the thought of leaving them alone. It was then that I resolved not to terminate the meetings, and to continue on with the few. When I returned to my home, I received a telepathic message from the Temple of Chapultepec. I was commanded to leave the house and to immediately go to the forest of Chapultepec.

I obeyed the command and left the house, towards that marvelous forest which the Master Huiracocha speaks of in his novel *Rosy Cross*.

THE CASTLE OF CHAPULTEPEC, MEXICO CITY

The Castle of Chapultepec with its thousands of little lights was shining marvelously. The avenues and the central stairway were deserted and the doors hermetically locked. To enter into the forest of Chapultepec during the midnight hours is difficult because the guards and policemen are alert and vigilant. Therefore, it could happen that if some Gnostic Rosicrucian student were to venture into the forest, he could be mistaken for a thief. The zeal of the guards is great, because in the Castle of Chapultepec there are immense treasures. Let us remember the dinnerware of Emperor Maximillian, all solid gold, and the colonial treasures contained in the halls of the palace. This is the most magnificent palace in Mexico.

To narrate how I was able to enter the forest of Chapultepec at midnight is not important. The fact is that I entered; that is all. I walked along the avenue, turning at the hill of Chapultepec, continuing in the direction of the fountains that were constructed by President Madero. The path was deserted and the night dark... I spent some time waiting for a prearranged signal. It seemed like a very long time to me; however, finally someone arrived who spoke on my behalf, and everything was arranged.

The superior adept of the temple commanded me to enter; thus, without further formality I went in. The temple is situated inside the hill of Chapultepec. In other times, this temple was visible to the Aztecs, but afterwards, with the arrival of the Spaniards, the temple entered into Jinn state. The empire of light and faith of the Nahuas is within this temple.

Two guardians, holding unsheathed swords, guard the entrance; thus, nobody is able to enter without superior orders.

That was a night of immense happiness for me. The temple was filled with a light of immaculate whiteness. It was light imbibed with life and Spirit, light that casts no shadows. This light comes from a tabernacle chalice. Wrapped within such a light, the soul feels filled with a truly indescribable happiness.

An angel entered the temple with me and took a seat. The superior adept of the temple showed us some very beautiful paintings filled with life and movement. These paintings are very abundant in the White Lodges. Franz Hartmann already commented in his book entitled *With the Adepts* about this kind of painting, which he saw in a Rosicrucian temple in Bohemia. The figures in these kinds of pictures are full of life and movement. This is called the royal art of Nature.

The superior of the temple, noticing our admiration for the paintings, addressed the angel and then myself, saying, "You are forbidden to touch these paintings." The angel faithfully obeyed the command. However, I frankly, felt tempted to touch them... They were so beautiful... A severe reminder from the master, given in time, was sufficient, "I have already told you, sir, that you are forbidden to touch these paintings."

I excused myself by answering, "Certainly, I do not intend to touch them."

That night, the temple shone with ineffable glory. It is impossible to describe such beauty with human words. The roof, the walls, were all made with solid gold. Nonetheless, something filled me with amazement. I had heard so much talk about Theosophy, Rosicrucianism, Hermeticism, Yoga, etc., and indeed, here I was, in the midst of a Jinn-stated Gnostic Rosicrucian temple. However, there was only a small group of ladies and gentlemen, who like myself, had also been invited to the gathering in the temple.

I remembered the lecture halls of some professors of esotericism, always filled with thousands of people. I remembered the temples of the world, filled with thousands of human beings. I remembered the lodges that call themselves Rosicrucian with their millions of affiliates. Nonetheless, here, now, in the midst of an authentic temple of the White Lodge, the few who were present could be counted on the fingers of one hand. Then I understood everything. At first, many people came to our esoteric meetings. As time passed, the number who attended notably decreased, and now only a few thirsty for wisdom and love were coming to us. When I understood this, I spontaneously exclaimed, "The temples, lodges and schools of the world are always filled with many people, because Satan has enticed them. However, only few are those who come into the temples of true divine wisdom." This is how I spoke, with a voice that amazed me; thus, when I spoke, I noticed that the superior of the temple was nodding in approval.

Then he added, "Thus, this is how it is, Satan has enticed them." Immediately after having confirmed my words, the master commanded the angel to go up to the choir of musicians and singers in order to sing. The angel obeyed, and after having ascended to the choir, he sang the history of the centuries in opera.

The angel, from the doctrinal point of view, placed himself mentally in the time of the future fifth round[224] of planetary evolution. In that future age, the physical-chemical Earth will already be nothing more than a cadaver, a new moon. Then all the evolving life will develop within the ethereal plane or ethereal region of our Earth. The seven root races of flesh and bone will no longer exist. These races will have become extinct.

The angel sang with a voice so ineffable and sweet that it resembled *The Magic Flute* of Mozart. My whole being went into

---

224 Modern humanity is the fifth root race (of seven) in the fourth round. Read *The Revolution of Beelzebub* by Samael Aun Weor.

ecstasy. To hear an angel sing is something that you can never forget in your life.

The angel, situated mentally in the future Earth of the fifth round, narrated in opera the history of terrestrial evolution. He mentioned all the prophets that have been sent to the Earth. With a melodious voice he narrated the history of the seven root races of the world, the apocalypse of the present fifth root race, the continents that existed in the past and their general destruction, the great cataclysms of the Earth, the great wars, the superhuman efforts that had been made by the great avatars to save humanity, the crucifixion of the martyr of Golgotha, etc. Subsequently, he lamented with pain the few that had been saved. Only a few had managed to be born as angels. The rest, the great majority of human beings, were swallowed up by the Abyss. Thus, from the billions of souls that entered evolution and devolution on the planet Earth, only a handful of creatures were fit for the angelic state.

"For many are called, but few are chosen."
—Christian Bible, Matthew 22:14

When the angel reached this part of his ineffable opera, I felt profoundly moved and amazed. Frankly, I had believed that the case of only a few being saved and the great majority being lost only applied to Earth, and in the past mahamanvantara to the Earth-Moon; I believed that in the rest of the worlds, things were different. The angel pointed out this error when he said, "And this that has happened on Earth will always be repeated on all the worlds of the infinite space." When the angel finished his ineffable song I understood why so many people had attended my meetings, and why, from the many who began, only a few remained with me. Now I am willing to continue with the few. I am no longer interested in having a room full of people. Indeed, many are they who begin, but few are those who arrive.

The perfect matrimony is the path of the razor's edge. To affiliate oneself with a school, lodge, order etc., is something very easy. To study yoga, hermeticism, philosophy, astrology, is very beautiful and easy. Nevertheless, to be born as an angel is something terribly difficult. The angel must be born of the sexual seed. Behold, this is precisely where the difficulty lies. The wheat seed germinates easily. Indeed, many seeds are lost, but the majority germinate and become ears of wheat which give forth the grain with which the multitudes are nourished. To sow corn seeds is also something easy. Many seeds are lost, but the great majority are not; they germinate and produce corn. The most difficult is the seed of angels. This seed is carried by the human being in their sexual glands, and very rarely does it germinate.

We have concluded this book emphatically affirming that only with the perfect matrimony can we achieve the germination of this seed and give birth to the fruit. This fruit is the angel. Here is where the problem and the difficulty lies.

It so happens that people think that by belonging to this or that faith, to such and such religion, or to one or another sect, that they are already saved. Naturally, this is false. A seed never germinates because of what a person believes or stops believing. An insect is never born because of what a human being thinks or stops thinking. A person is never born from the parchment of theory. This subject matter is sexual, and in this, the angel is no exception.

The members of all religions, schools, sects, and beliefs say, "For many are called, but few are chosen." People from all over the world repeat it and presume (as is normal) that they are the chosen ones. Nobody considers themselves lost. They believe that with their belief, theory, study etc., they are already saved. However, this is a false and absurd thing, because the problem of being born cannot be the result of beliefs, theories, or concepts. The reality is different. To be born is a totally sexual problem.

Sexual Magic is taught in the esoteric heart of the great religions. Unfortunately, people do not investigate it, they do not inquire. That is the problem.

People do not like Sexual Magic because it means the sacrifice of oneself, of one's animal passions. Rare is the one who can be truly steadfast in Sexual Magic. Many begin with curiosity; however, after a few days, they can no longer tolerate it, and then give themselves over to fornication. These are the weak

SELENE, THE MOON OF EARTH

who afterwards go about saying that Sexual Magic is harmful. These are the degenerated seeds that do not germinate.

Sex is the path that leads human beings to final liberation. If someone thinks that there may be a different path for Realization of the Self, they are obviously totally mistaken. This is the law for all the continents, worlds, and spaces.

We will talk now a little about Selene. Certainly, today the Moon is a cadaver. However, before it died, it was a world that had very beautiful seas, luxuriant vegetation, all kinds of people, etc. Unfortunately, the lunar multitudes became demons. Only a small handful of human creatures achieved practical adepthood. On our planet Earth, the outcome will be likewise. Only a small group of people will be born as angels. We can affirm without fear of error, that the humanity of Earth will be swallowed up by the Abyss.

The Theosophists are mistaken when they affirm that all human beings will reach liberation. This concept is not accepted by the White Lodge because it is false. Those who think that by believing in something or other they will be saved are mistaken. This concept is false. Those who believe that with the bellows-system of pranayama and philosophy they can be saved are mistaken. Nobody can save themselves without being born, and nobody can be born without sex.

I have concluded this book with immense sorrow for humanity. It is lamentable that the Abyss swallows up so many people. I write with pain, because I know that humanity does not accept the perfect matrimony. I conclude this book perfectly convinced that those who truly know how to take advantage of it are very few. People do not like these things. Everyone thinks that with their particular belief, religion, order, or school, they can save themselves, and there is no way of convincing them that they are mistaken. In the future fifth round, all those who do not accept the perfect matrimony will become demons, inhabitants of the Abyss. In the future fifth round, those who accept the perfect matrimony will be angels.

We are at the end of the Aryan root race; we are beginning to live the Apocalypse of Saint John. Millions of human beings are entering into the Abyss. These poor people enter the Abyss convinced that they are doing very well. They believe that they are already the chosen ones, and that their beliefs have saved them. That is what they believe, and there is no way to prove the contrary to them. This is how they submerge themselves into the Abyss where, after many millions of years, they disintegrate slowly until becoming cosmic dust. This is the Second Death.

We conclude this book by stating: Only the one who becomes an angel is saved. The angel must be born within our very Selves. To be born is an absolutely sexual problem, and the only path is the path of the perfect matrimony.

Glossary

Absolute: Abstract space; that which is without attributes or limitations. Also known as sunyata, void, emptiness, Parabrahman, Adi-buddha, and many other names.

"The Absolute is the Being of all Beings. The Absolute is that which Is, which always has Been, and which always will Be. The Absolute is expressed as Absolute Abstract Movement and Repose. The Absolute is the cause of Spirit and of Matter, but It is neither Spirit nor Matter. The Absolute is beyond the mind; the mind cannot understand It. Therefore, we have to intuitively understand Its nature." —Samael Aun Weor, *Tarot and Kabbalah*

"In the Absolute we go beyond karma and the gods, beyond the law. The mind and the individual consciousness are only good for mortifying our lives. In the Absolute we do not have an individual mind or individual consciousness; there, we are the unconditioned, free and absolutely happy Being. The Absolute is life free in its movement, without conditions, limitless, without the mortifying fear of the law, life beyond spirit and matter, beyond karma and suffering, beyond thought, word and action, beyond silence and sound, beyond forms." —Samael Aun Weor, *The Major Mysteries*

Adultery: Etymologists say that the English word adultery comes from the Old French avoutrie, aoulterie, a noun of condition from avoutre / aoutre, and from the Latin adulterare "to corrupt," meaning, "debauch; falsify, debase." The term adulterate is used correctly when describing a lie or a corruption of something that was pure. Thus, broadly speaking, an act of adultery is an act that makes purity into impurity.

In the scriptures of Judaism and Christianity, the word adultery is usually placed as the translation for נאף na'aph: "To perform voluntary violation of the marriage bed." This word does not mean just adultery in a limited, literal sense, but is far more broad.

Strictly defined, adultery is sexual infidelity: to lust after someone other than one's partner, or to have sex with multiple partners.

"Three evil deeds [that create suffering] depending upon the body are: killing, stealing, and committing adultery." —Buddha, from The Practice of Dhyâna

"Have nought to do with adultery; for it is a foul thing and an evil way." —Mohammed, from Qu'ran, Sura XVII, The Night Journey, Mecca

"The husband receives his wife from the gods; he does not wed her according to his own will; doing what is agreeable to the gods, he must always support her while she is faithful. "Let mutual fidelity continue until death;" this may be considered as a summary of the highest law for husband and wife." —Laws of Manu 9.95, 101

Throughout the world, adultery is commonly defined as "sexual intercourse between a married person and someone else" and while there are many varieties of interpretation on this point, the scriptures are actually quite clear about what adultery is:

"Adultery can be committed with the eyes." —Jewish, Leviticus Rabba 23

"Commit no adultery. This law is broken by even looking at the wife of another with a lustful mind." —Buddha

"Ye have heard that it was said by them of old time, Thou shalt not commit adultery: But I say unto you, That whosoever looketh on a woman to lust after her hath committed adultery with her already in his heart." —Jesus, in Matthew 5

"But I say unto you, That whosoever shall put away his wife, saving for the cause of fornication, causeth her to commit adultery: and whosoever shall marry her that is divorced committeth adultery." —Jesus, in Matthew 5

"Immorality is not confined to action; it is rooted in the very thought. It can be effectively eliminated not by merely restraining the external organs, as the hypocrites do, but by making the mind and heart pure. "Whosoever looketh on a woman to lust after her hath committed adultery with her already in the heart." Sin is in the mind; the body is a mere tool of the mind." —Swami Sivananda, *Life and Teachings of Lord Jesus* (1959)

"Adultery is the cruel result of the lack of love. The woman who is truly in love would prefer death to adultery. The man who commits adultery is not truly in love. [...] There are also many women who, under the pretext of supposed profound Realization of the Self, unite with any male. What all these passionate women really want is to satiate their carnal desires. The world is always the world, and since we have been divulging the Great Arcanum there have appeared, as one might expect, those swine who trample the doctrine and then die poisoned by the bread of wisdom. The cult of Sexual Magic can only be practiced between husband and wife. [...] We must clarify that Sexual Magic can only be practiced between husband and wife. The adulterer and the adulteress inevitably fail. You can only be married when there is love. Love is law, but it must be conscious love." —Samael Aun Weor, *The Perfect Matrimony*

Akash: (Sanskrit आकाश; or akasa) "Space, sky, atmosphere, vacuity, ether, free or open space, subtle and ethereal fluid, heaven, god brahma." From akash, "to be visible, appear, shine, be brilliant."

"A subtle agent that penetrates and permeates the whole space." —Samael Aun Weor, *The Perfect Matrimony*

The most subtle level of matter. The solar light comes to earth and everything on earth transforms that light. Prana is the light from the Absolute. When it passes through the law of seven it becomes the Akasha. Akasha is further modified into the tattvas and the elements.

Akasha is the name of the first tattva, the primordial substance that inundates the entire space; all the other tattva (Fire-Tejas, Air-Vayu, Water-Apas and Earth-Prithvi) are modifications of these cosmic waters, all of them live and work within Akasha. All forms, thoughts, dreams and ideas of the universe live in Akasha. There is no living thing in the universe that can exist without Akasha or multiply its species without it. Akasha is the substance from which every other substance emerges; Akasha is that which every other tattva emerges from; Akasha is where everything is in potency, and Akasha is where everything is in activity. Thus, Akasa appears in various positions. Wherever there is any room for any substance, there is Akasha.

"By dint of His will, the Lord, the undecaying substratum or reality of the universe, gave the first impetus to Nature to shake off her state of primal equipoise and to be gradually and successfully evolved into those categories and elements which were necessary for the formation of the present universe. The first evolute is Akasa. Why should Akasa be the first evolute? Because, without space, nothing can exist. Prana acted on Akasa. There was Spandana or vibration. Wherever there is vibration, there must be motion. Motion is the quality of air. Therefore, air came out of Akasa. Motion produced heat. Therefore, fire was born of Vayu or air. When there is heat, water is produced. On a hot day, the body perspires. Hence, water was born of fire. Wherever there is water, there is food. Earth is Annam or food. Therefore, earth was born of water. The subtler the element, the more powerful it is. Water is more powerful than earth, because it is more subtle than earth. Water removes away earth. Fire is more powerful than water, because it is more subtle than water. Fire dries up all water. Air is more powerful than fire, because it is more subtle than fire. Air blows up fire. Ether or Akasa is more powerful than air, because it is more subtle than air. Air rests in Akasa. Akasa is the support for air. Air is born of Akasa, fire is born of air, water is born of fire, earth is born of water. During cosmic Pralaya, earth is reduced or involved into water, water into fire, fire into air, and air into Akasa." —Swami Sivananda

"According to the Hindu Philosophy the whole nature is composed of two principal substances. One of them is called the Akasa or ether and the other, Prana or energy. These two may be said to correspond to matter and force of the modern scientists. Everything in this universe that possesses form or that has material existence, is evolved out of this omnipresent and all-pervasive subtle substance 'Akasa'. Gas, liquid and solid, the whole universe, consisting of our solar system and millions of huge systems like ours and in fact every kind of existence that may be brought under the word 'created', are the products of this one subtle and invisible Akasa and at the end of each cycle return to the starting point. In the same way, all the way of forces of nature that are known to man; gravitation, light, heat, electricity, magnetism all those that can be grouped under the generic name of 'energy', physical creation, nerve-currents, all such as are known as animal forces and thought and other intellectual forces also, may be said to be the manifestations of the cosmic Prana. From Prana, they spring into existence and in Prana, they finally subside. Every kind of force in this universe, physical or mental can be resolved into this original force. There can be nothing new except these two factors in some one of their forms. Conservation of matter and conservation of energy are the two fundamental laws of nature. While one teaches that the sum total of Akasa forming the universe, is constant, the other teaches that the sum total of energy that vibrates the universe, is also a constant quantity. At the end of each cycle the different manifestations of energy quiet down and become potential: so also the Akasa which becomes indistinguishable: but at the beginning of the next cycle the energies start up again and act on the Akasa so as to involve the various forms. Accordingly, when the Akasa changes and becomes gross or subtle, Prana also changes and becomes gross or subtle. As the human body is only a microcosm to a Yogi, his body composed of the nervous system and the internal organs of perception represent to him, the microcosmic Akasa, the nerve-currents and thought-currents, and the cosmic Prana. To understand the secrets of their workings and to control them is, therefore, to get the highest knowledge and the conquest of the universe." —Swami Sivananda

Alchemy: Al (as a connotation of the Arabic word Allah: al-, the + ilah, God) means "The God." Also Al (Hebrew) for "highest" or El "God." Chem or Khem is from kimia (Greek) which means "to fuse or cast a metal." Also from Khem, the ancient name of Egypt. The synthesis is Al-Kimia: "to fuse with the highest" or "to fuse with God."

Aquarius: An era of time under the influence of the zodiacal sign of Aquarius that will last for approximately 2,140 years. The new Aquarian era began with the celestial conjunction of February 4-5, 1962. On February 4-5, 1962, exactly when there was a new moon AND a full solar eclipse, there was also an extraordinary celestial conjunction of the seven primary planets with the Earth. The Sun, the Moon, Mercury, Venus, Mars, Jupiter, and Saturn were all visibly grouped close together, and their orbits were aligned with the Earth. This event signaled a change of era, similar to how the hands of a clock move into a new day. The Earth had completed an era of approximately 2,140 years under the influence of Pisces, and then entered an era influenced by Aquarius.

When the age of Aquarius arrived, humanity entered into a very new situation. With the new celestial influence we saw the arrival of a huge shift in society: mass rebellion against the old ways, sexual experimentation, giant social earthquakes shaking up all the old traditions. We also saw the arrival in the West of a strong spiritual longing, and deep thirst for true, authentic spiritual experience. These two elements: 1) rebellion to tradition and 2) thirst for spiritual knowledge are a direct effect of the influence of Aquarius, the most revolutionary sign of the zodiac. Aquarius is the Water Carrier, whose occult significance is knowledge, the bringer of knowledge. With the new age came a sudden revealing of all the hidden knowledge. The doors to the mysteries were thrown open so that humanity can save itself from itself. Of course, the Black Lodge, ever-eager to mislead humanity, has produced so much false spirituality and so many false schools that it is very difficult to find the real and genuine path.

"The majority of the tenebrous brothers and sisters of Aquarius are wicked people who are going around teaching black magic." —Samael Aun Weor, *The Major Mysteries*

"The age of sex, the new Aquarian Age, is at hand. The sexual glands are controlled by the planet Uranus which is the ruling planet of the constellation of Aquarius. Thus, sexual alchemy is in fact the science of the new Aquarian Age. Sexual Magic will be officially accepted in the universities of the new Aquarian Age. Those who presume to be messengers of the new Aquarian Age, but nevertheless hate the Arcanum A.Z.F., provide more than enough evidence that they are truly impostors, this is because the new Aquarian Age is governed by the regent of sex. This regent is the planet Uranus. Sexual energy is the finest energy of the infinite cosmos. Sexual energy can convert us into angels or demons. The image of truth is found deposited in sexual energy. The cosmic design of Adam Christ is found deposited in sexual energy." —Samael Aun Weor, *The Perfect Matrimony*

To learn more about the Aquarian era, read *Christ and the Virgin* by Samael Aun Weor.

Arcanum: (Latin. plural: arcana). A secret, a mystery. The root of the term "ark" as in the Ark of Noah and the Ark of the Covenent.

Arcanum A.Z.F.: The practice of sexual transmutation as couple (male-female), a technique known in Tantra and Alchemy. Arcanum refers to a hidden truth or law. A.Z.F. stands for A (agua, water), Z (azufre, sulfur), F (fuego, fire), and is thus: water + fire = consciousness. . Also, A (azoth = chemical element that refers to fire). A & Z are the first and last letters of the alphabet thus referring to the Alpha & Omega (beginning & end).

Astral: This term is derived from "pertaining to or proceeding from the stars," but in the esoteric knowledge it refers to the emotional aspect of the fifth dimension, which in Hebrew is called Hod.

Astral Body: What is commonly called the astral body is not the true astral body, it is rather the lunar protoplasmatic body, also known as the kama rupa (Sanskrit, "body of desires") or "dream body" (Tibetan rmi-lam-gyi lus). The true astral body is solar (being superior to lunar nature) and must be created, as the Master Jesus indicated in the Gospel of John 3:5-6, "Except a man be born of water and of the Spirit, he cannot enter into the kingdom of God. That which is born of the flesh is flesh; and that which is born of the Spirit is spirit." The solar astral body is created as a result of the Third Initiation of Major Mysteries (Serpents of Fire), and is perfected in the Third Serpent of Light. In Tibetan Buddhism, the solar

astral body is known as the illusory body (sgyu-lus). This body is related
to the emotional center and to the sephirah Hod.

"Really, only those who have worked with the Maithuna (White Tantra)
for many years can possess the astral body." —Samael Aun Weor, *The
Elimination of Satan's Tail*

Astral Light: "There has been an infinite confusion of names to express one
and the same thing. The chaos of the ancients; the Zoroastrian sacred
fire, or the Antusbyrum of the Parsees; the Hermes-fire; the Elmes-fire
of the ancient Germans; the lightning of Cybele; the burning torch of
Apollo; the flame on the altar of Pan; the inextinguishable fire in the
temple on the Acropolis, and in that of Vesta; the fire-flame of Pluto's
helm; the brilliant sparks on the hats of the Dioscuri, on the Gorgon
head, the helm of Pallas, and the staff of Mercury; the πυρ ασβεστον the
Egyptian Phtha, or Ra; the Grecian Zeus Cataibates (the descending);
the pentecostal fire-tongues; the burning bush of Moses; the pillar of fire
of the Exodus, and the "burning lamp" of Abram; the eternal fire of the
"bottomless pit"; the Delphic oracular vapors; the Sidereal light of the
Rosicrucians; the AKASA of the Hindu adepts; the Astral light of Eliphas
Levi; the nerve-aura and the fluid of the magnetists; the od of Reichen-
bach; the fire-globe, or meteor-cat of Babinet; the Psychod and ectenic
force of Thury; the psychic force of Sergeant Cox and Mr. Crookes; the
atmospheric magnetism of some naturalists; galvanism; and finally,
electricity, are but various names for many different manifestations, or
effects of the same mysterious, all-pervading cause--the Greek Archeus, or
Αρχαιοσ. [...] The thaumaturgists of all periods, schools, and countries,
produced their wonders, because they were perfectly familiar with the im-
ponderable--in their effects--but otherwise perfectly tangible waves of the
astral light. They controlled the currents by guiding them with their willpower. The wonders were both of physical and psychological character;
the former embracing effects produced upon material objects, the latter
the mental phenomena of Mesmer and his successors. This class has been
represented in our time by two illustrious men, Du Potet and Regazzoni,
whose wonderful powers were well attested in France and other countries.
Mesmerism is the most important branch of magic; and its phenomena
are the effects of the universal agent which underlies all magic and has
produced at all ages the so-called miracles. The ancients called it Chaos;
Plato and the Pythagoreans named it the Soul of the World. According
to the Hindus, the Deity in the shape of Æther pervades all things. It is
the invisible, but, as we have said before, too tangible Fluid. Among other
names this universal Proteus--or "the nebulous Almighty," as de Mirville
calls it in derision--was termed by the theurgists "the living fire," the
"Spirit of Light," and Magnes. This last appellation indicates its magnetic
properties and shows its magical nature. For, as truly expressed by one of
its enemies--μαγος and μαγνες are two branches growing from the same
trunk, and shooting forth the same resultants. Magnetism is a word for
the derivation of which we have to look to an incredibly early epoch. The

stone called magnet is believed by many to owe its name to Magnesia, a
city or district in Thessaly, where these stones were found in quantity. We
believe, however, the opinion of the Hermetists to be the correct one. The
word Magh, magus, is derived from the Sanskrit Mahaji, the great or wise
(the anointed by the divine wisdom). [...] Now, what is this mystic, primordial substance? In the book of Genesis, at the beginning of the first
chapter, it is termed the "face of the waters," said to have been incubated
by the "Spirit of God." Job mentions, in chap. xxvi., 5, that "dead things
are formed from under the waters, and inhabitants thereof." In the
original text, instead of "dead things," it is written dead Rephaim (giants,
or mighty primitive men), from whom "Evolution" may one day trace our
present race. In the Egyptian mythology, Kneph the Eternal unrevealed
God is represented by a snake-emblem of eternity encircling a water-
urn, with his head hovering over the waters, which it incubates with his
breath. In this case the serpent is the Agathodaimon, the good spirit; in
its opposite aspect it is the Kakodaimon--the bad one. In the Scandinavian Eddas, the honey-dew--the food of the gods and of the creative, busy
Yggdrasill--bees--falls during the hours of night, when the atmosphere
is impregnated with humidity; and in the Northern mythologies, as the
passive principle of creation, it typifies the creation of the universe out
of water; this dew is the astral light in one of its combinations and possesses creative as well as destructive properties. In the Chaldean legend of
Berosus, Oannes or Dagon, the man-fish, instructing the people, shows
the infant world created out of water and all beings originating from
this prima materia. Moses teaches that only earth and water can bring a
living soul; and we read in the Scriptures that herbs could not grow until
the Eternal caused it to rain upon earth. In the Mexican Popol-Vuh man
is created out of mud or clay (terre glaise), taken from under the water.
Brahma creates Lomus, the great Muni (or first man), seated on his lotus,
only after having called into being, spirits, who thus enjoyed among mortals a priority of existence, and he creates him out of water, air, and earth.
Alchemists claim that primordial or pre-Adamic earth when reduced to
its first substance is in its second stage of transformation like clear-water,
the first being the alkahest proper. This primordial substance is said to
contain within itself the essence of all that goes to make up man; it has
not only all the elements of his physical being, but even the "breath of
life" itself in a latent state, ready to be awakened. This it derives from
the "incubation" of the Spirit of God upon the face of the waters--chaos;
in fact, this substance is chaos itself. From this it was that Paracelsus
claimed to be able to make his "homunculi"; and this is why Thales,
the great natural philosopher, maintained that water was the principle
of all things in nature. What is the primordial Chaos but Æther? The
modern Ether; not such as is recognized by our scientists, but such as it
was known to the ancient philosophers, long before the time of Moses;
Ether, with all its mysterious and occult properties, containing in itself
the germs of universal creation; Ether, the celestial virgin, the spiritual
mother of every existing form and being, from whose bosom as soon as

"incubated" by the Divine Spirit, are called into existence Matter and Life, Force and Action. Electricity, magnetism, heat, light, and chemical action are so little understood even now that fresh facts are constantly widening the range of our knowledge. Who knows where ends the power of this protean giant--Ether; or whence its mysterious origin?--Who, we mean, that denies the spirit that works in it and evolves out of it all visible forms?" —H.P.Blavatsky, *Isis Unveiled*

"The Astral Light is the battlefield between white and black magicians. The Astral Light is the clue of all empires and the key of all powers. It is the great universal agent of life. All the columns of angels and demons live within the Astral Light..." —Samael Aun Weor, *The Revolution of Beelzebub*

Atom: While modern science studies atoms as the basic unit of matter, they are ignoring the two other essential aspects of each atom: energy and consciousness.

"Every atom is a trio of matter, energy and consciousness. The consciousness of every atom is always an intelligent elemental. If the materialists are not capable of seeing those elementals, it is because they still do not know the scientific procedures that allow us to see them. We have special methods in order to see those creatures. Indeed, the atom is a truly infinitely small planetary system. Those planetary systems of the atoms are formed by ultra-atomic ternaries that spin around their centers of gravitation. The atom with its Alpha, Beta, and Gamma rays is a trio of matter, energy and consciousness." —Samael Aun Weor, *Sexology, the Basis of Endocrinology and Criminology*

Thus understood as being more than mere matter, atoms have great significance for all living creatures, since atoms form the basis for all living things. That is why the spiritual classic *The Dayspring of Youth* by M explains that atoms are "Minute bodies of intelligence possessing the dual attributes of Nature and man." While there are many types and levels of such atomic intelligences, both positive and negative, some of particular importance are Aspiring atoms, Destructive atoms, the Nous atom, Informer atoms, Scholar atoms, etc.

"Life will not be fully understood until we recognise the living forces within us and transplant atoms of a higher nature into the body. This will eventually help humanity to become the personification of justice. Our atomic centres are similar to the starry clusters in the sky, and each atom is a minute intelligence revolving within its own atmosphere. When we aspire we unite ourselves to atoms that have preceded us in evolution; for they evolve as we evolve: this body being their university, and they prepare the path for us to follow." —*The Dayspring of Youth* by M

"The atom of the Father is situated in the root of the nose; this is the atom of willpower. The seven serpents ascend by means of willpower, by dominating the animal impulse. The atom of the Father is situated in the root of the nose; this is the atom of willpower. The seven serpents ascend by means of willpower, by dominating the animal impulse. The atom of the Son is in the pituitary gland, whose exponent is the Nous atom (the Son of Man) in the heart. The angelic atom of the Holy Spirit shines in the pineal gland, within the chakra Sahasrara. The atom of the Father governs or controls the right ganglionary chord Pingala within which the solar atoms, the positive force, ascends. The atom of the Son governs the Sushumna canal, within which the neutral forces ascend. The atom of the Holy Spirit governs the Ida canal, within which the negative forces ascend. This is why it is related with our creative sexual forces and with the rays of the moon, which are intimately related with the reproduction of the races. Each of the seven chakras from the spinal medulla is governed by an angelic atom." —Samael Aun Weor, *Kabbalah of the Mayan Mysteries*

Centers, Seven: The human being has seven centers of psychological activity. The first five are the Intellectual, Emotional, Motor, Instinctive, and Sexual Centers. However, through inner development one learns how to utilize the Superior Emotional and Superior Intellectual Centers. Most people do not use these two at all.

Chakra: (Sanskrit) Literally, "wheel." The chakras are subtle centers of energetic transformation. There are hundreds of chakras in our hidden physiology, but seven primary ones related to the awakening of consciousness.

"The Chakras are centres of Shakti as vital force... The Chakras are not perceptible to the gross senses. Even if they were perceptible in the living body which they help to organise, they disappear with the disintegration of organism at death." —Swami Sivananda, *Kundalini Yoga*

"The chakras are points of connection through which the divine energy circulates from one to another vehicle of the human being." —Samael Aun Weor, *Aztec Christic Magic*

Chastity: Although modern usage has rendered the term chastity virtually meaningless to most people, its original meaning and usage clearly indicate "moral purity" upon the basis of "sexual purity." Contemporary usage implies "repression" or "abstinence," which have nothing to do with real chastity. True chastity is a rejection of impure sexuality. True chastity is pure sexuality, or the activity of sex in harmony with our true nature, as explained in the secret doctrine. Properly used, the word chastity refers to sexual fidelity or honor.

"The generative energy, which, when we are loose, dissipates and makes us unclean, when we are continent invigorates and inspires us. Chastity is the flowering of man; and what are called Genius, Heroism, Holiness, and the like, are but various fruits which succeed it." —Henry David Thoreau, *Walden*

Christ: Derived from the Greek Christos, "the Anointed One," and Krestos, whose esoteric meaning is "fire." The word Christ is a title, not a personal name.

"Indeed, Christ is a Sephirothic Crown (Kether, Chokmah and Binah) of incommensurable wisdom, whose purest atoms shine within Chokmah, the world of the Ophanim. Christ is not the Monad, Christ is not the Theosophical Septenary; Christ is not the Jivan-Atman. Christ is the Central Sun. Christ is the ray that unites us to the Absolute." —Samael Aun Weor, *Tarot and Kabbalah*

"The Gnostic Church adores the saviour of the world, Jesus. The Gnostic Church knows that Jesus incarnated Christ, and that is why they adore him. Christ is not a human nor a divine individual. Christ is a title given to all fully self-realized masters. Christ is the Army of the Voice. Christ is the Verb. The Verb is far beyond the body, the soul and the Spirit. Everyone who is able to incarnate the Verb receives in fact the title of Christ. Christ is the Verb itself. It is necessary for everyone of us to incarnate the Verb (Word). When the Verb becomes flesh in us we speak with the verb of light. In actuality, several masters have incarnated the Christ. In secret India, the Christ Yogi Babaji has lived for millions of years; Babaji is immortal. The great master of wisdom Kout Humi also incarnated the Christ. Sanat Kumara, the founder of the great College of Initiates of the White Lodge, is another living Christ. In the past, many incarnated the Christ. In the present, some have incarnated the Christ. In the future many will incarnate the Christ. John the Baptist also incarnated the Christ. John the Baptist is a living Christ. The difference between Jesus and the other masters that also incarnated the Christ has to do with hierarchy. Jesus is the highest Solar initiate of the cosmos..." —Samael Aun Weor, *The Perfect Matrimony*

Clairvoyance: A term invented by occultists, derived from the French clair "clear," and voyance "seeing."

Clairvoyance is simply the perception of non-physical imagery, such as imagination. Inferior forms include hallucinations, dreams, daydreaming, fantasy, memory, etc. Superior forms provide perception of other dimensions, free of the limitations of physical spacetime.

"There exist clairvoyance and pseudo-clairvoyance. The Gnostic student must make a clear differentiation between these two forms of extrasensory perception. Clairvoyance is based on objectivity. However, pseudo-clairvoyance is based on subjectivity. Understand that by objectivity we mean spiritual reality, the spiritual world. Understand that by subjectivity we mean the physical world, the world of illusion, that which has no reality. An intermediate region also exists, this is the Astral World, which can be objective or subjective according to the degree of spiritual development of each person." —Samael Aun Weor, *The Perfect Matrimony*

"Positive clairvoyance is achieved only with a great intellectual culture and a great esoteric discipline. The highest cultured people, who are submitted to the most rigorous intellectual disciplines, only achieve the truly positive clairvoyance. The illuminated intellect is the outcome of positive clairvoyance." —Samael Aun Weor, *Sexology: Fundamental Notions of Endocrinology and Criminology*

Consciousness: The modern English term consciousness is derived primarily from the Latin word conscius, "knowing, aware." Thus, consciousness is the basic factor of perception and understanding, and is therefore the basis of any living thing. Since living things are not equal and have a great deal of variety, so too does consciousness: it has infinite potential for development, either towards the heights of perfection or towards the depths of degeneration.

"Wherever there is life, there is consciousness. Consciousness is inherent to life as humidity is inherent to water." —Samael Aun Weor, *Sexology, the Basis of Endocrinology and Criminology*

"It is vital to understand and develop the conviction that consciousness has the potential to increase to an infinite degree." —The 14th Dalai Lama

"Light and consciousness are two phenomena of the same thing; to a lesser degree of consciousness, corresponds a lesser degree of light; to a greater degree of consciousness, a greater degree of light." —Samael Aun Weor, *The Esoteric Treatise of Hermetic Astrology*

Cup of Hermes: A Hermetic symbol of the sexual power, mentioned by Hermes Trismegistus in his twelfth book.

"Hermes Trismegistus, that thrice great god, the real incarnation of the god Osiris, gave us the marvelous science of Alchemy." —Samael Aun Weor, *The Mysteries of Life and Death*

A reference to ῥυτόν rhyton, a drinking cup or horn; the word is derived from rheo, meaning 'flow through'. These were used all over Eurasia for drinking wine, even in Tibet. They usually had a conical, phallic shape, or were crafted with a ram, goat, or bull's head (symbols of masculine fertility). Dionysus, god of wine and sexual transmutation, is often seen with a rhyton. Significantly, when filled with wine, a rhyton could not be put down or it would spill its contents. One had to hold it upright with great awareness in order to avoid "spilling the wine."

Devolution: (Latin) From devolvere: backwards evolution, degeneration. The natural mechanical inclination for all matter and energy in nature to return towards their state of inert uniformity. Related to the Arcanum Ten: Retribution, the Wheel of Samsara. Devolution is the inverse process of evolution. As evolution is the complication of matter or energy, devolution is the slow process of nature to simplify matter or energy by applying forces to it. Through devolution, protoplasmic matter and energy descend, degrade, and increase in density within the infradimensions of nature to finally reach the center of the earth where they attain their ultimate state of inert uniformity. Devolution transfers the psyche, moral values, consciousness, or psychological responsibilities to inferior degradable organisms (Klipoth) through the surrendering of our psychological values to animal behaviors, especially sexual degeneration.

Divine Mother: The Divine Mother is the eternal, feminine principle, which is formless, and further unfolds into many levels, aspects, and manifestations.

"Devi or Sakti is the Mother of Nature. She is Nature Itself. The whole world is Her body. Mountains are Her bones. Rivers are Her veins. Ocean is Her bladder. Sun, moon are Her eyes. Wind is Her breath. Agni is Her mouth. She runs this world show. Sakti is symbolically female; but It is, in reality, neither male nor female. It is only a Force which manifests Itself in various forms. The five elements and their combinations are the external manifestations of the Mother. Intelligence, discrimination, psychic power, and will are Her internal manifestations." —Swami Sivananda

"Among the Aztecs, she was known as Tonantzin, among the Greeks as chaste Diana. In Egypt she was Isis, the Divine Mother, whose veil no mortal has lifted. There is no doubt at all that esoteric Christianity has never forsaken the worship of the Divine Mother Kundalini. Obviously she is Marah, or better said, RAM-IO, MARY. What orthodox religions did not specify, at least with regard to the exoteric or public circle, is the aspect of Isis in her individual human form. Clearly, it was taught only in secret to the Initiates that this Divine Mother exists individually within each human being. It cannot be emphasized enough that Mother-God, Rhea, Cybele, Adonia, or whatever we wish to call her, is a variant of our own individual Being in the here and now. Stated explicitly, each of us has our own particular, individual Divine Mother." —Samael Aun Weor, *The Great Rebellion*

"Devi Kundalini, the Consecrated Queen of Shiva, our personal Divine Cosmic Individual Mother, assumes five transcendental mystic aspects in every creature, which we must enumerate:

1. The unmanifested Prakriti

2. The chaste Diana, Isis, Tonantzin, Maria or better said Ram-Io

3. The terrible Hecate, Persephone, Coatlicue, queen of the infemos and death; terror of love and law

4. The special individual Mother Nature, creator and architect of our physical organism

5. The Elemental Enchantress to whom we owe every vital impulse, every instinct." —Samael Aun Weor, *The Secret of the Golden Flower*

Drukpa: (Also known variously as Druk-pa, Dugpa, Brugpa, Dag dugpa or Dad dugpa) The term Drukpa comes from from Dzongkha and Tibetan ('brug yul), which means "country of Bhutan," and is composed of Druk, "dragon," and pa, "person." In Asia, the word refers to the people of Bhutan, a country between India and Tibet. Drukpa can also refer to a large sect of Buddhism which broke from the Kagyug-pa "the Ones of the Oral Tradition." They considered themselves as the heirs of the indian Gurus: their teaching, which goes back to Vajradhara, was conveyed through Dakini, from Naropa to Marpa and then to the ascetic and mystic poet

Milarepa. Later on, Milarepa's disciples founded new monasteries, and new threads appeared, among which are the Karmapa and the Drukpa. All those schools form the Kagyug-pa order, in spite of episodic internal quarrels and extreme differences in practice. The Drukpa sect is recognized by their ceremonial large red hats, but it should be known that they are not the only "Red Hat" group (the Nyingmas, founded by Padmasambhava, also use red hats). The Drukpas have established a particular worship of the Dorje (Vajra, or thunderbolt, a symbol of the phallus). Samael Aun Weor wrote repeatedly in many books that the "Drukpas" practice and teach Black Tantra, by means of the expelling of the sexual energy. If we analyze the word, it is clear that he is referring to "Black Dragons," or people who practice Black Tantra. He was not referring to all the people of Bhutan, or all members of the Buddhist Drukpa sect. Such a broad condemnation would be as ridiculous as the one made by those who condemn all Jews for the crucifixion of Jesus.

Eden: (Hebrew עֵדֶן) Eden means "bliss, pleasure, delight." In the book of Genesis written by Moses [Moshe], Eden is a symbol with many levels of meaning. Of primary importance, in the book of Genesis / Bereshit, the primeval state of humanity is depicted in the Garden of Eden. This story symbolizes that when the man and the woman are performing the sexual act, they are in that moment in the Garden of Eden, enjoying that bliss, delight, or voluptuousness, and it is in that state when the serpent (Lucifer) appears in order to tempt them.

"Eden is the Ethereal World. Eden is sex itself. The Ethereal World is the abode of the sexual forces. The Ethereal World is Eden. We were driven out of Eden through the doors of sex, thus we can return to Eden only through the doors of sex. We cannot enter into Eden through false doors; we must enter into Eden through the doors out of which we were driven. The governor of Eden is the Lord Jehovah." —Samael Aun Weor, *The Major Mysteries*

Ego: The multiplicity of contradictory psychological elements that we have inside are in their sum the "ego." Each one is also called "an ego" or an "I." Every ego is a psychological defect which produces suffering. The ego is three (related to our Three Brains or three centers of psychological processing), seven (capital sins), and legion (in their infinite variations).

"The ego is the root of ignorance and pain." —Samael Aun Weor, *The Esoteric Treatise of Hermetic Astrology*

"The Being and the ego are incompatible. The Being and the ego are like water and oil. They can never be mixed... The annihilation of the psychic aggregates (egos) can be made possible only by radically comprehending our errors through meditation and by the evident Self-reflection of the Being." —Samael Aun Weor, *The Pistis Sophia Unveiled*

Elementals: Creatures who have not yet created the soul; in other words, they have consciousness ("anima," raw, unformed soul) as given by nature, and have evolved mechanically through the lower kingdoms. Their physical bodies are minerals, plants, animals, and humanoids (intellectual animals); internally they have the appearance of people (gnomes, sprites, elves, fairies, mermaids, dwarves). However, in common usage the term elementals refers to the creatures of the three lower kingdoms: mineral, plant and animal, and out of politeness we call the intellectual animals "human," even though they have not become human yet.

"Just as visible Nature is populated by an infinite number of living creatures, so, according to Paracelsus, the invisible, spiritual counterpart of visible Nature (composed of the tenuous principles of the visible elements) is inhabited by a host of peculiar beings, to whom he has given the name elementals, and which have later been termed the Nature spirits. Paracelsus divided these people of the elements into four distinct groups, which he called gnomes, undines, sylphs, and salamanders. He taught that they were really living entities, many resembling human beings in shape, and inhabiting worlds of their own, unknown to man because his undeveloped senses were incapable of functioning beyond the limitations of the grosser elements. The civilizations of Greece, Rome, Egypt, China, and India believed implicitly in satyrs, sprites, and goblins. They peopled the sea with mermaids, the rivers and fountains with nymphs, the air with fairies, the fire with Lares and Penates, and the earth with fauns, dryads, and hamadryads. These Nature spirits were held in the highest esteem, and propitiatory offerings were made to them. Occasionally, as the result of atmospheric conditions or the peculiar sensitiveness of the devotee, they became visible." —Manly P. Hall, *The Secret Teachings of All Ages*

"Each elemental of Nature represents certain powers of the blessed goddess mother of the world. Thus, whosoever knows how to handle the powers of nature that are enclosed within each herb, within each root and each tree, is the only one who can be a true magician and doctor. Thought is a great force, yet everything is dual in creation. Thus, if we want to make perceptible any hidden intention, a physical instrument that serves as the clothing for that idea is necessary. This instrument is the plant that corresponds to our intention. Only the one who knows the secret of commanding the elementals of plants can be a magician." — Samael Aun Weor, *Esoteric Medicine and Practical Magic*

Eleusis: "The most famous of the ancient religious Mysteries were the Eleusinian, whose rites were celebrated every five years in the city of Eleusis to honor Ceres (Demeter, Rhea, or Isis) and her daughter, Persephone. The initiates of the Eleusinian School were famous throughout Greece for the beauty of their philosophic concepts and the high standards of morality which they demonstrated in their daily lives. Because of their excellence, these Mysteries spread to Rome and Britain, and later the initiations were given in both these countries. The Eleusinian Mysteries, named for the community in Attica where the sacred dramas were first presented, are generally believed to have been founded by Eumolpos about fourteen hundred years before the birth of Christ, and through the Platonic system of philosophy their principles have been preserved to modern times. The rites of Eleusis, with their Mystic interpretations of Nature's most precious secrets, overshadowed the civilizations of their time and gradually absorbed many smaller schools, incorporating into their own system whatever valuable information these lesser institutions possessed. Heckethorn sees in the Mysteries of Ceres and Bacchus a metamorphosis of the rites of Isis and Osiris, and there is every reason to believe that all so-called secret schools of the ancient world were branches from one philosophic tree which, with its root in heaven and its branches on the earth, is--like the spirit of man--an invisible but ever-present cause of the objectified vehicles that give it expression. The Mysteries were the channels through which this one philosophic light was disseminated, and their initiates, resplendent with intellectual and spiritual understanding, were the perfect fruitage of the divine tree, bearing witness before the material world of the recondite source of all Light and Truth. The rites of Eleusis were divided into what were called the Lesser and the Greater Mysteries. According to James Gardner, the Lesser Mysteries were celebrated in the spring (probably at the time of the vernal equinox) in the town of Agræ, and the Greater, in the fall (the time of the autumnal equinox) at Eleusis or Athens. It is supposed that the former were given annually and the latter every five years. The rituals of the Eleusinians were highly involved, and to understand them required a deep study of Greek mythology, which they interpreted in its esoteric light with the aid of their secret keys. The Lesser Mysteries were dedicated to Persephone. In his Eleusinian and Bacchic Mysteries, Thomas Taylor sums up their purpose as follows: "The Lesser Mysteries were designed by the ancient theologists, their founders, to signify occultly the condition of the unpurified soul invested with an earthy body, and enveloped in a material and physical nature." —Manly P. Hall, *The Secret Teachings of All Ages*

Elohim: [אלהים] An Hebrew term with a wide variety of meanings. In Christian translations of scripture, it is one of many words translated to the generic word "God," but whose actual meaning depends upon the context.

Significantly, the word Elohim is always used in acts of creation.

"Said Rabbi Abbi: "The higher or celestial world with its accompanying spheres, though invisible to mortal sight, has its reflection and analogue, namely, the lower world with its circumambient spheres, according to the saying, 'As above, so below.' The works of the Holy One in the celestial world are the type of those in the terrestrial world. The meaning of the [first three] words [of the Bible], Brashith, bara אלהים Elohim is this: brasahith, i.e., the celestial world, gave rise or origin to אלהים Elohim, the visible divine name that then first became known. Thus אלהים Elohim was associated with the creation of the world, as Brashith was connected with the creation of the celestial or invisible world, that being the type, thus the antetype, or in other words, one was the reflection and analogue of the other, and therefore it is written, 'Ath hashamayim, veath ha-aretzs' (the heavens and the earth). The heaven on high produced and gave rise to the earth below." —Zohar

1. In Kabbalah, אלהים is a name of God the relates to many levels of the Tree of Life. In the world of Atziluth, the word is related to divnities of the sephiroth Binah (Jehovah Elohim, mentioned especially in Genesis), Geburah, and Hod. In the world of Briah, it is related beings of Netzach and Hod.

2. El [אל] is "god," Eloah [אלה] is "goddess," therefore the plural Elohim refers to "gods and goddesses," and is commonly used to refer to Cosmocreators or Dhyan-Choans. Humanity was created by the Elohim, to become Elohim:

"And אלהים Elohim said, 'Let us make man in our image, after our likeness...' So אלהים Elohim created Adam in their own image, in the image of אלהים Elohim created they them; male and female created they them." —Bereshit / Genesis 1

3. Similiarly, El [אל] is "god," Eloah [אלה] is "goddess," and the plural Elohim can also mean "god-goddess," an androgynous divinity, a self-realized master (ie. a Beni-Elohim, "child of God."] Such beings can manifest the male or female aspects as needed.

"Observe that in any place of scripture where the male and female are not found united together, the Holy One is said not to dwell or be present with His blessing..." —Zohar

4. Yam [ים] is "sea" or "ocean." Therefore אלהים Elohim can be אלה-ים "the sea god" [Neptune, Poseidon] or "the sea goddess" [i.e. Venus-Aphrodite, Stella Maris, etc.]

"The word אלהים Elohim is composed of two words אל EL and הים Ha-Yam, which signify The-Sea-God or The-Water-God. The word הים Ha-Yam "the Sea" has the same letters as ימה Yamah "sea", by which the scripture teaches that all division of opinion [in the head], symbolized by the feminine term sea ימה Yamah, is right and just when its object is the glory of אלה Elah the divine [female], as then אל-הים El-Ha-Yam, "The-Sea-God" becomes united to אלה-ים Elah-Yam "the Sea Goddess... When the waters became separated, then אלהים Elohim interposed and became the point of union between them, and harmony prevailed and dissension ceased. The waters above the firmament, the male part אל EL ; those below, the female אלה Elah." —Zohar

5. Elohim אלהים means El אל, Elah אלה [god, goddess] united by Yam ים the sexual waters, at the end of the word אלהים Elohim.

6. The word אלהים Elohim also addresses the first triangle of the Tree of Life. The word אל El points at Kether. The word אלה Eleh points at חכמה Chokmah. Eleh אלה means "these," which is plural because the will of Chokmah expresses the multiplicity of אל El, the unity. And the final syllable of אלהים Elohim, is ים Yam which means "sea"; ים is also use to indicate masculine plural, ים Yom relates to Binah, the Holy Spirit, the

third sephirah of the first triangle. So, the word אלהים Elohim embraces the Holy Trinity.

7. Elohim can refer to the creative principle, symbolized in Kabbalah as the sephirah Binah, and in Christianity as the Holy Spirit, and in Hinduism as Shiva-Shakti. This is hidden in the Hebrew as:

"The word Elohim is a plural formed from the feminine singular ALH, Eloh, by adding IM to the word. But inasmuch as IM is usually the termination of the masculine plural, and is here added to a feminine noun, it gives to the word Elohim the sense of a female potency united to a masculine idea, and thereby capable of producing an offspring. Now, we hear much of the Father and the Son, but we hear nothing of the Mother in the ordinary religions of the day. But in the Qabalah we find that the Ancient of Days conforms Himself simultaneously into the Father and the Mother, and thus begets the Son. Now, this Mother is Elohim. Again, we are usually told that the Holy Spirit is masculine. But the word RVCh, Ruach, Spirit, is feminine, as appears from the following passage of the Sepher Yetzirah: "AChTh RVCh ALHIM ChIIM, Achath (feminine, not Achad, masculine) Ruach Elohim Chiim: "One is She the Spirit of the Elohim of Life. "—*The Kabbalah Unveiled* [1912], S. L. Macgregor Mathers

"Each one of us has his own Interior Elohim. The Interior Elohim is the Being of our Being. The Interior Elohim is our Father-Mother. The Interior Elohim is the ray that emanates from Aelohim." —Samael Aun Weor, *The Gnostic Bible: The Pistis Sophia Unveiled*

Eros: (Greek Ερως, Roman Cupid, Amor) An ancient Greek symbol of love related to the fundamental force of existence (love, sex). Sadly, as with most esoteric symbols, the interpretation and depiction of Eros was perverted over time.

"In the sense in which he is usually conceived, Eros is the creature of the later Greek poets; and in order to understand the ancients properly we must distinguish three Erotes: viz. the Eros of the ancient cosmogonies, the Eros of the philosophers and mysteries, who bears great resemblance to the first, and the Eros whom we meet with in the epigrammatic and erotic poets, whose witty and playful descriptions of the god, however, can scarcely be considered as a part of the ancient religious belief of the Greeks. Homer does not mention Eros, and Hesiod, the earliest author that mentions him, describes him as the cosmogonic Eros. First, says Hesiod (Theog. 120, &c.), there was Chaos, then came Ge, Tartarus, and Eros, the fairest among the gods, who rules over the minds and the council of gods and men. In this account we already perceive a combination of the most ancient with later notions. According to the former, Eros was one of the fundamental causes in the formation of the world, inasmuch as he was the uniting power of love, which brought order and harmony among the conflicting elements of which Chaos consisted. In the same metaphysical sense he is conceived by Aristotle (Metaph. i. 4); and similarly in the Orphic poetry (Orph. Hymn. 5; comp. Aristoph. Av. 695) he is described as the first of the gods, who sprang from the world's egg. In Plato's Symposium (p. 178,b) he is likewise called the oldest of the gods. It is quite in accordance with the notion of the cosmogonic Eros, that he is described as a son of Cronos and Ge, of Eileithyia, or as a god who had no parentage, and came into existence by himself. (Paus. ix. c. 27.)" —Dictionary of Greek and Roman Biography and Mythology

"I call, great Eros, the source of sweet delight, holy and pure, and charming to the sight; darting, and winged, impetuous fierce desire, with Gods and mortals playing, wandering fire : agile and twofold, keeper of the keys of heaven and earth, the air, and spreading seas; of all that earth's fertile realms contains, by which the all parent Goddess life sustains, or dismal Tartaros is doomed to keep, widely extended, or the sounding deep; for thee all nature's various realms obey, who rulest alone, with universal sway. Come, blessed power, regard these mystic fires, and far avert unlawful mad desires." —Orphic Hymn 58 to Eros (C3rd B.C. to 2nd A.D.)

Essence: From Chinese 體 ti, which literally means "substance, body" and is often translated as "essence," to indicate that which is always there throughout transformations. In gnosis, the term essence refers to our consciousness, which remains fundamentally the same, in spite of the many transformations it suffers, especially life, death, and being trapped in psychological defects. A common example given in Buddhism is a glass of water: even if filled with dirt and impurities, the water is still there; its original pure essence is latent and ultimately unchanged by the presence of filth. However, one would not want to drink it that way. Just so with the Essence (the consciousness): our Essence is trapped in impurities; to use it properly, it must be cleaned first.

"Singularly radiating is the wondrous Light;
Free is it from the bondage of matter and the senses.
Not binding by words and letters.
The Essence [體] is nakedly exposed in its pure eternity.
Never defiled is the Mind-nature;
It exists in perfection from the very beginning.
By merely casting away your delusions
The Suchness of Buddhahood is realized." —Shen Tsan

"Zen, however, is interested not in these different "fields" but only in penetrating to 體 the Essence, or the innermost core of the mind for it holds that once this core is grasped, all else will become relatively insignificant, and crystal clear... only by transcending [attachment] may one come to the innermost core of Mind—the perfectly free and thoroughly nonsubstantial illuminating-Voidness. This illuminating-Void character, empty yet dynamic, is the Essence (Chinese: 體 ti) of the mind... The Essence of mind is the Illuminating-Void Suchness." —G.C.Chang, *The Practice of Zen* (1959)

"Without question the Essence, or consciousness, which is the same thing, sleeps deeply... The Essence in itself is very beautiful. It came from above, from the stars. Lamentably, it is smothered deep within all these "I's" we carry inside. By contrast, the Essence can retrace its steps, return to the point of origin, go back to the stars, but first it must liberate itself from its evil companions, who have trapped it within the slums of perdition. Human beings have three percent free Essence, and the other ninety-seven percent is imprisoned within the "I's"." —Samael Aun Weor, *The Great Rebellion*

"A percentage of psychic Essence is liberated when a defect is disintegrated. Thus, the psychic Essence which is bottled up within our defects will be completely liberated when we disintegrate each and every one of our false values, in other words, our defects. Thus, the radical transformation of ourselves will occur when the totality of our Essence is liberated. Then, in that precise moment, the eternal values of the Being will express themselves through us. Unquestionably, this would be marvelous not only for us, but also for all of humanity." —Samael Aun Weor, *The Revolution of the Dialectic*

Evolution: "It is not possible for the true human being (the Self-realized Being) to appear through the mechanics of evolution. We know very well that evolution and its twin sister devolution are nothing else but two laws which constitute the mechanical axis of all Nature. One evolves to a certain perfectly defined point, and then the devolving process follows. Every ascent is followed by a descent and vice-versa." —Samael Aun Weor, *Treatise of Revolutionary Psychology.*

"Evolution is a process of complication of energy." —Samael Aun Weor, *The Perfect Matrimony*

Fornication: Originally, the term fornication was derived from the Indo-European word gwher, whose meanings relate to heat and burning. Fornication means to make the heat (solar fire) of the seed (sexual power) leave the body through voluntary orgasm. Any voluntary orgasm is fornication, whether between a married man and woman, or an unmarried man and woman, or through masturbation, or in any other case; this is explained by Moses: "A man from whom there is a discharge of semen, shall immerse all his flesh in water, and he shall remain unclean until evening. And any garment or any leather [object] which has semen on it, shall be immersed in water, and shall remain unclean until evening. A woman with whom a man cohabits, whereby there was [a discharge of] semen, they shall immerse in water, and they shall remain unclean until evening." —Leviticus 15:16-18

Primarily, to fornicate is to spill the sexual energy through the orgasm. Those who "deny themselves" restrain the sexual energy, and "walk in the midst of the fire" without being burned. Those who restrain the sexual energy, who renounce the orgasm, remember God in themselves, and do not defile themselves with animal passion, "for the temple of God is holy, which temple ye are."

"Whosoever is born of God doth not commit sin; for his seed remaineth in him: and he cannot sin, because he is born of God." —1 John 3:9

This is why neophytes always took a vow of sexual abstention, so that they could prepare themselves for marriage, in which they would have sexual relations but not release the sexual energy through the orgasm. This is why Paul advised:

"...they that have wives be as though they had none..." —I Corinthians 7:29

"A fornicator is an individual who has intensely accustomed his genital organs to copulate (with orgasm). Yet, if the same individual changes his custom of copulation to the custom of no copulation, then he transforms himself into a chaste person. We have as an example the astonishing case of Mary Magdalene, who was a famous prostitute. Mary Magdalene became the famous Saint Mary Magdalene, the repented prostitute. Mary Magdalene became the chaste disciple of Christ." —Samael Aun Weor, *The Revolution of Beelzebub*

Fourth Way: (or Fourth Path) There are four basic kinds of spiritual schools:

- The path of the Fakir: those who seek union with God through willpower and physicality; this includes those who practice Hatha Yoga, physical austerities (tapas), etc.

- The path of the Monk: those who seek union with God through emotion, the heart; this includes those who practice Bhakti Yoga, whose religion is prayer, or music or devotional practices.

- The path of the Yogi: those who seek union with God through the intellect, the brain; this includes those who practice Jnana Yoga, who study and memorize theories and doctrines, or through various forms of meditation.

- The path of the well-balanced human being: includes those schools and religions which unify all three paths in one, under the equilibrating influence of chastity, and guided by the Three Factors: birth, death and sacrifice.

Many people believe the Fourth Way was founded by Gurdjieff and is unique to him, whereas he was merely a student and teacher of that tradition.

"When referring to the schools of the Fourth Way, we find that Gurdjieff, Ouspensky, and Nicoll had written what they knew, but their expositions suffer from many mistakes. For example, Gurdjieff committed the error of mistaking the Kundalini with the abominable Kundabuffer organ, and Ouspensky committed the same error. We cannot desist recognizing the existence of that blind fohatic force that has people hypnotized; yet this one has nothing to do with the Kundalini, but with the Kundabuffer that is the lunar fire. The Bible refers to the forty-four fires, but only two great fires can be spoken of: Kundalini and Kundabuffer. The Kundalini is the Pentecostal fire, the lightning of Vulcan ascending through the dorsal spine, the positive fire that crystallizes in worlds and suns. Its antithesis is the Kundabuffer, the negative fire that crystallizes in those psychological aggregates, those quarrelling and screaming "I's" that we carry within and which are negative crystallizations that have people immersed into unconsciousness. Gurdjieff also committed the error of not speaking about the Lunar Bodies that everyone has. He only says that we must transform the Being and that we must build the Solar Bodies. Ouspensky speaks about the Second Birth, but his teachings are incomplete. To begin with, the Solar Bodies have to be built in the Ninth Sphere, thus reaching the Second Birth. But neither Gurdjieff nor Ouspensky give the clue. The school of the Fourth Way is very ancient; it comes from the archaic lands. It is the foundation of the great mysteries and is found alive in Gnosticism, and in the religions of the Egyptians, Lemurians, Atlanteans, Phoenicians, etc. One has to tread the path by that Fourth Way. We need to march with equilibrium in science, philosophy, art, and religion. In the staged arts of long ago, the individual would receive information in his three brains: motor, emotional, and intellectual. In the schools of today however, only the intellectual brain receives information. Neurosis and the sick states of the mind are due to this. Mental disequilibrium is avoided by balancing the three brains." —Samael Aun Weor, *Tarot and Kabbalah*

Gnosis: (Greek) Knowledge.

1. The word Gnosis refers to the knowledge we acquire through our own experience, as opposed to knowledge that we are told or believe in. Gnosis - by whatever name in history or culture - is conscious, experiential knowledge, not merely intellectual or conceptual knowledge, belief, or theory. This term is synonymous with the Hebrew "daath" and the Sanskrit "jna."

2. The tradition that embodies the core wisdom or knowledge of humanity.

"Gnosis is the flame from which all religions sprouted, because in its depth Gnosis is religion. The word "religion" comes from the Latin word "religare," which implies "to link the Soul to God"; so Gnosis is the very pure flame from where all religions sprout, because Gnosis is knowledge, Gnosis is wisdom." —Samael Aun Weor from the lecture entitled *The Esoteric Path*

"The secret science of the Sufis and of the Whirling Dervishes is within Gnosis. The secret doctrine of Buddhism and of Taoism is within Gnosis. The sacred magic of the Nordics is within Gnosis. The wisdom of Hermes, Buddha, Confucius, Mohammed and Quetzalcoatl, etc., etc., is within Gnosis. Gnosis is the doctrine of Christ." —Samael Aun Weor, *The Revolution of Beelzebub*

God: "All nations have their first god, or gods, as androgynous; it could not be in any other way, since they used to consider their distant primal ancestors, their dual-sex forefathers, as divine beings and holy gods, just as the Chinese do today. Indeed, the artificial conception of an anthropomorphic Jehovah who is exclusivist, independent of his own work, sitting up there on a throne of tyranny and despotism, throwing lightning and thunder against this miserable human ant hill, is the outcome of ignorance, mere intellectual idolatry. This erroneous conception of the truth has unfortunately taken possession of both the western philosopher and the religious person who is affiliated to any of those sects that are completely lacking the Gnostic elements. What the Gnostics of all times have rejected is not the unknown God, one and always present in Nature, or Nature in abscondito, but the God of the orthodox dogma, the horrific vengeful deity of the law of Talion ("an eye for an eye, a tooth for a tooth"). The Absolute Abstract Space, the Unknowable God, is neither a limitless void nor a conditioned fullness, but both things in unison. The Gnostic esotericist understands that revelation comes from divine beings, from manifested lives, but never from the one life not manifestable. The Unknowable Seity is the Absolute Abstract Space, the rootless root of all that has been, is, or shall be." —Samael Aun Weor, *The Secret Doctrine of Anahuac*

"The love that all mystic institutions of the world feel for the divine is noticeable: for Allah, Brahma, Tao, Zen, I.A.O., INRI, God, etc. Religious esotericism does not teach atheism of any kind, except in the sense that the Sanskrit word nastika encloses: no admission of idols, including that anthropomorphic God of the ignorant populace. It would be an absurdity to believe in a celestial dictator who is seated upon a throne of tyranny and throws lightning and thunderbolts against this sad human ant hill. Esotericism admits the existence of a Logos, or a collective Creator of the universe, a Demiurge architect. It is unquestionable that such a Demiurge is not a personal deity as many mistakenly suppose, but rather a host of Dhyan Chohans, Angels, Archangels, and other forces. God is Gods. It is written with characters of fire in the resplendent book of life that God is the Army of the Voice, the great Word, the Verb. "In the beginning was the Word, and the Word was with God, and the Word was God. All things were made by him, and without him was not any thing made that was made." (John 1:1-3) For this reason, it is evident that any authentic human being who really achieves perfection enters into the Current of Sound, into the Celestial Army constituted by the Buddhas of Compassion, Angels, Planetary Spirits, Elohim, Rishi- Prajapatis, etc. It has been said to us that the Logos sounds and this is obvious. The Demiurge, the Verb, is the multiple, perfect unity. Whosoever adores the Gods, whosoever surrenders worship unto them, is more capable of capturing the deep significance of the diverse divine facets of the Demiurge architect. When humanity began to mock the Holy Gods, then it fell mortally wounded into the gross materialism of this Iron Age." —Samael Aun Weor, *The Three Mountains*

"If when you address "God" you mean that puppet painted by some dead sects? That puppet has no existence. That puppet is created by our misleading fantasy ... It is better if we think of the manifested unity, which is the Army of the Word; you yourself are part of that Army of the Word

— better said, the superior part of your self in the Tree of Life, the Kether of the Hebrew Kabbalah, an igneous and divine particle, is therefore a fragment of the great manifested unity, which is not an individual and who has no head or feet, but is an ocean, essential with space, life, free in its movement. In turn, that manifested unity comes from the unmanifested unity. The unmanifested is endless! Can you find an end to space? For it is the same space. Where can you mark an end to space? Therefore, if we think this way, we will understand better. Because if you talk to me about a God in the sky, a gentleman with a long beard that reaches his navel, seated on a throne of tyranny, throwing thunderbolts against all of this wretched human anthill — well, frankly, I do not accept it. Indeed, in relation to that puppet, you could ask, "Who made this puppet?" Well, of course, when one comes to know a tyrant puppet like that, one has to grab it from his beard, right? But that puppet does not exist. That is a misleading fantasy. We must begin to understand that in the depths, there in the most profound depths of our being, we are just particles of the great ocean of universal life, and that is all. So, this is how we must understand God, in that manner and not in an anthropomorphic way. Anthropomorphism has caused a lot of damage. Many Russians, those Russian astronauts precisely, when they got to space in their famous rockets, the famous Russian rockets, they said: "Where is God, we have not found him anywhere here." Why? Because humanity was taught idolatry. Humans were taught that God is a gentleman up there in the sky, seated on the throne of tyranny. So, that is misleading, that is false..."
—Samael Aun Weor, *Alchemical Symbolism of the Nativity of Christ*

"Certainly, Elohim is translated as "God" in the various authorized and revised versions of the Bible. Not only from the esoteric point of view, but also linguistically, it is an incontrovertible fact that the term Elohim is a feminine noun with a plural masculine ending. The correct translation of the noun Elohim in its strict sense is "goddesses and gods." —Samael Aun Weor, *The Secret Doctrine of Anahuac*

Hermes Trismegistus: (Greek: Ἑρμῆς ὁ Τρισμέγιστος, "thrice-great Hermes"; Latin: Mercurius ter Maximus).

"Hermes Trismegistus (who was the author of the divine Pymander and some other books) lived some time before Moses. He received the name of Trismegistus, or Mercurius ter Maximus, i. e. thrice greatest Intelligencer, because he was the first intelligencer who communicated celestial and divine knowledge to mankind by writing.

"He was reported to have been king of Egypt; without doubt he was an Egyptian; nay, if you believe the Jews, even their Moses; and for the justification of this they urge, 1st, His being well skilled in chemistry; nay, the first who communicated that art to the sons of men; 2dly, They urge the philosophic work, viz. of rendering gold medicinal, or, finally, of the art of making aurum potabile; and, thirdly, of teaching the Cabala, which they say was shewn him by God on Mount Sinai: for all this is confessed to be originally written in Hebrew, which he would not have done had he not been an Hebrew, but rather in his vernacular tongue. But whether he was Moses or not, it is certain he was an Egyptian, even as Moses himself also was; and therefore for the age he lived in, we shall not fall short of the time if we conclude he flourished much about the time of Moses; and if he really was not the identical Moses, affirmed to be so by many, it is more than probable that he was king of Egypt; for being chief philosopher, he was, according to the Egyptian custom, initiated into the mysteries of priesthood, and from thence to the chief governor or king. He was called Ter Maximus, as having a perfect knowledge of all things contained in the world (as his Aureus, or Golden Tractate, and his Divine Pymander shews) which things he divided into three kingdoms, viz. animal, vegetable, and mineral; in the knowledge and comprehension of which three he excelled and transmitted to posterity, in enigmas and symbols, the profound secrets of nature; likewise a true description of the Philosopher's Quintessence, or Universal Elixir, which he made as the receptacle of all celestial and terrestrial virtues. The Great Secret of the philosophers he discoursed on, which was found engraven upon a Smaragdine table, in the valley of Ebron." - Quoted from The Magus by Francis Barrett (London, 1801)

Human: Although the words human or human being are used generally to refer to the people of this planet, the real meaning of the word human is far more demanding. Human is derived from Latin humanus "of man, human," also "humane, philanthropic, kind, gentle, polite; learned, refined, civilized." In classical philosophy, we are not yet human beings, but have the potential to become so. A famous illustration of this is the story of Diogenes wandering around crowded Athens during this day with an illuminated lantern, searching for "anthropos" (a real human being), yet failing to find even one.

In general, there are three types of human beings:

1. The ordinary person (called human being out of respect), more accurately called the "intellectual animal."

2. The true human being or man (from Sanskrit manas, mind; this does not indicate gender): someone who has created the soul (the solar bodies), symbolized as the chariot of Ezekiel or Krishna, the Wedding Garment of Jesus, the sacred weapons of the heroes of mythology, etc. Such persons are saints, masters, or buddhas of various levels.

3. The superhuman: a true human being who has also incarnated the Cosmic Christ, thus going beyond mere sainthood or buddhahood, and into the highest reaches of liberation. These are the founders of religions, the destroyers of dogmas and traditions, the great rebels of spiritual light.

According to Gnostic anthropology, a true human being is an individual who has conquered the animal nature within and has thus created the soul, the Mercabah of the Kabbalists, the Sahu of the Egyptians, the To Soma Heliakon of the Greeks: this is "the Body of Gold of the Solar

Man." A true human being is one with the Monad, the Inner Spirit. It can be said that the true human being or man is the inner Spirit (in Kabbalah, Chesed. In Hinduism, Atman).

"Every spirit is called man, which means that only the aspect of the light of the spirit that is enclothed within the body is called man. So the body of the spirit of the holy side is only a covering; in other words, the spirit is the actual essence of man and the body is only its covering. But on the other side, the opposite applies. This is why it is written: "you have clothed me with skin and flesh..." (Iyov 10:11). The flesh of man is only a garment covering the essence of man, which is the spirit. Everywhere it is written the flesh of man, it hints that the essence of man is inside. The flesh is only a vestment for man, a body for him, but the essence of man is the aspect of his spirit." —Zohar 1A:10:120

A true human being has reconquered the innocence and perfection of Eden, and has become what Adam was intended to be: a king or queen of nature, having power over nature. The intellectual animal, however, is controlled by nature, and thus is not a true human being. Examples of true human beings are all those great saints of all ages and cultures: Jesus, Moses, Mohammed, Krishna, and many others whose names were never known by the public.

Hydrogen: (From *hydro-* water, *gen-* generate, genes, genesis, etc.) The hydrogen is the simplest element on the periodic table and in Gnosticism it is recognized as the element that is the building block of all forms of matter. Hydrogen is a packet of solar light. The solar light (the light that comes from the sun) is the reflection of the Okidanok, the Cosmic Christ, which creates and sustains every world. This element is the fecundated water, generated water (hydro). The water is the source of all life. Everything that we eat, breathe and all of the impressions that we receive are in the form of various structures of hydrogen. Samael Aun Weor often will place a note (Do, Re, Mi...) and a number related with the vibration and atomic weight (level of complexity) with a particular hydrogen. For example, Samael Aun Weor constantly refers to the Hydrogen Si-12. "Si" is the highest note in the octave and it is the result of the notes that come before it. This particular hydrogen is always related to the forces of Yesod, which is the synthesis and coagulation of all food, air and impressions that we have previously received. Food begins at Do-768, air begins at Do-384, and impressions begin at Do-48.

Initiation: Initiation comes from the Latin words initiare "originate, initiate," from initium "a beginning." Initiations are moments that mark the beginning of a new stage of development, thus in the development of the consciousness there are initiations it must pass through in order to rise.

Throughout our history, the real initiations have not been taught publicly. In this new era, for the first time, we can learn about the initiations the consciousness must pass through.

Initiations are stages of spiritual development. Initiation is internal, spiritual, and not physical. The process whereby the Innermost (the Inner Father) receives recognition, empowerment and greater responsibilities in the Internal Worlds, and little by little approaches His goal: complete Self-realization, or in other words, the return into the Absolute. Initiation NEVER applies to the "I" or our terrestrial personality.

"There are nine Initiations of Minor Mysteries and seven great Initiations of Major Mysteries. The INNERMOST is the one who receives all of these Initiations. The Testament of Wisdom says: "Before the dawning of the false aurora upon the earth, the ones who survived the hurricane and the tempest were praising the INNERMOST, and the heralds of the aurora appeared unto them." The psychological "I" does not receives Initiations. The human personality does not receive anything. Nonetheless, the "I" of some Initiates becomes filled with pride when saying 'I am a Master, I have such Initiations.' Thus, this is how the "I" believes itself to be an Initiate and keeps reincarnating in order to "perfect itself", but, the "I" never ever perfects itself. The "I" only reincarnates in order to satisfy desires. That is all." —Samael Aun Weor, *The Aquarian Message*

Initiations of Major Mysteries: The qualifications of the consciousness as it ascends into greater degrees of wisdom. The first five Initiations of Major Mysteries correspond to the creation of the real Human Being. Learn more by studying these books by Samael Aun Weor: *The Perfect Matrimony, The Three Mountains,* and *The Revolution of Beelzebub.*

"High initiation is the fusion of two principles: Atman-Buddhi, through the five principal Initiations of Major Mysteries. With the first we achieve the fusion of Atman-Buddhi, and with the fifth, we add the Manas to this fusion, and so the septenary is reduced to a trinity: "Atman-Buddhi Manas." There are a total of Nine Initiations of Major Mysteries." —Samael Aun Weor, *The Zodiacal Course*

"We fulfill our human evolution with the five Initiations of Major Mysteries. The remaining three Initiations and the degree of "Lord of the World" are of a "Super-Human" nature." —Samael Aun Weor, *Esoteric Medicine and Practical Magic*

Initiations of Minor Mysteries: The probationary steps required of all who wish to enter into the path of Self-realization. These nine tests are given to all disciples who begin to perform the Gnostic work in themselves. Only those who complete these tests can receive the right to enter into the Major Mysteries. For more information, read *The Perfect Matrimony.*

"Remember that each one of the nine Initiations of Lesser Mysteries has a musical note and an instrument which produces it." —Samael Aun Weor, *The Revolution of Beelzebub*

"To want to rapidly become fused with the Innermost without having passed through the nine initiations of Lesser Mysteries is akin to wanting to receive a doctor's degree in medicine without having studied all the required years at university, or like wanting to be a general without having passed through all the military ranks." —Samael Aun Weor, *The Zodiacal Course*

"Throughout the Initiations of Lesser Mysteries, the disciple has to pass through the entire tragedy of Golgotha..." —Samael Aun Weor, *The Zodiacal Course*

Innermost: "Our real Being is of a universal nature. Our real Being is neither a kind of superior nor inferior "I." Our real Being is impersonal, universal, divine. He transcends every concept of "I," me, myself, ego, etc., etc." —Samael Aun Weor, *The Perfect Matrimony*

Also known as Atman, the Spirit, Chesed, our own individual interior divine Father.

"The Innermost is the ardent flame of Horeb. In accordance with Moses, the Innermost is the Ruach Elohim (the Spirit of God) who sowed the waters in the beginning of the world. He is the Sun King, our Divine Monad, the Alter-Ego of Cicerone." —Samael Aun Weor, *The Revolution of Beelzebub*

Intellectual Animal: The current state of humanity: animals with intellect.

When the Intelligent Principle, the Monad, sends its spark of consciousness into Nature, that spark, the anima, enters into manifestation as a simple mineral. Gradually, over millions of years, the anima gathers experience and evolves up the chain of life until it perfects itself in the level of the mineral kingdom. It then graduates into the plant kingdom, and subsequently into the animal kingdom. With each ascension the spark receives new capacities and higher grades of complexity. In the animal kingdom it learns procreation by ejaculation. When that animal intelligence enters into the human kingdom, it receives a new capacity: reasoning, the intellect; it is now an anima with intellect: an Intellectual Animal. That spark must then perfect itself in the human kingdom in order to become a complete and perfect human being, an entity that has conquered and transcended everything that belongs to the lower kingdoms. Unfortunately, very few intellectual animals perfect themselves; most remain enslaved by their animal nature, and thus are reabsorbed by Nature, a process belonging to the devolving side of life and called by all the great religions "Hell" or the Second Death.

"The present manlike being is not yet human; he is merely an intellectual animal. It is a very grave error to call the legion of the "I" the "soul." In fact, what the manlike being has is the psychic material, the material for the soul within his Essence, but indeed, he does not have a Soul yet." — Samael Aun Weor, *The Revolution of the Dialectic*

Internal Worlds: The many dimensions beyond the physical world. These dimensions are both subjective and objective. To know the objective internal worlds (the astral plane, or Nirvana, or the Klipoth) one must first know one's own personal, subjective internal worlds, because the two are intimately associated.

"Whosoever truly wants to know the internal worlds of the planet Earth or of the solar system or of the galaxy in which we live, must previously know his intimate world, his individual, internal life, his own internal worlds. Man, know thyself, and thou wilt know the universe and its gods. The more we explore this internal world called "myself," the more we will comprehend that we simultaneously live in two worlds, in two realities, in two confines: the external and the internal. In the same way that it is indispensable for one to learn how to walk in the external world so as not to fall down into a precipice, or not get lost in the streets of the city, or to select one's friends, or not associate with the perverse ones, or not eat poison, etc.; likewise, through the psychological work upon oneself we learn how to walk in the internal world, which is explorable only through Self-observation." —Samael Aun Weor, *Treatise of Revolutionary Psychology*

Through the work in Self-observation, we develop the capacity to awaken where previously we were asleep: including in the objective internal worlds.

Karma: (Sanskrit, literally "deed"; derived from kri, "to do...") The law of cause and effect.

"Be not deceived; God is not mocked: for whatsoever a man soweth, that shall he also reap." —Galatians 6:7

Kundalini: "Kundalini, the serpent power or mystic fire, is the primordial energy or Sakti that lies dormant or sleeping in the Muladhara Chakra, the centre of the body. It is called the serpentine or annular power on account of serpentine form. It is an electric fiery occult power, the great pristine force which underlies all organic and inorganic matter. Kundalini is the cosmic power in individual bodies. It is not a material force like electricity, magnetism, centripetal or centrifugal force. It is a spiritual potential Sakti or cosmic power. In reality it has no form. [...] O Divine Mother Kundalini, the Divine Cosmic Energy that is hidden in men! Thou art Kali, Durga, Adisakti, Rajarajeswari, Tripurasundari, Maha-Lakshmi, Maha-Sarasvati! Thou hast put on all these names and forms. Thou hast manifested as Prana, electricity, force, magnetism, cohesion, gravitation in this universe. This whole universe rests in Thy bosom. Crores of salutations unto thee. O Mother of this world! Lead me on to open the Sushumna Nadi and take Thee along the Chakras to Sahasrara Chakra and to merge myself in Thee and Thy consort, Lord Siva. Kundalini Yoga is that Yoga which treats of Kundalini Sakti, the six centres of spiritual energy (Shat Chakras), the arousing of the sleeping Kundalini Sakti and its union with Lord Siva in Sahasrara Chakra, at the crown of the head. This is an exact science. This is also known as Laya Yoga. The six centres are pierced (Chakra Bheda) by the passing of Kundalini Sakti to the top of the head. 'Kundala' means 'coiled'. Her form is like a coiled serpent. Hence the name Kundalini." —Swami Sivananda, *Kundalini Yoga*

"Kundalini is a compound word: Kunda reminds us of the abominable "Kundabuffer organ," and lini is an Atlantean term meaning termination. Kundalini means "the termination of the abominable Kundabuffer organ." In this case, it is imperative not to confuse Kundalini with Kund-abuffer." —Samael Aun Weor, *The Great Rebellion*

These two forces, one positive and ascending, and one negative and de-scending, are symbolized in the Bible in the book of Numbers (the story of the serpent of brass). The Kundalini is "The power of life."- from the Theosophical Glossary. The sexual fire that is at the base of all life.

"The ascent of the Kundalini along the spinal cord is achieved very slowly in accordance with the merits of the heart. The fires of the heart control the miraculous development of the sacred serpent. Devi Kundalini is not something mechanical as many suppose; the igneous serpent is only awakened with genuine Love between husband and wife, and it will never rise up along the medullar canal of adulterers." —Samael Aun Weor, *The Secret of the Golden Flower*

"The decisive factor in the progress, development and evolution of the Kundalini is ethics." —Samael Aun Weor, *The Revolution of Beelzebub*

"Until not too long ago, the majority of spiritualists believed that on awakening the Kundalini, the latter instantaneously rose to the head and the initiate was automatically united with his Innermost or Internal God, instantly, and converted into Mahatma. How comfortable! How comfort-ably all these theosophists, Rosicrucians and spiritualists, etc., imagined High Initiation." —Samael Aun Weor, *The Zodiacal Course*

"There are seven bodies of the Being. Each body has its "cerebrospinal" nervous system, its medulla and Kundalini. Each body is a complete organism. There are, therefore, seven bodies, seven medullae and seven Kundalinis. The ascension of each of the seven Kundalinis is slow and difficult. Each canyon or vertebra represents determined occult powers and this is why the conquest of each canyon undergoes terrible tests." — Samael Aun Weor, *The Zodiacal Course*

Left-hand: In traditional cultures (especially Asian), the right hand is uti-lized for positive, clean, upright actions, such as eating, making offerings, etc., while the left hand is used for hidden, unclean, or harmful actions. This tradition emerged from the ancient esoteric knowledge, unknown to the public, in which the followers of the light (divinity, purity) cor-respond to the "right-hand of God" while the adherents of impurity and desire fall to the left, into disgrace. These contrary paths are rooted in Sanskrit terms. Dakshinachara (Sanskrit) literally means "upright in con-duct" but is interpreted as "Right-Hand Path." Vamacara literally means "black magic," or "behaving badly or in the wrong way," and is used to refer to "Left-Hand Path" or "Left-path" (Sanskrit: Vamamarga). These two paths are explained in Kabbalah as well.

In modern times, those who follow the left-hand path have worked hard to make their path seem respectable and equal to the right, by claiming the two need each other to exist. This argument is based on the lie that left-hand initiates pursue the darkness of the Uncreated Light, the Abso-lute (which is pure, divine), yet the reality is that their degeneration and harmful acts propel them into the darkness of the abyss, the hell realms, to be cleansed of their impurity. Followers of the left-hand path believe they can outwit Divinity.

"And he shall separate them one from another, as a shepherd divideth his sheep from the goats. And he shall set the sheep on his right, but the goats on his left." —Matthew 25: 32-33

"Then the people of the right hand —Oh! how happy shall be the people of the right hand! And the people of the left hand —Oh! how wretched shall be the people of the left hand!" —Qur'an, Surah Al-Waqiah (The Inevitable) [56:8-9]

The widespread of the use of these terms in the West originated with H. P. Blavatsky.

It is important to note that physical handedness has nothing to do with one's spiritual level, value, or destiny. The persecution of left-handedness is just an ignorant form of discrimination.

"In symbolism the body is divided vertically into halves, the right half being considered as light and the left half as darkness. By those unacquainted with the true meanings of light and darkness the light half was denominated spiritual and the left half material. Light is the symbol of objectivity; darkness of subjectivity. Light is a manifestation of life and is therefore posterior to life. That which is anterior to light is darkness, in which light exists temporarily but darkness permanently. As life precedes light, its only symbol is darkness, and darkness is considered as the veil which must eternally conceal the true nature of abstract and undifferentiated Being.

"In ancient times men fought with their right arms and defended the vital centers with their left arms, on which was carried the protecting shield. The right half of the body was regarded therefore as offensive and the left half defensive. For this reason also the right side of the body was considered masculine and the left side feminine. Several authorities are of the opinion that the present prevalent right-handedness of the race is the outgrowth of the custom of holding the left hand in restraint for defensive purposes. Furthermore, as the source of Being is in the primal darkness which preceded light, so the spiritual nature of man is in the dark part of his being, for the heart is on the left side.

"Among the curious misconceptions arising from the false practice of associating darkness with evil is one by which several early nations used the right hand for all constructive labors and the left hand for only those purposes termed unclean and unfit for the sight of the gods. For the same reason black magic was often referred to as the left-hand path, and heaven was said to be upon the right and hell upon the left. Some philosophers further declared that there were two methods of writing: one from left to right, which was considered the exoteric method; the other from right to left, which was considered esoteric. The exoteric writing was that which was done out or away from the heart, while the esoteric writing was that which--like the ancient Hebrew--was written toward the heart." —Manly P. Hall, *The Secret Teachings of All Ages*

Lemuria: The people of Lemuria were the third root race of this terrestrial round. They inhabited the huge continent Mu in the Pacific Ocean. In the early stages of their time, they were hermaphrodites, yet gradually passed through the division of sexes, thus being the source of the stories in many myths and scriptures.

The Lemurians existed before the Atlanteans, but have been confused with them by some groups. About this, H.P. Blavatsky said, "In our own day we witness the stupendous fact that such comparatively recent personages as Shakespeare and William Tell are all but denied, an attempt being made to show one to be a nom de plume, and the other a person who never existed. What wonder then, that the two powerful races -- the Lemurians and the Atlanteans -- have been merged into and identified, in time, with a few half mythical peoples, who all bore the same patronymic?" (The Secret Doctrine, 1888)

"It is clear that the Miocene Epoch had its proper scenario on the ancient Lemurian land, the continent that was formerly located in the Pacific Ocean. Remnants of Lemuria are still located in Oceania, in the great Australia, and on Easter Island (where some carved monoliths were found), etc." —Samael Aun Weor, *Gnostic Anthropology*

"The third root race was the Lemurian race, which inhabited Mu, which today is the Pacific Ocean. They perished by fire raining from the sun (volcanoes and earthquakes). This Root Race was governed by the Aztec God Tlaloc. Their reproduction was by means of gemmation. Lemuria was a very extensive continent. The Lemurians who degenerated had, afterwards, faces similar to birds; this is why some savages, when remembering tradition, adorned their heads with feathers." —Samael Aun Weor, *The Kabbalah of the Mayan Mysteries*

Logos: (Greek, plural Logoi) means Verb or Word. In Greek and Hebrew metaphysics, the unifying principle of the world. The Logos is the manifested deity of every nation and people; the outward expression or the effect of the cause which is ever concealed. (Speech is the "logos" of thought). The Logos has three aspects, known universally as the Trinity or Trimurti.

4. The First Logos. Represents the active / projective principle, such as: Aztec: Tepeu K'Ocumatz; Buddhist: Dharmakaya; Christian: The Father; Egyptian: Osiris-Ra; Gnostic: The 10th Aeon; Hindu: Brahma; Mayan: Huracan Kakulha; Nordic: Odin

5. The Second Logos represents the passive / receptive principle, such as: Aztec: Ehekatl Quetzalcoatl; Buddhist: Sambogokaya; Christian: The Son; Egyptian: Horus; Gnostic: The 9th Aeon; Hindu: Vishnu; Mayan: Chipí Kakulha; Nordic: Balder

6. The Third Logos represents the creative principle, such as: Aztec: Tlaloc Quetzalcoatl; Buddhist: Nirmanakaya; Chris-

tian: The Holy Spirit; Egyptian: Osiris-Isis; Gnostic: The 8th
Aeon; Hindu: Shiva; Mayan: Raxa Kakulha; Nordic: Thor

One who incarnates the Logos becomes a Logos.

"The Logos is not an individual. The Logos is an army of ineffable beings." —Samael Aun Weor, *Sexology, the Basis of Endocrinology and Criminology*

Lucifer: (Latin: lux, lucis, luce, luci, and lucu: "light"; fer, fero: "to bear,
carry, support, lift, hold, take up"; these synthesize as "Bearer of Light")
Before Milton (17th c), Lucifer had never been a name of the devil. One of
the early Popes of Rome bore that name, and there was even a Christian
sect in the fourth century which was called the Luciferians. Lucifer, the
"carrier of the light," is Prometheus, the divinity who brings the life-giv-
ing fire to humanity, yet is punished for this act, and is only freed when
that fire incarnates as Herakles ("the aura of Hera"), the hero (bodhisattva; i.e. Jesus, Krishna, Moses, etc) who liberates the Christic fire from its
bondage in the stone (the mountain / Mercury).

"We need to whitewash the devil with maximum expedited urgency. This
is only possible through fighting against our own selves, by dissolving all
those conjunctions of psychological aggregates that constitute the "I,"
the "myself," the "itself." Only by dying in ourselves can we whitewash
the brass and contemplate the Sun of the Middle Night (the Father).
This signifies that we must defeat all temptations and eliminate all of the
inhuman elements that we carry within (anger, greed, lust, envy, pride,
laziness, gluttony, etc, etc, etc.). A trainer in the psychological gymnasium
of human existence is always required. The divine Daimon, quoted many
times by Socrates, is the very shadow of our own individual Spirit. He is
the most extraordinary psychological trainer that each one of us carries
within. He delivers us into temptation with the purpose of training us,
teaching us. Only in this way is it possible for the precious gems of virtue
to sprout from our psyche. Now I question myself and I question you.
Where is the evil of Lucifer? The results speak for themselves. If there are
no temptations there are no virtues. Virtues are more grandiose when
temptations are stronger. What is important is not to fall into temptation. That is why we have to pray to our Father, saying, "Lead us not into
temptation." —Samael Aun Weor, *Tarot and Kabbalah*

Lumisial: "A place of light." A Gnostic Lumisial is a generator of spiritual
energy, a Gnostic school which maintains the ancient initiatic Three
Chamber structure. The source of power is the Cosmic Christ, and the
means to receive and transform it are within the Second and Third
Chambers.

"We are therefore working, my dear brethren, to initiate the Era of Aquarius. We are working in order to save what is possible, meaning, those who
allow themselves to be saved. This is why it is necessary that we shape our
Gnostic Movements and that we organize them each time better; that
we establish the Three Chambers. Our Gnostic Movements must have

exactly Three Chambers. Each Lumisial must have Three Chambers for the instruction of our students. Our Gnostic Centers receive a name in a very pure language that flows like a river of gold that runs in the sunny, thick jungle; that name is LUMISIALS." - Samael Aun Weor, *The Final Catastrophe and the Extraterrestrials*

Magic: The word magic is derived from the ancient word "mag" that means priest. Real magic is the work of a priest. A real magician is a priest.

"Magic, according to Novalis, is the art of influencing the inner world consciously." —Samael Aun Weor, *The Secret of the Golden Flower*

"When magic is explained as it really is, it seems to make no sense to fanatical people. They prefer to follow their world of illusions." —Samael Aun Weor, *The Revolution of Beelzebub*

Maithuna: The Sanskrit word मिथुन maithuna is used in Hindu Tantras (esoteric scriptures) to refer to the sacrament (sacred ritual) of sexual union between husband and wife. Maithuna or Mithuna has various appearances in scripture:

- Mithuna: paired, forming a pair; copulation; the zodiacal sign of Gemini in Vedic Astrology, which is depicted as a man and woman in a sexual embrace
- Mithunaya: to unite sexually
- Mithuni: to become paired, couple or united sexually

By means of the original Tantric Maithuna, after being prepared psychologically and spiritually and initiated by a genuine teacher (guru), the couple learns how to utilize their love and spiritual aspiration in order to transform their natural sexual forces to purify the mind, eliminate psychological defects, and awaken the latent powers of the consciousness. The man represents Shiva, the masculine aspect of the creative divine, and the woman represents Shakti, the feminine aspect and the source of the power of creation.

This method was kept in strictest secrecy for thousands of years in order to preserve it in its pure form, and to prevent crude-minded people from deviating the teaching, other people, or harming themselves. Nonetheless, some degenerated traditions (popularly called "left-hand" traditions, or black magic) interpret Maithuna or sacramental sexuality according to their state of degeneration, and use these sacred teachings to justify their lust, desire, orgies, and other types of deviations from pure, genuine Tantra.

Krishna: "And I am the strength of the strong, devoid of lust and attachment. O best of the Bharatas, I am sex not contrary to dharma." —Bhagavad Gita 7.11

"The Tantric student must be endowed with purity, faith, devotion, dedication to Guru, dispassion, humility, courage, cosmic love, truthfulness, non-covetousness, and contentment. Absence of these qualities in the practitioner means a gross abuse of Shaktism. Sexual intercourse

by a man with a woman who is not lawful to him is a sin. The Vaidika Dharma is very strict on this point. It forbids not merely actual Maithuna but Ashtanga or eightfold Maithuna namely Smaranam (thinking upon it), Kirtanam (talking of it), Keli (play with women), Prekshanam (making eyes at women), Guhya-bhashanam (talking in private with women), Sankalpa (wish or resolve for sexual union), Adhyavasaya (determination towards it), Kriyanishpatti (actual accomplishment of the sexual act). A Tantric can have copulation with his wife. He calls his wife his Shakti. Wife is a house-goddess Griha-lakshmi or Griha-devata united to her husband by the sacramental Samskara of marriage. She should not be regarded as an object of enjoyment. She is his partner in life (Ardhangini). The union of a man and his wife is a veritable sacred scriptural rite."
—Swami Sivananda, *Tantra Yoga*

Master: In spirituality, the word master means "a worker or artisan qualified to teach apprentices." That is, they are a teacher, a helper, not a tyrant or authority to be worshipped.

"And, behold, one came and said unto [Jesus], Good master, what good thing shall I do, that I may have eternal life? And he said unto him, Why callest thou me good? there is none good but one, that is, God." —Matthew 19

"But be not ye called Rabbi [master]: for one is your Master, even Christ; and all ye are brethren. And call no man your father upon the earth: for one is your Father, which is in heaven. Neither be ye called masters: for one is your Master, even Christ." —Jesus, in Matthew 23

Although many people claim to be "masters," the truth is that the terrestrial person is only a terrestrial person. The only one who can be a master is the Innermost, Atman, the Father, Chesed.

"It beseemeth not a man, that God should give him the Scriptures and the Wisdom, and the gift of prophecy, and that then he should say to his followers, 'Be ye worshippers of me as well as of God;' but rather, 'Be ye perfect in things pertaining to God, since ye know the Scriptures, and have studied deep.' God doth not command you to take the angels or the prophets as lords." —Koran 3:9

"The value of the human person which is the intellectual animal called human being is less than the ash of a cigarette. However, the fools feel themselves to be giants. Unfortunately, within all the pseudo-esoteric currents a great amount of mythomaniac people exist, individuals who feel themselves to be masters, people who enjoy when others call them masters, individuals who believe themselves to be Gods, individuals who presume to be saints. The only one who is truly great is the Spirit, the Innermost. We, the intellectual animals, are leaves that the wind tosses about... No student of occultism is a master. True masters are only those who have reached the Fifth Initiation of Major Mysteries [Tiphereth, the causal body]. Before the Fifth Initiation nobody is a master." —Samael Aun Weor, *The Perfect Matrimony*

"You [if you have reached levels of initiation] are not the master, you are only the sinning shadow of He who has never sinned. Remember that only your internal Lamb is the master. Remember that even though your internal God is a Hierarch of fire, you, poor slug, are only a human being and as a human being you will always be judged. Your internal Lamb could be a planetary God, but you, poor slug of the mud, do not forget, always remember that you are only the shadow of your God. Poor sinning shadow..! Do not say "I am this God" or "I am that master," because you are only a shadow that must resolve to die and be slaughtered in order not to serve as an obstacle for your internal God. It is necessary for you to reach supreme humbleness." —Samael Aun Weor, *The Aquarian Message*

"Do not accept external masters in the physical plane. Learn how to travel in the astral body, and when you are skillful in the astral, choose an authentic master of Major Mysteries of the White Brotherhood and consecrate unto him the most absolute devotion and the most profound respect." —Samael Aun Weor, *The Zodiacal Course*

Meditation: "When the esotericist submerges himself into meditation, what he seeks is information." —Samael Aun Weor

"It is urgent to know how to meditate in order to comprehend any psychic aggregate, or in other words, any psychological defect. It is indispensable to know how to work with all our heart and with all our soul, if we want the elimination to occur." —Samael Aun Weor, *The Gnostic Bible: The Pistis Sophia Unveiled*

"1. The Gnostic must first attain the ability to stop the course of his thoughts, the capacity to not think. Indeed, only the one who achieves that capacity will hear the Voice of the Silence.

"2. When the Gnostic disciple attains the capacity to not think, then he must learn to concentrate his thoughts on only one thing.

"3. The third step is correct meditation. This brings the first flashes of the new consciousness into the mind.

"4. The fourth step is contemplation, ecstasy or Samadhi. This is the state of Turiya (perfect clairvoyance)." —Samael Aun Weor, *The Perfect Matrimony*

Nirvana: (Sanskrit, "extinction" or "cessation"; Tibetan: nyangde, literally "the state beyond sorrow") In general use, refers to the permanent cessation of suffering and its causes, and therefore refers to a state of consciousness rather than a place. Yet, the term can also apply to heavenly realms, whose vibration is directed related to the cessation of suffering. In other words, if your mind-stream has liberated itself from the causes of suffering, it will naturally vibrate at the level of Nirvana (heaven).

"When the Soul fuses with the Inner Master, then it becomes free from Nature and enters into the supreme happiness of absolute existence. This state of happiness is called Nirvana. Nirvana can be attained through millions of births and deaths, but it can also be attained by means of a shorter path; this is the path of "initiation." The Initiate can reach Nirvana in one single life if he so wants it." —Samael Aun Weor, *The Zodiacal Course*

Orgasm: In sexuality, the word orgasm refers to a climactic peak of sexual, electrical forces, in which the nervous system is over-charged with sexual energy, resulting in a "short circuit" or massive, damaging release of energy. Orgasm is primarily energetic, and is not always accompanied by the expulsion of sexual fluids.

In scriptures, the orgasm is called fornication. The word fornication comes from a root that means "to burn." Read What is Fornication?

The orgasm is the "forbidden fruit" of the tree of knowledge (daath) from the Garden of Eden (Eden is Hebrew for "pleasure, bliss").

Every religion in the world originally taught chastity, brahmacharya, the importance of preserving the sexual energy so it can be utilized for regeneration and spiritual birth, thus every religion required the renunciation of the orgasm. In this way, the energy that provided the minor pleasure of the orgasm is harnessed and transformed, thereafter producing the ecstasies of the soul (consciousness), called samadhi, satori, manteia, etc.

"Speak unto the children of Israel, and say unto them, When any man hath an ejaculation of semen [orgasm] out of his flesh, because of his ejaculation he is filthy... And if a woman have a discharge [of energy; orgasm]... she shall be in her impurity seven days: and whosoever toucheth her shall be unclean until the even... Thus shall ye separate the children of Israel from their uncleanness, that they die not in their uncleanness, when they defile my tabernacle [sexual organs] that is in the midst of them [their body]." —Leviticus 15

"Ejaculation of semen brings death, preserving it within brings life. Therefore, one should make sure to retain the semen within." —Siva Samhita

"Whosoever is born of God doth not commit sin; for his σπέρμα sperma [seed] remaineth in him: and he cannot sin, because he is born of God." —1 John 3:9

"To be aroused but not ejaculate is what is called "returning the Ching." When the Ching is returned to benefit the body, then the tao of life has been realized." —Su Nu Ching (300 BC)

The path of chastity requires retaining the sexual energy by avoiding the orgasm. The physical matter (semen) is the vehicle for that energy; by restraining the matter we restrain the energy so that the energy can be transmuted into a more elevated, powerful force. But do not mistake the physical matter for what it carries. Many people seek ways to continue indulging in the energetic sensations of the orgasm while retaining the physical matter: this is a deception, and results in the strengthening of desire rather than the elimination of desire. To acheive chastity, one needs to be focused on ensuring that the sexual energy is transmuted, and not lost through the sensations of the orgasm, which may or may not be accompanied by physical matter.

Resurrected Master: A master who has completed the Second Mountain (thereby eliminating the entirety of their defects), has died physically, and has resurrected in a new physical body. The story of Jesus of Nazareth provides a clear example. After resurrection the master enters the Third Mountain, the Mountain of Ascension. This type of master has no ego (pride, lust, anger, etc), but still needs to work a lot in order to gain the right to enter into the Absolute.

"Every resurrected master has solar bodies, but does not have lunar bodies. The resurrected masters have powers over fire, air, water and the earth. Resurrected masters can transmute physical lead into physical gold. The resurrected masters govern life and death. They can conserve the physical body for millions of years. They know the quadrature of the circle and the perpetual movement. They have the universal medicine, and speak the very pure language of the divine tongue which, like a golden river, flows delightfully through the thick, sunny jungle." - Samael Aun Weor, *The Esoteric Treatise of Hermetic Astrology*

"The [number of] resurrected masters can be counted on the fingers of the hands. [...] Hermes, Cagliostro, Paracelsus, Nicholas Flamel, Quetzalcoatl, St. Germain, Babaji, etc., preserved their physical bodies for thousands, and even millions of years, without death harming them. They are resurrected masters." - Samael Aun Weor, *Alchemy and Kabbalah in the Tarot*

"Indeed, there is no resurrection without death, nor a dawn within nature (or within the human being) without darkness, sorrows, and nocturnal agony preceding them, which makes their light more adorable." —Samael Aun Weor, *The Three Mountains*

"After the resurrection, the master does not die again. He is eternal. With this immortal body, he can appear and disappear instantaneously. Masters can make themselves visible in the physical world at will.

"Jesus the Christ is a Resurrected Master who for three days had his physical body in the Holy sepulcher. After the resurrection, Jesus appeared before the disciples who were on their way to the village of Emmaus and dined with them. After this, he was before the unbelieving Thomas, who only believed when he put his fingers in the wounds of the holy body of the great master.

"Hermes, Cagliostro, Paracelsus, Nicholas Flamel, Quetzalcoatl, St. Germain, Babaji, etc. preserved their physical body thousands and even millions of years ago without death harming them. They are resurrected masters." —Samael Aun Weor, *Tarot and Kabbalah*

"All the masters who have resurrected live with their physical bodies for millions of years... Only the initiates who have reached these summits can live and direct the current of life of the centuries. Only here the initiate no longer needs a spouse. The initiate's physical body remains in Jinn state; this is the gift of Cupid. Nevertheless, the initiate can become visible and tangible in this tridimensional world wherever is necessary, and works in the physical world under the commands of the White Lodge. As a Resurrected Master, the initiate commands the great life; he has power over the fire, air, water, and earth. Yes, all of Nature kneels before him and obeys him. He can live among men, and becomes a human-god.

"Naturally, it is indispensable to undergo the ordeals of the Arcanum Thirteen in order to reach these summits (Second Mountain). The physical body must be embalmed for death. The supper at Bethany corresponds to this event of the Arcanum Thirteen. Thus, after the body has been embalmed for death, it is submitted to a special evolution for the tomb that develops within the numbers thirty and thirty-five, which when added together give the Arcanum Eleven (the tamed lion); yes, we have to tame nature and overcome it.

"Thus, when the body is ready for the sepulcher, the processes of death and resurrection occur. In this case, the Angels of Death do not cut the silver cord; this is how the initiate dies but does not die. The physical brain of the initiate is submitted to a special transformation: it becomes more subtle, delicate, and radiant.

"The supper at Bethany relates with these processes of Jesus Christ.

"Now when Jesus was in Bethany, in the house of Simon the leper, There came unto him a woman having an alabaster jar of very precious ointment, and poured it on his head, as he sat at meat. But when his disciples saw it, they had indignation, saying, To what purpose is this waste? For this ointment might have been sold for much, and given to the poor. When Jesus understood it, he said unto them, Why trouble ye the woman? for she hath wrought a good work upon me. For ye have the poor always with you; but me ye have not always; for in that she hath poured this ointment on my body, she did it for my burial. Verily I say unto you, wherever this gospel shall be preached in the whole world, there shall also this, that this woman hath done, be told for a memorial of her." - Matthew, 26: 6-13 - Samael Aun Weor, *The Major Mysteries*

Root Races: "Every planet develops seven root races and seven subraces. Our planet Earth already developed five root races; it needs to develop two more root races. After the seven root races, the planet Earth, already transformed by cataclysms over the course of millions of years, will become a new moon." —Samael Aun Weor, *The Kabbalah of the Mayan Mysteries*

The seven root races of this planet Earth are:

- Polar
- Hyperborean
- Lemurian
- Atlantean
- Aryan (present)
- Koradi (future)
- (Seventh) (future)

Furthermore, each root race has seven subraces.

Satan: (Hebrew שטן, opposer, or adversary) Although modern Christians have made Satan into a cartoon character, the reality is very different. Within us, Satan is the fallen Lucifer, who is born within the psyche of every human being by means of the sexual impulse that culminates in the orgasm or sexual spasm of the fornicators. Satan, the fallen Lucifer, directs the lustful animal currents towards the atomic infernos of the human being, thus it becomes the profoundly evil adversary of our Innermost (God) and human values within our own psyche. This is why it is often identified with the leader of the fallen angels or fallen human values (parts) of our consciousness trapped within the animal mind (legions of egos, defects, vices of the mind) in other words, Satan is the Devil or "evil" adversary of God that everybody carries within their own psychological interior. The spiritual aspirant has to conquer Satan and transform him back into Lucifer, which is Latin for "bearer of Light." This was once known in Christianity (even some popes were named Lucifer), but over the centuries Christianity degenerated.

Second Death: A mechanical process in nature experienced by those souls who within the allotted time fail to reach union with their inner divinity (i.e. known as self-realization, liberation, religare, yoga, moksha, etc). The Second Death is the complete dissolution of the ego (karma, defects, sins) in the infernal regions of nature, which after unimaginable quantities of suffering, proportional to the density of the psyche, in the end purifies the Essence (consciousness) so that it may try again to perfect itself and reach the union with the Being.

"He that overcometh (the sexual passion) shall inherit all things; and I will be his God (I will incarnate myself within him), and he shall be my son (because he is a Christified one), But the fearful (the tenebrous, cowards, unbelievers), and unbelieving, and the abominable, and murderers, and whoremongers, and sorcerers, and idolaters, and all liars, shall have their part in the lake which burneth with fire and brimstone: which is the second death. (Revelation 21) This lake which burns with fire and brimstone is the lake of carnal passion. This lake is related with the lower animal depths of the human being and its atomic region is the abyss. The tenebrous slowly disintegrate themselves within the abyss until they die. This is the second death." —Samael Aun Weor, *The Aquarian Message*

"When the bridge called "Antakarana," which communicates the divine triad with its "inferior essence", is broken, the inferior essence (trapped into the ego) is left separated and is sunk into the abyss of destructive forces, where it (its ego) disintegrates little by little. This is the Second Death of which the Apocalypse speaks; this is the state of consciousness called "Avitchi." —Samael Aun Weor, *The Zodiacal Course*

" The Second Death is really painful. The ego feels as if it has been divided in different parts, the fingers fall off, its arms, its legs. It suffers through a tremendous breakdown." —Samael Aun Weor, from the lecture *The Mysteries of Life and Death*

Secret Enemy: "The Nous atom is sometimes called by the occultist the white or good principle of the heart. We will now speak of its opposite: the dark atom or Secret Enemy. In many ways its activities are similar to the Nous atom; for it has legions of atomic entities under its command; but they are destructive and not constructive. This Secret Enemy resides in the lower section of the spine, and its atoms oppose the student's attempts to unite himself to his Innermost. The Secret Enemy has so much power in the atmosphere of this world that they can limit our thoughts and imprison our minds... The Secret Enemy works in every way to deny us any intelligence that would illuminate our minds, and would seek to stamp man into a machine cursed with similarity and a mind lacking all creative power... Man easily degenerates when in the power of the Secret Enemy; it preys upon the burning furnace of his desires, and when he weakens he is lost and sometimes cannot regain contact with his Innermost for two or three lives wherein he works out the karma of his evil desires." —M, *The Dayspring of Youth*

Self-realization: The achievement of perfect knowledge. This phrase is better stated as, "The realization of the Innermost Self," or "The realization of the true nature of self." At the ultimate level, this is the experiential, conscious knowledge of the Absolute, which is synonymous with Emptiness, Shunyata, or Non-being.

Semen: In sacred sexuality, the word semen has a much deeper and profound meaning that the words as used in everyday language. In common usage, the word semen usually means, "The smaller, usually motile male reproductive cell of most organisms that reproduce sexually." Yet, this usage is relatively recent, and ignores the true importance of the word.

The English word semen originally meant 'seed of male animals' in the 14th century, and it was not applied to human males until the 18th century. It came from Latin semen, "seed of plants," from serere `to sow.' The Latin goes back to the Indo-European root *se-, source of seed, disseminate, season, seminar, and seminal. The word seminary (used for religious schools) is derived from semen and originally meant 'seedbed.'

That the semen is the source of all virtue is known from the word "seminal," derived from the Latin "semen," and which is defined as "highly original and influencing the development of future events: a seminal artist; seminal ideas."

In the esoteric tradition of pure sexuality, the word semen refers to the sexual energy of the organism, whether male or female. This is because male and female both carry the "seed" within: in order to create, the two "seeds" must be combined.

"According to Yogic science, semen exists in a subtle form throughout the whole body. It is found in a subtle state in all the cells of the body. It is withdrawn and elaborated into a gross form in the sexual organ under the influence of the sexual will and sexual excitement. An Oordhvareta Yogi (one who has stored up the seminal energy in the brain after sublimating the same into spiritual energy) not only converts the semen into Ojas, but checks through his Yogic power, through purity in thought, word and deed, the very formation of semen by the secretory cells or testes or seeds. This is a great secret." —Swami Sivananda

Sephirah: (or sefira; Hebrew) plural: Sephiroth. The "Sefirot" (סְפִירוֹת), singular "Sefirah" (סְפִירָה), from ספר ("to count") literally means "counting" or "enumeration", yet given the flexibility of Hebrew has other roots, such as sefer (text), sippur (recounting a story), sappir (sapphire, brilliance, luminary), separ (boundary), and safra (scribe). A sephirah is a symbol used in Kabbalah to represent levels of manifestation ranging from the very subtle to the very dense, and which apply to everything that exists, from the grandest scale to the most minute. Generally, these levels are represented in a structure of ten sephiroth called "the Tree of Life." This ten-sphered structure is a simplified arrangement of more complex renderings.

"The ten Sephiroth of universal vibration emerge from the Ain Soph, which is the microcosmic star that guides our interior. This star is the real Being of our Being. Ten Sephiroth are spoken of, but in reality there are twelve; the Ain Soph is the eleventh, and its tenebrous antithesis is in the abyss, which is the twelfth Sephirah. These are twelve spheres or universal regions that interpenetrate each other without confusion." — Samael Aun Weor, *Tarot and Kabbalah*

Sexual Magic: The word magic is derived from the ancient word magos "one of the members of the learned and priestly class," from O.Pers. magush, possibly from PIE *magh- "to be able, to have power." [Quoted from Online Etymology Dictionary].

"All of us possess some electrical and magnetic forces within, and, just like a magnet, we exert a force of attraction and repulsion... Between lovers that magnetic force is particularly powerful and its action has a far-reaching effect." —Samael Aun Weor, *The Secret of the Golden Flower*

Sexual magic refers to an ancient science that has been known and protected by the purest, most spiritually advanced human beings, whose purpose and goal is the harnessing and perfection of our sexual forces. A more accurate translation of sexual magic would be "sexual priesthood." In ancient times, the priest was always accompanied by a priestess, for they represent the divine forces at the base of all creation: the masculine and feminine, the Yab-Yum, Ying-Yang, Father-Mother: the Elohim. Unfortunately, the term "sexual magic" has been grossly misinterpreted by mistaken persons such as Aleister Crowley, who advocated a host of degenerate practices, all of which belong solely to the lowest and most perverse mentality and lead only to the enslavement of the consciousness, the worship of lust and desire, and the decay of humanity. True, upright, heavenly sexual magic is the natural harnessing of our latent forces, making them active and harmonious with nature and the divine, and which leads to the perfection of the human being.

"People are filled with horror when they hear about sexual magic; however, they are not filled with horror when they give themselves to all kinds of sexual perversion and to all kinds of carnal passion." —Samael Aun Weor, *The Perfect Matrimony*

Solar Bodies: The physical, vital, astral, mental, and causal bodies that are created through the beginning stages of alchemy/tantra and that provide a basis for existence in their corresponding levels of nature, just as the physical body does in the physical world. These bodies or vehicles are superior due to being created out of solar (Christic) energy, as opposed to the inferior, lunar bodies we receive from nature. Also known as the Wedding Garment (Christianity), the Merkabah (Kabbalah), To Soma Heliakon (Greek), and Sahu (Egyptian).

"All the masters of the White Lodge, the angels, archangels, thrones, seraphim, virtues, etc. are garbed with the solar bodies. Only those who have solar bodies have the Being incarnated. Only someone who possesses the Being is an authentic human being." —Samael Aun Weor, *The Esoteric Treatise of Hermetic Astrology*

Soul: The modern definition and usage of this word "soul" is filled with contradictions, misconceptions, and misuse. In Gnosis (the heart of all religions), the meaning is very precise. The English word comes from the Old English sawol, meaning the "spiritual and emotional part of a person."

In Kabbalah, the spiritual and emotional part of the person is related to the sephiroth Hod (emotion), Netzach (mind), Tiphereth (will; Human Soul), and Geburah (consciousness; Divine Soul). Furthermore, these sephiroth undergo stages of growth, explained as five types or levels of soul: nephesh, neshemah, ruach, chaiah, and yechidah.

In Hinduism and Buddhism, the word soul is usually related to the Sanskrit word Atman, defined as "self." (See Atman for more information). Yet, this word has been misinterpreted for centuries.

The teaching of the Buddha explains that there is no "soul" in the sense of a permanent, eternally existing element beyond the body that defines a person. Samael Aun Weor uses the word soul in the way that Buddhism uses the word "body" (of which there are physical and nonphysical bodies); each, even when created and refined, is merely a vehicle, and as such is impermanent. What is eternal is what uses those bodies.

In reality, the common person does not have a "soul" yet; they have the essence or seed of the soul, which must be grown through the "second birth." As Jesus explained, "With patience ye shall possess thy souls." (Luke 21) Thus, the development of the soul is the mere beginning of the path to full development. Afterward, there are far greater works to accomplish.

The term "soul" should not be confused with "spirit," which refers to a higher aspect of the Innermost (Atman; Chesed).

Subjective: "What do modern psychologists understand as 'objective?' They understand it to be that which is external to the mind: the physical, the tangible, the material.

"Yet, they are totally mistaken, because when analysing the term "subjective," we see that it signifies "sub, under," that which is below the range of our perceptions. What is below our perceptions? Is it not perhaps the Infernal Worlds? Is it not perhaps subjective that which is in the physical or beneath the physical? So, what is truly subjective is what is below the limits of our perceptions.

"Psychologists do not know how to use the former terms correctly.

"Objective: the light, the resplendence; it is that which contains the Truth, clarity, lucidity.

"Subjective: the darkness, the tenebrous. The subjective elements of perception are the outcome of seeing, hearing, touching, smelling and tasting. All of these are perceptions of what we see in the third dimension. For example, in one cube we see only length, width and height. We do not see the fourth dimension because we are bottled up within the ego. The subjective elements of perception are constituted by the ego with all of its "I's." —Samael Aun Weor, *Tarot and Kabbalah*

Tantra: Sanskrit for "continuum" or "unbroken stream." This refers first (1) to the continuum of vital energy that sustains all existence, and second (2) to the class of knowledge and practices that harnesses that vital energy, thereby transforming the practitioner. There are many schools of Tantra, but they can be classified in three types: White, Grey and Black. Tantra has long been known in the West as Alchemy.

"In the view of Tantra, the body's vital energies are the vehicles of the mind. When the vital energies are pure and subtle, one's state of mind will be accordingly affected. By transforming these bodily energies we transform the state of consciousness." —The 14th Dalai Lama

Tree of Knowledge of Good and Evil: (Hebrew) From Hebrew: עץ tree. דעת (Daath) "knowledge." טוב "goodness." רע "pollution" or "impurity."

One of two trees in the Garden of Eden, the Tree of Knowledge in Hebrew is Daath, which is related to the sexual organs and the study of sexuality, known also as Alchemy / Tantra. The full name "Tree of Knowledge of Goodness and Impurity" indicates that Daath, sexual "knowledge," leads to either "goodness" or "impurity."

Tree of Life: (Hebrew) Although the Hebrew term is plural ("Tree of Lives") it is usually rendered singular.

"And out of the ground made the LORD God to grow every tree that is pleasant to the sight, and good for food; the tree of life also in the midst of the garden, and the tree of knowledge of good and evil." —Genesis 2:9

This tree represents the structure of the soul (microcosm) and of the universe (macrocosm).

"The Tree of Life is the spinal medulla. This tree of wisdom is also the ten sephiroth, the twenty-two creative Major Arcana, letters, sounds and numbers, with which the Logos (God) created the universe." —from Alcione, a lecture by Samael Aun Weor

Venustic Initiation: After completing the serpents of fire and entering the direct path, the bodhisattva begins the Venustic Initiations, which are the Seven Serpents of Light of the First Mountain plus one more related with the Sephirah Binah. Read *The Three Mountains*.

"The Venustic Initiation is only for true human beings, never for intellectual animals. Let "true human beings" be understood as those who already created the solar bodies. Let "intellectual animals" be understood as all of humanity, all the people who only have lunar bodies. The Venustic Initiation is the true nativity of the tranquil heart. The Venustic Initiation is for the few; it is a grace from the Solar Logos. In Nirvana, there are many Buddhas who—in spite of their great perfections—have never reached the Venustic Initiation." —Samael Aun Weor, *Light from Darkness*

"...the Venustic Initiation that has eight grades. The first Venustic Initiation is just the superior octave of the first initiation of fire. The second Venustic Initiation is the superior octave of the second initiation of fire. The third Venustic Initiation is the superior octave of the third initiation of fire. The fourth Venustic Initiation is the fourth superior octave of the fourth initiation of fire. The fifth Venustic Initiation is the fifth superior octave of the fifth initiation of fire; after this come the three initiations (the total is eight) that are related with the First Mountain (that is the First Mountain). In the Second Mountain one has to begin the work with the Moon, with Mercury, with Venus, with the Sun, Mars, Jupiter, Saturn, Uranus and Neptune, to then achieve Perfection in Mastery (it is the Mountain of the Resurrection), and the Third Mountain is the Ascension, to finally crystallize (in oneself) the Second and First Logos, and to receive the Inner Atomic Star." —Samael Aun Weor, The Master Key

White Lodge or Brotherhood: That ancient collection of pure souls who maintain the highest and most sacred of sciences: White Magic or White Tantra. It is called White due to its purity and cleanliness. This "Brotherhood" or "Lodge" includes human beings of the highest order from every race, culture, creed and religion, and of both sexes.

Yoga: (Sanskrit) "union." Similar to the Latin "religare," the root of the word "religion." In Tibetan, it is "rnal-'byor" which means "union with the fundamental nature of reality."

"The word YOGA comes from the root Yuj which means to join, and in its spiritual sense, it is that process by which the human spirit is brought into near and conscious communion with, or is merged in, the Divine Spirit, according as the nature of the human spirit is held to be separate from (Dvaita, Visishtadvaita) or one with (Advaita) the Divine Spirit." — Swami Sivananda, *Kundalini Yoga*

"Patanjali defines Yoga as the suspension of all the functions of the mind. As such, any book on Yoga, which does not deal with these three aspects of the subject, viz., mind, its functions and the method of suspending them, can he safely laid aside as unreliable and incomplete." —Swami Sivananda, *Practical Lessons In Yoga*

"The word yoga means in general to join one's mind with an actual fact..." —The 14th Dalai Lama

"The soul aspires for the union with his Innermost, and the Innermost aspires for the union with his Glorian." —Samael Aun Weor, *The Revolution of Beelzebub*

"All of the seven schools of Yoga are within Gnosis, yet they are in a synthesized and absolutely practical way. There is Tantric Hatha Yoga in the practices of the Maithuna (Sexual Magic). There is practical Raja Yoga in the work with the chakras. There is Gnana / Jnana Yoga in our practices and mental disciplines which we have cultivated in secrecy for millions of years. We have Bhakti Yoga in our prayers and Rituals. We have Laya Yoga in our meditation and respiratory exercises. Samadhi exists in our practices with the Maithuna and during our deep meditations. We live the path of Karma Yoga in our upright actions, in our upright thoughts, in our upright feelings, etc." —Samael Aun Weor, *The Revolution of Beelzebub*

"Yoga does not consist in sitting cross-legged for six hours or stopping the beatings of the heart or getting oneself buried underneath the ground for a week or a month. These are all physical feats only. Yoga is the science that teaches you the method of uniting the individual will with the Cosmic Will. Yoga transmutes the unregenerate nature and increases energy, vitality, vigour, and bestows longevity and a high standard of health." —Swami Sivananda, *Autobiography*

"Brahmacharya [sexual purity] is the very foundation of Yoga." —Swami Sivananda

"The Yoga that we require today is actually ancient Gnostic Christian Yoga, which absolutely rejects the idea of Hatha Yoga. We do not recommend Hatha Yoga simply because, spiritually speaking, the acrobatics of this discipline are fruitless; they should be left to the acrobats of the circus." —Samael Aun Weor, *The Yellow Book*

"Yoga has been taught very badly in the Western world. Multitudes of pseudo-sapient Yogis have spread the false belief that the true Yogi must be an infrasexual (an enemy of sex). Some of these false yogis have never even visited India; they are infrasexual pseudo-yogis. These ignoramuses believe that they are going to achieve in-depth realization only with the yogic exercises, such as asanas, pranayamas, etc. Not only do they have such false beliefs, but what is worse is that they propagate them; thus, they misguide many people away from the difficult, straight, and narrow door that leads unto the light. No authentically initiated Yogi from India would ever think that he could achieve his inner self-realization with pranayamas or asanas, etc. Any legitimate Yogi from India knows very well that such yogic exercises are only co-assistants that are very useful for their health and for the development of their powers, etc. Only the Westerners and pseudo-yogis have within their minds the belief that they can achieve Self-realization with such exercises. Sexual Magic is practiced very secretly within the Ashrams of India. Any true yogi initiate from India works with the Arcanum A.Z.F. This is taught by the great Yogis from India that have visited the Western world, and if it has not been taught by these great, initiated Hindustani Yogis, if it has not been published in their books of Yoga, it was in order to avoid scandals. You can be absolutely sure that the Yogis who do not practice Sexual Magic will never achieve birth in the superior worlds. Thus, whosoever affirms the contrary is a liar, an impostor." —Samael Aun Weor, *Alchemy and Kabbalah in the Tarot*

Index

About the Author

His name is Hebrew סמאל און ואור, and is pronounced "sam-ayel on vay-or." You may not have heard of him, but Samael Aun Weor changed the world.

In 1950, in his first two books, he became the first person to reveal the esoteric secret hidden in all the world's great religions, and for that, accused of "healing the ill," he was put in prison. Nevertheless, he did not stop. Between 1950 and 1977 — merely twenty-seven years — not only did Samael Aun Weor write over sixty books on the most difficult subjects in the world, such as consciousness, kabbalah, physics, tantra, meditation, etc., in which he deftly exposed the singular root of all knowledge — which he called Gnosis — he simultaneously inspired millions of people across the entire span of Latin America: stretching across twenty countries and an area of more than 21,000,000 square kilometers, founding schools everywhere, even in places without electricity or post offices.

During those twenty-seven years, he experienced all the extremes that humanity could give him, from adoration to death threats, and in spite of the enormous popularity of his books and lectures, he renounced an income, refused recognitions, walked away from accolades, and consistently turned away those who would worship him. He held as friends both presidents and peasants, and yet remained a mystery to all.

When one reflects on the effort and will it requires to perform even day to day tasks, it is astonishing to consider the herculean efforts required to accomplish what he did in such a short time. But, there is a reason: he was a man who knew who he was, and what he had to do. A true example of compassion and selfless service, Samael Aun Weor dedicated the whole of his life to freely helping anyone and everyone find the path out of suffering. His mission was to show all of humanity the universal source of all spiritual traditions, which he did not only through his writings and lectures, but also through his actions. He said,

"I, the one who writes this book, am not anyone's master, and I beg people to not follow me. I am an imperfect human just like anyone else, and it is an error to follow someone who is imperfect. Let every one follow their "I am [their Innermost]...

"I do not want to receive visitors. Unquestionably, I am nothing more than a postman, a courier, a man that delivers a message... It would be the breaking point of silliness for you to come from your country to the capital city of Mexico with the only purpose of visiting a vulgar postman, an employee that delivered you a letter in the past... Why would you waste your money for that? Why would you visit a simple courier, a miserable postman? It is better for you to study the message, the written teachings delivered in the books...

"I have not come to form any sect, or one more belief, nor am I interested in the schools of today, or the particular beliefs of anyone! ...

"We are not interested in anyone's money, nor are we interested in monthly fees, or temples made out of brick, cement or clay, because we are conscious visitors in the cathedral of the soul and we know that wisdom is of the soul.

"Flattery tires us, praise should only belong to our Father (who is in secret and watches over us minutely).

"We are not in search of followers; all we want is for each person to follow his or her self—their own internal master, their sacred Innermost— because he is the only one who can save and glorify us.

"I do not follow anyone, therefore no one should follow me...

"We do not want any more comedies, pretenses, false mysticism, or false schools. What we want now are living realities; we want to prepare ourselves to see, hear, and touch the reality of those truths..." —Samael Aun Weor

Your book reviews matter.

Glorian Publishing is a very small non-profit organization, thus we have no money to spend on marketing and advertising. Fortunately, there is a proven way to gain the attention of readers: book reviews. Mainstream book reviewers won't review these books, but you can.

The path of liberation requires the daily balance of three active factors:

- birth of virtue
- death of vice
- sacrifice for others

Writing book reviews is a powerful way to sacrifice for others. By writing book reviews on popular websites, you help to make the books more visible to humanity, and you might help save a soul from suffering. Will you do your part to help us show these wonderful teachings to others? Take a moment today to write a review.

Donate

Glorian Publishing is a non-profit publisher dedicated to spreading the sacred universal doctrine to suffering humanity. All of our works are made possible by the kindness and generosity of sponsors. If you would like to make a tax-deductible donation, you may send it to the address below, or visit our website for other alternatives. If you would like to sponsor the publication of a book, please contact us at help@glorian.org.

Glorian Publishing
PO Box 209
Clinton, CT 06413 US
Phone: (844) 945-6742
VISIT US ONLINE AT glorian.org